THE HOLY SPIRIT IN LUKE-ACTS

Marco C.D. Wittenberg

The Holy Spirit in Luke-Acts

The Role of the Reader

Summum

Cover design: Brainstorm
Typesetting: Gewoon Geertje

ISBN 978 94 927 0102 2

Copyright © Summum Academic Publications, Kampen, The Netherlands. All rights reserved. No part of this publication may be reproduced, translated, stored in a retrieval system, or transmitted in any form by any means, electronic, mechanical, photocopying, recording or otherwise, without prior written permission from the publisher.

*"There is a great difference between
our receiving power from the Holy Ghost
and our receiving the Holy Ghost as our power"*

- Albert Benjamin Simpson (1843-1919) -
Founder of the Christian & Missionary Alliance

TABLE OF CONTENTS

ACKNOWLEDGEMENTS		1
ABBREVIATIONS		3
INTRODUCTION		5

CHAPTER 1: FORSCHUNGSBERICHT — 13

1.1 Introduction — 13
1.2 The Holy Spirit in Luke-Acts: Main Areas of Consensus — 14
   1.2.1 Luke as Historian, Theologian and Storyteller — 14
   1.2.2 The Background of the Holy Spirit in Luke-Acts — 19
   1.2.3 The Relation between the Holy Spirit and Mission in Luke-Acts — 24
   1.2.4 Conclusion — 25
1.3 The Holy Spirit in Luke-Acts: Theological Disagreements — 25
   1.3.1 Introduction — 25
   1.3.2 The Theological Framework of Luke-Acts — 26
   1.3.3 Water-Baptism and the Holy Spirit in Luke-Acts — 27
   1.3.4 Baptism in the Spirit: the Holy Spirit as a necessary and subsequent experience after conversion — 28
   1.3.5 Conclusion — 30
1.4 The Holy Spirit in Luke-Acts: Pneumatological Disagreements — 30
   1.4.1 Introduction — 30
   1.4.2 The Holy Spirit in Luke-Acts designated as "Soteriological Spirit" — 33
   1.4.3 The Holy Spirit in Luke-Acts designated as "Eschatological Spirit" — 35
   1.4.4 The Holy Spirit in Luke-Acts designated as "Missiological Spirit" — 37
   1.4.5 The Holy Spirit in Luke-Acts designated as "Charismatic Spirit" — 42
   1.4.6 Conclusion — 46
1.5 Towards Understanding: The Role of the Reader — 46
   1.5.1 Introduction — 46
   1.5.2 Establishing the role of the reader — 47
   1.5.3 Establishing different readers — 47
   1.5.4 Conclusion — 48
1.6 Conclusion — 48

CHAPTER 2: THE ROLE OF THE READER, UMBERTO ECO AND LUKE-ACTS — 50

2.1 Introduction — 50
2.2 The Role of the Reader in Recent Research — 51
2.3 The Role of the Reader according to Umberto Eco — 56
2.4 Umberto Eco and Luke-Acts — 57
2.5 Umberto Eco's model of the cooperative reader — 60
  2.5.1 The actualized text — 61
  Box 3: Expression — 61
  Box 1: Codes and subcodes — 62
  Box 2: Circumstances of utterance — 63
  2.5.2 The substantial properties of the text (intensions) — 63
  Box 4: Discursive structures — 63
  Box 6: Narrative structures — 64
  Box 8: Actantial structures — 65
  Box 9: Elementary ideological structures — 65
  2.5.3 Preliminary deductions and possible implications (extensions) — 66
  Box 5: Bracketed extensions — 66
  Box 7: Forecasts and inferential walks — 66
  Box 10: World structures — 67
2.6 Applying Eco's model to Luke-Acts — 68
  2.6.1 The "literary knots" in Luke's πνεῦμα texts — 68
  2.6.2 How to apply Eco's model to the "literary knots" — 69
2.7 Conclusion — 70

CHAPTER 3: THE MODEL APPLIED (1): MAX M.B. TURNER — 73

3.1 Introduction — 73
3.2 The infancy narratives (Luke 1-2) — 73
  3.2.1 The actualized text — 73
  3.2.2 The substantial properties of the text — 77
  3.2.3 Preliminary deductions and possible implications — 80
3.3 The ministry of John the Baptist (Luke 3:1-20) — 81
  3.3.1 The actualized text — 81
  3.3.2 The substantial properties of the text — 82
  3.3.3 Preliminary deductions and possible implications — 84
3.4 The baptism and subsequent testing of Jesus (Luke 3:21-22, 4:1-14) — 84
  3.4.1 The actualized text — 84

	3.4.2 The substantial properties of the text	86
	3.4.3 Preliminary deductions and possible implications	87
3.5	Jesus' inauguration address (Luke 4:14-30)	88
	3.5.1 The actualized text	88
	3.5.2 The substantial properties of the text	90
	3.5.3 Preliminary deductions and possible implications	91
3.6	Jesus' general sayings about the Spirit (Luke 10:21, 11:13, 12:10-12)	93
	3.6.1 The actualized text	93
	3.6.2 The substantial properties of the text	93
	3.6.3 Preliminary deductions and possible implications	94
3.7	The promise of the Spirit (Luke 24 – Acts 1)	94
	3.7.1 The actualized text	94
	3.7.2 The substantial properties of the text	95
	3.7.3 Preliminary deductions and possible implications	96
3.8	Pentecost: the outpouring of the Spirit (Acts 2)	96
	3.8.1 The actualized text	96
	3.8.2 The substantial properties of the text	97
	3.8.3 Preliminary deductions and possible implications	102
3.9	The Samaritans (Acts 8)	102
	3.9.1 The actualized text	102
	3.9.2 The substantial properties of the text	103
	3.9.3 Preliminary deductions and possible implications	105
3.10	The Damascus event (Acts 9)	106
	3.10.1 The actualized text	106
	3.10.2 The substantial properties of the text	106
	3.10.3 Preliminary deductions and possible implications	107
3.11	The Cornelius' household (Acts 10)	108
	3.11.1 The actualized text	108
	3.11.2 The substantial properties of the text	108
	3.11.3 Preliminary deductions and possible implications	110
3.12	The Ephesian disciples (Acts 19)	111
	3.12.1 The actualized text	111
	3.12.2 The substantial properties of the text	111
	3.12.3 Preliminary deductions and possible implications	113
3.13	Conclusion	114
	3.13.1 The Role of the Reader: Max M.B. Turner	114
	3.13.2 Lukan Pneumatology according to Max M.B. Turner	115

CHAPTER 4: THE MODEL APPLIED (2): ROBERT P. MENZIES 117

4.1	Introduction	117
4.2	The infancy narratives (Luke 1-2)	118
	4.2.1 The actualized text	118
	4.2.2 The substantial properties of the text	110
	4.2.3 Preliminary deductions and possible implications	121
4.3	The ministry of John the Baptist (Luke 3:1-20)	122
	4.3.1 The actualized text	122
	4.3.2 The substantial properties of the text	122
	4.3.3 Preliminary deductions and possible implications	124
4.4	The baptism and subsequent testing of Jesus (Luke 3:21-22, 4:1-14)	125
	4.4.1 The actualized text	125
	4.4.2 The substantial properties of the text	125
	4.4.3 Preliminary deductions and possible implications	127
4.5	Jesus' inauguration address (Luke 4:14-30)	128
	4.5.1 The actualized text	128
	4.5.2 The substantial properties of the text	128
	4.5.3 Preliminary deductions and possible implications	130
4.6	Jesus' general sayings about the Spirit (Luke 10:21, 11:13 [11:20], 12:10-12)	130
	4.6.1 The actualized text	130
	4.6.2 The substantial properties of the text	131
	4.6.3 Preliminary deductions and possible implications	132
4.7	The promise of the Spirit (Luke 24 – Acts 1)	133
	4.7.1 The actualized text	133
	4.7.2 The substantial properties of the text	133
	4.7.3 Preliminary deductions and possible implications	135
4.8	Pentecost: the outpouring of the Spirit (Acts 2)	136
	4.8.1 The actualized text	136
	4.8.2 The substantial properties of the text	136
	4.8.3 Preliminary deductions and possible implications	139
	Excursus: Acts 2:38	140
4.9	The Samaritans (Acts 8)	141
	4.9.1 The actualized text	141
	4.9.2 The substantial properties of the text	141
	4.9.3 Preliminary deductions and possible implications	142

4.10	The Damascus event (Acts 9)	143
	4.10.1 The actualized text	143
	4.10.2 The substantial properties of the text	143
	4.10.3 Preliminary deductions and possible implications	144
4.11	The Cornelius' household (Acts 10)	145
	4.11.1 The actualized text	145
	4.11.2 The substantial properties of the text	145
	4.11.3 Preliminary deductions and possible implications	147
4.12	The Ephesian disciples (Acts 19)	147
	4.12.1 The actualized text	147
	4.12.2 The substantial properties of the text	148
	4.12.3 Preliminary deductions and possible implications	149
4.13	Conclusion	150
	4.13.1 The Role of the Reader: Robert P. Menzies	150
	4.13.2 Lukan Pneumatology according to Robert P. Menzies	152

CHAPTER 5: THE MODEL APPLIED (3): William S. Kurz		**155**
5.1	Introduction	155
5.2	Methodology: Kurz' dynamic reading of Luke-Acts	156
	5.2.1 Introduction	156
	5.2.2 The expression of the text	156
	5.2.3 Codes and subcodes in the text	157
	5.2.4 Circumstances of utterance	158
	5.2.5 Conclusion	159
5.3	The infancy narratives (Luke 1-2)	160
	5.3.1 The actualized text	160
	5.3.2 The substantial properties of the text	160
	5.3.3 Preliminary deductions and possible implications	161
5.4	The ministry of John the Baptist (Luke 3:1-20)	163
	5.4.1 The actualized text	163
	5.4.2 The substantial properties of the text	163
	5.4.3 Preliminary deductions and possible implications	163
5.5	The baptism and subsequent testing of Jesus (Luke 3:21-22, 4:1-14)	164
	5.5.2 The substantial properties of the text	165
	5.5.3 Preliminary deductions and possible implications	166
5.6	Jesus' inauguration address (Luke 4:14-30)	167
	5.6.1 The actualized text	167
	5.6.2 The substantial properties of the text	167
	5.6.3 Preliminary deductions and possible implications	169

5.7	Jesus' general sayings about the Spirit (Luke 10:21, 11:13, 12:10-12)	170
5.8	The promise of the Spirit (Luke 24 – Acts 1)	171
	5.8.1 The actualized text	171
	5.8.2 The substantial properties of the text	171
	5.8.3 Preliminary deductions and possible implications	174
5.9	Pentecost: the outpouring of the Spirit (Acts 2)	174
	5.9.1 The actualized text	174
	5.9.2 The substantial properties of the text	175
	5.9.3 Preliminary deductions and possible implications	178
5.10	The Samaritans (Acts 8)	178
	5.10.1 The actualized text	178
	5.10.2 The substantial properties of the text	179
	5.10.3 Preliminary deductions and possible implications	181
5.11	The Damascus event (Acts 9)	181
	5.11.1 The actualized text	182
	5.11.2 The substantial properties of the text	182
	5.11.3 Preliminary deductions and possible implications	184
5.12	The Cornelius' household (Acts 10)	184
	5.12.1 The actualized text	184
	5.12.2 The substantial properties of the text	186
	5.12.3 Preliminary deductions and possible implications	187
5.13	The Ephesian disciples (Acts 19)	188
5.14	Conclusion	190
	5.14.1 The Role of the Reader: William S. Kurz	190
	5.14.2 Lukan Pneumatology according to William S. Kurz	191

CHAPTER 6: THE ROLE OF THE READER:
LIMITS AND POSSIBILITIES OF INTERPRETATION   **193**

6.1	Introduction	193
6.2	Luke 1-2: The Infancy Narratives	198
6.3	Luke 3: The Promise of John the Baptist	201
6.4	Luke 4: Jesus' inaugural address	204
6.5	Acts 2: Pentecost	207
6.6	Acts 8: The Samaritans	212
6.7	Acts 10: Cornelius' Household	218
6.8	Conclusion	221
	Max Turner	221
	Robert Menzies	222
	William Kurz	223

CONCLUSION	227
APPENDIX 1: *PNEUMA* AND ITS DERIVATES IN THE GOSPEL OF LUKE	235
APPENDIX 2: *PNEUMA* AND ITS DERIVATES IN THE BOOK OF ACTS	239
APPENDIX 3: THE HOLY SPIRIT IN LUKE-ACTS AND GERMAN INFLUENCES	245
BIBLIOGRAPHY	249

ACKNOWLEDGEMENTS

This book is a slightly revised version of my PhD dissertation defended in 2016 at VU University in Amsterdam. Several people have supported and encouraged me during the period of reading, studying and writing and I am most grateful for them. But first things first: before I mention some of the names of people who are of meaning in my life and were of great help to fulfil this project, I would like to express my sincerest gratefulness to our Lord God and Father, the One who was, who is, and who is to come. I am deeply convinced that He is the One who created me, gave me the intellectual abilities and possibilities to study and to eventually pursue a PhD degree in theology. It is my prayer that this present work will be of benefit for the church in general and the individual believer in specific.

My sincere thanks are due to both of my supervisors, Dr. Bert Jan Lietaert Peerbolte and Dr. Kees van der Kooi who tirelessly and patiently kept reading and rereading the drafts of each chapter and provided me with constructive feedback. In addition I mention Dr. Arie Zwiep, who has been my professor in the early stages of my studies in theology and who learned me how to write and rewrite. I am especially grateful for his meticulous work of going through my dissertation in the final stage.

A special thanks for Dr. Pieter Rouwendal who accepted this work to be published with Summum Academic Publications. And I specifically mention the four Dutch foundations who contributed financially to make this publication possible: Stichting Zonneweelde, Jurriaanse Stichting, Sormanifonds and the Gilles Hondius Foundation. Thank you for your generous donations.

A special thanks to my parents who taught me to pursue those things I am enthusiast about and who taught me to work in a disciplined and organized manner. This is still of great help for me every day.

Last, but certainly not least, my gratitude belongs to my wife Patricia and our children. She made it possible for me to constantly set time apart to study, read, write and rewrite. She has been and still is the best what happened to me. The pillar besides me and from time to time *gegenüber* me. May the Lord bless you and keep you so that you will continue to be a rich blessing to others. It is to you Patricia that I dedicate this work.

Rev. dr. Marco Wittenberg
Amstelveen, June 2018

ABBREVIATIONS[1]

AGAJU	Arbeiten zur Geschichte des antiken Judentums und des Urchristentums
AJPS	*Asian Journal of Pentecostal Studies*
AncB	Anchor Bible
AdvSem	Advances in Semiotics
BAFCS	The Book of Acts in its First Century Setting
BDAG	W. Bauer, F.W. Danker, *A Greek-English Lexicon of the New Testament and Other Early Christian Literature* (Chicago: University of Chicago Press, ³2000)
BECNT	Baker Exegetical Commentary on the New Testament
BTB	*Biblical Theology Bulletin*
BTNTS	Biblical Theology of the New Testament Series
CBC	Collegeville Bible Commentary
CBR	*Currents in Biblical Research*
EKK	Evangelisch-Katholischer Kommentar zum Neuen Testament
EQ	*Evangelical Quarterly*
ExpTim	*Expository Times*
HNT	Handbuch zum Neuen Testament
HThK	Herders theologischer Kommentar zum Neuen Testament
ICC	International Critical Commentary
JBL	*Journal of Biblical Literature*
JGRChJ	*Journal of Greco-Roman Christianity and Judaism*
JPT	*Journal of Pentecostal Theology*
JPTSub	Journal of Pentecostal Theology Supplement Series
JSNT	*Journal for the Study of the New Testament*
JSNTSup	Journal for the Study of the New Testament Supplement Series
JSOT	*Journal for the Study of the Old Testament*
KEK	Kritisch-Exegetischer Kommentar über das Neue Testament
LNTS	Library of New Testament Studies
NCBC	New Collegeville Bible Commentary
NICNT	The New International Commentary on the New Testament

---

1 I have used the guidelines of the SBL Handbook of Style: P.H. Alexander (ed.), The SBL Handbook of Style. For Ancient, Near Eastern, Biblical and Early Christian Studies (Peabody, MA: Hendrickson, 2014), 68-152.

NIGTC	New International Greek Testament Commentary
NovT	*Novum Testamentum*
NovTSup	Supplements to Novum Testamentum
NTOA	Novum Testamentum et orbis antiquus
NTT	New Testament Theology
RBL	Review of Biblical Literature
RNT	Regensburger Neues Testament
SBL	Society of Biblical Literature
SBT	Studies in Biblical Theology
SJT	*Scottish Journal of Theology*
SNTS	Society for New Testament Studies
SNTSMS	Society for New Testament Studies Monograph Series
SPg	Sacra Pagina
StNT	Studien zum Neuen Testament
SUNT	Studien zur Umwelt des Neuen Testaments
SwJT	*Southwestern Journal of Theology*
TANZ	Texte und Arbeiten zum neutestamentlichen Zeitalter
TPQ	Theologisch-praktische Quartalschrift
TU	Texte und Untersuchungen zur Geschichte der altchristlichen Literatur
VE	*Vox Evangelica*
WBC	Word Biblical Commentary
WUNT	Wissenschaftliche Untersuchungen zum Neuen Testament
ZDPV	Zeitschrift des Deutschen Palästina-Vereins

INTRODUCTION

In search for a Lukan Pneumatology
One of the intriguing questions within theology and biblical studies is why there are several, different and often opposed interpretations of the same biblical text. And are these different interpretations all equally valid, legitimate and plausible? These are questions one stumbles upon whether active in academics, church ministry or pastoral activity. These are questions related to the biblical text on the one hand and the reader / interpreter of the biblical text on the other hand. This is in short what this dissertation is about: the role of the reader in his interpretation of the biblical text. What is the extent of the role of the reader? Can he or she make anything out of the text? *Create* meaning so to say. Or is it the text itself that has the last word and determines the right meaning? Or should we perhaps go back to the author of the text for the correct interpretation? These are all difficult, but valid, questions in the search for meaning and for the right interpretation of a biblical text. These questions put us on the intersection of biblical exegesis and hermeneutics. That is why in this present study there will be an interaction between these two theological disciplines. The text and author of the text (exegesis) on the one hand and the present day reader (hermeneutics) on the other hand. Both disciplines are needed for the interpretation of the biblical text.

One of the poignant issues that scholars, pastors and lay Christians stumble upon is the role and working of the Holy Spirit. The Holy Spirit seems to be elusive, untouchable, and doctrines about the Holy Spirit and the working of the Holy Spirit vary. Especially when it concerns the role and working of the Holy Spirit in the narrative of Luke-Acts. In construing a possible pneumatology of Luke-Acts, scholars have seldom reached agreements in their conclusions. It seems that quite often the exegetical outcome of a certain study is predetermined by a theological or denominational bias of the scholar. This suggests that the role of the reader is of significant importance during the process of reading and interpreting texts. And in addition this raises the question whether such a theological or denominational bias is allowed by the text of Luke-Acts. To put it differently: when is an interpretation right or wrong? And is there a clear dividing line between right or wrong? What criteria are used and why? This present study will provide an answer to these questions.

In general there have been numerous studies published on the Holy Spirit. Most of these studies are taken from a certain angle: a first distiction is made between the Old and the New Testament.[2] Within the New Testament a further distiction becomes visible: especially Paul, John and Luke are treated separately when it concerns their writings about the Holy Spirit. As the table below shows, Paul and Luke are the ones who deal extensively with the Spirit:[3]

	Total occurances of πνεῦμα	Meaning (Holy) Spirit
Matthew	19	12
Mark	23	6
Luke-Acts	106	75
Gospel and letters of John1	36	33
Pauline letters2	145	125

The Gospel of Luke together with the Book of Acts cover approximately 27% of the New Testament writings and provide us with a consistent narrative in which the Holy Spirit is frequently mentioned. These statistics demonstrate the importance of this two volume work for the whole of the New Testament and for pneumatology. In regard to pneumatology the Gospel of Luke and the Book of Acts are frequently quoted within charismatic or Pentecostal circles. The distinctive Pentecostal doctrine of *Baptism in the Spirit* is almost solely based on data derived from the Book of

---

2 See for instance: W.C. Kaiser, 'The Indwelling Presence of the Holy Spirit in the Old Testament' *EQ* 82 (2010), pp.308-315; C.J.H. Wright, *Knowing the Holy Spirit through the Old Testament* (Oxford/Downers Grove, IL: Monarch/IVP, 2006); J.M. Hamilton Jr., *God's Indwelling Presence: The Holy Spirit in the Old & New Testaments* (Nashville: B&H Academic, 2006); G. Beynon, *Experiencing the Spirit: New Testament Essentials for Every Christian* (Leicester: IVP, 2006); J.C. Thomas, *The Spirit of the New Testament* (Leiden: Deo, 2005); K. Warrington, *Discovering the Holy Spirit in the New Testament* (Peabody, MA: Hendrickson, 2005); M.M.B. Turner, *The Holy Spirit and Spiritual Gifts Then and Now* (Carlisle: Paternoster, 1996); W. Hildebrandt, *An Old Testament Theology of the Spirit of God* (Grand Rapids, MI: Baker Academic, 1993). For an overview of the Holy Spirit in the letters of Paul see: G.D. Fee, *God's Empowering Presence: The Holy Spirit in the Letters of Paul* (Peabody, MA: Hendrickson, 1994).
3 W.F. Moulton, A.S. Geden and H.K. Moulton, *A Concordance to the Greek Testament* (Edinburgh: T&T Clark, 1978), 819-823.

Acts.[4] It is only in the Book of Acts that we read about Pentecost, the outpouring of the Holy Spirit, an important event to pay attention to while searching for a Lukan Pneumatology. Considering all this it should not come as a surprise that Luke-Acts provide an excellent arena to search for the distinctive role of the reader in construing a Lukan Pneumatology.

Setting the parameters for this study
Methodology of the study
The elements of interest in this study are Lukan pneumatology and the role of the reader. As already stated above these elements are situated in the areas of exegesis and hermeneutics. In these disciplines diverse methods were and are used. Historical criticism, source criticism, literary criticism and reader-response strategies are just a few. This research is foremost an exploration of the role of the reader: how is the specific Lukan text concerning the Holy Spirit read and interpreted? This exploration of the role of the reader in regard to a possible Lukan pneumatology is captivated in a research question, which is expressed as follows:

> What is the role of the reader in construing a Lukan pneumatology?

To come to a satisfying answer to this research question I have formulated four sub-questions:

1. What is the *status quaestionis* concerning Lukan pneumatology?
2. What is a useful method for determining the role of the reader in a narrative text?
3. How can we understand the differences within Lukan pneumatology while focusing on three specific readers?
4. What is the role of the reader in Lukan pneumatology?

These four sub questions will all be addressed in the different chapters of this study, a brief outline of these chapters will be given below. To gain a good grasp of the differences in interpretation and the possible influences of a certain denominational background, three different scholars will be discussed. All three are experts on the topic of Luke-Acts and/or pneumatology and all three have published in these areas. Subsequently Max

---

4 See for the 16 fundamental truths of the international Assemblies of God: http://www.ag.org/top/beliefs/ statement_of_fundamental_truths/sft_full.cfm#7. Truths number 7 and 8 deal explicitly with the Holy Spirit.

Turner, Robert Menzies and William Kurz will be discussed. All three are from a different denominational background: Max Turner is an ordained Baptist minister and professor emeritus at London School of Theology; Robert Menzies is a Pentecostal scholar and missionary; William Kurz is a Catholic Priest and New Testament professor at Marquette University. These three scholars with their respective backgrounds will prove to be of great interest to gain insight in the various interpretive choices that are made during the reading process. As a result the specific role of the reader in the process of interpreting can be determined.

Assumptions of the study
This study offers *a* certain treatment of the Spirit texts in Luke-Acts, using *a* certain model and discussed through a limited selection of only three scholars. The aim of this study is not to be all comprehensive, that is simply impossible. In addition I am aware of my own background and of my own reading of the Lukan narrative and of the three scholars. At this point, at the beginning of this study it seems only proper to briefly elaborate on my own assumptions before embarking on the journey of determining the role of the reader in construing a Lukan pneumatology.

The Gospel of Luke and the Book of Acts will be studied together as Luke-Acts. This approach is based
on the assumption that there is a narrative and theological unity between the two works.[5] In addition I will use "Luke" to refer to the author of Luke-Acts. In doing so I make no assumptions to the author's actual identity, but I use the term for the sake of convenience.

The role of Luke as author of Luke-Acts is a combined role of theologian, historian and storyteller at the same time. In assuming so I follow the scholarly consensus about these various roles as elaborated upon in the first chapter of this study. This combined role is also of importance of the typical genre of Luke-Acts. It is not the aim of this study to treat the genre of Luke-Acts, however it is my assumption that Luke wrote a two volume narrative (story), based upon history and with theological purposes in mind. In the development of this study I will use systematic the-

---

5 Contra Mikael Parsons and Richard Pervo, *Rethinking the Unity of Luke-Acts* (Minneapolis, MN: Fortress, 1993) and Patricia Walters, *The Assumed Authorial Unity of Luke and Acts. A Reassessment of the Evidence* (Cambridge: Cambridge University, 2008). For a positive evaluation of the unity of Luke and Acts see: Howard Marshall, "Acts and the 'Former Treatise'" in: Bruce Winter and Andrew Clarke (eds.), *The Book of Acts in its Ancient Literary Setting* (BAFCS volume 1; Grand Rapids, MI / Carlisle: Eerdmans / Paternoster: 1993), 163-182.

ological terminology such as pneumatology, soteriology, missiology, eschatology. This terminology is used for the sake of convenience. With this terminology I do not mean that the original author of Luke-Acts had a full blown systematic theology in mind or that he used these terms as contemporary theologians do. The same is true when I use terms as "soteriological Spirit, missiological Spirit and eschatological Spirit". These are terms to designate the way scholars interpret the first and foremost working of the Spirit, for example: the Spirit is only for salvation or the Spirit is only a power for missions. So these terms are also used for the sake of convenience and not to suggest that the original author had such a systematical theological mindset.

A last remark concerns my use of "he" when I refer to the reader in general. For the sake of brevity I use "he", but it is possible and equally valid to read "she" as well.

Procedure of this study
Chapter one is a *Forschungsbericht* on Lukan Pneumatology. Forty-five years of research, from 1970 until 2015, will be discussed. The main focus in this chapter is on the very few agreements and the most prominent disagreements that scholars have about the Spirit in Luke-Acts. The Gospel of Luke and the Book of Acts are indeed a 'storm center' when it comes to all the different opinions, exegetical choices and pastoral applications which are made in relation to the working of the Holy Spirit.[6] The Holy Spirit as depicted in Luke-Acts forms the cornerstone for a Pentecostal Pneumatology.[7] The close correlation between receiving the Spirit and water baptism and/or laying on of hands in Luke-Acts are 'proof texts' for sacramentalists and confirmationalists.[8] And then there is still

---

6 The term 'storm center' is from W.C. van Unnik, 'Luke-Acts: A Storm Center in Contemporary Scholarship' in: L.E. Keck and J.L. Martyn, eds., *Studies in Luke-Acts* (Nashville, TN: Abingdon, 1966), 15-32.

7 In addition to the above mentioned fundamental truths of the international Assemblies of God (see above in note 5) Luke-Acts is sometimes also used as a canon within the canon by Pentecostals, see: Kenneth J. Archer, *A Pentecostal Hermeneutic for the Twenty-First Century: Spirit, Scripture and Community* (JPTSS 28; London; New York: T&T Clark, 2004), 138-139 and also Max M.B. Turner, *Power From On High: The Spirit in Israel's Restoration and Witness in Luke-Acts* (JPTSS 9; Sheffield: Sheffield Academic, 1996), 48.

8 For instance: N. Adler, *Taufe und Handauflegung. Eine exegetisch theologische Untersuchung von Apg, 8, 14-17* (NTAbh 19, heft 3; Münster: Aschendorf, 1951). The doctrine of Confirmation suggests the Spirit is received after conversion through the sacrament of Confirmation.

the widespread influence of James Dunn's dissertation from 1970 who first and foremost argues that the Spirit in Luke-Acts is the soteriological Spirit.[9] At the end of this overview of agreements and disagreements the conclusion is that it will prove to be all the more worthwhile to take a closer look at the role of the reader while he interprets the Lukan texts concerning the Spirit.

Chapter two introduces the shift in hermeneutical approaches from author-oriented to text-oriented and eventually reader-oriented methods. Umberto Eco developed and described a model which provides insight in the specific steps and thoughts a reader makes while reading and processing a text. This model is extensively described in this second chapter and is very suitable for the narrative of Luke-Acts, because Luke-Acts is a story. All the πνεῦμα texts in Luke-Acts are subsequently clustered in ten clusters which provide the outline for next three chapters in which the three mentioned scholars will be discussed.

Chapter three is an assessment of the work of Max Turner on the Holy Spirit in Luke-Acts. Turner, a prolific author is professor emeritus at London School of Theology and he has published in abundance on Luke-Acts as well as on the Holy Spirit. Characteristic for his work on the Holy Spirit in Luke-Acts is the way in which he meticulously treats every text and passage. In combination with his wide knowledge of the Old Testament background of the "Spirit of prophecy" he proves to be an interesting reader to discuss.

In *chapter four* the work of Pentecostal scholar Robert Menzies will be discussed. The subject of his 1991 PhD dissertation was Lukan Pneumatology and provides the basis for his reading and interpretation of the Lukan πνεῦμα texts. Menzies' thorough knowledge of Pentecostal doctrine and his heart for missions result in an engaged reader and interpreter of the Lukan texts. He however has a distinctive view on the Holy Spirit in Luke-Acts, which is in certain ways opposed to that of Max Turner.

---

9 James D.G. Dunn, *Baptism in the Holy Spirit: A Re-examination of the New Testament Teaching on the Gift of the Spirit in Relation to Pentecostalism Today* (London: SCM, 1970). Dunn later admitted frankly that he saw the Spirit in Luke-Acts through Pauline spectacles, but still held to his view of the Spirit in Luke-Acts as being foremost the soteriological Spirit. See: James D.G. Dunn, 'Baptism in the Spirit: A Response to Pentecostal Scholarship on Luke-Acts', *JPT* 3 (1993), 6.

Chapter five turns to the last scholar under scrutiny and this is the Roman Catholic scholar William S. Kurz. He published several books on Luke-Acts, including a recent commentary on the Book of Acts.

His work is characterized by a combination of scholarly work with a direct application for the church today. His reading and interpretation of the Lukan πνεῦμα texts is colored by his Roman Catholic background and Kurz does not hesitate to encourage individual Christians and the Catholic church to respond in faith to these Lukan texts.

In *chapter six* the limits and possibilities of interpretations will be discussed. The criteria for a cooperative and responsible interpretation will be set and subsequently six fundamental passages (three from the Gospel of Luke and three from the Book of Acts) in Luke-Acts will be briefly discussed. This eventually leads to an assessment of the three scholars in which their respective roles as readers of the Lukan narrative will be discussed.

This study closes with the *conclusion* of this research. My findings will be briefly summarized and I will provide a workable set of criteria to come to a responsible interpretation of the Spiritpassages in Luke-Acts.

---

10 Due to the different genre of Revelation I only mention the Gospel and the letters of John. For the number of occurrences see G.M. Burge, The Anointed Community. The Holy Spirit in the *Johannine Tradittion* (Grand Rapids, MI: Eerdmans, 1987), 41-43.
11 Here I did not make a distinction between the disputed and the undisputed letters of Paul, so this counting of πνεῦμα is within all the thirteen New Testament letters designated to Paul. The numbers are based on Fee, Gods Empo*wering Presence*, 14-15.

CHAPTER 1
FORSCHUNGSBERICHT

1.1 Introduction

In the abundance of pneumatological studies on Luke-Acts, excellent overviews have been given.[1] Most of them better than I could do. So it is not my intention to rewrite or rehearse the work that others already have done. The footnote below and the bibliography at the end of this study provide detailed information of research done during the past century. My intention here is to focus on the main areas of consensus and of disagreement among the different scholars. By taking this angle as a point of departure, at the end of this chapter it will become clear what is "solid ground" (consensus) and what is still disputed and contested within Lukan Pneumatology.

---

1   Robert P. Menzies, *The Development of Early Christian Pneumatology with Special Reference to Luke-Acts* (JSNTS 54; Sheffield: Sheffield Academic, 1991), 18-46; Max M.B. Turner, *Power from on High: The Spirit in Israel's Restoration and Witness in Luke-Acts* (JPTSS 9; Sheffield: Sheffield Academic, 1996), 20-79; Scott Cunningham, *Through Many Tribulations: The Theology of Persecution in Luke-Acts* (JSNTS 142; Sheffield: Sheffield Academic, 1997), 23-42; Ju Hur, *Dynamic Reading of the Holy Spirit in Luke-Acts* (Sheffield: Sheffield Academic, 2001), 13-26; Matthias Wenk, *Community-Forming Power: The Socio-Ethical Role of the Spirit in Luke-Acts* (Sheffield: Sheffield Academic, 2001), 13-43; François Bovon, *Luke the Theologian: Fifty-Five Years of Research (1950-2005)* (Trans. Ken McKinney: Waco, TX: Baylor University, 2006), 225-272; Martin W. Mittelstadt, *Reading Luke-Acts in the Pentecostal Tradition* (Cleveland, TN: CPT, 2010); Aaron Kuecker, *The Spirit and the "Other": Social Identity, Ethnicity, and Intergroup Reconciliation in Luke-Acts* (New York, London: T&T Clark, 2011), 1-17; William P. Atkinson, *Baptism in the Spirit. Luke-Acts and the Dunn debate* (Eugene, OR: Pickwick, 2011); Jonathan Kienzler, *The Fiery Holy Spirit: The Spirit's Relationship with Judgment in Luke-Acts* (JPTSS; Winona Lake, IN: Eisenbrauns/Deo, 2015). In addition see the recent and extensive commentaries on Acts: Richard I. Pervo, *Acts: A Commentary* (Hermeneia; Augsburg, MN: Fortress, 2008); Craig S. Keener, *Acts An Exegetical Commentary* (4 vols.; Grand Rapids, MI: Baker Academic, 2012-2015).

When it comes to consensus, already in 1998 Max Turner summed up five topics of agreement:[2]

1. The Old Testament background of Luke's Spirit material;
2. The Spirit "as uniting motif and driving force within Lukan salvation history";
3. The Spirit in Luke-Acts is the "Spirit of prophecy";
4. The Spirit in Luke-Acts has relatively little to do with the "spiritual, ethical and religious renewal of the individual";
5. Luke expands his Pneumatology beyond that of Judaism in attributing Christocentric functions to the Spirit.

However, when closer examined these five points of consensus are only superficial agreements. Directly after his summary of these points, Aaron Kuecker shows his disagreements or as he calls it "deficits" on the study of the Spirit in Luke-Acts.[3]

In 1966 Willem Cornelis van Unnik discussed the debate in New Testament scholarship whether Luke should be treated as a historian or as a theologian.[4] So before something can be said about the Lukan concept of the Spirit, it is necessary to take some time and elaborate on Luke as a historian, a theologian and a storyteller. Scholars do agree about exactly these three roles of Luke.

1.2 The Holy Spirit in Luke-Acts: Main Areas of Consensus
1.2.1 Luke as Historian, Theologian and Storyteller
Luke as a historian. Traditionally Luke has been seen as a historian.[5]

---

2 Max M.B. Turner, "The Spirit of Prophecy as the Power of Israel's Restoration and Witness." in: I. Howard Marshall and David Peterson, eds., *Witness to the Gospel: The Theology of Acts* (Grand Rapids, MI: Eerdmans, 1998), 328-333. Aaron Kuecker reflects on these five points of agreement: Kuecker, *The Spirit and the "Other"*, 2-3. See also Kuecker's Ph.D. Thesis (Scotland: University of St. Andrews, 2008), 16-17 (downloadable at http://research-repository.st-andrews.ac.uk/ handle/ 10023/532). For a short treatment of prominent German influence on Lukan Pneumatology see appendix 3.
3 Kuecker, *The Spirit and the "Other"*, 17-20.
4 Willem C. van Unnik, "Luke-Acts: A Storm Center in Contemporary Scholarship" in: L.E. Keck and J.L. Martyn, eds., *Studies in Luke-Acts* (Nashville, TN: Abingdon, 1966), 15-32.
5 D.A. Carson, D.J. Moo and L. Morris, *An Introduction to the New Testament* (Leicester/Grand Rapids, MI: Apollos/Zondervan, 1992, ²1994), 122-123; D. Marguerat, *The First Christian Historian: Writing the "Acts of the Apostles"* (orig. French, transl. K. McKinney, G.J. Laughery and R. Bauckham; SNTS 121; Cambridge: University, 2002). Marguerat combines historical criticism with narrative criticism to find out what Lukes

With the turn from the 19th to the 20th century there were two different currents of research visible: a conservative (mostly British) and a less conservative (mostly German) current. [6] The historical reliability of primarily the Book of Acts became a measuring rod for conservatism. Numerous studies about Luke-Acts as (some sort of) history followed, all closely knitted together with the question of the genre of the Book of Acts.[7] Methodologically source-criticism was used and along rough lines the argument was that Luke never attended or heard any of the speeches in Acts, so how could this material be trustworthy? Let alone be historically correct? If you add to this the obvious redactional phrases and summaries, one might start to wonder about Luke's abilities as a historian. On the other hand it is argued that Luke made use of reliable sources and used his own redactional creativity to make the speeches fit in correctly into the whole of the story. Earl Richard proved in his excellent discussion of Acts 6:1 – 8:4 how speech and narrative are an integral part of the

---

theological agenda was. T.E. Philips, "The Genre of Acts: Moving Toward a Consensus?", *CBR 4.3* (2006), 365-366; M. Hengel, "Der Historiker Lukas und die Geographie Palästinas in der Apostelgeschichte" *ZDPV 98* (1983); M. Dibelius, and K.C. Hanson (ed.), *The Book of Acts: Form, Style and Theology* (Orig. German; transl. M. Ling; Minneapolis: Fortress, 2004), 14-31. See for the importance of the preface to the Gospel of Luke L.C.A. Alexander, *The Preface to Luke's Gospel: Literary Convention and Social Context in Luke 1.1-4 and Acts 1.1* (SNTSMS 78; Cambridge: University, 1993).

6   Names attached to both of these currents are for instance: F.F. Bruce, I.H. Marshall, C.J. Hemer, L. Goppelt and M. Hengel (conservative) and M. Dibelius, H. Conzelmann, E. Haenchen, J. Bihler and M. Sabbe (less conservative). See for more background information: Philips, "Genre of Acts", 365-366; T. Penner, *In Praise of Christian Origins: Stephen and the Hellenists in Lukan Apologetic Historiography* (ESEC; New York, London: T&T Clark, 2004), 1-3 and H.W. Neudorfer, *Der Stephanuskreis in der Forschungsgeschichte seit F.C. Baur* (Giessen, Basel: Brunnen Verlag, 1983), 10-11.

7   For example: T. Penner, *In Praise of Christian Origins*; C.K. Rothschild, *Luke-Acts and the Rhetoric of History: An Investigation of Early Christian Historiography* (WUNT 2.Reihe 175; Tübingen: Mohr Siebeck, 2004); D.W. Palmer, "Acts and the Ancient Historical Monograph" in: Winter, B.W. and Clark, A.D. (eds.), *The Book of Acts in its Ancient Literary Setting* (BAFCS 1; Grand Rapids, MI: Eerdmans, 1994), 1-29; L.C.A. Alexander, "Acts and Ancient Intellectual Biography" in: B.W. Winter and A.D. Clark, (eds.), *The Book of Acts in its Ancient Literary Setting* (BAFCS 1; Grand Rapids, MI: Eerdmans, 1994), 31-64; R.I. Pervo, *Profit with Delight: The Literary Genre of the Acts of the Apostles* (Philadelphia: Fortress, 1987); E. Plümacher, *Lukas als hellenistischer Schriftsteller: Studien zur Apostelgeschichte* (SUNT 9; Göttingen: Vandenhoeck & Ruprecht, 1972).

whole of the Book of Acts and are the work of one and the same author.[8] It looks like one's own prejudices about the trustworthiness of Luke's sources determine whether or not Luke is reliable. Attached to this there are a lot of additional questions, such as: What kind of history was written by Luke? Is it the same history as 21st century history? Is there any difference between the Gospel and Acts or should we take both books as two volumes of one written work? What about questions dealing with normativity? Is a historical precedent in Luke-Acts normative for today or is it pure descriptive? And what about a "canon within a canon"? And how to determine what is descriptive and what is normative? Here we come to the point when questions asked are not pure historical questions, but also hermeneutical, theological and literary questions. It soon became clear that Luke was more than just a historian. In 1970 the book by Ian Howard Marshall, *Luke: Historian and Theologian*, was published.[9] Marshall starts with a short discussion on different methodological approaches towards Luke-Acts. Then, in chapter two, he extensively treats the nature of history and the writing of history. In chapter three he continues to discuss Luke's sources. For the Gospel Luke used the Gospel of Mark and "Q", for Acts it is not possible to determine any sources which Luke could have used.[10] The way one looks at the speeches in Acts is important to ones understanding of Luke as a historian and a theologian.[11] Marshall concludes:

a. Luke uses history to promote his theology;[12]
b. Luke is a historian who does not hesitate to include miraculous or supernatural events in his narrative;[13]

---

8   Earl Richard, *Acts 6:1-8:4 The Authors Method of Composition* (SBLDS 41; Missoula, MT: Scholars, 1978).
9   I. Howard Marshall, *Luke: Historian and Theologian* (Grand Rapids, MI: Zondervan, 1970). This monograph shows the historical and theological value of Luke's work.
10 This is not the place to discuss the Q-hypothesis. See for more background information on Mark and Q as sources and the Lukan *Sondergut*: Bart D. Ehrman, *The New Testament: A Historical Introduction to the Early Christian Writings* (New York: Oxford University, ⁴2007), 83-91 and Udo Schnelle, *Einleitung in das neue Testament* (Göttingen: Vandenhoeck & Ruprecht, 1994), translated in English by M.E. Boring, *The History and Theology of the New Testament Writings* (Augsburg: Fortress, 1998), 151-257.
11 Marshall finds it likely that Luke incorporated the speeches in Acts because preaching was an essential element and integral part of the activity of the early church. Marshall, *Luke: Historian and Theologian*, 73.
12 Marshall, *Luke: Historian and Theologian*, 19.
13 Marshal, *Luke: Historian and Theologian*, 28-30. Taken from Lukes perspective these events were an essential and integral part of the history he was writing.

c. Luke gives a particular interpretation to historical events which would not be shared by a secular modern historian.[14]

Luke as a theologian. In the preface to his commentary on Luke, Marshall writes it is justified to publish a new commentary on Luke, since the one by John M. Creed (1930)[15] did not *regard Luke as a theologian in his own right* (italics are mine).[16] A lot had changed during those 45 years and more and more scholars agreed on Luke being a theologian. A few pages later Marshall comments on the purpose of the Gospel and argues "Of all the Evangelists he is the most conscious of writing as a historian, yet throughout his work the history is the vehicle of the theological interpretation in which the significance of Jesus is expressed."[17] So here we see the shift in the treatment of Luke. History is the means of telling the theological story of Jesus. This is exactly the point of view Marshall advocates in his 1970 book, *Luke: Historian and Theologian*, in which he starts the discussion on the theology of Luke from chapter four. Influential works about Luke the theologian are the books by Hans Conzelmann,[18] Ernst Haenchen[19] and Oscar Cullmann.[20] Keyword in Conzelmann's approach is *Heilsgeschichte*, salvation-history. Due to the delay of the parousia, Luke was forced to write about history and made the period of the church fit into it. This is how Conzelmann came to the division of three different periods of time: (1) the preparation for Jesus' ministry; (2) Jesus' ministry and (3) the period since the ascension of Jesus. Where Conzelmann makes more use of the Gospel than of Acts, Haenchen focuses on Acts. In his opinion Luke is first and foremost a theologian who wishes to edify the church. He thinks Luke paints an idealized picture of the early church, where the preaching of the word of God ties the period of Jesus to the period of the church. It is here where the term "early Catholicism" (*Früh-*

---

14 Marshall, *Luke: Historian and Theologian*, 56.
15 J.M. Creed, *St. Luke* (London: MacMillan, 1930).
16 I. Howard Marshall, *The Gospel of Luke: A Commentary on the Greek Text* (NIGTC; Grand Rapids, MI: Paternoster/Eerdmans, 1978), 15.
17 Marshall, *The Gospel of Luke*, 35.
18 Hans Conzelmann, *Die Mitte der Zeit: Studien zur Theologie des Lukas* (Tübingen: Mohr Siebeck, ¹1953, ⁷1993) and *Grundriss der Theologie des Neuen Testaments* (München: Kaiser, 1967).
19 Ernst Haenchen, *Die Apostelgeschichte* (KEK III¹⁶; Göttingen: Vandenhoeck & Ruprecht, 1956, ⁷1977).
20 Oscar Cullmann, *Heil als Geschichte: Heilsgeschichtlichte Existenz im Neuen Testament* (Tübingen: Mohr Siebeck, 1965).

katholizismus) comes to the surface. Cullmann does not limit the term salvation-history only to Luke-Acts, but sees it throughout the whole of the New Testament and states that Luke did not invent this, but that it was already a part of Christian thinking. Luke did not write to come to some sort of "early Catholicism", but Luke's writings are a consistent development of the message of Jesus.[21] Marshall states it somewhat sharper when he writes:

> "Consequently, while we freely admit the presence of salvation-history in Luke-Acts, the idea is not distinctive of Luke, nor was it his theological purpose to bring it to expression [...] Luke's concern is with the saving significance of the history rather than with the history itself as bare facts."[22]

This brings Marshall to the conclusion that Luke's theology is a theology of salvation.[23] A quarter of a century later, Joel B. Green underwrites this conclusion in his works on the Gospel of Luke.[24]

Luke as a storyteller. In the opening chapter of his study on Stephen and the Hellenists, Todd Penner marks the work of Henry Cadbury, *The Making of Luke-Acts* (1927), as groundbreaking because he began to view Luke-Acts as a literary product.[25] Cadbury compared the letters of Paul with Luke in the way they made use of common literary conventions: the opening and closing of Paul's letters were common in his days, so were certain Lukan literary characteristics.[26] In 1974 the book by Charles Talbert, *Literary Patterns, Theological Themes and the Genre of Luke-Acts*, was published.[27] More recently in the *Reading the New Testament* commentary series (of which Talbert is the editor) Talbert's commentaries on

---

21 Marshall, *Luke: Historian and Theologian*, 83.
22 Marshall, *Luke: Historian and Theologian*, 84-85.
23 Prominently based on the use of the words σῴζω, σωτήρ, σωτηρία and σωτήριον. Marshall, *Luke: Historian and Theologian*, 92.
24 Joel B. Green, *The Theology of the Gospel of Luke* (NTT 3; Cambridge: Cambridge University, 1995); Joel B. Green, *The Gospel of Luke* (NICNT; Grand Rapids, MI: Eerdmans, 1997), 21-22. For other recent theologies on Luke-Acts see: Darrell L. Bock, *A Theology of Luke and Acts: God's Promised Program, Realized for All nations* (BTNTS; Grand Rapids, MI: Zondervan, 2012) and Paul Kragt, *The Theology of Luke-Acts: Jesus as Prophet* (Ebook; Amazon digital services, 2015).
25 Todd Penner, *In Praise of Christian Origins*, 1-2.
26 Henry J. Cadbury, *The Making of Luke-Acts* (New York: MacMillan, 1927), 194.
27 Charles H. Talbert, *Literary Patterns, Theological Themes and the Genre of Luke-Acts* (SBLMS 20; Missoula, MT: Scholars, 1974).

Luke and on the Book of Acts were published.[28] This shows the shift that has taken place within Lukan research: more and more the focus became on the *story* of Luke-Acts. The work of Richard Pervo, *Profit with Delight: The Literary Genre of the Acts of the Apostles* gave the literary research on Luke-Acts a further stimulus.[29] Literary characteristics as style, parallelisms, figures of speech, patterns of repetition became important and prominent in recent research.[30] The unity of both works of Luke was stressed, the importance of the prologue, *hearing* the story instead of *reading* it, renewed interest in the genre of Luke-Acts and the use of modern literary approaches to study Luke-Acts.[31] To summarize the literary work: Luke's theological aims were presented in a *story*.[32] This research shows that Luke was a storyteller. Or perhaps it is better to say that Luke was a *narrative theologian*, just as for instance Kenneth Bailey calls Jesus a *metaphorical theologian*.[33]

1.2.2 The Background of the Holy Spirit in Luke-Acts

It is generally acknowledged that Luke used the Old Testament as a background for his two-volume work. But what about the period of second

---

28 Charles H. Talbert, *Reading Luke. A Literary and Theological Commentary* (RNT; New York: Crossroad, 1982; Macon, GA: Smyth & Helwys, 22002) and *Reading Acts. A Literary and Theological Commentary on the Acts of the Apostles* (RNT; New York: Crossroad, 1997; Macon, GA: Smyth & Helwys, 22005). For a short overview of Talbert's influence on the study of Luke-Acts see F.S. Spencer, "Acts and Modern Literary Approaches" in: B.W. Winter and A.D. Clark, *The Book of Acts in its Ancient Literary Setting* (BAFCS 1; Grand Rapids, MI: Eerdmans, 1994), 386-391.
29 R.I. Pervo, *Profit with Delight: The Literary Genre of the Acts of the Apostles* (Philadelphia: Fortress, 1987).
30 See for instance: S.M. Praeder, "Jesus-Paul, Peter-Paul and Jesus-Peter Parallelisms in Luke-Acts: A History of Reader Response", *SBL Seminar Papers, vol. 23* (1984), 23-39.
31 A. Cornils, *Vom Geist Gottes erzählen: Analysen zur Apostelgeschichte* (TANZ 44; Tübingen: Francke, 2006).
32 Robert C. Tannehill, *The Narrative Unity of Luke-Acts: A Literary Interpretation*, (Philadelphia, Minneapolis: Fortress, 1986, 1990). For a short discussion of Tannehill's two volume commentary see Spencer, "Acts and Modern Literary Approaches", 393-396. See also: P. Borgman, *The Way According to Luke: Hearing the Whole Story of Luke-Acts* (Grand Rapids, MI: Eerdmans, 2006); Wilfrid J. Harrington, *Reading Luke for the First Time* (Mahwah, NJ: Paulist, 2015).
33 Kenneth E. Bailey, *Jesus Through Middle Eastern Eyes. Cultural Studies in the Gospels* (London: SPCK, 2008), 279.

Temple Judaism? The monographs by Menzies,[34] Levison[35] and a response on Menzies' thesis by Turner,[36] shed some light on the development of early Jewish / Christian Pneumatology. Overall there seems to be consensus about the terminology "Spirit of prophecy", but the way this terminology is exactly interpreted differs.

Robert P. Menzies. In part I of his monograph Menzies treats respectively the Diaspora, Palestinian, Qumran and Rabbinic literature, followed by part II in which he discusses Lukan Pneumatology and in part III he concludes with two chapters on the origin of Pauls soteriological Pneumatology. In short, Menzies comes to the conclusion that the Jews of the pre-Christian era generally regarded the gift of the Spirit as a *donum superadditum*. The gift of the Spirit was not soteriological, but given to individuals for a special task. Despite several exceptions Menzies is determined that Luke used this concept of the Spirit as a background for writing Luke- Acts.[37]

Max M.B. Turner. In part II of his *Power from on High*, Turner analyzes the "Spirit of Prophecy" in Judaism and as a background to Luke-Acts, in which his primary sparring partner is Robert Menzies. Turner's major point of disagreement in his response to Menzies is that Menzies takes the "Spirit of prophecy" as a *rigidly fixed concept* (italics are mine, choice of words is Turner's).[38] As a background to Lukan Pneumatology Menzies sees the Spirit of prophecy predominantly as the Spirit who inspires speech and that is why he dismisses other, more charismatic workings of the Spirit such as works of power, miracles and ethical renewal. As a background to Lukan Pneumatology Menzies sees the Spirit of prophecy predominantly as the Spirit who inspires speech and that is why he dis-

---

34 R.P. Menzies, *The Development of Early Christian Pneumatology with Special Reference to Luke-Acts* (JSNTS 54; Sheffield: Sheffield Academic, 1991), 52-112.
35 J.R. Levison, *The Spirit in First Century Judaism* (AGAJU 29; Leiden: Brill, 1997) and J.R. Levison, *Filled with the Spirit* (Grand Rapids, MI: Eerdmans, 2009).
36 Max M. B. Turner, *Power From On High: The Spirit in Israel's Restoration and Witness in Luke-Acts* (JPTSS 9; Sheffield: Sheffield Academic, 1996), 82-138.
37 The author of Wisdom sees the Spirit as soteriological; Philo comes close to this perspective; The Qumran community viewed the role of the Spirit to draw near to God (...) reception of the Spirit is necessary for one to know God and live within the community of salvation. See Menzies, *Development*, respectively 67, 76 and 89-90. For more on Menzies' view see below in chapter four.
38 Turner, *Power from on High*, 83.

misses other, more charismatic workings of the Spirit such as works of power, miracles and ethical renewal. In addition to this, soteriological workings of the Spirit could not have functioned as a background to Luke. According to Menzies the background of the Holy Spirit in Luke-Acts is limited to the Spirit of prophecy, the Spirit who (only) inspires speech. That is why Menzies sees three different pneumatologies come to the surface: one of inspired speech, a charismatic Pneumatology and a soteriological Pneumatology.[39] Turner, on the contrary, does not limit the background of Lukan Pneumatology to "inspired speech" alone, but also sees charismatic and spiritual/ethical renewal as characteristics of the "Spirit of Prophecy" and so "broadens" the background of Lukan Pneumatology. Turner concludes:

> "There is, therefore, in Judaism neither the sharp difference between the "Spirit of Prophecy" and the "charismatic Spirit" elucidated by Menzies; nor the equally sharp one he posits between the former and the "soteriological Spirit."[40]

John R. Levison. In his 1997 book on the Spirit in first-century Judaism,[41] Levison focuses on the writings of three early Jewish authors: Philo Judaeus[42], Pseudo-Philo[43] and Flavius Josephus.[44] His conclusions are:

a. An adequate explanation of first-century exegesis must take into consideration both the biblical text and related conceptions and interpretations that circulated during the Greco-Roman era;[45]

---

39 Menzies writes "Thus I shall distinguish Luke's "prophetic" Pneumatology from the "charismatic" perspective of the primitive church on the one hand, and Paul"s "soteriological" understanding of the Spirit on the other", Menzies, *Development*, 48.
40 Turner, *Power From On High*, 138. For Turner's substantiation of this conclusion see 103-137.
41 John R. Levison, *The Spirit in First Century Judaism* (AGAJU 29; Leiden, New York: Brill, 1997).
42 Philo Judaeus was an Alexandrian philosopher and statesmen, born between 20-10BC and died approximately   in 50CE.
43 Pseudo-Philo is the pseudonymous writer of *Liber Antiquitatem Biblicarum*, written during the first century
CE, in which the Jewish scriptures are retold from creation to the death of Saul.
44 Flavius Josephus was a Jewish general, born 37CE and died approximately around 100CE.
45 Levison, *The Spirit in First Century Judaism*, 79.

b. Palestinian interpretations of the Spirit derive almost nothing from their Greco-Roman context, while Diaspora interpretation of the Spirit cannot be understood without recourse to Greco-Roman prophetic phenomena, such as ecstasy and intellectual illumination;[46]
c. Jewish and Greco-Roman elements in first century Judaism function in unity with each other.[47]

In short, Levison holds to the view that there is a difference between Palestinian and Greco-Roman interpretations of the Spirit.[48] Next to this there is Platonic influence in describing ecstasy and intellectual illumination to the working of the Spirit in a individual.[49] At the end of his book Levison writes "...that a diversity of portraits of the spirit co-exist in the biblical interpretations of these three authors. [...] Each of these biblical interpreters preserves an astounding *variety of effects* of the spirit's presence."[50] To put it in other words, the work of Levison makes it abundantly clear there was not a one-and-only view of the Spirit in first century Judaism. Later on he concludes "it is ill-advised to attempt to ascertain for each first century author one dominant conception of the spirit."[51] Despite these conclusions, Levison himself does state that prophecy is the most pervasive effect of the Spirit. This caused different scholars to write about the Holy Spirit as the Spirit of prophecy. This is confirmed by Levison's study, although he strongly emphasizes the importance of the use of qualifying statements as "in the main" or "pre-eminently".[52] A few pages later Levison refers to the work of Menzies and warns for reconstructing an early Christian Pneumatology by focusing on one dominant effect of the Spirit.[53] All this underscores the consensus about the terminology of the "Spirit of prophecy" and at the same time demonstrates that the exact interpretation of such terminology can differ between various scholars.

---

46 Levison, *The Spirit in First Century Judaism*, 161-164.
47 Levison, *The Spirit in First Century Judaism*, 211.
48 Levison, *The Spirit in First Century Judaism*, 129.
49 Levison, *The Spirit in First Century Judaism*, 164.
50 Levison, *The Spirit in First Century Judaism*, 238 and later again on 240 (italics are Levison's).
51 Levison, *The Spirit in First Century Judaism*, 242.
52 Levison, *The Spirit in First Century Judaism*, 248.
53 Levison, *The Spirit in First Century Judaism*, 253.

A short note has to be made here on the book by Craig Keener,[54] published in the same year as Levison's *The Spirit in First Century Judaism*. Keener traces two streams of Jewish understandings of the Spirit, each stream with their subcategories. Both streams are respectively labeled as "Spirit of Purification" and "Spirit of Prophecy". Although at the beginning of his book Keener admits a third stream of "inspired insight" distinctive from prophecy would also be possible.[55] In a rather short overview (only 20 pages) Keener presents these two streams in early Judaism. Levison is critical in his review of Keener's book: the division in two streams is perhaps too easy for such a complicated matter as the Spirit in early Judaism.[56]

In his more recent book on the Spirit,[57] Levison develops his view on the Spirit and writes in three parts respectively on the Spirit in Israelite, Jewish and Christian literature. As a point of departure and framework to write within, Levinson uses the work of Hermann Gunkel.[58] Important for the background of Luke-Acts is Levison's conclusion in part II of his work about the false conception that the Spirit was quenched during second Temple Judaism.[59] In Greco-Roman literature there were images of fire used for the Spirit and ecstasy subscribed to the Spirit.[60] The Christian view of the Spirit and the Hebrew view of the Spirit are related, but also distinctive. Is the Spirit the Spirit of God given within the human being? Or is it an additional empowering for a specific task? It is here that we arrive in the area of disagreement.

To conclude this subsection on the background of Lukan Pneumatology we have seen the dividing line between agreement and disagreement is a very thin one. The terminology of "Spirit of prophecy" is widely used and shows a certain measure of agreement. However, the exact interpretation of this terminology differs. Menzies opts for a "one-and-only" interpretation.

---

54 C. S. Keener *The Spirit in the Gospels and Acts: Divine Purity and Power* (Peabody, MA: Hendrickson, 1997).
55 Keener, *The Spirit in the Gospels and Acts*, 4.
56 J.R. Levison, "Bookreview of *The Spirit in the Gospels and Acts: Divine Purity and Power*" *RBL* (1998).
57 J.R. Levison, *Filled with the Spirit* (Grand Rapids, MI: Eerdmans, 2009).
58 H. Gunkel, *Die Wirkungen des heiligen Geistes nach der populären Anschauung der apostolischen Zeit und der Lehre des Apostel Paulus* (Göttingen: Vandenhoeck & Ruprecht, 1899).
59 Levison, *Filled with the Spirit*, 116.
60 Levison, *Filled with the Spirit*, 170.

Turner takes a more mediating position while Levison leaves us actually in the dark concerning Luke's background, because there was a wide variety of views on the Spirit and the working of the Spirit in the pre-Christian era.

1.2.3 The Relation between the Holy Spirit and Mission in Luke-Acts
In his 2007 article about baptism in the Holy Spirit, Arie Zwiep mentions among the then current areas of consensus the "power-for-mission" character of the Spirit.[61] This mission motif is also briefly mentioned in Turner's article, "The Spirit of Prophecy as the Power of Israel's Restoration and Witness",[62] and made Hans von Baer to see three different epochs in Luke-Acts.[63]

In general terms scholars agree on the relation between the Spirit and mission in Luke-Acts. Just as is the case with the terminology "Spirit of prophecy", it is the question *how* this relation between mission and Spirit is interpreted. Zwiep suggests to qualify this relation with the adverb "predominantly" to tackle the instance in Acts 11:17 where Peter refers to the gift of the Spirit in a context of salvation.[64] On the other hand Robert Menzies uses the term "exclusively" to define the relation between Spirit and mission, taking a more narrow position in *Spirit and Power* (2000).[65] In his previous work, *The Development of Early Christian Pneumatology* (1991), Menzies is more careful and concludes "…the Spirit comes upon them all as the source of prophetic inspiration, granting special insight and inspiring speech."[66]

In reaction to the work of James Shelton, *Mighty in Word and Deed*,[67] Max Turner writes about the Spirit in Luke-Acts as being *mission-oriented*.[68] His three main objections against Shelton (and also Menzies) are:

---

61 Arie W. Zwiep "Luke's Understanding of Baptism in the Holy Spirit. An Evangelical Perspective", *PentecoStudies* 6 (2007), 130. Revised and reprinted in: A.W. Zwiep (ed.), *Christ, the Spirit and the Community of God: Essays on the Acts of the Apostles* (WUNT 2. Reihe 293; Tübingen: Mohr Siebeck, 2010), 100-119.
62 Turner, "Spirit of Prophecy", 329.
63 Hans von Baer, *Der Heilige Geist in den Lukasschriften* (Stuttgart: Kohlhammer, 1926).
64 Zwiep, "Luke's Understanding of Baptism in the Holy Spirit", 130, 142n.14.
65 Robert P. Menzies and William W. Menzies, *Spirit and Power. Foundations of Pentecostal Experience* (Grand Rapids, MI: Zondervan, 2000).
66 Menzies, *Development*, 278.
67 James B. Shelton, *Mighty in Word and Deed: The Role of the Holy Spirit in Luke-Acts* (Peabody, MA: Hendrickson, 1991).
68 Max M.B. Turner, "'Empowerment for Mission?' The Pneumatology of Luke-Acts: An Appreciation and Critique of James B. Shelton's *Mighty in Word and Deed*", *VE* 24 (1994), 103-122.

a. Only the two texts of Luke 24:47-49 and Acts 1:8 are in favour of the "exclusively empowerment-for-mission" position;[69]
b. Lukes ties the gift of the Spirit very closely to conversion and baptism;[70]
c. The restriction of the gift of the Spirit as *exclusively* for mission leads to a reductionist view of salvation in Luke-Acts.[71]

So again there is scholarly consensus on the relation between Spirit and mission in Luke-Acts, but the further interpretation of this consensus varies per scholar. One way or the other, the relation between Spirit and mission is somehow a first hint to read Luke's two volume work in the framework of a "theology of salvation" as already was mentioned by Howard Marshall and later by Joel Green.[72]

1.2.4 Conclusion
So far we have seen that there is scholarly consensus when it comes to the three roles Luke represents:

historian, theologian and storyteller. During the past century all three of these different roles were accentuated. During the last decades especially the roles of theologian and storyteller became intertwined and it is quite safe to speak of Luke as being a narrative theologian. That the Spirit in Luke-Acts is closely knitted to the mission of the church is beyond doubt. Discussion arises how to describe the relation between Spirit and mission: is this an exclusively or a predominantly relation?

Perhaps the most "contested" agreement is that of Luke's background of his concept of the Spirit. On a superficial level scholars do agree Luke used the Old Testament (LXX) as a background and agree on the usage of the term "Spirit of prophecy". However on a more profound level it soon becomes clear that the role of the respective reader plays an important part how to understand this Spirit of prophecy. We can conclude this is a fragile consensus.

1.3 The Holy Spirit in Luke-Acts: Theological Disagreements
1.3.1 Introduction
Before embarking on the specific pneumatological disagreements, I will highlight a few differing theological points of view in relation to Luke-Acts.

---

69 Turner, "Empowerment for Mission?", 114-116.
70 Turner, "Empowerment for Mission?", 117.
71 Turner, "Empowerment for Mission?", 117-119.
72 See above in §1.2.1 under *Luke as a theologian*.

No one starts reading or theologizing unbiased we all have our own presuppositions which we take with us in the process of reading. Through the years there has been (and still is) some scholarly debate on typical Lukan issues. Above we have already seen that in regard to the background of the Holy Spirit in Luke-Acts the consensus is very superficial. In this next section I briefly elaborate on three Lukan theological topics, which all three do influence one's view on the working of the Spirit in Luke-Acts.

1.3.2 The Theological Framework of Luke-Acts
There is scholarly debate whether there is a distinctive Lukan theological framework which fits the story of Luke-Acts. One of the questions to be answered concerns if there are certain clearly marked periods of time in Luke's two volume work. The origin of these distinctive periods of time within Luke-Acts stems from Hans von Baer, *Der Heilige Geist in den Lukasschriften* and was picked up in the groundbreaking work on Lukan Theology by Hans Conzelmann, *Die Mitte der Zeit*.[73] They both argue there are three clearly marked and distinctive periods of time to discover in Luke-Acts. Scholars do agree on the uniting effect of the Spirit in Luke-Acts, however they disagree on the question if Luke's theological framework consist of three sharply distinct periods of time. For example it is James Shelton's thesis that the Lukan phrases on the Spirit break down these divisions (contra Dunn and Conzelmann).[74] Turner nuances this in distinguishing between the non-eschatological content of the three periods (Conzelmann) and the three phases Joseph Fitzmyer sees with Jordan and the Ascension as borders.[75] Turner finds the linguistic basis of Shelton too small for a breakdown of divisions, he himself sees the differences on a phenomenological level. Despite the same language Luke is using, there is a qualitative difference between the working of the Spirit in the birth narratives, in the life of Jesus and in that of the disciples.[76]

---

73 H. von Baer, *Der Heilige Geist in den Lukasschriften* (Stuttgart: Kohlhammer, 1926); H. Conzelmann, *Die Mitte der Zeit. Studien zur Theologie des Lukas* (Tübingen: Mohr Siebeck, ¹1953, ⁷1993).
74 J.B. Shelton, *Mighty in Word and Deed: The Role of the Holy Spirit in Luke-Acts* (Peabody, MA: Hendrickson, 1991). 16, 25, 161.
75 M.M.B. Turner, ""Empowerment for Mission"? The Pneumatology of Luke-Acts: An Appreciation and Critique of James B. Shelton's Mighty in Word and Deed", VE 24 (1994). 110 and J. Fitzmyer, Luke the Theologian: Aspects of His Teaching (London: Chapman, 1989). 61-63 and J. Fitzmyer, *The Gospel According to Luke I-IX* (AncB 28; New York: Doubleday, 1981), 179-192.
76 Turner, "Empowerment for Mission?", 112.

John Nolland is not at all convinced of three sharply delineated periods in Luke-Acts. He argues that for Luke the same story keeps repeating only with different key-persons and developing to a climax. This repetition serves as some kind of "water-mark" and "places the emphasis on continuity and repetition in the unfolding of salvation-history."[77]

Darrell L. Bock passes by the three periods of time in a few short sentences, proposing an alternative namely to view Luke's theology in just two periods: an era of promise and an era of inauguration.[78] John the Baptist then serves as the pivotal figure between the two era's. Luke 7:24-30 provides the basis for Bock's argumentation and his main problem with Conzelmann's division is the sharp distinction between the period of Jesus and the period of the disciples/church. Seen from a literary point of view the many parallels Luke uses between Jesus and his disciples show a continuation and proof it is one era, the era of inauguration. Bock does use the terminology "already-not-yet" to explain the difference between inauguration and fulfillment.[79]

We can safely conclude that there is no consensus among scholars whether there is or is not a sharp division of three epochs of time in Luke-Acts.

1.3.3 Water-Baptism and the Holy Spirit in Luke-Acts

Although this is not the place to give an extensive treatment on water-baptism in Luke-Acts, a few remarks are necessary.[80] In the work by James Dunn, already mentioned above, it is argued that in the terminology of spirit-baptism the *metaphor* of water-baptism is used. The linkage between both is the word baptism, in spirit-baptism as a metaphor and in water-baptism in its literal meaning of immersion.[81] However, one cannot escape the close correlation between water baptism and receiving the Spirit in the Gospel and especially in Acts. Friedrich Avemarie starts the topic of baptism and Spirit with the title 'Ein klassischer Streitpunkt konfessioneller Exegese', in

---

77 J. Nolland, "Salvation-history and eschatology", in: I.H. Marshall and D. Peterson (eds.), *Witness to the Gospel*, 70-76.
78 D.L. Bock, *Luke 1:1-9:50* (BECNT 3A; Grand Rapids, MI: Baker Academic, 1994). 28.
79 See also A.W. Zwiep, *The Ascension of the Messiah*, 169-171. He writes "As is clear from the larger study of Luke-Acts (e.g. the Jesus-Paul and Jesus-Peter parallelisms) Luke's focus is more on that which connects the two periods than that which divides them."
80 See for an extensive treatment on water-baptism and its history: E. Ferguson, *Baptism in the Early Church. History, Theology, and Liturgy in the First Five Centuries* (Grand Rapids, MI: Eerdmans, 2009).
81 Contra sacramentalists: Dunn, *Baptism in the Holy Spirit*, 22, 32-33.

other words: there has been a long controversy in explaining the relation between water-baptism and Lukan Pneumatology.[82] He writes that there are two possibilities: either there is an indissoluble unity between water-baptism and receiving the Spirit or the combination of these events are coincidental in Acts. These opposite positions show there is no scholarly consensus in this matter. Avemarie observes that one's theological or denominational background colors one's interpretation of the relevant passages.[83] And later he writes that the position one takes in the relation between water-baptism and receiving the Spirit also determines whether the Spirit in Luke-Acts is seen as soteriological, missiological or charismatic.[84]

In this issue we again notice the importance of exegesis and the leading role hermeneutics play in explaining and applying the different passages and determining the distinctive role of the Spirit in Luke-Acts. This illustrates the crucial role of the reader.

1.3.4 Baptism in the Spirit: the Holy Spirit as a necessary and subsequent experience after conversion

One of the most hotly debated topics within Lukan Pneumatology is the issue of 'baptism in the Holy Spirit'. This means that in addition to the reception of the Holy Spirit at conversion, a second reception of the Spirit is necessary and normative. This issue or doctrine of the 'Baptism in the Holy Spirit' was a reason for James Dunn to write his 1970 dissertation which in response led to several Pentecostal studies. Besides the importance of this topic for theologians and for the study of the New Testament, there is a wide-ranging pastoral importance. It touches the so called 'ordo salutis'; it touches the practice of teaching and applying biblical instruction in churches; and it touches the personal life of believers and the unity within Christian communities.

The origin of the modern Pentecostal movement started with the *Azusa Street Revival*, 1906-1909, where under the leadership of Charles Parham and William Seymour the doctrine of baptism in the Holy Spirit was taught and experienced.[85] In the same year Dunn's *Baptism in the*

---

82 F. Avemarie, *Die Tauferzählungen der Apostelgeschichte* (WUNT 139; Tübingen: Mohr Siebeck, 2002), 129.
83 Avemarie mentions the Catholic scholar Adler, Pentecostal scholars Menzies, Shelton, Stronstad and Ervin. A middle position is taken by Turner and Penney. From a Catholic-Charismatic perspective the name of Haya-Prats is mentioned. Avemarie, *Tauferzählungen*, 129-130.
84 Avemarie, *Tauferzählungen*, 136.
85 Long before 1906 there were also different 'Pentecostal-like' movements, accentuating the

Holy Spirit was published, the dissertation of Frederick Dale Bruner was also published: *A Theology of the Holy Spirit. The Pentecostal Experience and the New Testament Witness*.[86] He describes in part I the Pentecostal movement, its origins and its doctrine of the Holy Spirit. Then in part II he extensively discusses the data from the Book of Acts and ends with a systematic survey and treatment of the relevant passages in the first and second letter to the Corinthians. The exegetical basis for the doctrine of 'baptism in the Spirit' rests upon a couple of texts, most of them found in the Book of Acts. Acts 2:4 is the starting point, the twelve disciples and the 120 waiting Christians receive the Holy Spirit at Pentecost. According to Bruner's description op the Pentecostal doctrine this must have been a subsequent filling, because the apostles were already Christians: the initiatory reception of the Spirit took place in John 20:22.[87] Acts 2:38 is explained in three stages: repentance, baptism and receiving the Holy Spirit. This means the *first* reception of the Spirit takes place at the stage of repentance, water-baptism upon which the second reception of the Spirit follows. The Samaritan episode, Paul's conversion, Cornelius' household and the Ephesian disciples (respectively Acts 8, 9, 10 and 19) all confirm this line of reasoning. Add to this the example of Jesus himself, his birth by the Holy Spirit and the subsequent filling with the Spirit at his baptism, and we have in a nutshell the classical Pentecostal doctrine of the baptism in the Holy Spirit.[88] Note that this is Bruner's description of the Pentecostal doctrine of 'Baptism in the Holy Spirit'. He himself holds another view.[89] Within the forty-five years that passed since the publication of Bruner's dissertation, there have not been many changes in this line of reasoning.[90] James Dunn argued thoroughly against this line

---

work of the Holy Spirit. For a short overview see F.D. Bruner, *A Theology of the Holy Spirit. The Pentecostal Experience and the New Testament Witness* (Grand Rapids, MI: Eerdmans, 1970), 35-55. See also the work by Paul L. King, *Genuine Gold: The Cautiously Charismatic Story of the Early Christian and Missionary Alliance* (Tulsa, OK: Word & Spirit, 2006), who not only elaborates on spirit-baptism, but on evidential tongues as well.

86 Bruner, *Theology of the Holy Spirit*.
87 Bruner, *Theology of the Holy Spirit*, 63.
88 For a lengthier discussion of the relevant passages see Bruner, *Theology of the Holy Spirit*, 63-69.
89 Bruner, *Theology of the Holy Spirit*, 225-284.
90 See for instance the conclusion in R.P. Menzies' dissertation, *The Development of Early Christian Pneumatology with Special Reference to Luke-Acts* (JSNTS 54; Sheffield: Sheffield Academic, 1991), 316 and also his later work in co-authorship with his father W.W. Menzies, *Spirit and Power. Foundations of Pentecostal Experience* (Grand Rapids, MI: Zondervan, 2000), 103-120.

of reasoning, starting with his dissertation. But also from within Pentecostal circles there is not a full consensus about the doctrine of a subsequent filling with the Spirit. Gordon D. Fee, a Pentecostal scholar and known for his work on textual criticism and exegesis, takes the more traditional Evangelical point of view. In an article in *Pneuma* he addresses the issue and states it is the *intense experience* of the Pentecostal which confirms for him that the baptism in the Holy Spirit is from God. After this experience he looks for confirmation in Scripture.[91] Basically Fee's question is whether or not one has the right hermeneutical approach or not. Fee's main objections to the Pentecostal hermeneutic procedure are the use of the analogy of the baptism of Jesus and to take the biblical precedents in the Book of Acts normative. In response father and son Menzies argue that "the crucial issue centers not on hermeneutics and historical precedent, but rather on exegesis and the nature of Luke's Pneumatology."[92] Once again we see the importance of methodology and the necessity of openness about one's presuppositions, argumentation and ways of approaching the text.

1.3.5 Conclusion
To summarize briefly, we have seen there are debated theological issues which run through the reading and interpreting of the narrative of Luke-Acts: whether or not Luke differentiatea between epochs or not, the exact relationship between water-baptism and spirit-baptism, and the topic of this spirit-baptism or also called baptism in/with the spirit. Each of these issues color one's approach of Luke-Acts. And as a consequence they color one's understanding of Lukan Pneumatology, which we address in the next section.

1.4 The Holy Spirit in Luke-Acts: Pneumatological Disagreements
1.4.1 Introduction
The origins of the discussion on Lukan Pneumatology can be found around the turn of the 19th into the 20th century when in 1926 the monograph by Hans von Baer[93] was published as a response to the works of

---

91 G. D. Fee, "Baptism in the Holy Spirit: The Issue of Separability and Subsequence", *Pneuma* 7 (1985), 87-99. See also by Fee, *Gods Empowering Presence. The Holy Spirit in the Letters of Paul* (Peabody, MA: Hendrickson, 1994) and on hermeneutics: G.D. Fee, "Hermeneutics and Historical Precedent – A Major Problem in Pentecostal Hermeneutics", in: R.P. Spittler, (ed.) *Perspectives on the New Pentecostalism* (Grand Rapids, MI: Baker, 1976), 118-132 and also *Gospel and Spirit: Issues in New Testament Hermeneutics* (Peabody, MA: Hendrickson, 1991).
92 R.P. Menzies and W.W. Menzies, *Spirit and Power,* 118.
93 H. von Baer, *Der Heilige Geist in den Lukasschriften* (Stuttgart: Kohlhammer, 1926).

Hermann Gunkel[94] and Hans Leisegang.[95] The issue in this debate was whether the Holy Spirit in Luke-Acts should be understood as "the Spirit empowering for mission" (later termed as *missiological*) or as "the Spirit offering sonship and new covenant life" (later termed as *soteriological*). Different answers were and are given to this issue, varying from a *both/and* to an *either/or* point of view.[96]

This issue still dominates the current debate on Lukan Pneumatology. A pivotal year in the research concerning Lukan Pneumatology turned out to be 1970. This year the dissertation of James D.G. Dunn was published, *Baptism in the Holy Spirit: a Re-examination of the New Testament Teaching on the Gift of the Spirit in Relation to Pentecostalism Today*.[97] In this work Dunn argues that the Spirit in Luke-Acts is the Spirit of sonship, the soteriological Spirit.[98] During the years following his dissertation Dunn would adjust his point of view slightly, but still holds the view that the Spirit in Luke-Acts is *primarily* the soteriological Spirit.[99]

Dunn's work provoked the Pentecostal movement to think through their theology of "baptism in/with the Spirit" as a second blessing or *donum superadditum* and to come with answers. And so they did. To

---

94 H. Gunkel, *Die Wirkungen des Heiligen Geistes nach der populären Anschauung der apostolischen Zeit und der Lehre des Apostels Paulus* (Göttingen: Vandenhoeck & Ruprecht, 11888, 31909). See for some background information on Gunkel the introduction in J.R. Levison, *Filled with the Spirit* (Grand Rapids, MI: Eerdmans, 2009), xiv-xxvi.

95 H. Leisegang, *Der Heilige Geist: Das Wesen und Werden der Mystisch-Intuitiven Erkenntnis in der Philosophie und Religion der Griechen* (Berlin: Teubner, 1919) and *Pneuma Hagion: Der Ursprung des Geistesbegriffs der synoptischen Evangelien aus der griechischen Mystik* (Leipzig: Hinrichs, 1922). For an extensive discussion on these monographs and the foundation of Lukan Pneumatology see M.M.B. Turner, *Power From On High: The Spirit in Israel's Restoration and Witness in Luke-Acts* (JPTSS 9; Sheffield: Sheffield Academic, 1996), 20-37.

96 For a brief historical overview see Turner, *Power From On High*, 20-37 and G.D. Fee, "Review on Max Turners *Power From On High*" RBL 11/30 (1998), 1.

97 J. D. G. Dunn, *Baptism in the Holy Spirit: a Re-examination of the New Testament Teaching on the Gift of the Spirit in Relation to Pentecostalism Today* (London: SCM, 1970).

98 Dunn, *Baptism in the Spirit*, 40-43, 90-102.

99 J. D. G. Dunn "Baptism in the Spirit: A Response to Pentecostal Scholarship on Luke-Acts", *JPT* 3 (1993) pp.3-27, where Dunn combines the "Spirit of prophecy" with the soteriological Spirit. Although the latter is still prominent.

name only a few: Gonzala Haya-Prats,[100] Howard M. Ervin,[101] Roger Stronstad,[102] James B. Shelton[103] and Robert P. Menzies.[104] A middle road in the debate was taken by Max Turner, who wrote extensively about Lukan Pneumatology, starting with his 1980 dissertation at Cambridge University.[105]

Next to the discussion on the distinctive working of the Spirit in Luke-Acts, more and more research was done from a *narrative-critical* point of

---

100   G. Haya-Prats, *L'Esprit force de l'*église (Paris: Cerf, 1975). This is the French translation of the Spanish dissertation of Haya-Prats from the Pontifical Gregorian University of Rome in 1967, titled *El Espiritu Santo en los Hechos de los Apostoles* (The Holy Spirit in the Acts of the Apostles). An English translation has been published in November 2010 edited by Paul Elbert and translated by Scott Ellington: *Empowered Believers. The Holy Spirit in the Book of Acts* (Eugene, OR: Cascade, 2010). Strictly speaking the work of Haya-Prats is not an answer to Dunn's dissertation, but it has been widely used by Pentecostal scholars to provide answers and think through their theology.

101   H.M. Ervin, *Conversion-Initiation and the Baptism in the Holy Spirit. A Critique of James D.G. Dunn's "Baptism in the Holy Spirit"* (Peabody, MA: Hendrickson, 1984); H.M. Ervin, *Spirit-Baptism: A Biblical Investigation* (Revision of: *These are not Drunken, As Ye Suppose*, 1968; Peabody, MA: Hendrickson, 1987).

102   To name just a few of his works: R. Stronstad, *The Charismatic Theology of St. Luke* (Peabody, MA: Hendrickson, 1984); R. Stronstad, "The Holy Spirit in Luke-Acts", *Paraclete* 23 (1989); R. Stronstad, "The Charismatic Theology of St Luke Revisited (Special Emphasis upon being Baptized in the Holy Spirit)", in: Studebaker (ed.) *Defining Issues in Pentecostalism* (Eugene, OR: Pickwick, 2008).

103   J. B. Shelton, ""Filled with the Holy Spirit" and "full of the Holy Spirit": Lucan Redactional Phrases", in: Elbert (ed.) *Faces of renewal: Studies in Honour of Stanley M. Horton* (Peabody, MA: Hendrickson, 1988); J.B. Shelton, *Mighty in Word and Deed: The Role of the Holy Spirit in Luke-Acts* (Peabody, MA: Hendrickson, 1991); J.B. Shelton, "A Reply to James D.G. Dunn's *Baptism in the Spirit. A Response to Pentecostal Scholarship on Luke-Acts*", *JPT* 4 (1994).

104   To name just a few: R.P. Menzies, *The Development of Early Christian Pneumatology with Special Reference to Luke-Acts* (JSNTS 54; Sheffield: Sheffield Academic, 1991); R.P. Menzies, "Spirit and Power in Luke-Acts: A Response to Max Turner", *JSNT* 49 (1993); R.P. Menzies, *Empowered for Witness: The Spirit in Luke-Acts* (Sheffield: Sheffield Academic, 1994); R.P. Menzies, "Luke and the Spirit: A Reply to James Dunn", *JPT* 4 (1994) W.W. Menzies and R.P. Menzies, *Spirit and Power: Foundations of Pentecostal Experience* (Grand Rapids, MI: Zondervan, 2000); R.P. Menzies, "Luke's Understanding of Baptism in the Holy Spirit. A Pentecostal Perspective", *PentecoStudies* 6-2 (2007).

105   M.M.B. Turner, *Luke and the Spirit: Studies in the Significance of Receiving the Spirit in Luke-Acts* (PhD dissertation: Cambridge, 1980). For more titles of Turners work on Lukan Pneumatology see the bibliography.

view. To name just a few contributors: John Kilgallen,[106] Robert Tannehill,[107] Richard Pervo,[108] William Kurz,[109] William H. Shepherd,[110] Charles Talbert,[111] Paul Borgman,[112] Anja Cornils,[113] and Ute Eva Eisen.[114]

This short overview shows the abundance of scholarly work done on Lukan Pneumatology, all from different angles. One will not be surprised to find out the disagreements are abundant as well. In this section I will describe the four prominent and different designations of the Spirit in Luke-Acts.

1.4.2 The Holy Spirit in Luke-Acts designated as "Soteriological Spirit"
Probably the most known proponent of seeing the Spirit in Luke-Acts as the *soteriological* Spirit is James D.G. Dunn. Other terms he uses are conversion-initiation, entrance into the new covenant, Spirit of sonship. The main thesis is: *There is only one coming of the Spirit in the life of the believer*, this is with his or her conversion. The Spirit initiates him or her into the new covenant. The underlying exegetical work for this thesis is Dunn's published dissertation: *Baptism in the Spirit* (1970). Already in the preface of this work, Dunn states it is a *New Testament* study.[115] In this preface he describes in short the historical development of the Pentecostal doctrine of Baptism in the Spirit. Starting with pietistic Protestantism, the

---

106 J. Kilgallen "Acts: Literary and Theological Turning Points", *BTB* 7 (1977).
107 R.C. Tannehill, *The Narrative Unity of Luke-Acts: A Literary Interpretation* (2 vols.; Philadelphia, Minneapolis: Fortress, 1986-1990).
108 R.I. Pervo, *Profit with Delight: The Literary Genre of the Acts of the Apostles* (Philadelphia: Fortress, 1987).
109 W.S. Kurz, "Narrative Approaches to Luke-Acts", *Bib* 68 (1987); W.S. Kurz, *Reading Luke-Acts: Dynamics of Biblical Narrative* (Louisville, KY: Westminster/John Knox, 1993).
110 W.H. Shepherd, *The Narrative Function of the Holy Spirit as a Character in Luke-Acts* (SBL 147; Atlanta, GA: Scholars, 1994).
111 C.H. Talbert, *Literary Patterns, Theological Themes and the Genre of Luke-Acts* (SBL Monograph Series 20; Missoula, MT: Scholars, 1974); C.H. Talbert, *Reading Luke: A Literary and Theological Commentary* (RNT; Macon, GA: Smith & Helwys, ²2002); C.H. Talbert, *Reading Acts. A Literary and Theological Commentary on the Acts of the Apostles* (RNT; New York: Crossroad, 1997; Macon, GA: Smyth & Helwys, ²2005).
112 P. Borgman, *The Way According to Luke: Hearing the Whole Story of Luke-Acts* (Grand Rapids, MI: Eerdmans, 2006).
113 A. Cornils, *Vom Geist Gottes erzählen: Analysen zur Apostelgeschichte* (TANZ 44; Tübingen: Francke, 2006).
114 U.E. Eisen, *Die Poetik der Apostelgeschichte: Eine narratologische Studie* (NTOA 58; Fribourg/Göttingen: Academic/Vandenhoeck & Ruprecht, 2006).
115 Dunn, *Baptism*, viii.

Puritans, John Wesley and the "higher or deeper life" messages in the 19th century one arrives at the year 1906 which was more or less the start of current day Pentecostalism.[116]

Dunn's work is a New Testament study and therefore focuses on the whole corpus of the New Testament. His thesis *there is only one coming of the Spirit* is therefore based on all the writings of the New Testament, including Luke-Acts. Although Dunn's treatment of Luke-Acts is extensive (the first hundred pages are devoted to the Gospels and Acts), he was (and still is) blamed for 'treating Luke's view of the Spirit through Pauline spectacles.'[117] There has been a development in Dunn's point of view and in responding to his (foremost) Pentecostal interlocutors he slightly adjusted his view. In his 1993 article, "Baptism in the Spirit: A Response to Pentecostal Scholarship on Luke-Acts"[118] Dunn agrees on the terminology of Spirit of prophecy and even sees this Spirit as responsible for inspired witness and speech (p.8). "But is this the whole story?", Dunn asks himself on page 9. And he continues questioning whether it is fair, exegetically speaking, to limit the Spirit in Luke-Acts solely to the Spirit of Prophecy. Is not this Spirit the same Spirit of salvation? His argument is that Pentecostals make a dissociation between the functions of the Spirit. A dissociation Luke does not make according to Dunn. His objection lies in the adverbs "only" and "exclusively" as we also have seen above in §1.2.3.[119] Dunn goes as far as to acknowledge Luke's visible (or perhaps we should say *audible*) sign of the reception of the Spirit is speaking in tongues, but he opposes the Pentecostal doctrine of a second and subsequent filling with the Spirit on the basis of (a) Luke's way of describing the Spirit, namely in enthusiastic, extraordinary and supernatural phenom-

---

116 Dunn, *Baptism*, 1-2. I am referring to the Azusa Street Revival, see also R.P. and W.W. Menzies, *Spirit and* Power, 16-17.
117 H.D. Hunter, *Spirit-Baptism: A Pentecostal Alternative* (Lanham, MD: University of America, 1983; Eugene, OR: Wipf & Stock, ²2009); H. Ervin, *Conversion-Initiation and the Baptism in the Holy Spirit: An Engaging Critique of James D.G. Dunn's Baptism in the Holy Spirit* (Peabody, MA: Hendrickson, 1984); R. Stronstad, *The Charismatic Theology of St. Luke* (Peabody, MA: Hendrickson, 1984); J.B. Shelton, *Mighty in Word and Deed. The Role of the Holy Spirit in Luke-Acts* (Peabody, MA: Hendrickson, 1991); R.P. Menzies, *The Development of Early Christian Pneumatology with Special Reference to Luke-Acts* (JSNTS 54; Sheffield: Sheffield Academic, 1991). See also the discussion in N. Baumert "Charism and Spirit-Baptism: Presentation of an Analysis", *JPT 12-2* (2004) pp.158-160.
118 J.D.G. Dunn, 'Baptism in the Spirit: A Response to Pentecostal Scholarship on Luke-Acts', *JPT* 3 (1993), 3-27.
119 Dunn, 'Baptism in the Spirit: A Response', 9-10.

ena and (b) putting a question in Luke's mind he simply was not asking! The Pentecostal question is "what is the outward sign of the (second) reception of the Spirit?" According to Dunn Luke was not answering this question when writing Luke-Acts, he was just describing the enthusiastic start of the early Christian community.[120]

Dunn's argumentation for viewing the Spirit in Luke-Acts as primarily soteriological is based on the following exegetical observations:[121]

1. John's baptism is purely preparatory;
2. The multiple Spirit experiences in Jesus' life are not about phases in his life, but about phases in salvation-history;
3. Pentecost is the inauguration of the new age, not a personal experience per se, but a salvation-historical experience;
4. Apparently there is a distinction between authentic and inauthentic Christianity, as shown by the Samaritan episode in Acts 8 and the Ephesian disciples in Acts 19. Only authentic Christians receive the Spirit;
5. Saul as well as Cornelius received the Spirit, that is the Spirit of salvation, only once;
6. The Spirit is first of all soteriological; as a consequence there is empowerment for ministry.

1.4.3 The Holy Spirit in Luke-Acts designated as "Eschatological Spirit"
Already from the start of Luke's Gospel there is a certain eschatological undertone: there is active movement of the Spirit within the birth narratives in Luke 1-2. John the Baptist preaches about "the one who will come" embedded in strong judgmental terminology (coming wrath, ax at the root of the trees, fire, baptize with holy Spirit and fire, winnowing fork, unquenchable fire, Luke 3:7-17). The public confirmation of Jesus' anointment with the Spirit happens through the reading of a Messianic text from Isaiah (Luke 4:18-19). In the Pentecost episode in Acts 2 Peter quotes the prophecy of Joel with tree alterations which all three confirm

---

120 J.D.G. Dunn, *Jesus and the Spirit: A Study of the Religious and Charismatic Experience of Jesus and the First Christians as Reflected in the New Testament* (London: SCM, 1975), 189-193.
121 In my previous work on the Spirit in Luke-Acts I have discussed all the relevant passages in Luke-Acts and the exegetical choices made by Dunn, see: Marco C.D. Wittenberg, *Lukan Pneumatology. Forty Years of Research, 1970-2010* (Unpublished M.Phil. thesis; Amsterdam: VU University, 2011), 28-33.

it is the eschatological Spirit which has been poured out.[122] Turner writes that from a Jewish point of view there was a longing and an expectation for the eschatological Spirit of Prophecy which also was distinctly soteriological.[123]

Eschatology in Luke-Acts is a wholly different subject which has kept scholars busy for some time.[124] Once again, a person's view on Lukan eschatology has all to do with hermeneutical presuppositions. For instance, did Luke write the Gospel already with the Book of Acts in mind? Did Luke write because of some "early Catholicism" (*Frühkatholizismus*)? Had both of Luke's volumes to do with providing an answer to the delayed parousia of Jesus (*Parusieverzögerung*)? Or, at the other end of the spectrum, there are those who still see an expectation of an imminent return of the Lord. And even dare to speak about a scholarly consensus of this view.[125] Perhaps because the opinions about Pneumatology as well as eschatology differ widely, there has not much been written about Lukan Pneumatology in correlation with his eschatology.[126]

---

122 The three alterations in Acts 2:17-19 are: "in the last days (ἐν ταῖς ἐσχάταις ἡμέραις)" instead of "after these things" and an addition of "and they shall prophecy (καὶ προφητεύσουσιν)" and "and signs on the earth below (καὶ σημεῖα ἐπὶ τῆς γῆς κάτω)". See L.T. Johnson, *The Gospel of Luke* (SPg 3; Collegeville, MN: Liturgical, 1991), 18-19.

123 M.M.B. Turner, "The Spirit in Luke-Acts: A Support or a Challenge to Classical Pentecostal Paradigms?" *VE* 27 (1997), 83-86. Turner has a rather broad view of salvation in opposition to R.P. Menzies who has a narrow view of salvation. This difference in view explains some of the disagreements between both.

124 See for instance the German influence in this subject: J. Weiss, *Die Predigt Jesu vom Reich Gottes* (Göttingen: Vandenhoeck & Ruprecht, [1]1892, [2]1900, [3]1964); A. Schweitzer, *Von Reimarus zu Wrede. Eine Geschichte der Leben-Jesu-Forschung* (Tübingen: Mohr Siebeck, 1906, [6]1951); E. Grässer, *Das Problem der Parusieverzögerung in den synoptischen Evangelien und in der Apostelgeschichte* (Berlin: Töppelman, 1957); H. Conzelmann, *Die Mitte der Zeit. Studien zur Theologie des Lukas* (Tübingen: Mohr Siebeck, [3]1960, [7]1993). For a discussion of the topic in English see for instance A.W. Zwiep, *The Ascension of the Messiah in Lukan Christology* (NovTSup. 87; Leiden, New York, Köln: Brill, 1997), 175-180.

125 So C.H. Talbert, "Shifting Sands. The Recent Study of the Gospel of Luke" in: J.L. Mays, *Interpreting the Gospels* (Philadelphia: Fortress, 1981), 197-213. See also the article by J. Nolland, in which he takes distance from a delayed parousia view: J. Nolland, "Salvation-History and Eschatology" in: I.H. Marshall, and D. Peterson (eds.), *Witness to the Gospel. The Theology of Acts* (Grand Rapids, MI: Eerdmans, 1998), 63-81.

126 For a bibliography on Luke-Acts and eschatology see: http://benbyerly.wordpress.com/bibliographies/luke-acts-eschatology-by-date/

J. Rodman Williams wrote a short article in the early eighties in which he outlines eight different topics of the Spirit related to eschatology.[127] Unfortunately he writes in a very broad sense and does not specifically address Luke-Acts. In 1999 Veli-Matti Kärkkäinen wrote the article "Mission, Spirit and Theology"[128] in which he mentions that "eschatology has been the mother of Pentecostal missiology". This makes clear the close connection between eschatology, missiology and Pneumatology and later Kärkkäinen writes that "Luke's distinctive Pneumatology speaks for a prophetic community empowered by the Spirit for missionary service".[129] Apparently there is some eschatological urgency which stimulates one for missions, all through guidance and empowerment by the Holy Spirit. This is in fact the practice of the past century within Pentecostal and charismatic circles. However, seen from a biblical theological and exegetical point of view, the question remains: "Was this also Luke's agenda when writing Luke-Acts?" If so, then there should also be an urgency within Luke-Acts to proclaim the Gospel because of the imminent parousia.

1.4.4 The Holy Spirit in Luke-Acts designated as "Missiological Spirit"
Despite the rather broad consensus on the relation between the Spirit and mission (see above in §1.2.3), the ways part when this relation is described. Words as "exclusively", "predominantly" or "mission-oriented" show the scholar's point of view in this debate. During the last forty-five years the major proponents of viewing the Spirit in Luke-Acts "exclusively" as the missiological Spirit are Robert P. Menzies and James B. Shelton.

Robert P. Menzies. In his 1991 Aberdeen dissertation, *The Development of Early Christian Pneumatology with Special Reference to Luke-Acts*,[130] Menzies defends the thesis that the Spirit in Luke-Acts is a second blessing

---

127 J.R. Williams, 'The Holy Spirit and Eschatology', *Pneuma* 3-2 (1981), 54-58.
128 V.M. Kärkkäinen, 'Spirit, Mission and Eschatology. An Outline of a Pentecostal-Charismatic Theology of Mission', *Mission Studies* 16-1 (1999), 73-94. See also his more recent works: V.M. Kärkkäinen, *Pneumatology: The Holy Spirit in Ecumenical, International and Contextual Perspective* (Grand Rapids, MI: Baker Academic, 2002); V.M. Kärkkäinen and A. Yong, *Towards a Pneumatological Theology: Pentecostal and Ecumenical Perspectives on Ecclesiology, Soteriology and Theology of Mission* (Lanham, MD: University Press of America, 2002).
129 Kärkkäinen, 'Spirit, Mission and Eschatology', 77-78.
130 R.P. Menzies, *The Development of Early Christian Pneumatology with Special Reference to Luke-Acts* (JSNTS 54; Sheffield: Sheffield Academic, 1991).

which is exclusively meant as an empowerment for mission.[131] His argumentation develops from the intertestamental period to the period of Luke-Acts. The background of Lukan Pneumatology is a concept of the Spirit as a second blessing, an additional gift for empowerment. In his conclusion he writes "the soteriological dimension is entirely absent from the Pneumatology of Luke."[132] In regard to these statements we can place Menzies on one of the edges of Lukan Pneumatology. The one side being totally consistent with Pauline and Johannine Pneumatology, that is the Spirit is the soteriological Spirit. And on the other hand, totally opposite, we have a very distinctive Lukan Pneumatology which has nothing to do with soteriology. Also in his later works Menzies is consistent to this latter point of view.[133]

In his Ph.D. dissertation, Menzies also treats the different episodes in Acts 2, 8, 9, 10 and 19 like Dunn did before.[134] I will extensively discuss Menzies' interpretation of these passages in chapter four below. For now it suffices to state that Menzies interprets the working of the Spirit in Luke-Acts exclusively as an empowerment for mission

James B. Shelton. A somewhat moderate view is taken by James Shelton. His thesis is that the Spirit in Luke-Acts acts primarily as an empowerment for mission. So he uses *primarily* instead of Menzies' *exclusively*. This point of view leaves space to attribute other workings or charismata to the Spirit in Luke-Acts. Since his 1982 dissertation from the University of Stirling, Shelton studies the working of the Holy Spirit.[135] In the conclusion of this work he concludes that Luke's terminology "filled with the Spirit" and "full of the Spirit" are parallels and states that Jesus functions

---

131 Menzies, *Development*, pp.278-279, 316-318; Turner, *Power from on High*, pp.63-66, 399; A.W. Zwiep, 'Luke's Understanding of Baptism in the Holy Spirit. An Evangelical Perspective', in: A.W. Zwiep, *Christ, the Spirit and the Community of God: Essays on the Acts of the Apostles* (WUNT 2.Reihe 293; Tübingen: Mohr Siebeck, 2010), 100-105.
132 Menzies, *Development*, 316.
133 R.P. Menzies, "Luke's Understanding of Baptism in the Holy Spirit. A Pentecostal Perspective", *PentecoStudies* 6 (2007); See also the interview in the Dutch Newspaper *Nederlands Dagblad* (16th February 2006); W.W. Menzies and R.P. Menzies, *Spirit and Power: Foundations of Pentecostal Experience* (Grand Rapids, MI: Zondervan, 2000), especially the chapters in which they answer Max Turner and James Dunn.
134 Menzies, *Development*, 246-277.
135 J.B. Shelton, *"Filled with the Holy Spirit": A Redactional Motif in Luke's Gospel* (Unpublished doctoral thesis from the University of Stirling, 1982).

as an archetype for his disciples.¹³⁶ There are of course some minor distinctions, but overall Jesus functions as archetype.¹³⁷ The main function of the Holy Spirit in Luke-Acts is to inspire for speaking. However, also miracles are described to the Spirit's working (chapter VI; with the remark that miracles happen through words being spoken), witness (chapter VII), prayer and mission (chapter VIII). So according to Shelton the primary role of the Spirit is to inspire for speech.¹³⁸

Almost ten years later Shelton writes his book *Mighty in Word and Deed*, in which he critically engages the Lukan Pneumatology debate.¹³⁹ He is careful not to exclude conversion or the soteriological function of the Spirit, but states it is Luke's primary interest to describe the role of the Holy Spirit in inspiring speech and empowering for witness.¹⁴⁰ As his methodology Shelton uses *redaction-criticism*, which both has its weakness and strengths.¹⁴¹ He is not convinced Luke had three sharply marked epochs in mind, on the contrary he argues Luke's writing on salvation-history is a fluid process, without clean cut borders. And precisely Lukan Pneumatology shows this.¹⁴² In using the same terminology of "filled with the Spirit" and "full of the Spirit" in the Book of Acts (the church) and before Jesus' birth (the infancy narratives), Shelton argues that Luke shows this is exactly the same working of the Spirit, namely: inspired speech. To put it in other words: Luke is using the mold of Acts to write the infancy narratives.

Shelton maintains that redaction-criticism is the most appropriate method to a right understanding of Luke and his conclusion is that "for Luke, the dominant function of the Spirit is empowerment for mission, especially in relation to effective witness".¹⁴³

---

136 See also M.M.B. Turner, "Spirit Endowment in Luke-Acts: Some Linguistic Considerations", *VE* 12 (1981) and J.B. Shelton, "Filled with the Holy Spirit and full of the Holy Spirit: Lucan Redactional Phrases" in: P. Elbert, (ed.) *Faces of Renewal: Studies in Honour of Stanley M. Horton* (Peabody, MA: Hendrickson, 1988), 81-107.
137 Shelton, *Redactional Motif*, 464-466.
138 Shelton, *Redactional Motif*, 305-306.
139 J.B. Shelton, *Mighty in Word and Deed: The Role of the Holy Spirit in Luke-Acts* (Peabody, MA: Hendrickson, 1991).
140 Shelton, *Mighty in Word and Deed*, 127-135, 161. And also M.M.B. Turner, "Empowerment for Mission? The Pneumatology of Luke-Acts: An Appreciation and Critique of James B. Shelton's Mighty in Word and Deed", *VE* 24 (1994), 106.
141 Turner, "Empowerment for Mission?", 103-107 and see the review of Shelton's book by J.C. Thomas, *Pneuma* 15-1 (1993), 125-128.
142 See the discussion in Turner, "Empowerment for Mission?", 110-113.
143 Shelton, *Mighty in Word and Deed*, 161.

Some other proponents who view the Spirit in Luke-Acts as the missiological Spirit are: John Michael Penney, Youngmo Cho and Dennis M. Hamm. A few remarks on the works of these three scholars will suffice for this *Forschungsbericht*.

John M. Penney. His originally Th.M. thesis was published in 1997 as *The Missionary Emphasis in Lukan Pneumatology*.[144] His statement is made with this title. Penney claims to treat Luke on his own merits, states that the Pauline and Johannine concepts of the Spirit are not absent in Luke-Acts, but that Luke's primary role of the Spirit is missions. The prophetic Spirit calls Gods people to prophesy (witness) and the Spirit empowers them for mission.[145] He is convinced of the unity of Luke-Acts and understands the purpose of Luke-Acts to be concerned with salvation and mission. Penney is convinced that the exact role of the Spirit in Luke-Acts is missionary, but he does not limit it to missions alone and thus leaves space for other interpretations of the Spirit's role.

Youngmo Cho. Cho is Assistant Professor of New Testament Studies at the Asia Life University in Daejon, South Korea. In 2005 his book *Spirit and Kingdom in the Writings of Luke and Paul: An Attempt to Reconcile these Concepts* was published.[146] As the title already suggests, he tries to combine the topics of Spirit and Kingdom and his case for the Spirit in the Lukan writings is that Luke limited the Spirit as a power for mission. Two years earlier, Cho wrote an extensive article focusing on the topic of Spirit and Kingdom in Luke-Acts, with the suggestive subtitle *Proclamation as the Primary Role of the Spirit in Relation to the Kingdom of God in Luke-Acts*.[147] In this article he elaborates on the relation between Spirit and Kingdom in Luke-Acts. He argues that in Luke-Acts there is not an equation between Spirit and Kingdom, as is the case in the writings of Paul.[148] After this, Cho demonstrates that the Spirit is the driving force behind the proclamation of the Kingdom of God. This is the case with

---

144   J.M. Penney, *The Missionary Emphasis of Lukan Pneumatology* (JPTSS 12; Sheffield: Sheffield Academic, 1997).
145   Penney, *Missionary Emphasis*, 113-118.
146   Y. Cho, *Spirit and Kingdom in the Writings of Luke and Paul: An Attempt to Reconcile these Concepts* (Waynesboro, GA: Paternoster, 2005).
147   Y. Cho, 'Spirit and Kingdom in Luke-Acts: Proclamation as the Primary Role of the Spirit in Relation to the Kingdom of God in Luke-Acts', *AJPS* 6-2 (2003), 173-197.
148   Contra James Dunn, *The Christ and the Spirit: Pneumatology* (Grand Rapids, MI: Eerdmans,1998), 137- 138; Y. Cho 'Spirit and Kingdom in Luke-Acts', 173-178.

Jesus, his disciples, Philip and Paul. Just like Shelton and in opposition to Menzies, Cho is careful to designate the Spirit's role as *primarily* for proclamation. To conclude in Cho's own words:

> "To make an equation of the Spirit with the kingdom has apparently oversimplified the true relationship between the two and does not exactly echo Luke's perspective. Luke does not regard the Spirit as the source of the manifestation of the kingdom of God or as the life of the kingdom in its entirety as in Paul. For Luke the primary role of the Spirit in relation to the kingdom of God is presented in qualified terms: principally as the power for the proclamation of the kingdom. The Spirit as an empowering force inspires people to proclaim the kingdom so that others have an opportunity to enter into it."[149]

Dennis M. Hamm. In an original and provocative article, Dennis M. Hamm writes about the "spirit-driven-mission" of the church in Luke-Acts.[150] Hamm, a Catholic Scholar teaching at Creighton University, starts with the words of the angel Gabriel in Luke 1:31-33, in which he promises that the throne of David will be given to the son of Mary and that he will reign the house of Jacob forever. Together with the words of Jesus during the last supper in which Jesus promises his disciples a place at his table in his kingdom (Luke 22:24-30), Hamm ties them to the Pentecost speech in Acts 2 and the communal narrative in Acts 4:24-31, where the references to David are the catchwords:

> "As the restored Israel of the end time, they are heirs of the promise to Israel. In the full context of Luke-Acts that means they share Israel's mission to be a light to the nations. [...] God will accomplish this daunting task through the power of the Holy Spirit accessed through prayer."[151]

Hamm illustrates this by elaborating on "the little Pentecost" in Acts 4 and concludes "[...] after gathering in prayer, empowered by the Holy Spirit to live a robust community life and to reach out in a mission of

---

149 Y. Cho, 'Spirit and Kingdom in Luke-Acts', 197.
150 D.M Hamm, 'The Mission Has a Church: Spirit, World and Church in Luke-Acts', in: B.E. Hinze, *The Spirit in the Church and the World* (Maryknoll, NY: Orbis, 2004), 68-80. In 2005 a commentary on the Acts of the Apostles by Dennis Hamm was published: D.M. Hamm, *The Acts of the Apostles* (NCBC; Collegeville, MN: Liturgical, 2005).
151 Hamm, *The Mission Has a Church*, 74-75.

healing and bold preaching."¹⁵² So we might deduce from Hamm's own words that he sees the Spirit in Luke-Acts as the missiological Spirit. He uses the term "en-spirited" church and in all this he accentuates the prominence of prayer within the church.¹⁵³ When we carefully read Hamm's words we can see he does not limit the Spirit's work to mission alone. The words "to live a robust community life" can be understood as the outcome of the working of the soteriological Spirit (entrance into a new community, ethical renewal). To conclude: Hamm's focus is on the mission which is Spirit-driven, but if we focus on the Spirit then mission is one of many other consequences.

Summarizing this subsection, we can conclude that the Spirit in Luke-Acts interpreted as the "missiological Spirit" has different nuances varying from exclusively missiological to a Spirit driven mission (including soteriological and ethical aspects).

1.4.5 The Holy Spirit in Luke-Acts designated as "Charismatic Spirit"
It is fair to begin this section with the short work of Roger Stronstad, *The Charismatic Theology of St. Luke*, originally written as a Master's thesis at Regent College in 1975.¹⁵⁴ This work proved to be groundbreaking from a Pentecostal point of view in the sense that it challenged James Dunn's thesis of Luke's soteriological Spirit. After the short monograph of Stronstad, many other Pentecostal contributions followed.¹⁵⁵ Stronstad starts with the problem of methodology: as where Paul *teaches*, Luke *narrates* about the Holy Spirit. So once again it signals the importance for determining the genre and purpose of a particular writing, before interpreting it. Mentioning I.H. Marshall's work, *Luke: Historian and Theologian*, Stronstad agrees that Luke is a historian and writes with a theological

---

152 Hamm, *The Mission Has a Church*, 75.
153 Hamm, *The Mission Has a Church*, xvii, 68, 78.
154 R. Stronstad, *The Charismatic Theology of St. Luke* (Peabody, MA: Hendrickson, 1984, ²2012).
155 For example: H.M. Ervin, *Spirit-Baptism: A Biblical Investigation* (Revision of: *These are not Drunken, As Ye Suppose*, 1968; Peabody, MA: Hendrickson, 1987); J.B. Shelton, *Mighty in Word and Deed*; R.P. Menzies, *Development*; W. Atkinson, "Pentecostal Responses to Dunn's Baptism in the Holy Spirit: Luke-Acts", *JPT* 6 (1995); A. Yong, *Discerning the Spirit(s): A Pentecostal-Charismatic Contribution to Christian Theology of Religions* (JPTSS 20; Sheffield: Sheffield Academic, 2000); F.D. Macchia, *Baptized in the Spirit: A Global Pentecostal Theology* (Grand Rapids, MI: Zondervan, 2006).

aim.[156] The paradigmatic narrative sections within Luke-Acts are normative for today, according to Stronstad.[157] As paradigmatic he determines the infancy narratives, Jesus' inauguration narrative and the Pentecostal narrative (respectively Luke 1-2, Luke 3-4:40 and Acts 2). His main thesis is that the Spirit is being transferred upon others, building on Old Testament parallels from Moses to the seventy elders and from Elijah to Elisha. In describing the Pentecost event he elaborates on the exact content of the charismatic Spirit and writes "[…] Pentecost is a complex phenomenon. A fivefold description illuminates the meaning of the Pentecost event. It is at once a clothing, a baptizing, an empowering, a filling and an outpouring of the Holy Spirit. No single term adequately denotes the meaning of the gift of the Spirit […]."[158] However, in contrast to his own fivefold description Stronstad focuses mainly on the prophetic gift of the Spirit (as Turner rightly observes).[159]

At the end of chapter four Stronstad concludes that Pentecost is not the birth of the church, because this view stems from a discontinuity between the periods of Israel, Jesus and the Church and from a soteriological view of the Spirit.[160] He just demonstrated that the Spirit in Acts is the charismatic Spirit, but he did not *disprove* any of the soteriological functions of the Spirit in Acts. In a short treatment of Acts 8, the gift of the Spirit to the Samaritans, Stronstad argues (contra Dunn) it is not about Samaritans entering the Church, but about equipping them for discipleship. The Jerusalem apostles transfer the Spirit upon the Samaritans.[161] But Stronstad himself wrote earlier in discussing the Old Testament background that "at key periods in Israel's history the transfer of leadership […] is typically accompanied by a complementary transfer or gift of the Spirit."[162] Complementary to what? To the soteriological function of the Spirit? Later he writes about the unique place of Luke's charismatic theology and stresses the discontinuity between the Old and

---

156 For a short description of Marshall's book see above in §1.2.1.
157 Stronstad, *Charismatic Theology*, 8-9.
158 Stronstad, *Charismatic Theology*, 61.
159 Turner, *Power from on High*, 62.
160 Stronstad, *Charismatic Theology*, 62.
161 Just as was the case in the Old Testament between Moses and the elders (Num.11:16-30), between Elijah and Elisha (2 Kgs 2:9-18) and in the New Testament between Jesus and his disciples. This "transfer of the Spirit" is the main point of Stronstad's argumentation.
162 Stronstad, *Charismatic Theology*, 23-24.

the New Testament.¹⁶³ It is here that Stronstad contradicts himself in discussing the possible continuity or discontinuity between the Old and New Testament. When it comes to Pentecost as the origin of the church (and thus the Spirit as soteriological), Stronstad opts for continuity with the Old Testament and with it continuity in the charismatic working of the Spirit, thereby eliminating a possible soteriological view of the Spirit. However, he argues, there are significant differences between the Old and New Testament, so discontinuity should be stressed.

In the conclusion of chapter five Stronstad writes that the major narratives in Acts " [...] demonstrate that all who receive the Gospel, either simultaneously or subsequently, also receive the charismatic gift of the Spirit."¹⁶⁴ This at least suggests a view of the Spirit in Luke-Acts which is both soteriological and charismatic, but not charismatic alone.

Stronstad offers a clear overview of the working of the Spirit and the best point in his thesis is that he does not limit the working of the Spirit, despite his emphasis on the prophetic gift. Unfortunately he gives too little attention to the possible soteriological working of the Spirit in Luke-Acts.

In his second book on Luke-Acts, *The Prophethood of All Believers*, Stronstad elaborates on the charismatic theology of Luke and designates Jesus as the anointed prophet who by transferring the Spirit creates a community of prophets.¹⁶⁵ Once again he argues Pentecost is not the birth of the church, but it "is vocational to baptize and empower the community of God to witness as prophets."¹⁶⁶ At the same time he writes about Pentecost as "an epochal event in the history of salvation" without adequately explaining his view on continuity or discontinuity between the Old and the New Testament.¹⁶⁷ Stronstad sees Jesus as the charismatic prophet and as such He is performing miracles and his speech is inspired. Those elements are complementary to the office of a charismatic prophet (contra Shelton, who sees the Holy Spirit as the one effecting miracles and inspiring speech).¹⁶⁸ In addition Stronstad differs from R.P. Menzies in regard to the meaning of the words Spirit (πνεῦμα) and power

---

163 Stronstad, *Charismatic Theology*, 79, he writes about "significant differences".
164 Stronstad, *Charismatic Theology*, 73.
165 R. Stronstad, *The Prophethood of all Believers: A Study in Luke's Charismatic Theology* (JPTSS; Sheffield: Sheffield Academic, 1999).
166 Stronstad, *Prophethood*, 70.
167 Stronstad, *Prophethood*, 66, 70.
168 Stronstad, *Prophethood*, 38; J.B. Shelton, *Mighty in Word and Deed: The Role of the Holy Spirit in Luke-Acts* (Peabody, MA: Hendrickson, 1991), 4.

(δύναμις). Whereas Stronstad sees these words as more or less interchangeably (comparing Luke 24:49 and Acts 1:8), Menzies states "δύναμις is mediated by the Spirit but not equivalent to it."[169] In chapters five and six of his work Stronstad shows that the charismatic Spirit is being transferred to individual prophets in which especially Stephen next to Paul gets a great deal of attention because of the parallels between Stephen and Jesus.[170]

To conclude Stronstad's contribution: Luke writes a charismatic theology in which Jesus is the anointed and charismatic prophet who transfers the charismatic Spirit upon his apostles and so creates a community of charismatic prophets.

When discussing the charismatic Spirit in his monograph, *Power from on High*, Turner focuses solely on the work of Gonzalo Haya-Prats, *L'Esprit force de l'église*, because (in Turner's opinion) Stronstad's work is about the Spirit of prophecy instead of the charismatic Spirit.[171] Haya-Prats does not limit the Spirit's working to prophecy alone. He includes aspects such as joy, courage and praise. On the other hand he excludes miracles from the working of the Spirit. The tension between the Spirit of mission versus the Spirit as a source for Christian life is solved by distinguishing *ordinary* religious life from *inspired* religious life. So, according to Gonzalo Haya-Prats, there exists an ordinary religious life which is not gifted or fueled by the Spirit and there is an extraordinary religious life (an intensification) which is inspired by the Spirit. It is this latter life which instigates mission.[172]

---

169 Stronstad, *Prophethood*, 61; Menzies, *Development*, 204 and R.P. Menzies, *Empowered for Witness: The Spirit in Luke-Acts* (Sheffield: Sheffield Academic, 1994), 114-117. On the discussion Spirit and/or power see also J. Kremer, *Pfingstbericht und Pfingstgeschehen. Eine exegetische Untersuchung zu Apg 2,1-13* (Stuttgarter Bibelstudien 63/64; Stuttgart: KBW, 1973), 179 and 186-188. See also the helpful table of the macro-structure of Luke 24:36-53 and Acts 1-14 in Zwiep, *Ascension*, 118.

170 Stronstad, *Prophethood*, 85-90, 100-101. Stronstad sees Stephen as the charismatic prophet par excellence (p.100) and explains the parallels from a theological point of view. However it remains the question whether Luke meant the example of Stephen as an elaboration on the theme of "charismatic prophecy" or whether he used the Stephen episode for different reasons in his narrative. For an alternative view see M.C.D. Wittenberg, *Stefanus: de voorbeeldige volgeling? Een literair onderzoek naar parallellen rondom de steniging van Stefanus, Handelingen 7:54-8:1a* (Unpublished M.Th. Thesis; VU University: Amsterdam, 2009).

171 Turner, *Power from on High*, 62, 72-78. For additional information and the translation in English of Haya-Prats' work see above in §1.3.1.

172 See the discussion in Turner, *Power from on High*, 74.

In his treatment of the universality of the Spirit Haya-Prats makes a distinction between (as Turner terms it) an "eschatological/fruitbearing" and a "historical/kerygmatic" aspect of the Spirit. The first aspect is universal, given to the whole community of God. The second aspect is first for the disciples and later on for divinely chosen evangelists.[173] This distinction seems a rather arbitrary choice.

1.4.6 Conclusion
To conclude this section: we have seen, just as in the previous section, that there are many disagreements regarding Lukan Pneumatology. There continues to be debate about how to designate the Spirit in Luke-Acts. Whether it be soteriological, eschatological, missiological or charismatic, all these show the specific angle from which scholars approach the topic of Lukan Pneumatology. And all these show a certain Lukan characteristic of the Spirit in the narrative of Luke-Acts. The way these typifications of the Spirit are reached all vary and depend on methodology, the (conscious or unconscious) usage of other New Testament writers and denominational background. So far we have seen a very superficial consensus and a wide range of different interpretations concerning Luke's theology and the working of the Spirit in Luke-Acts. A recurring theme in understanding this wide range of different interpretations is the specific role of the reader. It is this specific role of the reader that we will now turn to.

1.5 Towards Understanding: The Role of the Reader
1.5.1 Introduction
When one takes notice of the mentioned disagreements a feeling of disappointment and incomprehension may occur. How is it possible that one-and-the-same text form the basis of such wide ranging and differing theological interpretations? What causes these different interpretations? Is Luke's two volume story so poorly written that everyone can use it for his or her own theological point of view? I do not think so. For the greater benefit of theology and the believing Christian community it is of utmost importance that there is understanding. Not only understanding of each other's theological positions, but also understanding how those positions are reached and formulated. That brings us at the role of the reader. The reader of the text determines, along the process of reading, the interpretation. And the consequences of these interpretations. The reader of

---

173 Turner, *Power from on High*, 75-76.

Luke-Acts plays an important part: the story is read, re-read, interpreted and eventually used to construe some sort of Lukan Pneumatology. If we want to gain understanding of all the different positions regarding the working of the Holy Spirit in Luke-Acts, we should focus on the role of the reader.

1.5.2 Establishing the role of the reader
An intriguing question is of course how to determine the role of the reader. In a way the role of the reader is dependend on the kind of text in front of him. Some texts are very strict in how a reader should use the text or respond to a text. A classical example are the guidelines to use some electrical device. If the reader intends to reach his purpose, then the text should be followed very secure and there are no alternative interpretations possible. A poetic text however, is open for different possible interpretations: the same text can invoke different feelings and interpretations by different readers. In view of the fact that the two volume work of Luke-Acts is a *narrative* (Luke is a storyteller), we do need a model specifically designed for narrative texts. Umberto Eco has provided such a model which in a certain way visualizes the role of the reader. His model is developed for narrative texts, so that makes it suitable for application to the narrative of Luke-Acts. In the next chapter I will elaborate on the role of the reader and explain the model of Umberto Eco, which he calls "the model of the cooperative reader". In addition to this I will also explain the manner in which I will apply this model to the Lukan pneumatological texts.

1.5.3 Establishing different readers
Because the topic of Lukan Pneumatology will not benefit from randomly picked scholars to assess, I did use some criteria in whom to choose. First of all, the topic is about Lukan Pneumatology. So there should be theological expertise in Lukan theology or pneumatology, preferably in both. Second, we do take our own theological background with us in reading and interpreting a text. So there should be different backgrounds and/or denominations present in the scholars assessed. And in the third place there is a wide variety in methodology concerning biblical texts: source criticism, redaction criticism, narrative criticism are just a view. It will be best if different methodologies are represented in the chosen scholars.

With these three criteria in mind, I have come to assess the next three scholars: Max M.B. Turner, Robert P. Menzies and William S. Kurz. All three of these scholars will be discussed in a different chapter. Each of these chapters will start with an introduction on the scholar in question. All three scholars have different views on the working of the Holy Spirit in Luke-Acts, so they are all the more worthwhile to assess and then to understand how they have come to construe their different Lukan Pneumatologies.

1.5.4 Conclusion
Agreements and disagreements alike, all depend on the role of the reader in question. Agreements tend to unite, disagreements tend to divide. For the greater benefit of not only theology in general, but as well as for the believing community of Christians, it is necessary that mutual understanding is gained. To gather insight in this specific role of the reader we will use the model designed by Umberto Eco within the boundaries of the Lukan pneumatological texts. The work of readers from different backgrounds, but all with expertise in Luke-Acts and/or Pneumatology, will be subjected to this model. The reader plays an important role in interpreting texts, but this same reader also plays an important role in understanding other readers. Both of these roles will be the interest of the subsequent chapters.

1.6 Conclusion
So far in this *Forschungsbericht* we have seen that there is an abundance of literature on Luke-Acts relating to the work of the Spirit, starting roughly around the turn of the 19th century into the 20th century with the works of Hans von Baer, Hermann Gunkel and Hans Leisegang.[174] The question whether the Spirit was missiological or soteriological dominated the debate. We saw that in the years following there slowly grew a consensus on the different roles of Luke. He nowadays is treated as theologian, historian and storyteller alike. Concerning the background of Luke and the relation between the Spirit and mission in Luke-Acts there is also consensus, but not perhaps as firm as we might expect.

The year 1970 proved to be pivotal, with the publishing of James Dunn's dissertation and the subsequent (predominantly Pentecostal) responses to this publication. The disagreements on the working of the Holy Spirit in Luke-Acts surfaced rather quickly and still dominate the

---

174 For views on the working of the Holy Spirit before the 19th century, see the overview in Part II of the book by Anthony C. Thiselton, *The Holy Spirit – In Biblical Teaching, through the Centuries, and Today* (Grand Rapids, MI: Eerdmans, 2013), 163-292 and chapter XII in his *Systematic Theology* (Grand Rapids, MI: Eerdmans, 2015), 290-310.

present day debate. Various theological assumptions and sometimes personal religious preferences all color the interpretation of the present day reader. That brings us to the specific and important role the reader plays in reading, analyzing and interpreting the text. In our case this is the narrative of Luke-Acts with a special focus on the Holy Spirit in this narrative. In the next chapter I will elaborate on the specific model of Umberto Eco, the model of the cooperative reader, and I will identify and cluster the most important πνεῦμα texts in Luke-Acts.

CHAPTER 2

THE ROLE OF THE READER, UMBERTO ECO AND LUKE-ACTS

2.1 Introduction

For centuries the focus of interpretation has been on the author of the text: what exactly did he mean when he wrote his text? It is here that the so-called *Einleitungs-* and *Einführungsfragen* are important. Murray Krieger used the metaphor of a window to designate the focus on the author of the text.[1] The text functions as a window and through the window we gain insight into the original circumstances and conditions in which the text was written. It was (and in some circles still is) widely assumed that this is the only proper way to discover the one-and-only and objective meaning of the biblical text. This stance is often referred to as the *authorial intention* of the text.[2]

However, from the 1940s (New Criticism) to the 1960s (Structuralism) literary critics focused on the text alone in search for meaning.[3] Next to Nietzsche's declaration of the "death of God", it was Roland Barthes

---

1 Murray Krieger, *A Window to Criticism: Shakespeare's Sonnets and Modern Poetics* (Princeton: Princeton University, 1964), 3-70. See also Norman R. Peterson, *Literary Criticism for New Testament Critics* (Philadelphia, PA: Fortress, 1978), 24-33 and Mark Allen Powell, "Narrative Criticism" in: Joel B. Green, ed., *Hearing the New Testament. Strategies for Interpretation* (Grand Rapids, MI: Eerdmans, 1995, ²2010), 241.
2 See for instance Gordon D. Fee and Douglas Stuart, *How to Read the Bible for all Its Worth. A Guide to Understanding the Bible* (Grand Rapids, MI: Zondervan, 1982, ³2003), 26-27, who write: "The reason one must *not begin* with the here and now is that *the only proper control for hermeneutics is to be found in the original intent of the biblical text.* (…) A *text cannot mean what it never meant.*" (Their italics).
3 Thomas S. Eliot, *Selected Essays 1917-1932* (New York: Harcourt Brace, 1932); John C. Ranson, *The New Criticism* (Norfolk, CT: New Directions, 1941); Leonard Bloomsfield, *Language* (London: Allen & Unwin, 1933, ¹³1976); Cleanth Brooks, *Modern Poetry and the Tradition* (Chapel Hill, NC: North Carolina University, 1939) and *The Well Wrought Urn: Studies in the Structure of Poetry* (|New York: Harcourt Brace,1947); René Wellek and Austin Warren, *Theory of Literature* (Harmondsworth, Middlesex: Penguin, 1973); Roman Jakobson, *Selected Writings* ('s-Gravenhage: Mouton, 1962-1988); Claude Lévi-Strauss, *Les Structures élémentaires de la parenté (Berlin, New York: Mouton de Gruyter, 1947, ²2002);* Ferdinand de Saussure, *Cours de linguistique générale* (publ. par Charles Bally et Albert Sechehaye; Paris, Payot: 1980).

who declared the "death of the author".[4] Consequence was a focus on the text itself, separated from the author. Murray Krieger uses the metaphor of a mirror to designate this process. Meaning is acquired to look into the text and the text alone. The text serves as a mirror: by looking into the text, the reader understands the text and himself.

After the shift from the original author to the text as we have it in front of us, it was only a small step to focus on the reader. Naturally the reader plays an important part in the communication process (author → text → reader). Actually the reader is necessary for the text to become meaningful in the life of the reader. It is here that reader-response strategies come into focus to determine the role of the reader during the process of interpretation.

2.2 The Role of the Reader in Recent Research

A solid introduction to reader-response criticism is a volume of essays edited by Jane P. Tomkins: *Reader-Response Criticism: From Formalism to Post-Structuralism*.[5] Next to this Umberto Eco's *The Role of the Reader: Explorations in the Semiotics of Texts*[6] and more recently *Interpretation and Overinterpretation*,[7] edited by Stefan Collini with contributions from Umberto Eco, Richard Rorty, Jonathan Culler and Christine Brooke-Rose, provide collections of essays on the subject of the response of the reader. There are various opinions concerning the role of the reader in interpreting texts. At one end of the spectrum there are those who argue that the meaning is in the text self (as is the case, e.g. in biblical literalism),[8] at the other

---

4 Friedrich Wilhelm Nietzsche, *Gesammelte Werke* (Köln, Anaconda: 2012); Roland Barthes, *Le bruissement de la langue, Essais critiques IV* (Paris: Seuil, 1984), 63-70.
5 Jane P. Tomkins (ed.), *Reader-Response Criticism: From Formalism to Post-Structuralism* (Baltimore, MD: John Hopkins University, 1980). For general works on reception theory see: Robert C. Holub, *Reception Theory: A Critical Introduction* (London; New York: Methuen, 1984) and Robert C. Holub, *Crossing Borders: Reception Theory, Poststructuralism, Deconstruction* (Madison: University of Wisconsin, 1992). A recent two volume work on hermeneutics in general has been published in Dutch: Arie W. Zwiep, *Tussen Tekst en Lezer. Een historische inleiding in de bijbelse hermeneutiek* 1 en 2 (Amsterdam: VU University, 2009-2013).
6 Umberto Eco, *The Role of the Reader: Explorations in the Semiotics of Texts* (Advances in Semiotics; Bloomington, London: Indiana University, 1979).
7 Stefan Collini (ed.), *Interpretation and Overinterpretation* (Cambridge: Cambridge University, 1992).
8 See Zwiep, *Tussen tekst en lezer II*, 328-332; Walter A. Elwell (ed.), *Evangelical Dictionary of Theology* (Grand Rapids, MI: Baker, 2001), 694; Kevin J. Vanhoozer, *Is There a Meaning in this Text? The Bible, the Reader, and the Morality of Literary Knowledge* (Grand Rapids, MI: Zondervan, 1998).

end we find those who argue that (only) the reader gives meaning to the text, the text itself is lacking stability (for instance Stanley Fish, Norman Holland and David Bleich).⁹ Both ends can respectively be designated as "text-centered" and "reader-centered" with a lot of positions in between, in which a certain cooperation between text and reader is promoted.¹⁰ The most promising position for theology in general and especially biblical studies is somewhere in the middle. All three—author, text and reader—are necessary for communication. Without an author or a text there is nothing to communicate. But without a reader there is no one to interpret. Proper communication demands all three. However, the issue of the role of the reader is a more complicated matter than just an interaction between author, text and reader. During the past decades different types of readers—and therefore different roles of readers—have been developed. A few examples are: the implied reader, the ideal or informed reader and the empirical reader. A short overview will provide some information.

The concept of an *implied reader* originates from Wolfgang Iser (1926-2007).¹¹ Iser earned his PhD degree in *Anglistik* in 1950 at the University of Heidelberg and after earning the German *Habilitation* in 1957 became full professor.¹² Iser's influence on literary theory started with his appointment as professor at the University of Konstanz in 1967 where he together with Hans Robert Jauss (1921-1997) developed the German *Rezeptionsästhetik*. Their influence was firmly established during the 1970s, when Iser's books *Der implizite Leser* and *Der Akt des Lesens* were published.¹³

---

9   Stanley E. Fish, *Is there a Text in this Class? The Authority of Interpretive Communities* (Cambridge, MA: Harvard University, 1980); Norman Holland, "Unity, Identity, Text, Self" in: Tomkins, *Reader-Response Criticism*, 118-133 and David Bleich, "Epistemological Assumptions in the Study of Response" in: Tomkins, *Reader-Response Criticism*, 134-163.

10 Eco describes these ends as "two poles" in Eco, *The Limits of Interpretation*, 24. See also David Robey, "Introduction: Interpretation and Uncertainty" in *Illuminating Eco. On the Boundaries of Interpretation* (ed. C. Ross, R. Sibley; Warwick Studies in the Humanities; Hampshire, Burlington, VT: Ashgate, 2004), 1-10.

11 Wolfgang Iser, *Der implizite Leser: Kommunikationsformen des Romans von Bunyan bis Beckett* (München: Fink, 1972); idem, *Der Akt des Lesens: Theorie ästhetischer Wirkung* (München: Fink, 1976); *The Range of Interpretation* (New York, NY: Colombia University, 2000). Both German books are translated in English.

12 See http://www.oac.cdlib.org/findaid/ark:/13030/tf9d5nb5jw/admin/#bioghist-1.2.3 for a full biography on Wolfgang Iser.

13 Influential books by Hans Robert Jauss are: *Literaturgeschichte als Provokation* (Frankfurt am Main: Suhrkamp, 1970) and *Ästhetische Erfahrung und literarische Hermeneutik* (Frankfurt am Main: Suhrkamp, 1982).

When it comes to the implied reader Iser states, in the introduction of *Der implizite Leser*, that the term *implied reader* incorporates two things:

> "Damit ist zweierlei gesagt: 1. Die Struktur kann und wird historisch immer unterschiedlich besetzt sein. 2. Der implizite Leser meint den im Text vorgezeichneten Aktcharakter des Lesens und nicht eine Typologie möglicher Leser."[14]

The potential meaning has to be actualized by the implied reader. This means that the dominant theme is discovery (*Entdeckung*). The author takes the reader into account while writing his text. Apparently there are structures or hints within the text that have to be discovered by the reader. As such the reading process is creating meaning (*Sinnkonstitution*) or establishing a new reality which is within the text. Iser states: " […] dann wird Sinn zu einer Sache der Entdeckung."[15]

Iser is clear about the purpose of the essays in *Der implizite Leser*: they are concerned with the historically changing contents of the discovery, "…ohne daß sie den Sachverhalt selbst theoretisieren."[16] Although Iser's work was groundbreaking, he did not develop a specific theory or theoretical model for the implied reader.

As Anthony Thiselton has pointed out, Iser's implied reader is based on construing something which lies beyond immediate perception: the reader regularly fills in what he presupposes and thus construes.[17] Other terminology used to designate this process is "filling in the gaps or blanks", "actualization", "concretizing dimensions of meaning".[18] Especially Stanley Fish criticizes Iser in his essay "Why No One's Afraid of Wolfgang

---

14 Iser, *Der implizite Leser*, 8-9; *The Implied Reader*, xii.
15 Iser, *Der implizite Leser*, 9; *The Implied Reader*, xiii.
16 Iser, *Der implizite Leser*, 9; *The Implied Reader*, xiii.
17 Anthony C. Thiselton, *New Horizons in Hermeneutics* (Grand Rapids, MI: Zondervan, 1992), 516-517. Reprinted in idem, *Thiselton on Hermeneutics: Collected Works with New Essays* (Grand Rapids, MI: Eerdmans, 2006), 491.
18 Max Turner states that the reader does not create meaning when "filling in the gaps", but rather shares the same presupposition pool as the author. This implies a shared understanding of the social world and context of the author and the text. As such the study of the "behind-the-text-issues" stays important and is necessary to rightly fill in the gaps or understand the text. Max M.B. Turner, "Historical Criticism and Theological Hermeneutics of the New Testament" in: Joel B. Green, Max Turner (eds.), *Between Two Horizons. Spanning New Testament Studies & Systematic Theology* (Grand Rapids, MI: Eerdmans, 2000), 49.

Iser".[19] According to Fish, Iser is not radical enough and tries to satisfy both objectivists (more text oriented) and pluralists (more reader oriented).

The implied reader is actually the reader which the author had in mind during the writing process. The author obviously assumes an *ideal reader*: a reader who understands and grasps everything that the author intends. It then seems that the implied reader and the ideal reader coincide. Thiselton rightly points out that such an ideal reader remains "hypothetically ideal", because the real reader (or empirical reader) cannot exhaustively understand what the original author meant.[20]

In contrast to Iser who focuses on the individual reader, Stanley Fish writes about *interpretive communities*. No single reader stands on his own, but every reader is part of an interpretive community. Such an interpretive community has certain strategies of reading and interpreting, which explains why different readers can show interpretive similarities while reading the same text (because they belong to the same interpretive community).[21] Apparently the reader approaches a text with a preconditioned set of interpretive strategies which are leading in the interpretive community to which he belongs. This leads Fish to speak of an *informed reader* (or ideal reader).[22] In contrast to Iser's "discovering the meaning", Fish speaks of the reader "producing meaning". In such a way meaning involves the activity of the reader instead of activity of the author. Stability is not to be found in the text, but in the interpretive community. The informed reader of Fish must have *literary competence*, by which Fish means that he is capable and experienced as a reader.[23] In this way Fish places the constraints of interpretation foremost in the reader.

Next to these different opinions and models about author, text and reader, there are those who shift their focus on the so called *empirical reader*. This refers to the *actual* or *real* reader. Eventually when it comes to reading and understanding texts it is the flesh-and-blood person who actually reads and therefore is the (empirical) reader. The Dutch theologian Hans de Wit launched a project where some 120 small groups from 25 different countries read and studied the same biblical passage: John 4, the Samaritan woman at the well. The book *Through the Eyes of Another:*

---

19 Stanley Fish, "Why No One's Afraid of Wolfgang Iser", in: idem, *Doing What Comes Naturally* (Duke University, 1989).
20 Thiselton, *New Horizons*, 517 and idem, *Thiselton on Hermeneutics*, 491.
21 Fish, *Is There a Text*, 167.
22 Fish, *Is There a Text*, 15.
23 Fish, *Is There a Text*, 48-49.

Intercultural Reading of the Bible presents the results of this three year research.[24] This project clearly showed how actual readers from different cultural, social, economic and denominational backgrounds add something to the reading and understanding of this Bible chapter. De Wit mentions two objections to the different hermeneutical theories of the reader, both of which led the focus on the empirical reader:

> "First there was the objection that people spoke endlessly about the reader but actually engaged the reader very little in conversation, and little empirical research was done. [...]. A second objection was that proper reading was very normatively formulated by hermeneuticians, philosophers and linguists, and that much was demanded of the ideal -often Western and well-educated- readers."[25]

The reason for De Wit's empirical research is that the Bible needs response, because "without response the Scripture ceases to be a source of revelation."[26] This present study focuses on this response by examining the role of three leading scholars in the field of Luke-Acts. However, as already mentioned in the introduction and demonstrated in the subsequent *Forschungsbericht*, scholars have seldom reached agreements in their conclusions on Lukan pneumatology. It seems like the exegetical outcome is more than often predetermined by a theological bias of the scholar. The poignant question is whether every response to Scripture is possible, without harming the text. This question shows the need to investigate the role of the reader and exactly determine this role to conclude whether a scholar goes beyond the limits of a text, and as such harms a text, or not. In my opinion it is the model of the cooperative reader by Umberto Eco who can help investigate and value the role of the reader.

2.3 The Role of the Reader according to Umberto Eco

To do justice to the role of each individual reader, a certain model is necessary. In the study of narrative texts, Umberto Eco provides us with such a model. Iser, Fish, Thiselton and De Wit provide narrative-critical theories, but not a model. Eco developed the model of *the cooperative reader*,

---

24 J.H. de Wit et al., *Through the Eyes of Another. Intercultural Reading of the Bible* (Elkhart, IN: Institute of Mennonite Studies; Amsterdam, VU University, 2004).
25 J.H. de Wit, *"My God", she said, "ships make me so crazy." Reflections on Empirical Hermeneutics, Interculturality, and Holy Scripture* (Nappanee, IN: Evangel, 2008)
26 De Wit, *"My God", she said, "Ships make me so crazy."*, 22.

which will prove to be a workable model to show the role of the reader in interpreting narrative texts. In the next sections I will discuss Eco's model and demonstrate its suitability to use it on the Lukan πνεῦμα texts.

Umberto Eco (1932–2016) is a well-known Italian semiotician and novel writer. He is known by the general public through his bestselling novels *In the Name of the Rose*[27] and *Foucault's Pendulum*.[28] Next to being a novel writer Eco was professor emeritus of semiotics at the University of Bologna, Italy and served as president of the *Scuola Superiore di Studi Umanistici*, at the University of Bologna.[29] Eco published some works on semiotics, interpreting texts and the role of the reader in interpreting these texts.[30] Over the past years there has been a development in semiotics from studying signs (codes, structures, semantics) to the text (linguistics, grammar) to the reader and his response to the text.[31] Eco is one who takes a middle position when he states that a (narrative) text needs the cooperation of the reader. A text is written to be read and to invite a certain response from its readers. However, according to Eco this cooperation is not unlimited. There are limits of interpretation in each narrative. The author has put these limits in the text. The same is true about words being used. A word without context does not have a meaning. The context (whether in surrounding sentences or in the reader's mind) determines the meaning. Eco uses as an example the word "lion". The image we

---

27 Umberto Eco, *Il nome della rosa* (Letteraria Italiana; Milan: Bompiani, 1980), translated in multiple languages and made into a film in 1986 starring Sean Connery and Christian Slater.
28 Umberto Eco, *Il pendolo di Foucault* (Letteraria Italiana; Milan: Bompiani, 1988). More recent novels by Eco are: *Il cimitero di Praga* (Milan: Bompiani, 2010), *Baudolino* (Milan: Bompiani, 2000) and *L'isola del giorno prima* (Milan: Bompiana, 1994). All of these are translated in multiple languages.
29 See http://www.sssub.unibo.it. For Eco's curriculum vitae and extensive list of publications (1956-2011) see http://www.umbertoeco.it.
30 Umberto Eco, *A Theory of Semiotics* (Advances in Semiotics; Bloomington, IN: Indiana University, 1976, 1979); idem, *The Role of the Reader. Explorations in the Semiotics of Texts* (Advances in Semiotics; Bloomington, IN: Indiana University, 1979, 1984); idem, *Lector in fabula. La cooperationi interpretative nei testi narrativi* (Tascabili Bompiani 27; Milan: Bompiani, 1979, [11]2010); *Lector in fabula. De rol van de lezer in narratieve teksten* (trans. Y. Boeke, P. Krone: Amsterdam: Bert Bakker, 1989); idem, "The Theory of Signs and the Role of the Reader" *BMMLA 14.1 (1981)*: 35-45; *Semiotics and the Philosophy of Language* (Bloomington, IN: Indiana University, 1984, 1986); idem, *The Limits of Interpretation* (Advances in Semiotics; Bloomington, IN: Indiana University, 1990, 1994); idem, *Sulla Letteratura* (Milan: Bompiani, 2002); *On Literature* (trans. M. McLaughlin: New York: Harcourt, 2002).
31 Eco, "The Theory of Signs," 35.

have when reading the word "lion" differs if we read it in the context of jungle, zoo or circus.[32] This is a way in which the author of a text condenses the possible interpretations of his text. To give an example from Luke-Acts: if Luke uses the Greek word πνεῦμα, the context or adjective determines what kind of πνεῦμα is in view. Does Luke mean wind or spirit? What kind of spirit? Holy Spirit, evil spirit, unclean spirit, Spirit of Jesus, Spirit of the Lord are just a few possible examples from the corpus of Luke-Acts.

A helpful analogy Eco uses to explain his position is that of the game of chess.[33] There are different pieces used when playing chess. Each piece has its own rules of movement. The queen can move forward, backward, sideways and diagonally. A rook can only move forward, backward and sideways and a bishop can only move diagonally. However, each player will use the pieces in a different way. Within a given situation there are multiple options for the player on how to use his pieces: which piece he would like to move and in what direction.

The same is true when reading a narrative. Due to the set of presuppositions and foreknowledge of the reader (Eco likes to use the word "encyclopedia"), the reader determines which meaning he uses for a certain word when reading the text. In this way *the reader cooperates with the text* to determine the meaning. Within chess the board and the rules of the game provide the limits for the players; when reading a narrative text, it is the text itself and the encyclopedia of the reader who determine the limits of interpretation. This explains the different interpretations while reading the same text.

2.4 Umberto Eco and Luke-Acts

There continues to be scholarly discussion on several Lukan topics. In addition to the previous mentioned agreements and disagreements in the *Forschungsbericht*, scholars debate the literary genre, the purpose, the dating of Luke and Acts. Hermeneutically the discussion about interpretation and application influences Lukan scholarship. The question whether Luke-Acts needs to be read *descriptively* or *prescriptively* is still a hotly debated topic in some interpretive communities.[34] This touches the heart of the normativity question: some readers of Luke-Acts are biased in one or another way whether the text has normative demands or not.

---

32 Eco, *Lector in fabula* (Dutch translation), 25-27.
33 Eco, *Lector in fabula*, 152-154, 217-218.
34 Stephen Voorwinde, 'How Normative is Acts?', *Vox Reformata* (2010), 33-56.

The important question which needs to be asked first is whether Luke-Acts does have prescriptive (normative) pretentions or not. It is this question that also touches the heart of the ongoing debate between the various theological disciplines. Should the point of departure be the biblical texts? Should it be the history behind the biblical texts? Or should it be the (church) tradition or dogmatic stances articulated within the various denominations?[35] In both the disciplines of biblical studies and systematic theology, the reader plays an important role. Green briefly discusses the perspectives of Wolfgang Iser and Umberto Eco on reading, who both hold to the view that texts are not self-interpreting.[36] According to Iser and Eco texts are open to a range of meanings, though not an infinite range: there are limits of interpretation. Eco proposes a cooperation between reader, text and author. The author wrote his text to provoke something, to invite the reader to react.[37] Because Luke-Acts is a narrative and because there is no scholarly consensus on the working of the Holy Spirit in Luke-Acts, Lukan pneumatology will prove to be an excellent topic to study the role of the reader in his cooperation with the Lukan πνεῦμα texts.

The strength in Eco's model is a balanced view on the role of author, text and reader. All three are necessary in the process of reading and interpreting. All three have their own distinctive role. Eco's model of the cooperative reader gives attention to the text itself, to limits of interpretation placed (by the author) within the text and it gives attention to the role of the reader while reading/interpreting the text. Because of the balance between author, text and reader, this model prevents readers from focusing on only one aspect of the communication process. It is actually a combination of text criticism, historical-criticism and reader-response

---

35 Joel B. Green, "Scripture and Theology: Uniting the Two So Long Divided" in: J.B. Green and M.M.B. Turner (eds.), *Between Two Horizons. Spanning New Testament Studies & Systematic Theology* (Grand Rapids, MI: Eerdmans, 2000), 23-43; Robert P. Menzies and William W. Menzies, *Spirit and Power: Foundations of Pentecostal Experience* (Grand Rapids, MI: Zondervan, 2000), chapters 2-4 and Gordon D. Fee and Douglas Stuart, *How to Read the Bible for all Its Worth: A Guide to Understanding the Bible* (3d ed.; Grand Rapids, MI: Zondervan, 2003).

36 Green, "Scripture and Theology", 31-32.

37 This is especially true for the Lukan narrative, see: Joel B. Green, *The Theology of the Gospel of Luke* (NTT; 13d ed.; Cambridge: Cambridge University, 2010) 22-49. Green writes on p.23 "[…] the Third Evangelist presents the story of the Messiah's coming into the world […] *to invite response from his audience*" (emphasis is mine).

criticism. The model of Eco provides scholars with a "more holistic" model because of its attention to all three aspects of the communication process. While on the one hand doing justice to the importance of the author and the text, on the other hand it acknowledges the distinctive influence of the reader when interpreting and responding to the text. The possible result of applying Eco's "holistic" model to different Lukan scholars will lead to understanding and perhaps an appreciation of their distinctive interpretative choices.

In his work on semiotics and literary science Eco introduced the difference between an open and a closed text.[38] An open text gives opportunity for the reader to be substantially involved in the interpretation process. The author of the text decides the degree of cooperation of the potential reader. It is the author who decides where in his text he "controls" the interpretation, where he guides the reader in his interpretation or whether he leaves a certain aspect of his narrative open for different interpretations.[39] Examples of an open text are a poem, or a song, such as the Psalms. The reader is invited to cooperate with the text and join the writer/singer in praising, complaining or mourning. Interpretation is open to different nuances, mostly on an emotional level. On the contrary a closed text has clear-cut boundaries which guide the reader in his interpretation. An example of a closed text is a crime story: while reading the story it becomes clear who committed the crime and in what way he did it. The solution does not depend on the reader's choice, but is predetermined by the author.

In reality a text is often a combination of open and closed parts, as is also the case in Luke-Acts. In Acts 8:26-40 for example we read the story of Philip encountering the Ethiopian eunuch. A closed aspect in these verses is the fact that the Ethiopian is reading from the book of Isaiah. Luke makes explicitly clear which verses were read and the questions the Ethiopian had about these verses (Acts 8:32-34). The next verse however, verse 35, is quite open because it is only mentioned that Philip used these verses from Isaiah to explain the Gospel. How he explained it and what he exactly said is left open. According to the Eunuch's remark about baptism,

---

[38] Umberto Eco, *The Open Work* (trans. A. Cancogni) and *The Role of the Reader*. See also Zwiep, *Tussen tekst en lezer II*, 342.

[39] Eco, *Lector in fabula*, 77. Recently a volume was published on filling in one single gap in the Gospel of Luke: Bruce W. Longenecker, *Hearing the Silence: Jesus on the Edge and God in the Gap – Luke 4 in Narrative Perspective* (Eugene, OR: Cascade, 2012).

one may assume Philip talked about baptism, but the text does not explicitly state this. In regard to Lukan pneumatology the end of this pericope is also an open part when it is stated that "the Spirit of the Lord suddenly took Philip away". This is not explained in the context of these verses or even repeated in the whole corpus of Luke-Acts. It is open for the reader to interpret what exactly happened, although constrained by formal criteria of rapture categories.

Schematically Eco reflects the closed and open aspects of a text with these pictures:[40]

Picture [a] shows the structure of a closed text. With every "knot" there is only one possible interpretation. In this way the author limits the possibilities of interpreting his text and as such guides the reader to the meaning of the text. Picture [b] shows the structure of an open text. The "knots" in such an open text give multiple interpretive possibilities. It is here that the author encourages the cooperation of the reader in interpreting the text.

To understand the specific interpretation a scholar of Lukan pneumatology makes it is necessary to first determine the "literary knots" in the corpus of Luke-Acts. For example one might first need to determine those "knots" that have to do with the Holy Spirit. Secondly the personal interpretation of the scholar at these "knots" has to be determined. Every junction gives an opportunity to cooperate with the text and make a different interpretation. In section 2.6 the "literary knots" in the Lukan πνεῦμα texts will be discussed and a methodology to apply Eco's model will be provided. Before this it is necessary to take a closer look at Eco's model of the cooperative reader.

2.5 Umberto Eco's model of the cooperative reader
Graphically Eco's model consists of ten boxes and its difficulty lies in the fact that this model is not a linear model. In other words the way of

---

40 Eco, *Lector in fabula*, 158.

interpreting a text does not follow the normal linear way from one to two to three and so on. While reading (and interpreting) a text there is, within the reader, an interaction between the boxes from Eco's model. Different interpretive choices are made simultaneously. Interpreting a text is actually "reading between the lines", filling in blank spots with one's own ideas of meaning until such an idea is falsified or verified in the course of the story. The meaning of the ten different boxes in Eco's model will be explained below, next to a picture of this model (figure 1).[41] A rough division can be made between boxes 1-3, which deal with the actual text (linear manifestation); boxes 4, 6, 8 and 9 (intensions) which deal with the internal textual qualities and boxes 5, 7 and 10 (extensions) which are about possible implications outside the world of the text.

2.5.1 The actualized text
Box 3: Expression

Eco starts discussing his model with box 3: expression. This is the actual expression of the text in its physical constituency. With this Eco means the linear manifestation in which the text comes to the reader: a set of signs and symbols in a certain language which are read from a book or a screen. In the case of Luke-Acts the text is in a certain translation or in the original Greek language in which it was written. The author of a text uses a set of codes and subcodes (box 1) through which the reader can actually read and understand the text. It is here that textual criticism is important to determine as exact as possible the original text.

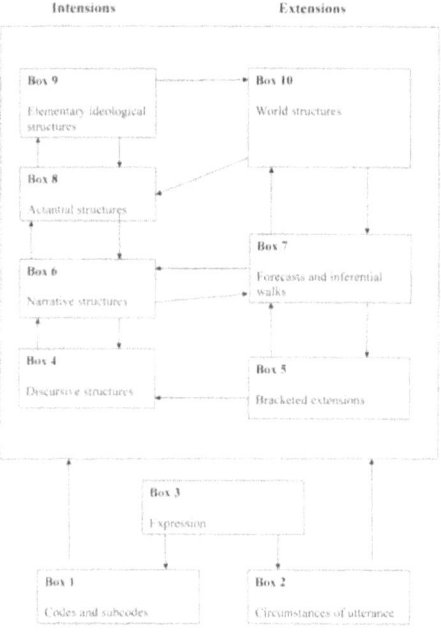

---

41 This model appears in Eco, *Lector in Fabula* (Dutch translation), 94 and *The Role of the Reader*, 14. See also Zwiep, *Tussen tekst en lezer II*, 347.

Box 1: Codes and subcodes
Proper communication between author-text-reader will be substantiated when the codes and subcodes, placed in the text by the author, will be recognized and understood by the reader. Issues like knowledge of the language, vocabulary and the order of reading (left to right, top to bottom) are evident. However, the author of the text presupposes a "model reader": a reader who understands his writing and expressions and due to their shared "presupposition pool" can understand and interpret the text properly.[42] Eco defines this complex system of codes and subcodes as *encyclopedia*.[43] The way in which the reader handles this complex system of codes and subcodes is then designated as *encyclopedic competence*.

In many texts the presupposed model reader is evident by using a certain vocabulary or literary style (e.g. children's books). In the process of actualizing the text, the reader uses his own set of codes and subcodes (the *encyclopedic competence* of the reader). As examples Eco mentions the basic dictionary a reader possesses, his knowledge of intertextuality, the meaning of words in a certain context (see the example of lion above), ambiguity and figures of speech. For instance: when a text speaks about "princess" the reader knows that a woman is meant.[44]

Besides the encyclopedic competence of the reader, the so called *ideological overcoding* plays a specific part in interpreting a text.[45] The reader approaches a text (consciously or unconsciously) from a personal ideological angle. This is particularly true when it concerns biblical texts. Raised in a certain denomination or interpretive community such as a church, the reader will take with him presuppositions about the biblical text in question. In the case of Luke-Acts there are certain denominations that treat this two volume work as their "canon within the canon".[46]

---

42 The term "presupposition pool" is Max Turners, see: Max M.B. Turner, "Historical Criticism and Theological Hermeneutics of the New Testament" in:J.B. Green, M.M.B. Turner (eds.), *Between Two Horizons. Spanning New Testament Studies & Systematic Theology* (Grand Rapids, MI: Eerdmans, 2000), 49-50.
43 Eco, *Lector in fabula*, 101; *The Role of the Reader*, 7.
44 Eco, *Lector in fabula*, 101-102; *The Role of the Reader*, 18.
45 Eco, *Lector in fabula*, 111-112; *The Role of the Reader*, 22.
46 For instance Kenneth J. Archer writes: "When it comes to Spirit Baptism, most Pentecostals grant Luke-Acts an equal if not superior position (even though it is narrative) to the Letters in the harmonization process". In: Kenneth J. Archer, *A Pentecostal Hermeneutic for the Twenty-First Century: Spirit, Scripture and Community* (JPTSS 28; London; New York: T&T Clark, 2004) 138-139.

On the other side of the spectrum it is the author of a text who incorporates ideologies within the text. The author keeps in mind a model-reader with an ideological competence so he can read and interpret the text properly. While actualizing the text the importance remains to determine case by case whether the author had readers in mind with such an ideological competence.

Box 2: Circumstances of utterance
Eco makes a difference between oral conversation and written text. Within a conversation elements like tone and gesture influence the circumstances in which a message is received. However, when reading a written text the reader is limited to the actual written text in front of him. The reader's first hypothesis is to accept that the author writes about their common world and experiences.[47] In continuation the reader determines the *genre* of the text: while reading or even before reading, the reader will make a decision about the text being a novel or a scientific work or history and so on. The reader's second hypothesis concerns the complex work of trying to determine the original place and circumstances of the author while writing his text.[48]

This is where Eco's model coincides with classical exegesis: answering introductory questions about authorship, addressees, date of writing, historical-cultural and social-economical background and issues of genre and literary forms.[49]

2.5.2 The substantial properties of the text (intensions)
Box 4: Discursive structures
With box 4 the transition is made from an encyclopedic meaning of the text to the textual meaning. The first signifies all the possible meanings the reader can find in his dictionary; the latter is the actual meaning of the words within the given text. A text is meant to be interpreted and as such has its own distinctive meaning. In theory a word can have an endless range of meanings, but in a certain text a word has a certain meaning. In determining the meaning of a word the reader searches for the *topic* of the text. This topic provides the basis for a meaning or some possible

---

47 Eco, *Lector in fabula*, 98.
48 Eco, *Lector in fabula*, 99.
49 See for instance Gordon D. Fee, *New Testament Exegesis. A Handbook for Students and Pastors* (3d ed.; Louisville, KY: Westminster/John Knox, 2002) and Stanley E. Porter (ed.), *Handbook to Exegesis of the New Testament* (Leiden, Brill: 1997).

meanings of the word. These possible meanings are all kept in mind, or as Eco says "narcotized", until a certain meaning can be actualized.[50] So the key in determining what the words mean is the topic of the text. The author of the text "guides" his model-reader in discovering the topic (or topics) of the text. This can be done by adding a title, making use of keywords or repetitions. To make things more complicated: a text does not necessarily have only one topic. There can be a hierarchy in topics: one main topic including some subtopics.[51]

Defining the topic is a matter of construing a hypothesis by the reader. The reader will ask himself the question "what is this text about?" and will then formulate for himself a provisional answer. On basis of this provisional answer he will actualize or narcotize certain meanings which are coherent with this provisional answer. In the process of reading, Eco calls this an *interpretive coherence* or *isotopy* and uses isotopy as an umbrella term.[52]

Box 6: Narrative structures
Topics and isotopies will guide the reader of the text in understanding the text: this is what the text is about, this is what happens in the story. However, beneath this interpretive level of the text there is the level of the structure of the text, the so-called framework of the text. It is here that Eco –in agreement with Russian formalists– distinguishes between the *plot* (sjuzet) and the *story* (fabula) of a text.[53] The plot of the text is the text as it is in front of the reader: the text with its timelines, descriptions, flashbacks and so on. In a narrative text the plot (*sjuzet*) coincides with the discursive structures (topics and isotopies).[54] While reading, the reader moves from discursive structures to the narrative structure, from plot (sjuzet) to story (fabula). The story of the text has to do with the overall structure *behind* the text: the narrative structure. Determining the narrative structure of the story is dependend on the intertextual competencies of the reader: it makes quite a difference if the reader already knows the story, or reads it for the first time.[55]

---

50 Eco, *Lector in fabula*, 114; *The Role of the Reader*, 27.
51 Eco, *Lector in fabula*, 119. Eco mentions "topic of a sentence, discursive topic, narrative topic and macro topic".
52 Eco, *Lector in fabula*, 120-133; Umberto Eco, "Two Problems in Textual Interpretation", *Poetics Today* (1980): 145-161; Zwiep, Tussen tekst en lezer II, 352-354.
53 Eco, *Lector in fabula*, 134; *The Role of the Reader*, 27; Zwiep, *Tussen tekst en lezer II*, 355.
54 Eco, *Lector in fabula*, 135.
55 Eco, *Lector in fabula*, 137.

To summarize: in box 4 the reader discovers what the text is about (topic or discursive structure) and then moves on to box 6, where he discovers the structure behind the text (narrative structure).

Box 8: Actantial structures
While continuing his reading process, the reader will constantly be busy actualizing structures and the meaning of words. He does so in collaboration with his own encyclopedic knowledge, his worldview and the knowledge of other (similar) narratives. All this means that during the reading process the reader actually "jumps" from box to box, back and forth. There is no neat linear process from box 1 to 2 and eventually box 10. Having distinguished the plot (box 4, discursive structures) and the story (box 6, narrative structures), the reader will try to move on to a more abstract level: actantial structures.[56] Eco intends that after plot and story are distinguished the reader will, on a deeper level, formulate some abstract terminology. Hereby characters in the narrative are reduced to propositions: subject | object, helper | opponent, beneficiary | benefactor, and so on. On this level the reader gains insight in what the story is really about. For instance in Luke 12 where Jesus warns his disciples for the hypocrisy of the Pharisees and declares that everything which is hidden will be made known, the deeper level (actantial structure) is that of a warning against hypocrisy in general.[57]

According to Eco to search for actantial structures and deduce them from the text is the only thing that really matters and as such the only thing that a *cooperative reader* should be doing.[58] The result of a critical reading of a narrative should be to produce a framework which shows these actantial structures. This can only be done after a thorough reading and re-reading of the text.

Box 9: Elementary ideological structures
The next step is to move from actantial structures to ideological structures. This occurs when the reader adds value judgments to the actantial structures.[59] Added value judgments can be: good versus bad, life versus death, genuine versus false, etcetera. To continue the example mentioned

---

56 Eco, *Lector in fabula*, 229-232; *The Role of the Reader*, 37-39.
57 John Nolland, *Luke 9:21-18:34* (WBC 35b; Dallas, TX: Word, 1993), 681-682 and Darrell L. Bock, *Luke volume 2* (BECNT 4; Grand Rapids, MI: Baker, 1996), 1144-1145.
58 Eco, *Lector in fabula*, 231.
59 Eco, *Lector in fabula*, 232-233; *The Role of the Reader*, 37-39.

above from Luke 12, the value judgment to add is that hypocrisy does not fit in the lives of genuine believers and followers of Christ. On the surface we have the story of Jesus teaching his disciples on hypocrisy and he takes the Pharisees as a negative example. In general hypocrisy is condemned, in that sense that all will be made known. The ideological aspect is that hypocrisy becomes a criterion for genuine discipleship.

2.5.3 Preliminary deductions and possible implications (extensions)
Box 5: Bracketed extensions
During the process of reading the reader gathers information by the codes and subcodes within the text. His preliminary assumption is that the world of the text is the actual world he lives in and thus the world he knows by way of his own codes and subcodes. If in the reading process some discrepancies with the actual world appear, such as a speaking stone, the reader will put this between brackets.[60] Believing or not-believing what he reads will be postponed until he finds other clues or directions in the story of the text. This searching for other clues is described in box 4 (discursive structures) where the topic of a certain text will determine whether the reader believes or disbelieves. If disbelieving is the case he will "jump" to box 10 (world structures).[61]

Box 7: Forecasts and inferential walks
While reading the text and actualizing a certain meaning of the different words and sentences, the reader discovers the plot (box 4) and the story (box 6) of the narrative. While, gradually, discovering plot and story, the reader will also predict a certain outcome or continuation of the story. For instance if a reader reads about a game of chess and he knows the rules of the game, the reader can predict a next move. This can be an adequate and just move, however only in continuing reading he will discover if it is the same move the author had in mind. So the reader of the narrative continually proposes certain outcomes, predicts these in his mind and when the narrative unfolds his *forecasts* or predictions will be verified or falsified.

To arrive at a hypothesis about the continuation of the narrative the reader uses his own encyclopedic knowledge and also takes notice of intertextuality within the narrative. For instance if in the narrative "x-does-so-and-so" and the result of this is "y", then the reader will con-

---

60 Eco, *The Role of the Reader*, 17.
61 Eco, *The Role of the Reader*, 17.

clude "if-x-takes-action-then-the-result-is-y."[62] To arrive at such a hypothesis, the reader uses other stories he knows. He actually "makes a trip outside the text" to gather some information only to return to his text with this information. Eco calls this *inferential walks*.[63]

Box 10: World structures
During the process of reading, the reader creates in his mind possible worlds. This is closely related to the *inferential walks* from box 7. As stated above, the reader will "wander" out of the text to relate to stories, places and worlds he already knows. For instance if the narrative mentions the city of Paris, then the reader relates to what he knows about Paris: it is the capital of France.[64] That is: Paris is the capital of France *in this (real) world*. The world of the text can be a different world. If the reader has ever been to Paris, his image will be richer because of certain details he remembers. If the text mentions impossibilities, for instance an apartment on the third story of the Eiffel Tower, or a stone which is speaking, then there occurs a discrepancy between the actual (*real*) world and the narrative world.[65] The reader must choose to cooperate with the author of the narrative to actualize the text and the possible worlds which the text mentions. The reader so to speak believes or disbelieves in the world of the narrative (or the reader chooses to narcotize certain features of the world of the text in order to first gain some more information). Believing in the world of the text will be beneficial for the cooperation between the reader and the author of the text. It will help to accomplish the goal the author has with the text. Whether the reader "believes" in the possible world from the text, depends on the encyclopedia of the reader. If, within the encyclopedia of the reader, it is possible for a human being to be swallowed by a large fish and three days later be spat out without any physical harm, then there is no discrepancy between the readers *real* world and the biblical story of Jonah.[66]

---

62 Example taken from Eco, *Lector in fabula*, 155.
63 Eco, *Lector in fabula*, 154-157; *The Role of the Reader*, 32.
64 Example taken from Eco, *Lector in fabula*, 168. On possible worlds, see also: Eco, *Limits of Interpretation*, 66-67.
65 Eco, *Lector in fabula*, 168; *The Role of the Reader*, 17; Zwiep, *Tussen tekst en lezer II*, 357.
66 Eco, *Lector in fabula*, 175.

2.6 Applying Eco's model to Luke-Acts
2.6.1 The "literary knots" in Luke's πνεῦμα texts
In comparison with the Gospels of Matthew, Mark and John, Luke's use of πνεῦμα exceeds them all. In total Luke uses πνεῦμα 106 times in the corpus of Luke-Acts. Of these 106 times the (Holy) Spirit is meant in 75 cases.[67] In theory these 75 πνεῦμα texts provide the scholar with 75 hypothetical knots. In practice some knots are more complicated than others. Generally speaking the scholarly attention is focused on the following clusters of πνεῦμα texts:

a. Luke 1-2, the infancy narratives. These texts are *Lukan Sondergut* and it is here that Luke writes about the working of the Spirit before Jesus' birth and during Jesus' infancy.
b. Luke 3-4:13 John the Baptist. Especially the promise spoken by John the Baptist about Jesus who will come and baptize with the Holy Spirit and fire, receive much attention from scholars. Subsequently the baptism of Jesus and the temptation in the wilderness follow.
c. Luke 4, the inauguration of Jesus ministry. Jesus' first public appearance in the synagogue of Nazareth is often seen as paradigmatic for his ministry throughout the Gospel. Luke's mixed citation from Isaiah gets much attention from scholars as well as the image of Jesus as the great prophet.
d. Luke 10-12, some general sayings about the Spirit. Some scholars treat these sayings of Jesus about the Holy Spirit, some leave them out of their research.
e. Luke 24 – Acts 1, the promise of the Spirit. In these two chapters, which serve (literary and theologically) as a bridge between Luke and Acts, the promise of the outpouring of the Holy Spirit is reiterated.
f. Acts 2, Pentecost. The actual outpouring of the Spirit followed by Peter's speech in which especially 2:38 receives much scholarly attention.
g. Acts 8, the Samaritan episode. The Samaritans respond positively to the Gospel preached by Philip. However, they receive the Holy Spirit only after Peter and John come from Jerusalem to lay on hands and pray with them.
h. Acts 9, the Damascus event. The issue here is whether Saul receives the Spirit during his encounter with Jesus on the Damascus road, or whether he receives the Spirit when Ananias lays on his hands and prays with Saul.
i. Acts 10, the Cornelius household. The Gentile household of Cornelius experiences the same outpouring of the Spirit as the apostles at Pentecost.

---

67 See appendix 1 and 2 for an overview of all the πνεῦμα texts in Luke-Acts.

This episode is a crux for the Gentile mission and as such redefines "the people of God."
j. Acts 19, the Ephesian disciples. In this episode the issue is whether these disciples were disciples of John the Baptist and as such were not converted. Or whether they already were followers of Jesus and receive the Holy Spirit here as an addition to their conversion.

These ten clusters of πνεῦμα texts are the most important for scholars in regard to their views of Lukan pneumatology. In each of the mentioned episodes above, decisive exegetical and interpretive choices are made. These choices serve as rudimentary building blocks for a Lukan pneumatology.

2.6.2 How to apply Eco's model to the "literary knots"
The above mentioned ten literary knots will form the basic structure of the next three chapters in which the work of Max Turner, Robert Menzies en William Kurz will be discussed. These ten clusters of Lukan πνεῦμα texts form the skeleton of Luke's writing on the Spirit. In regard to Eco's model of the cooperative reader, these ten clusters are the framework of the Lukan texts on the Spirit (box 6). This is the narrative structure, the structure behind the texts as it is in front of the reader. To do justice to this narrative structure of the Lukan texts on the Spirit, it only seems fair to use this also as a structure in the next chapters when the role of the reader will be examined.

Because of the interrelation between the different boxes in Eco's model (the reader "jumps" from box to box) it is not necessary or beneficial to discuss each box on its own terms in relation to each πνεῦμα text. Clustering the boxes seems again a good solution to come to a workable method. Eco's model can be divided in three categories: the text as we have it in front of us (boxes 1, 2 and 3), the different structures (or layers) of the text (boxes 4, 6, 8 and 9; Eco designates these as *intensions*) and the possible implications of the text (boxes 5, 7 and 10; Eco designates these as *extensions*).

For a proper understanding of the role of the reader it is necessary to question the reader on basis of these three categories. What is his opinion of the text itself? How does he understand the text in its different structures? And what exactly are the possible implications of the text for his actual world? In the next chapters these three categories will be labeled as follows:

a. The actualized text;
b. The substantial properties of the text;
c. Preliminary deductions and possible implications.

It is through these three categories that Eco's model of the cooperative reader will be applied to the three different readers and as such should provide a solid point of departure to distinguish the distinctive role of the readers in reading, interpreting and applying Luke's πνεῦμα texts.

2.7 Conclusion

Eco's model of *the cooperative reader* promises to be a rewarding method for the narrative of Luke-Acts. Rewarding because of the "holistic" scope of the model: it treats the text as it is in front of the reader, it focuses on the author in the sense of the interpretive limits of the text and it pays due attention to the role of the reader while reading and interpreting the text. As a novel writer and a semiotician Eco is well aware of the importance of author/text on the one hand and the reader on the other hand during the process of communication. His ten box model of the cooperative reader shows attention to all aspects of communication and is an excellent tool for narrative texts such as Luke-Acts.

When consequently applied this model of the cooperative reader will hopefully shed some light on the interpretive choices readers make when approaching a Lukan literary knot. As such this model will provide more insight on how exactly the three scholars discussed do understand and interpret the Lukan texts on the Holy Spirit.

CHAPTER 3

THE MODEL APPLIED (1):

MAX M.B. TURNER

3.1 Introduction

Max M.B. Turner is professor emeritus at London School of Theology and an ordained Baptist minister. After studying medicine and theology at Cambridge University, he completed his doctorate on Luke-Acts, also at Cambridge University.[1] He contributed substantially to the scholarly debate on the Holy Spirit in Luke-Acts. Several articles and two monographs on this subject were published.[2] His foremost sparring partners in the debate are James D.G. Dunn and Robert P. Menzies. In regard to the previous mentioned ten "literary knots" in Luke's πνεῦμα texts, Turner extensively discusses nine of them, and in addition he briefly comments on the general sayings of Jesus about the Spirit in chapters 10-12 from the Gospel of Luke. All these ten "literary knots" in Luke's πνεῦμα texts will be discussed in this chapter in the light of Eco's model of the cooperative reader. It is to be expected that in this way the specific role of the reader "Turner" will become clear.

3.2 The infancy narratives (Luke 1-2)

3.2.1 The actualized text

Concerning the text proper, Turner notes that the origins of Luke 1-2 are disputed. However, according to Turner four conclusions are justified:[3]

---

[1] For a more extensive biography on Max Turner see: Steve Walton, "An Introduction to Max Turner" in: I. Howard Marshall, Volker Rabens and Cornelis Bennema (eds.), *The Spirit and Christ in the New Testament & Christian Theology: Essays in Honor of Max Turner* (Grand Rapids, MI: Eerdmans, 2012), xvi-xx.

[2] For the more than ten articles see the bibliography at the end of this dissertation. The two monographs are: Max M.B. Turner, *Power from on High: The Spirit in Israel's Restoration and Witness in Luke-Acts*, (JPTS 9; Sheffield: Sheffield Academic, 1996), *The Holy Spirit and Spiritual Gifts Then and Now* (Carlisle: Paternoster, 1996).

[3] Turner, *Power from on High*, 140-143.

a. Luke did not get his infancy narratives from Matthew, or vice versa;[4]
b. The points of conceptual agreement between Luke and Matthew suggest their use of earlier traditions;[5]
c. The linguistic arguments favor the hypothesis that the traditions used in Luke 1-2 were Hebrew or Aramaic or a translation from these languages;[6]
d. It is probable that the parallel annunciation, birth and infancy accounts are from one single source.[7]

Besides these four conclusions, Turner does not engage in a debate about the so called *introductory questions*. Matters of the dating of the Gospel of Luke and the Book of Acts, the occasion and circumstances for writing and the genre of both writings are left aside.

Of great importance for Turner is the Jewish background of the role of the Spirit in Luke's writings. Turner extensively describes this background and proposes another definition of the term 'Spirit of prophecy' than other scholars.[8] It is already here that the role of the reader plays an important part in relation to Lukan Pneumatology. The various characteristics and attributes subscribed to the Spirit of prophecy do influence

---

4 This conclusion can be challenged if one for instance favors the so called "Two Gospel Hypothesis" or Griesbach Hypothesis, in which the Gospel of Luke is dependent on the Gospel of Matthew. For further reference see: M.D. Goulder, *Luke: A New Paradigm* (Sheffield: JSOT, 1989) and Mark S. Goodacre, *Goulder and the Gospels. An Examination of a New Paradigm* (JSNTS 133; Sheffield: Sheffield Academic, 1996); idem, *The Synoptic Problem. A Way Through the Maze* (London: T&T Clark, 2001); idem, *The Case Against Q* (Harrisburg, PA: Trinity, 2002).
5 Raymond E. Brown, *The Birth of the Messiah* (New York, NY: Doubleday, 1999), 34-35, lists eleven points of agreement: (1) the parents Joseph and Mary are engaged, but not involved in a sexual relationship; (2) Joseph is of Davidic descent; (3) the childbirth is announced by an angel; (4) and (5) the conception of the child is not through intercourse, but through the Holy Spirit; (6) and (7) an angel directs the child to be named Jesus and that He is to be Savior; (8) the birth takes place after the parents have come to live together; (9), (10) and (11) the birth takes place at Bethlehem during the reign of Herod the Great and the child is reared at Nazareth.
6 See the extensive footnote in Turner, *Power from on High*, 141, in which he elaborates on the debate whether Luke used Semitic sources or if there are Septuagintalisms in the infancy narratives.
7 Turner is cautious in regard to this conclusion. The strongly developed parallelism between John and Jesus in Luke 1-2 (where Jesus transcends John in matters of importance) is not continued in Luke 3-4. If Luke 1-2 were solely a Lukan redaction, one would expect the same strong parallelism in Luke 3-4. Turner, *Power from on High*, 142.
8 In *Power from on High*, Turner spends 56 pages on the Spirit of prophecy (chps. 3, 4 and 5). In *The Holy Spirit and Spiritual Gifts* this is 20 pages (chp.1).

the exegesis of the relevant Lukan passages. Scholars vary in what specific attributes *they* think can be subscribed to the Jewish Spirit of prophecy. By using the terminology 'Spirit of prophecy', Turner does not mean that the Spirit's activity is limited to prophecy alone. He argues that Jews meant something much wider. The Spirit acted as the organ of communication between God and a person.[9] According to Turner, the Spirit of prophecy inspires people with four different kinds of gifts:

a. Charismatic revelation and guidance;[10]
b. Charismatic wisdom;[11]
c. (Sometimes) invasively inspired prophetic speech;[12]
d. (Sometimes, but rarely) invasively inspired charismatic praise or worship.[13]

Besides this, Turner argues that generally speaking the Spirit was seen as the invisible activity of God in power and God's presence in revelation and wisdom. There was a future expectation of a universal outpouring of the Spirit on *all* of Israel's people and Turner opposes to an alleged *complete* withdrawal of the Spirit during the intertestamental period: the Spirit's working was rather relatively rare.[14]

In contrast to Eduard Schweizer,[15] Gonzalo Haya-Prats[16] and Robert Menzies,[17] Turner does include power to perform miracles, exorcisms

---

9   Turner, *Holy Spirit and Spiritual Gifts*, 8, and *Power from on High*, 89-90. Contra Menzies who states that Jews saw the Spirit of prophecy as a rigidly fixed concept (terminology is Turner's), idem, *Power from on High*, 83. For Menzies complete point of view see the next chapter of this dissertation.
10 Turner, *Power from on High*, 92-95, *Spirit and Spiritual Gifts*, 8-10.
11 Turner, *Power from on High*, 95-97, *Spirit and Spiritual Gifts*, 10-12.
12 Turner, *Power from on High*, 98-101, *Spirit and Spiritual Gifts*, 12-13.
13 Turner, *Spirit and Spiritual Gifts*, 13-14.
14 Turner, *Spirit and Spiritual Gifts*, 14-15.
15 E. Schweizer, 'πνεῦμα', in: G. Kittel and G. Friedrich, *Theologisches Wörterbuch zum Neuen Testament* (Stuttgart: Kohlhammer, 1933-1978) Bd.VI, 320-453.
16 Gonzalo Haya-Prats, *L'Esprit force de l'église* (Paris: Cerf, 1975). This is the French translation of the Spanish dissertation of Haya-Prats from the Pontifical Gregorian University of Rome in 1967, titled *El Espiritu Santo en los Hechos de los Apostoles*. An English translation has been published in 2011 edited by Paul Elbert and translated by Scott Ellington: *Empowered Believers. The Holy Spirit in the Book of Acts* (Eugene, OR: Cascade, 2011).
17 Robert P. Menzies, *The Development of Early Christian Pneumatology with Special Reference to Luke-Acts* (JSNTS 54; Sheffield: Sheffield Academic, 1991).

and healing to the working of the Spirit. In chapter four of *Power from on High*, Turner takes Robert Menzies as his primary sparring partner and elaborates why miraculous power (δύναμις) should be added to the working of the Spirit. Although miraculous power was rare during the intertestamental period, it cannot be totally dismissed as is the case in Menzies thesis.[18]

In addition to the discussion whether the Spirit of prophecy is also the source for miraculous power, there is the issue of ethical influence and salvation. Are these also concepts which can be ascribed to the Spirit of prophecy or not? Schweizer and Menzies do not thoroughly deny this ethical aspect of the Spirit of prophecy, but dismiss it as being untypical or insignificant. Turner disagrees and finds it an "oversimplified portrait of the Spirit of prophecy."[19] He argues that the gifts the Spirit can get a grasp on someone and encourages ethical transformation. He then respectively treats the LXX and Targums, Philo, The Twelve Patriarchs, Qumran and Rabbinical teaching to show the ethical influence of the Spirit of prophecy.[20]

The last issue to be discussed is the distinctive Lukan terminology used in combination with the Spirit. Luke uses the passive of the verb πληρόω (to fill), the adjective πλήρης (full of) and the passive of the verb πίμπλημι (to fill completely).[21] Turner argues that Luke uses *metaphorical language* contrary to *literal language* to describe the working of the Spirit in a person. Turner's ideological overcoding becomes clear in his concluding statement:

> "Luke does not believe all Christians to be 'full of the Spirit': this metaphor is used precisely to distinguish those whose lives are particularly marked by the work of the Spirit from ordinary Christians (cf. Acts 6.3!). And in Lukan terms the criterion for judging whether it is appropriate to speak of someone as 'full of the Spirit' is not whether he has a baptismal or she a confirmation certificate—nor even whether the person concerned has in the past experienced some 'second blessing—but whether the community of Christians *felt*

---

18 Turner's primary arguments are Menzies rejection of *2Baruch* and *4Ezra* and the influence of translations of the LXX and Targums. Turner, *Power from on High*, 106-110.
19 Turner, *Power from on High*, 121.
20 Turner, *Power from on High*, 123-132.
21 See for an extensive technical and grammatical explanation: Turner, *Power from on High*, 165-169 and idem "Spirit Endowment in Luke/Acts: Some Linguistic Considerations," *VE* 12 (1981): 45-63.

the impact of the Spirit through that person's life and *saw the Spirit's graces and gifts regularly expressed* through him or her."[22]

So in concluding this subsection on the actualized text, it becomes clear that Turner encounters the infancy narratives as being from a single traditional source, probably Hebrew, Aramaic or a translation from one of these. With regard to the concept of the Spirit of prophecy, Turner's opinion is that Luke has a rather broad view of the Spirit and the working of the Spirit. He establishes his opinion on his research concerning the Spirit of prophecy in the Old Testament and intertestamental period. In regard to linguistics Turner designates the Lukan terminology as *metaphorical* instead of *literal*. These three issues—the text proper, the background of the Spirit of prophecy and the Lukan terminology used in correlation with the Spirit— all three show Turner's ideological overcoding.

3.2.2 The substantial properties of the text
To discover the substantial properties of the text, boxes 4, 6, 8 and 9 will provide some answers. The textual meaning will be determined by ascertaining the topic of the text (box 4). From the topic the reader moves to a deeper level to determine the framework of the text. That is: the narrative structure which is behind the text (box 6). From this narrative structure the reader continues to give an abstract meaning to the text. It is here that characters become propositions (box 8). If the reader adds value judgments to this abstract structure then a certain elementary ideology comes forward (box nine).

The first conclusion drawn by Turner is that the infancy narratives are "previews of salvation" and that the major Lukan theological themes are introduced here.[23] The infancy narratives serve to understand the overall narrative of Luke-Acts. The narrator (author) uses these first two chapters as a guide to God's will and plan. He uses trustworthy characters to communicate this: the angel Gabriel (1:11, 19, 26) and people who are full of/filled with the Spirit (John, Zechariah, Elisabeth, Mary[24] and Simeon). So the infancy narratives are not only a preview of salvation, but also serve

---

22 Turner, *Power from on High*, 169 and idem, "Spirit Endowment", 55 (slightly different phrased).
23 Turner, *Power from on High*, 140. He borrows this terminology from R.C. Tannehill, *The Narrative Unity of Luke-Acts: A Literary Interpretation. Volume 1: The Gospel of Luke* (Philadelphia, PA: Fortress, 1986), 15.
24 Although it is not explicitly stated that Mary spoke the *Magnificat* (1:46-55) by inspiration of the Spirit, Turner assumes that she did: Turner, *Power from on High*, 143, n.13.

to legitimize the Gospel story that will follow.[25] Turner summarizes the content of the announcements (and as such the topic of the text) in three points:[26]

a. John will fulfill the eschatological role of Elijah and will prepare Israel for her salvation;
b. God will introduce Israel's long-promised salvation through Jesus. This salvation consists in the forgiveness of sins and the liberation (from enemies, oppressors and social injustice) and transformation (as a righteous worshipping community) of Israel;
c. This restored Israel will be a light to the nations.

Turner concludes that Luke works with an "essentially Jewish soteriological paradigm" and this means that salvation is not only release from guilt and assurance of life in some new creation, but also an ongoing participation in worship, life and witness in a restored (cleansed and transformed) community to become a light to the nations.[27]

In continuation Turner shows the framework of the text (box 6) and points to the structure of and intertextuality in the text. He argues that the Spirit references to Elizabeth (1:41), Zechariah (1:67) and Simeon (2:25-27) are not preludes to the Spirit experience at Pentecost or in the church. Rather the activities of the Spirit (invasive prophetic speech, charismatic revelation) are within the Old Testament and intertestamental range of gifts of the Spirit of prophecy.[28] A first exception occurs with John the Baptist, who is being filled with the Spirit from his mother's womb. According to Turner this is unparalleled in Judaism, just as the mentioning of the prophet Elijah (1:17), which makes the Spirit endowment of John the Baptist an "eschatological fulfillment of hopes for the return of Elijah."[29] This Elijianic figure would restore and unify Israel as a covenant people. As such John the Baptist serves as a hinge between the Old Testament eschatological prophecy and the coming of the promised Messiah. The closely paralleled structure and content of the birth stories

---

25 Turner, *Power from on High*, 143-144.
26 Turner, *Power from on High*, 144.
27 Turner, *Power from on High*, 145.
28 Turner, *Power from on High*, 148-149.
29 Turner, *Power from on High*, 151.

of John and Jesus confirm this transitional role of John.[30] According to Turner this analogy with John leads to a climax in 1:34-35. In addition to parallels with other biblical birth annunciations, the keyword for Turner is παρθένος which links this passage to the Isaiah 7 pericope.[31] Due to the Davidic-Messianic context this parallel is striking and 'guides' the reader to the issue of 'sonship' Christology, the role of the Spirit therein and its possible implications for eschatology and soteriology.[32] According to Turner, if divine sonship is promised in 1:32-33 at the enthronement, then 1:35 traces this back to the Messiah's conception by the Spirit.[33] It is here that we encounter the narrative structure behind the text: it seems that Luke grounds his theological prelude firmly in the Old Testament and the common intertestamental ideas about the Spirit. However, something totally new emerges, a concept which is "strikingly unusual" for Judaism, namely the working of the Holy Spirit before birth. Turner concludes:

a. The working of the Spirit is (in this context) equated with the power of the Most High;[34]
b. "...shall be called holy...' (1:35) assumes an ethical orientation of the working of the Spirit;[35]
c. ue to the allusions to Ex.40:35 (ἐπισκιάζω, overshadow) and Isaiah 32:15 (ὕψιστος, most high) the theme of a restored Israel and New Exodus are prominent in the birth annunciation, giving it an eschatological overtone;[36]
d. he Spirit's working is not limited to the conception alone: in the course of the narrative it becomes clear Jesus recognizes his special sonship (2:49-50) and excels in religious wisdom (2:40, 52), all through the Spirit;[37]

---

30 For detailed analysis of the parallel structure see: R.E. Brown, *The Birth of the Messiah* (New York, NY: Doubleday, 1999), 292-298; J.A. Fitzmyer, *The Gospel according to Luke I-IX* (New York: Doubleday, 1981), 313-321; Tannehill, *Narrative Unity*, 15-20; J. Nolland, *Luke 1-9:20* (WBC 35a; Dallas, TX: Word, 1989), 40-42; J.B. Green, *The Gospel of Luke* (NICNT; Grand Rapids, MI: Eerdmans, 1997), 47-51.
31 Turner, *Power from on High*, 154.
32 Turner, *Power from on High*, 155.
33 Turner, *Power from on High*, 156.
34 Turner, *Power from on High*, 156-158, contra Robert Menzies.
35 Turner, *Power from on High*, 158-159.
36 Turner, *Power from on High*, 159.
37 Turner, *Power from on High*, 1160-161..

e. Luke 1:35 should be seen as a keyverse to the understanding of Lukan Pneumatology. It serves as anticipation to the "gateway texts" in 24:49 and Acts 1:8, in which "the power of the Most High becomes the power from on high."[38]

To conclude this section on *intensions*, it becomes clear that Turner does not yet distract propositions or value judgments from the infancy narratives. Seen through the model of Eco this means that Turner leaves boxes 8 and 9 aside. He does not interpret beyond the meaning, topic and structure of the text to actualize these. Turner does not yet move to the deeper level to formulate propositions. The same is true for the next logical step (box 9) where ideological structures come in. Turner does not explicitly add value judgments to his findings. His primary concern is the framework of the text (box 6). Focusing on intertextuality, Turner shows on the one hand the dependency on the common Old Testament and intertestamental concept of the Spirit and on the other hand the totally new working of the Spirit at conception. Besides this Turner shows that the themes of a New Exodus, a restored eschatological Israel and a Davidic-Messianic Redeemer are all behind the textual meaning of the infancy narrative.

3.2.3 Preliminary deductions and possible implications

In this third phase of interpretation where deductions and implications come to the surface, Turner is reluctant to apply texts or discuss their significance for the present. In the second part of Turner's *The Holy Spirit and Spiritual Gifts*, he specifically addresses the church today, however, without reference to the infancy narratives.[39] Turner primarily gathers information from and about the text, fully aware of the intertextuality with Old Testament themes and the then leading view of the working of the Spirit. Turner chooses to cooperate with the author of the text in accepting the possibility of a virgin birth. His "inferential walks" concern the books of the Old Testament and the intertestamental period. In his "forecasts" Turner takes the infancy narratives as being Luke's theological prelude in which the themes of salvation, restoration and transformation are all colored by a Jewish concept of soteriology. This is preceded by the miraculous birth of John the Baptist who is only the precursor of the even more miraculous birth of Jesus. In both instances the Holy Spirit plays an

---

38 Turner, *Power from on High*, 162. Turner distances here from Eduard Schweizer, who does not give 1:35 such a prominent place within the interpretation of Lukan Pneumatology.
39 Turner, *Spirit and Spiritual Gifts*, 179-347.

important role, it is only in the birth story of the latter that the Holy Spirit is equated with the power of God. This power involves divine sonship, eschatological kingship and holiness (Luke 1:32-35).

3.3 The ministry of John the Baptist (Luke 3:1-20)
3.3.1 The actualized text
The key text discussed by Turner regarding the ministry of John the Baptist is Luke 3:16-17 in which John promises that a "Stronger One" will come, one who will baptize with Spirit and fire.[40] Turner spends three pages (170-172) to introduce the context of the promise, which he regards as redactional (following Fitzmyer[41] and Marshall[42]), and concludes that John the Baptist is more a transitional figure than the last prophet from the period of Israel (contra Conzelmann[43]). The remaining sixteen pages (172-189) relate to the promise of John in 3:16-17. Based on his own encyclopedic competence Turner observes four relevant issues in this text:

a. Mark's (shorter) version. This includes the "and fire" in the promise;[44]
b. The promise in Luke 3:16 forms a hendiadys with the subsequent phrase in 3:17, thus making the two one;[45]
c. According to Turner the meaning of βαπτίζω is "to immerse, to dip or to sink", whereas he follows the probable Aramaic origin which is לבט;[46]
d. The general meaning of πτύον is a fork-like shovel;[47] however Turner opts for the meaning of a spade.[48]

---

40 Parallel texts are: Mathew 3:11-12 and Mark 1:7-8, whereby Mark omits the 'and fire' part of the promise.
41 Fitzmyer, *Gospel according to Luke*, 451-452.
42 I.H. Marshall, *The Gospel of Luke* (NIGTC; Grand Rapids, MI: Eerdmans, Paternoster, 1978), 132-137.
43 H. Conzelmann, *Die Mitte der Zeit* (Tübingen: Mohr Siebeck, 1953), 16-20.
44 Turner does so on basis of Mark's neater parallel with John's baptism (water - Spirit) and leaving the "with fire" unexplained. See Turner, *Power from on High*, 173n.10.
45 Turner, *Power from on High*, 173n.11, 175, 184, idem, *Spirit and Spiritual Gifts*, 27. The baptism to which John refers is one baptism consisting in Spirit and fire, instead of two baptisms: one with Spirit (for the righteous) and one with fire (for the unrighteous).
46 Turner, *Power from on High*, 180-181.
47 BDAG, 895.
48 Turner, *Power from on High*, 171. Turner follows the interpretation of Robert L. Webb, "The Activity of John the Baptist's Expected Figure at the Threshing Floor (Mathew 3:12=Luke 3:17)", *JSNT* 43 (1991), 103-111 and *John the Baptizer and Prophet* (Sheffield: JSOT, 1991).

These four observations are the most important for Turner regarding the text proper. We can conclude that in this first phase of interpretation the role of the reader comes to the surface. Turner makes interpretive choices by designating 3:16-17 as a hendiadys, he follows the general meaning of βαπτίζω, but chooses not to do so with πτύον. All based on what he thinks is the best interpretation due to the direct context of the promise of John the Baptist. After examining the text proper we will now move on to boxes 4, 6, 8 and 9 (*intensions*) and see how Turner understands the topic and structure of the text and whether he will make some preliminary value judgments.

3.3.2 The substantial properties of the text
Turner combines a narrative-critical (reader-response) and a tradition-historical orientation to come to his interpretation of "baptism with Spirit and fire."[49] He observes that John is preaching to the whole of Israel, repentant and unrepentant. In contrast to his own baptism with water a stronger one will come who will baptize with Spirit and fire. Through the governing proposition ἐν only one baptism is promised to John's audience, one act which the repentant would experience as a blessing and the unrepentant as judgment/destruction.[50] Dunn and Webb argue that John the Baptist combined an eschatological outpouring of the Spirit with a Spirit-anointed Messiah. Turner opposes this view on the ground that God's Spirit was God himself and as such would threaten Jewish monotheism if the Messiah was sovereign over God's Spirit, sovereign in such a sense that he would bestow the Spirit on others.[51] Turner's exegesis and therewith the textual meaning of the text (box 4) depend foremost on the possible meanings of βαπτίζω and πτύον: they form the basis for his interpretation of Luke 3:16-17.

βαπτίζω. As noted above Turner views John's baptism with water in the normal and literal sense of the word, namely "to immerse, to dip or to sink".[52] However, βαπτίζω could also be used in a metaphorical sense, meaning "to deluge with" or "to overwhelm with."[53] The crux in interpre-

---

49 Turner, *Power from on High*, 176-177.
50 Turner, *Power from on High*, 177-179n.11. Contra Robert L. Webb, "Activity", 109-111 and idem, *John the Baptizer*, 289-295. See also Dunn, *Baptism*, 8-14.
51 Turner, *Power from on High*, 179-180.
52 For a thorough analysis of the meaning of words with the βαπτ-root see: Everett Ferguson, *Baptism in the Early Church. History, Theology, and Liturgy in the First Five Centuries* (Grand Rapids, MI: Eerdmans, 2009), 38-59.
53 Turner, *Power from on High*, 181-82 and idem "Spirit Endowment", 50-53.

tation lies in the meaning of "the baptism with Spirit and fire", what is meant here? Turner opposes to a literal meaning: immersing people literally in the Spirit. He also opposes a metaphorical meaning in which the Messiah would pour out an eschatological flood of Spirit and fire. And the suggested implication of "initiate" by James Dunn is also refuted by Turner.[54] Turner finds it more likely that the focus is not on the physical comparison between John's baptism and the baptism in Spirit and fire. He suggests the comparison (and thus the meaning in this context) should be made on the level of the *purpose* of both baptisms. The purpose of John's baptism is to wash and to cleanse repentant Israel from sin; the purpose of the baptism with Spirit and fire is a cleansing in the fuller sense, that is, an eschatological cleansing and restoration of Israel.[55] This does not mean that βαπτίζω always has the meaning of spiritual purification.[56] But based on the context (see below at πτύον) and the traditional expectation of the messianic figure (Isaiah 11:1-4, 4:4, 9:2-7, Malachi 3:2-3), an eschatological cleansing and restoration fits best in regard to the meaning of βαπτίζω here.

πτύον. Normally πτύον means a "fork-like shovel, a winnowing shovel". This was the kind of device which was used to toss the threshed grain into the wind so grain and chaff would be separated.[57] However in this case of the use of πτύον Turner follows the exegesis and interpretation suggested by Robert L. Webb, namely that of a *spade*.[58] Webb argues on basis of the context that the sifting of grain and chaff has already taken place and that the πτύον here is used to cleanse the threshing floor. So here πτύον means spade instead of winnowing fork, because it is not the sifting that is in view, but the cleansing. The already separated piles of grain and chaff are taken to their destination: respectively the granary and the fire.[59] This exegesis is substantiated by the meaning of the verb διακαθαίρω (διακαθαρίζω) which is *to clean out something*.[60]

---

54 Turner, *Power from on High*, 180-183, Dunn, *Baptism*, 19-22.
55 Turner, *Power from on High*, 183-184, idem, *Spirit and Spiritual Gifts*, 28.
56 Turner, *Power from on High*, 183n.43.
57 BDAG, 895.
58 Robert L. Webb, "The Activity of John the Baptist's Expected Figure at the Threshing Floor (Matthew 3.12 = Luke 3.17)", *JSNT* 43 (1991), 103-11 and idem, *John the Baptizer and Prophet* (JSNT.SS 62; Sheffield: JSOT, 1991).
59 Webb, "Activity", 105-107. Turner, *Power from on High*, 171-172n.7 and idem, *Spirit and Spiritual Gifts*, 28.
60 BDAG, 229; Abbott-Smith, 107.

To conclude this section, we have seen the reader's role in making interpretive decisions: Turner's interpretation of the Greek words βαπτίζω and πτύον differ from the general meaning of these words. Turner links this interpretation (and so to say John the Baptist's expectation) with prophecies from Isaiah (4:2-6, 9:2-6, 11:1-4) which point to the expectation of a Davidic Messiah. This is actually the story or narrative structure (box 6) behind the text. This Davidic Messiah is himself endowed with the Spirit to cleanse and restore Israel. Turner concludes that "the Spirit is clearly in some sense 'soteriologically necessary.'"[61]

3.3.3 Preliminary deductions and possible implications
At this stage of his monograph Turner still is very cautious to make any deductions and possible implications. He does give a foretaste when acknowledging that Luke saw the promise of John the Baptist fulfilled in an unexpected way. Acts 1:5 and 11:16 show this beyond any doubt, however Turner argues that these passages from Acts can only be properly understood if we interpret the promise of John the Baptist as the promise of a Davidic cleansing of Israel. The fulfillment of John's promise already began in the life and ministry of Jesus and saw its climax in Pentecost.[62]

3.4 The baptism and subsequent testing of Jesus (Luke 3:21-22, 4:1-14)
3.4.1 The actualized text
Turner views the Lukan account of Jesus' baptism as largely derived from Mark and perhaps a version in Q. Grammatically Turner points to three infinitives (ἀνεωχθῆναι, καταβῆναι and γενέσθαι) in the rather short account of Jesus' baptism.[63] Of seven alleged Lukan alterations Turner only accepts one, namely the insertion that Jesus prays right after his baptism. The other six are dismissed as being misunderstandings, stylistic changes, a literary motivation and one unlikely textual reading.[64]

Turner continues to discuss the episode of Jesus' testing. The opening verse parallels Matthew 4:1 and Mark 1:12-13, with slight alterations. Luke adds Jesus' return from the Jordan (ὑπέστρεψεν ἀπὸ τοῦ Ἰορδάνου) to connect the testing episode to the baptismal episode.[65] The phraseol-

---

61 Turner, *Power from on High*, 186.
62 Turner, *Power from on High*, 187 and idem, *Spirit and Spiritual Gifts*, 29.
63 Turner, *Power from on High*, 193.
64 Turner, *Power from on High*, 193-196.
65 These two episodes are interrupted by a rather lengthy genealogy in Luke 3:23-38. Turner, *Power from on High*, 201-202.

ogy "full of the holy Spirit" is characterized by Turner as a Lukanism and does not necessarily connote an inward working of the Spirit, but can be explained as a description of a person in whose life the Spirit was regularly and powerfully present.[66]

Instead of the Markan ἐκβάλλει Luke uses ἤγετο, but Turner (contrary to Robert Menzies) does not deduce any interpretive implications from this alteration.[67] Another modification Luke made is with the phrase in/by the Spirit. Luke has *in* the Spirit (ἐν τῷ πνεύματι) where Matthew has *by* the Spirit (ὑπὸ τοῦ πνεύματος). So from Luke's perspective Jesus was led in the Spirit, which can mean a.) the manner in which God led Jesus; or b.) a description of the powerful attendance of the Spirit.[68]

This modification from *by* to *in* was taken by Hans Conzelmann[69] and Eduard Schweizer[70] as proof that for Luke Jesus himself was acting and even was "Lord over the Spirit." Robert Menzies takes the "in the Spirit" as a stylistic variant and sees it as synonymous with Luke 2:26-27.[71] Turner agrees with this last possibility and thus interprets the "in the Spirit" as the Spirit being the one who leads Jesus. In addition to this, Turner expands the interpretation and also takes the dative to be a "dative of attendant circumstances" meaning Jesus was able to "manifest the Spirit". According to Turner the summary statement in 4:14 confirms this interpretation ("He returned *with* the power of God's Spirit").[72]

The last and according to Turner most important redactional change is that Luke states Jesus is being led *in* (ἐν) the wilderness and Mark and Matthew have Jesus led *into* (εἰς) the wilderness. The difference in interpretation is that in Mark and Matthew's description only the place *where* Jesus was tested is meant. Luke on the other hand describes that Jesus is continually being led through the Spirit's guidance.[73]

---

[66] Turner is highly cautious in this matter by keeping both options open, however it seems to me he prefers the last interpretation. Turner, *Power from on High*, 202n.47.
[67] Turner, *Power from on High*, 202n.50-51.
[68] The first option being a dative of sphere and the second being a dative of attendant circumstances. Turner, *Power from on High*, 203.
[69] H. Conzelmann, *Die Mitte der Zeit. Studien zur Theologie des Lukas* (Tübingen: Mohr Siebeck, 1953), 22.
[70] E. Schweizer, "πνεῦμα" in: TDNT, VI, 404-405.
[71] Menzies, *Development*, 156.
[72] Turner, *Power from on High*, 204 (emphasis is Turner's) and idem, "Spirit Endowment", 47.
[73] Turner, *Power from on High*, 204. It is possible to translate εἰς as well as *in*, see BDAG 288, so Turner's emphasis on this alteration is not totally undisputed.

3.4.2 The substantial properties of the text

When it comes to the next phase of interpretation, boxes 4 and 6 dominate in Turner's treatment of the texts. Above we have already seen different interpretive choices made concerning the Lukan phraseology of 'in the Spirit'. Turner relies heavily on the intertextuality of the text in particular allusions from the Lukan text to the Old Testament (LXX). In the baptismal account Turner focuses on the bodily form of the Spirit, that of a dove, and the voice from heaven:

> Based on Luke's knowledge of the LXX, Jewish messianism and the Church's Christology Luke would have detected allusions to Ps.2:7 and Isa. 42:1-2. Later in the Gospel (9:35, 23:35) Luke then deliberately changes his Markan source, whereas the word 'chosen' (ἐκλεκτός) functions as a keyword.[74] That Luke understood the 'You are my son' as an allusion to Ps.2:7 is highly probable because of Luke's own use of Ps. 2 in Acts 4:25-26 and 13:33. Because of the already instigated expectation of a Davidic Messiah in the infancy narratives and the promise of John the Baptist (3:15-17), it seems that this expectation comes to a fulfillment in the declaration 'You are my son'.[75]
>
> Turner understands the baptism of Jesus as "an empowering of the messianic son and servant to commence the promised cleansing/restoration of Zion."[76] He however does narcotize this interpretation: "we shall need to examine several other key passages before we can clarify this further."[77]

After an extensive genealogy the narrative continues with Jesus' testing while he is in the desert (place) and in the Spirit (attendant circumstance). In relation to the textual meaning (box 4) and the narrative structure behind this episode (box 6), Turner interprets as follows:

---

74 Turner, *Power from on High*, 197. The question not addressed by Turner in regard to Isa.42:1-2 is the identity of the servant of the Lord in Isaiah. Is this servant the people of Israel or is this servant the prophetic servant, the Messiah? See for instance Jaap Dekker, "Het verhaal van de knecht in het boek Jesaja", *Soteria* (4-2012), 7-19.

75 This is interpreted as an already existing status of Jesus, not as some sort of adoption by God. See Turner, *Power from on High*, 198n35, who follows Marshall, *The Gospel of Luke*, 155.

76 Turner, *Power from on High*, 201. Contra Dunn, who proposes Jesus enters a new epoch (198-199); contra Schweizer, who thinks of Jesus' installation as Son of God (199-200); contra Mainville, who sees this event as Jesus being the eschatological prophet, while he only becomes Messiah at the resurrection (200n.40).

77 Turner, *Power from on High*, 201. To narcotize is the term Eco uses to describe that a reader keeps a certain interpretation in mind until the right interpretation becomes clear from the remainder of the story, see above in §2.5.2.

This story of Jesus' testing in the desert is about the beginnings of Israel's restoration, her New Exodus. The narrative is not a counterpart to Adam's temptation and fall, but functions as an antitype to Israel's experience in the wilderness: Israel failed, Jesus overcomes. Turner does not use "New Exodus" in the limited sense of only the deliverance from Egypt, but also in the broader sense of the Old Testament background of release from captive exile (especially the prophecies from Deutero-Isaiah). So Jesus as the Davidic messianic Son "represents Israel in an eschatological replay of the wilderness testing of Moses and Israel."[78] The role of the Spirit in this episode according to Turner is a role of assistance and empowerment of Jesus. This includes the Spirit providing wisdom, strength, encouragement and ethical empowering. Luke 4:14 (Jesus returning in the power of the Spirit) confirms this role of the Spirit.[79]

3.4.3 Preliminary deductions and possible implications

Again, just as before, Turner barely makes any applications yet. He seems to stay with the text, the textual meaning and intertextuality. The next steps of interpretation to the abstract level where characters become propositions (box 8) or where value judgments are proposed (box 9) are not made. However, certain interpretive choices are made by Turner: only one of the seven alleged Lukan alterations is accepted; textual differences with Mark and Mathew are not treated as important for a right interpretation, but he gives rather much weight to the difference between ἐν (Luke) and εἰς (Mark and Matthew). This shows that despite Turner does not make any applications yet, he does give his imprint on the reading of the narrative.

In regard to Jesus' baptism Turner interprets Luke 3:21-22 not as a literal event, but as Jesus having a visionary experience.[80] The typical Lukan (and LXX) Spirit phraseology of the Spirit is "on, upon, by, through or in" someone or someone is "anointed by" or "full of" the Holy Spirit are all metaphorically interpreted: "God's Spirit is at work in and through the life of the one so described."[81]

To conclude this section it becomes clear that Turner so far seems to stay within the historical framework which the text and Luke's background (LXX) provide. He develops his line of reasoning and interpretation that a "New Exodus" has begun: where the people of Israel failed, the "Stronger One" will prevail and lead the people of Israel to her restoration.

---

78 Turner, *Power from on High*, 207 and idem, *Spirit and Spiritual Gifts*, 31.
79 Turner, *Power from on High*, 209-201.
80 Turner, "Spirit Endowment", 50-51 and idem, *Spirit and Spiritual Gifts*, 30.
81 Turner, "Spirit Endowment", 48.

3.5 Jesus' inauguration address (Luke 4:14-30)
3.5.1 The actualized text

An important key for understanding Luke's view of the Spirit is found in the Isaianic citation in Jesus' inaugural address. This citation "…involves some unusual features of omission, addition and alteration which are often attributed to Luke's distinctive view of the Spirit—especially by those who think 4.16-30 is a creative Lukan rewriting of Mk 6:1-6a."[82] So this is clearly an episode in which the role of the reader becomes decisive in establishing Luke's view of the Spirit or a Lukan pneumatology.

A textual issue to be solved is whether Luke solely used Mark 6:1-6 as a source and redacted it to his own theological purposes, or whether Luke used another available source. Turner is convinced of this last possibility. He lists seven arguments for Luke's use of non-Markan material:[83]

a. In 4:16 the Aramaic Ναζαρά is used, where Luke's preference is Ναζαρὲθ;
b. The citation in 4:18-19 is an embedded citation, not found elsewhere in Luke-Acts or the other Gospels;
c. he unnecessary repetitions in 4:20b indicate a source;
d. The "today" and "in your ears" in 4:21 are pre-Lukan;
e. The awkward transitions in 4:22, 23 and 4:24, 25-27 do not suggest a free Lukan composition;
f. rmally Luke tends to eliminate the "amen I say to you" sayings, however not here in 4:24;
g. The Jewish stoning procedure in 4:29 does not correspond with Luke's other use of this (Acts 7:56-60).

Based on these findings and the fact that there is little verbal contact with Mark's version and the quite different endings of both versions, Turner concludes: "…we are probably safest to assume that Luke had a parallel account to Mark of the preaching at Nazareth, and that he depended on that account largely, if not exclusively."[84] This parallel account is then recognized by Turner as one of Luke's other sources of tradition instead of being part of Q.[85]

---

82 Turner, *Power from on High*, 213-214.
83 See for the extensive list and argumentation: Turner, *Power from on High*, 216-217.
84 Turner, *Power from on High*, 217. In some of his arguments Turner follows Bruce Chilton, "Announcement in Nazara: An Analysis of Luke 4.16-21", in: R.T. France and D. Wenham (eds.), *Studies of History and Tradition in the Four Gospels, II* (Sheffield: JSOT, 1986), 147-172.
85 Turner, *Power from on High*, 219-220, especially notes 15 and 16 on 219.

After a thorough comparison between Isaiah 61:1-2 (LXX) and Luke 4:18-19, Turner comes to the following representation of the text:[86]

Luke 4:18	The Spirit of the Lord is upon me,	
	for he has anointed me	
	to preach Good News to 'the poor'.	
	he has sent me	
	{to heal the broken hearted}	
	to proclaim liberty to the captives	proclaim
	and sight to the blind	= κηρύξαι,
		liberty = ἄφεσιν
	<u>to set at liberty the oppressed</u> (Isa. 58:6d)	at liberty
		= ἐν ἀφέσει
Luke 4:19	and to *proclaim* the acceptable	proclaim
	year of the Lord	= κηρύξαι
	{and the day of vengeance of our God}.	

Turner concludes that this citation "belongs fundamentally to Luke's source, not to his own redactional activity."[87] This implies that for an interpretation of this citation, Turner will first turn to look at the tradition and the background of this citation before trying to interpret how Luke understood the passage. In contrast to Turners view there are scholars who see a Lukan redaction in this citation.[88] Especially the insertion of Isaiah 58:6d is explained as a Lukan addition because Luke saw the Spirit as a power to preach (κηρύξαι) which concerned forgiveness (ἀφέσις) of sins. Turner rejects this view on the omission of the word sins (ἁμαρτία) which always in Luke-Acts governs the meaning of ἀφέσις.[89]

The same line of reasoning applies to the omission of the phrase "to heal the broken hearted" where because of a narrow understanding of the Spirit of prophecy (power to preach rather than healing miracles), this

---

86 Turner, *Power from on High*, 221. The curly brackets indicate an omission from Isaiah 61:1-2, where the underlined words are an addition to the Isaianic text. The italicized word is a minor verbal change.
87 Turner, *Power from on High*, 226.
88 Among them is Menzies, *Development*, 171-173, who will be discussed in the next chapter of this dissertation.
89 Turner, *Power from on High*, 223.

omission is subscribed to Lukan redaction. Turner argues convincingly that the healing here is *metaphorical* and as such should have fitted very well within Luke's view of the Spirit. Surely no one would understand "to heal the broken hearted" as physical healing.[90] This strengthens Turner's point of view in which he sees Jesus' inaugural address as a citation from a traditional source. This citation seems a clear-cut case in which the determination of the original text directly determines the interpretation of the text.

3.5.2 The substantial properties of the text
To understand the text, Turner focuses on the background of the text and concludes that this is the background of Jewish eschatological Jubilee. The double reference of ἄφεσις points in this way as well as the Isaianic context and the Leviticus 25 imagery.[91] According to Turner different roles (priest, prophet, king, herald, servant and a royal Messiah) are then merged into the Spirit-anointed person. This Spirit empowers to declare and effect the liberation and restoration of Israel. Turner does not suggest that the historical Jesus pronounced a literal Jubilee, but that He used it as a "significant theological symbol" alongside the other well-known "the kingdom of God."[92]

Turner proposes that the "poor" (4:18) should be understood as oppressed Israel and that Jesus understood his miracles and healings as symbolizing Israel's promised liberation and restoration. The answer to John's question (7:18-22) confirms this understanding of the text.[93] In tradition the passages from Isa. 61:1-5 and 58:6 *thematically* (italics are Turner's) belonged together, focusing on Jubilee and New Exodus hopes.[94]

So in regard to the intensions of the text Turner sees the theme of Jubilee, the liberation and restoration of Israel, as the story of the text. This story of the text shows that the narrative structure behind the text is rooted in the Old Testament and the tradition. Here we come across an obvious move from the textual meaning (Jesus reading from a scroll in

---

90 Turner, *Power from on High*, 224-225.
91 Turner sees 11QMelchizedek as a confirmation of the Jubilee imagery, *Power from on High*, 227-229. See also Joseph A. Fitzmyer, T*he Gospel According to Luke* (I-IX) (New York: Doubleday, 198), 532 and David E. Aune, 'A Note on Jesus' Messianic Consciousness and 11QMelchizedek', *EvQ 45* (1973), 161-165.
92 Turner, *Power from on High*, 229, especially the comparison between Isa. 61 and the beatitudes (Mt.5, Lk.6).
93 Turner, *Power from on High*, 229-230, 250n.116.
94 Turner, *Power from on High*, 231.

the synagogue of Nazareth) to the underlying structure of the text (the theme of Jubilee). Turner does not yet make the next step to the abstract level (box 8) or adding value judgments (box 9).

3.5.3 Preliminary deductions and possible implications

Strictly speaking Turner does not yet move to boxes 5, 7 and 10. In his interpretation he focuses on the text and the story of the text. However, the world of the text (box 5) is thoroughly reviewed. In §4 of chapter nine (pp.233-264) Turner describes and interprets the significance of the Isaianic citation for Luke, thereby trying to get a grip on the world and thought of the original author of the text. Three core elements of the Isaianic citation are discussed respectively: the Christological focus, the missiological focus and Jesus' proclamation of liberty in relation to his miracles.

Christological focus.[95] According to Turner, Luke saw Jesus as a fusion between "the prophet-like-Moses" and "a Davidic-messianic-king". For Luke the last prophet was John the Baptist, with Jesus a new age had dawned. The picture of the messianic Son only comes back towards the end of the Gospel. Depending on the context and situation one of both pictures of Jesus emerges. In the context of Jesus' inaugural address it is the prophet-like-Moses who is anointed by the Spirit to liberate and restore.

Missiological focus.[96] Turner argues that Luke used a traditional source in which the Jubilee language prevailed, however Luke does not elaborate on this thema of Jubilee. Luke's focus instead is, as Turner calls it, "a New Exodus soteriology" in which the mission of the anointed prophet-king is to free people from poverty, captivity, blindness and oppression. The further development of this episode (4:14-30) shows that this message of Jesus involves willing participation. Rejection of this message is possible and leads to a shift from Jewish insiders to their outsiders (4:25-27). And in the end rejection of this message even leads to the death of the prophet (4:28-30).

Proclamation of liberty and Jesus' miracles.[97] Here we come across the interpretation of the relation Luke saw between the Spirit, proclaiming and the miracles performed by Jesus. Turner does not promote a distance between πνεῦμα and δύναμις.[98] He argues that for Luke power can be a

---

[95] Turner, *Power from on High*, 234-244.
[96] Turner, *Power from on High*, 244-250.
[97] Turner, *Power from on High*, 250-264.
[98] Max Turner, "The Spirit and the Power of Jesus' Miracles in the Lucan Conception", *NovT.* 33 (1991), 124-152.

quality of the Spirit's activity. Luke 1:35, 4:14 and Acts 10:38 are all convincing cases in which the Spirit is connected to miracles. As such for Luke the Spirit is God's empowering presence. In addition to this there is the issue of exorcisms performed by Jesus. Key texts here are Luke 11:20, where Luke attributes exorcisms to "the finger of God"[99] and 12:10-12 where Luke has a different context than Mark and Mathew for the logion about blasphemy against the Spirit. It is in these texts that the role of the reader is significant. Those in favor of a distance between πνεῦμα and δύναμις opt for a deliberate Lukan redaction because of this distance. Turner argues the other way around and proposes that Luke 12:10-12 should be interpreted in a more general way as being "present where the disciple encounter persistence in consummate and obdurate opposition to the influence of the Spirit which animates the preaching."[100] In case of the "finger of God" Luke simply meant the Spirit, but chooses to use an anthropomorphism which Turner understands as Luke's specific concern to portray Jesus as the Mosaic prophet-messiah. To conclude, for Turner this passage shows that Luke "considered the Spirit to be the chrism with which Jesus was (metaphorically) anointed (…) and more important, it suggests Luke understood the Spirit as the power operative through Jesus' proclamation and effective in acts expressive of his kerygma."[101]

The above summary of Turners interpretation of the significance of the Isaianic citation for Luke concerns, in Eco's terms, "the world of the text".[102] Until the opposite is proven, Turner understands Luke to carefully designate Jesus as the Davidic Messiah and the prophet-like-Moses. This is the interpretation Turner puts between brackets until the unfolding Lukan narrative will falsify or verify this interpretation (Eco: *forecasts*). The same is true concerning the role of the Spirit: until proven otherwise, Turner interprets the role of the Spirit in Luke as the effective power operating through Jesus' proclamation and acts. When it comes to applications and the actual world, Turner is careful not to draw any premature conclusions. Value judgments are postponed and it seems Turner's priority to gather information first.

---

99 For an extensive research done on the Lukan insertion of "the finger of God" see the published dissertation by Edward J. Woods, *The 'Finger of God' and Pneumatology in Luke-Acts* (JSNT.SS 205; Sheffield: Sheffield Academic, 2001).
100 Turner, *Power from on High*, 256, in accordance with Fitzmyer, *Gospel according to Luke*, 964.
101 Turner, *Power from on High*, 263.
102 Eco, *Lector in fabula*, 99-101. See also above in §2.5.

3.6 Jesus' general sayings about the Spirit (Luke 10:21, 11:13, 12:10-12)

3.6.1 The actualized text

Besides the accumulated πνεῦμα texts in the beginning of the Gospel of Luke, there are three instances of the use of πνεῦμα meaning holy Spirit. For matters of convenience I have called those 'general sayings about the Spirit'. Turner discusses these texts, however for obvious reasons not as extensive as the other clusters of πνεῦμα texts.

10:21. Only in one page Turner writes about this passage in which it is said that Jesus exulted in the Spirit. The variety in readings proves that this text is somehow obscure.[103] Turner interprets the dative noun ([ἐν] τῷ πνεύματι τῷ ἁγίῳ) as instrumental, that is: Jesus was inspired with joy by the Holy Spirit.

11:13. Turner discusses this verse and context in the 11th chapter of his *Power from on High*, entitled "The Circle of Jesus' Disciples and the Spirit."[104] Concerning the text proper, Turner opts for the variant
reading of 11:2 without πνεῦμα and for the reading πνεῦμα ἀγαθόν in 11:13.[105]

12:10-12. Contrary to Mark and Q, Luke has made some redactional changes concerning the passages about "blasphemy against the Spirit" (Mark 3:22-3, Q=Mt. 12:22-30). Luke does not put the saying in a context of exorcism, but in a context of failure to witness in times of trial. Turner does not further elaborate on Luke 12:10-12, instead he focuses on the "finger of God" phraseology from Luke 11.20.[106]

3.6.2 The substantial properties of the text

10:21. Turner understands Jesus' inspiration with joy from the context. The disciples just returned from their mission and by the ἐν αὐτῇ τῇ ὥρᾳ Luke joins these episodes. Turner then understands the Spirit as the source of charismatic wisdom which enables the joyful reception of the disciples' successful mission.[107]

11:13. Turner understands this episode and πνεῦμα text in close relation to the mission of the seventy (Luke 10:1-20) and points to the use of the serpent (ὄφις) and scorpion (σκορπίος) in both episodes. According to him these are symbols of demonic power and as such the story (Eco's

---

103 Turner, *Power from on High*, 264n.160.
104 Turner, *Power from on High*, 318-347, see especially 339-341.
105 Turner, *Power from on High*, respectively 337n.50 and 340n.61.
106 See also Turner, *Spirit and Spiritual Gifts*, 34-35.
107 Turner, *Power from on High*, 265.

narrative structure, box 6) is about God giving his good Spirit instead of demonic power to the disciples.

12:10-12. Based on the intertextuality of the whole narrative of Luke-Acts, Turner here points to Acts 6:10 (in which Stephen exceeds his opponents in wisdom and the Holy Spirit) and explains that Luke 12:10-12 and Luke 21:15 are used here.[108] So the story (narrative structure) in Luke-Acts is that in times of trial the Spirit grants words and wisdom.

3.6.3 Preliminary deductions and possible implications
10:21. On the abstract level Turner does not limit the Spirit's working to empowerment for mission alone, but interprets it as well to Jesus' own experience of sonship to God. Luke 10:21 is then used as one of these instances.[109] However Turner is very cautious to over-interpret this instance as an image of Jesus' own religious life before God. He describes it as "a psychological effect of the Spirit on Jesus", but does not derive any (theological) applications from it.[110]

11:13. The implication Turner draws from this episode is that Luke saw it somehow applicable to the pre-Easter mission of the disciples. This means that the Spirit of God was available for the followers of Jesus as some sort of "pre-Pentecost possibility".[111]

12:10-12. Turner does not actually make an application for the world today (Eco's boxes 5 and 10), he goes as far as to write that "for Luke, the Spirit is God's *power made manifest* in and through the Church. Not only does the Spirit give charismatic wisdom that empowers the witness (Luke 12.12; 22.15; 24.49; Acts 1.8; 6.10, etc.), but, through the Spirit (cf. Luke 4.18-20, Acts 10.38), God performs liberating 'signs and wonders' […]".[112]

3.7 The promise of the Spirit (Luke 24 – Acts 1)
3.7.1 The actualized text
In Luke 24:47-49 and Acts 1:4-5, 8 Jesus promises the Spirit to his disciples. The key terminology used in both episodes is "the promise of my/

---

108 Turner, *Power from on High*, 258, 305.
109 Turner, *Power from on High*, 405, 411.
110 Turner, *Power from on High*, 429.
111 Turner, *Power from on High*, 340.
112 Turner, *Power from on High*, 440. The italics are Turner's and in the quotation Turner has Luke 22:15, which should be 21:15.

the father" (τὴν ἐπαγγελίαν τοῦ πατρός [μου]).[113] These texts are treated by Turner in five pages (341-346) and in contrast to previous passages about the Spirit, Turner does not focus here on the text proper. He takes the text as it is and discusses its relevance for the continuing narrative in the Book of Acts and as some sort of matrix to understand Luke's Pneumatology.[114] Here we observe that Turner moves to boxes 5, 7 and 10 from Eco's model and elaborates on different interpretive choices.

3.7.2 The substantial properties of the text
On a textual level these passages from Luke 24 and Acts 1 form the transition from the Gospel to Acts. Luke 24 closes the Gospel account and Acts 1 not only opens the narrative of Acts, but also provides the program for it. Turner understands the text and therewith the function of it as an assurance that the disciples fully understand what will happen to them after Jesus ascended. The forty days of teaching on the Kingdom of God through the Spirit (Acts 1:2-3) are proof for Turner that the disciples did have "Christian faith" and so the Pentecost experience (Acts 2) cannot be interpreted as the moment of conversion for the disciples.[115] The (interpretive) role of the reader is prominent here. If the disciples in some way experienced or received the Spirit before Pentecost, this consequently means that their Pentecost experience was a second blessing or filling or baptism with the Spirit. Turner then continues to confirm the right emphasis of Pentecostal scholars who interpret this Spirit experience as a "prophetic empowering for witness" (see Luke 24:49 and Acts 1:8 where it is explicitly stated that the promise from the/my father contains power). This line of reasoning makes it obvious why especially Pentecostal scholars see the promise of the Spirit (fulfilled in Acts 2) as a *donum superadditum* (choice of words is Turner's). On an intertextual level this line of reasoning is strengthened by the deliberate parallelism Luke has created between the accounts of Jesus' baptism and Pentecost. In both instances people who are already in a full relationship with God, receive a "prophetic endowment of the Spirit in the context of prayer (Lk. 3.21-22//

---

113 Martin Salter joins four views as to what the promise of the Father refers to: Martin C. Salter, *The Power of Pentecost. An Examination of Acts 2:17-21* (Eugene, OR: Resource, 2012), 24-25.
114 See for instance the helpful macrostructure of Luke 24-Acts 1 in: Arie W. Zwiep, *The Ascension of the Messiah in Lukan Christology* (NT.S 87; Leiden, New York, Köln: Brill, 1997), 118.
115 Contra James Dunn, *Baptism*, 52-53, see Turner, *Power from on High*, 342.

Acts 2.1) at the beginning of a new phase in redemption history."[116] Turner interprets this as an important parallelism which helps to establish the continuance of Jesus' work into the period of the church.

3.7.3 Preliminary deductions and possible implications
However, interpretations and applications differ on the fact if this (the obvious parallelism between Jesus' baptism and the outpouring of the Spirit at Pentecost as a "prophetic empowering for witness") represents the whole story. Turner's stance in this is that it is certainly not the whole story.[117] Next to the empowerment for witness, Turner shows other characteristics of the working of the Spirit such as providing discernment, wisdom, guidance, encouragement and so forth. The allusion to Isaiah 32:15-20 in Acts 1:8 shows that the outpouring of the Spirit also generates refreshment, cleansing and restoration.[118] So Turner's implication of the Spirit's working is broader than for instance Menzies'. Later in *Power from on High* Turner explains that the gift of the Spirit is for *all* believers; however this does not imply that *all* believers receive the same gifts of the Spirit, especially not in an evidentialist way.[119] This shows that only after a thorough gathering of information applications are made by Turner. In his *The Holy Spirit and Spiritual Gifts*, Turner further elaborates on the meaning of the working of the Spirit for Christians and the church today.[120] After comparing the New Testament witness of Paul, John and Luke, Turner concludes that a so called "two-stage model of Spirit reception" has to be rejected in favor of a one-stage model of Spirit reception. This is not only based on the mentioned texts in this section (Luke 24 and Acts 1), but on an integrative approach of the pneumatology's of Paul, John and Luke.

3.8 Pentecost: the outpouring of the Spirit (Acts 2)
3.8.1 The actualized text
In Turner's discussion of Pentecost and Peter's subsequent speech (chapter 10 in *Power from on High*), he starts with the cautious statement that Peter's explanation of the Pentecost event "has perhaps greater claim than

---

116 Turner, *Power from on High*, 344.
117 Contra Menzies: R.P. Menzies, 'Luke and the Spirit: A Reply to James Dunn', *JPT* 4 (1994), 137. See also W.W. Menzies and R.P. Menzies, *Spirit and Power. Foundations of Pentecostal Experience* (Grand Rapids, MI: Zondervan, 2000), 82.
118 Turner, *Power from on High*, 345. See also Salter, *Power of Pentecost*, 25-27.
119 Turner, *Power from on High*, 444. Emphasis is Turners.
120 Turner, *Spirit and Spiritual Gifts*, 145-165.

Lk. 4:16-30 to be called 'the programmatic' text of Luke-Acts."[121] Turner comes to this statement because within Peter's speech all what is said about the Spirit is integrated with other aspects of Luke's theology. Turner treats the speech as coming from ancient tradition thereby leaving it an open question whether Peter actually held this speech at Pentecost or not. Simply because it cannot be proven Peter did or did not.[122] He assumes that Luke did not compose the *pesher* on Joel 3, or that he was responsible for the *midrashic* elements in the speech. After these introductory statements Turner continues to compare the form of the citation and notices six theologically important changes between the Joel text (LXX) and Acts 2:17-21.[123] These six are:

a. The replacement of the LXX μετὰ ταῦτα by the ἐν ταῖς ἐσχάταις ἡμέραις in Acts 2:17. Herewith the gift of the Spirit is identified as the eschatological promise;
b. 2:17 λέγει ὁ θεός is added. Turner argues this is pre-Lukan, because he does not elsewhere insert such affirmations within citations. However the addition serves the statement that the promise is the promise of the Father (Luke 24:49, Acts 1:4);
c. Twice, after men-servants and maid-servants in 2:18, μου is added. This shows that the gift is for God's servants, rather than for the sociological category of slaves;
d. The addition of καὶ προφητεύσουσιν in 2:18 forms together with 2:17c an *inclusio*, thereby confirming the gift as "the Spirit of prophecy";
e. In 2:19 ἄνω...σημεῖα...κάτω is added which interprets the Pentecost event and also prepares for 2:22;
f. The words from Joel 3:5b (*for on Mount Zion and in Jerusalem there will be deliverance, as the Lord has said, among the survivors whom the Lord calls*) are omitted by Luke. Because Peter uses the last words in Acts 2:39, Turner concludes it belonged to the original citation. In his opinion Luke dropped it here because of the fitting climax in 2:39 and because Luke already knew salvation was not limited to Jerusalem only.

3.8.2 The substantial properties of the text
Turner proceeds by addressing the purpose of Peter's speech, thereby interpreting the topic of the text. According to Turner Peter's speech

---
121 Turner, *Power from on High*, 267.
122 Turner, *Power from on High*, 268-269n.4. Contra Lüdemann and Haenchen.
123 Turner, *Power from on High*, 270.

explains the phenomena of Pentecost, especially glossolalia. The reference to dreams and visions in 2:17 confirms the Jewish expectation of the outpouring of the Spirit of Prophecy. However, this is not the only purpose. Peter's main purpose is Christological. The statement "all who call on the name of the Lord shall be saved" (Acts 2:21=Joel 3:5a), closes the Joel citation and prepares for Peter's argument that Jesus has been made Lord (2:36) and that Jesus is identified with the Lord God (2:39) in such a close manner that even repentance and baptism should take place while calling on the name of Jesus.[124]

It is here that we see Turner move between boxes 4 and 6 from Eco's model. Understanding the textual meaning is tightly woven to the topic and the story of the text. The frequent Old Testament citations show the importance of intertextuality.

Turner then continues to describe four stages which altogether build Peter's argument:

(1) The addition of ἄνω...σημεῖα...κάτω in 2:19 creates an antithetical parallelism (wonders, heaven, above // signs, earth, below) which interprets the apocalyptical language in verse 19c. The order (wonders, signs) is unusual in the LXX as well as for Luke. This unusual order correlates with the order in 2:22, "where Peter refers to God working wonders and signs through Jesus in his ministry."[125] If this Joel citation is entirely fulfilled in the Passion events is still a matter of scholarly debate[126], Turner chooses to interpret the wonders and signs stretching back to Jesus' earthly ministry as well as to the Passion events, which reinforce "the last days" from 2:17.[127] Another argument is to interpret "the wonders in the heaven" above as a correspondence to the Pentecost event itself. Jesus ascended *into heaven* (1:9-11) and noise and fire come *from heaven* (2:2-4). Turner interprets this Pentecost theophany as a Sinai allusion, strengthened by the *clouds of smoke* in 2:19.

(2) Peter then continues and uses Psalm 16 to demonstrate that it is Jesus and the resurrection of Jesus which David foresaw. This confirms Jesus as David's heir.[128]

---

124 Turner, *Power from on High*, 270-272.
125 Turner, *Power from on High*, 273.
126 For a brief overview see Salter, *Power of Pentecost*, 11-19.
127 Turner, *Power from on High*, 274.
128 The use of Psalm 16 in this way is debatable as Turners' footnote shows: Turner, *Power from on High*, 274n.19. The reader (and hearer) of Peter's speech will determine whether his application of Psalm 16 fits the overall argument.

(3) In 2:33 Peter claims that Jesus is lifted up/exalted (ὑψωθεὶς) to the right hand of God, referring to Jesus' ascension-exaltation to rule at God's right hand. Turner's interpretation is based on the context (2:34-35) in which it is made clear that it was not David who ascended into heaven. An issue of debate is whether the τῇ δεξιᾷ is meant as local (*to* the right hand of God) or as instrumental (*by* the right hand of God).[129] Based on the context Turner interprets it as local and argues that the promise of the throne of God to David's descendant in 2:30 points to the right hand of God.[130] Turner also points to Jesus own teaching in Luke 20:41-44 and 22:69.

(4) In this last stage Peter finishes the argument and claims that this human agent seated at the right hand of God is the Lord whose name has to be called on for salvation (Acts 2:21=Joel 3:5, and Acts 2:38 [in baptism]) and that He also is the one (in God's own place) who pours out the holy Spirit (Acts 2:33). In the Jewish understanding of the role of the Davidic Messiah, this was highly unusual and goes beyond their expectations. Turner explains Luke's theological reasoning as follows:

a. uke prepares his audience with the distinctive formula "the promise of the Father" in Luke 24:49 and Acts 1:4;
b. n Luke 24:49 Jesus refers to this promise as a "power from on high" and explicitly states He (Jesus) is the one who will send this power;
c. Acts 1:5 identifies this promise (power) with the promise of John the Baptist in Luke 3:16;
d. The fulfillment of this promise in Acts 2 relates the outpouring of the Spirit to Jesus in the same way as Judaism related it to God.

So far we have seen that Turner, based on the narrative structure and its intertextuality, comes to the interpretation of Peter's speech: the purpose of the speech is to equate God and Jesus and the Pentecost experience is the tangible proof for this.

---

129 Turner, *Power from on High*, 275n.20. In some of the Dutch Bible translations, both options are made effective (instrumental in the translations of NBG 1951 and HSV 2010; local in the translation of NBV 2004).

130 Turner here follows the interpretations of R.F. O'Toole, 'Acts 2:30 and the Davidic Covenant of Pentecost', *JBL* 102 (1983), 245-258 and D.L. Bock, *Proclamation from Prophecy and Pattern: Lucan Old Testament Christology* (Sheffield: JSOT, 1987), 181-186.

In addition to Turner's interpretation of Peter's Pentecost speech as a tangible proof that Jesus was the expected Davidic Messiah, he pushes the arguments a little further and also comes to the interpretation that Jesus was also the expected prophet-like-Moses.[131] Three arguments suggest this Mosaic background of Pentecost:

a. Normally Luke does not use detailed dating, so the dating in Acts 2:1 (Καὶ ἐν τῷ συμπληροῦσθαι τὴν ἡμέραν τῆς πεντηκοστῆς) points to Sinai connotations. The Jewish "feast of weeks" was a harvest festival in which the renewal of the covenant and the reception of the Law were celebrated;[132]

b. Turner sees in Acts 2:1-13 all kinds of allusions to Moses/Sinai (a holy theophany, a redemptive-historical event, a miraculous sound, something like fire, all resulting in a miraculous form of speech).[133] He is cautious not to see any literary dependence between Luke and a Sinai tradition, but he does see striking contacts.[134] The leading question for Turner is: "Would the Pentecost account strike a Jewish reader as sounding 'like' Sinai, despite the differences?"[135]

c. Turner's third argument focuses on a number of parallels between Pentecost and Sinai: the Joel citation as a fulfillment of the wishful longing in Num.11:29; apocalyptic language, especially that of wonders and signs; heaven, earth, fire, clouds of smoke (Ex.19:16-19); signs and wonders parallelisms between Moses and Jesus (Acts 2:22, 7:36); and Peter's final appeal to save themselves from this "corrupt generation" (Acts 2:40) alludes to the people of Israel in Ex.32:5-8.[136]

---

131 Contra Bock, *Proclamation*, 182-183.
132 Turner, *Power from on High*, 280-282. However, Menzies finds this connection "minor" (*Development*, 233) and Marshall is very cautious due to the fact that Philo and Josephus do not mention such an association between Pentecost and the Law: I.H. Marshall, 'The Significance of Pentecost', *SJT* 30 (1977), 349. It seems like Turner's hard evidence (his choice of words) comes from Rabbi Jose ben Halafta, 150 AD (Turner, *Power from on High*, 281).
133 Turner, *Power from on High*, 284.
134 Following J. Kremer, *Pfingstbericht und Pfingstgeschehen. Eine Exegetische Untersuchung zu Apg 2,1-13* (Stuttgart: KBW, 1973), 87-166, 238-252. Contra Menzies, who thinks the differences between Pentecost and the Sinai tradition are more striking than the similarities: Menzies, *Development*, 235-241. Here we clearly see the active role of the reader/interpreter engaging the same text, but drawing opposite conclusions.
135 Turner, *Power from on High*, 383.
136 Turner builds here on the work of H.S. Kim, *Die Geisttaufe des Messias: Eine kompositionsgeschichtliche Untersuchung zu einem Leitmotiv des lukanischen Doppelwerks* (Berlin: Lang, 1993), 162-168.

However, despite these parallels and allusions Turner does admit that:

> "No-one would wish to claim that these Mosaic features are presented in the surface structure of the argument, but they may inform the story's deep structure. For if the implicit 'story' in 2:33-34a is of Israel's ruler ascending to God where he receives a gift of great importance—which he then subsequently gives to his assembled waiting people in a theophanic context—then this whole part of the story is not essentially Davidic in character at all."[137]

This is an excellent example of what Eco describes in his model of "the cooperative reader". Turner does extensive research when it concerns the possible meaning and the textual meaning of the text (box 4). Based on the textual meaning, the topic of the text is determined (the Pentecost event and Peter's subsequent speech). Here we find Turner operating in box 6 of Eco's model. Turner then continues to move a layer deeper, in search of the narrative structure of the text and intertextuality to distinguish the purpose of Peter's speech. Eventually, when moving beyond this deeper layer of the text, Turner finds a parallel between the exalted Jesus and Moses under the surface of the text.

Most of Turner's argumentation here is built on a close linguistic parallel in Josephus *Antiquities* 3.77-78, where Josephus writes that Moses went up mount Sinai and he would return with a promise (ἐπαγγελίαν) of good things from God. Turner also points to the influence of the Mosaic ascent tradition on the Targum. While acknowledging this is late, Turner does argue that the Targum represents a much earlier tradition.[138] He argues that Peter connects Psalm 68 with the Moses/Sinai episode and assumes 68:18 means 'you ascended on high… and having received the gift of God (Torah) you gave gifts (the commandments) to men'. Peter saw this fulfilled in the Pentecost event, where Jesus ascended and received the promise of the Holy Spirit which he then poured out (Acts 2:33). Turner admits that this argument is difficult to prove or disprove, but he is convinced that Peter's speech not only shows that Jesus is the expected Davidic Messiah, but also the prophet-like-Moses.

---

137 Turner, *Power from on High*, 286.
138 Turner, *Power from on High*, 286-287. Turner here briefly discusses Psalm 68 (Pentecost Psalm) and sees influence on the citation in Ephesians 4:8.

3.8.3 Preliminary deductions and possible implications
So far, Turner is consistent in his focus on the text proper and the intensions of the text. He is meticulous in analyzing the text, he has a keen eye for intertextuality and he thoroughly composed some sort of "Davidic Messiah, Prophet-like-Moses, New Exodus" grid to interpret the Lukan πνεῦμα texts. However, when he comes to move beyond the intensions of the text, he, so to say, holds his breath and postpones the application of the text. The focus is primarily on the text and the story it presents. In Turner we see a scholar (and reader) who is thoroughly aware of the pitfalls in applying the text to fast or to easily. Up until now the conclusion is that Turner does (not yet) make any applications of the text in regard to the actual world. This will change in the following sections, when four important πνεῦμα passages will be discussed. These passages are used to prove one's interpretation (or disprove another one's) of the working of the Spirit in Luke-Acts.

3.9 The Samaritans (Acts 8)
3.9.1 The actualized text
After establishing the "norm" for Lukan pneumatology (Acts 2:38-39)[139], Turner dives right into the current debate between Confirmationists and Pentecostals. The issue at hand is the fact that the Samaritans believed the Christian message (8:4-6, 12-14), then were baptized (8:12), but only later received the gift of the Spirit after the apostles (Peter and John) laid hands on them (8:14-17). The burning question which addresses the heart of the matter is whether Lukan readers would interpret Acts 2:38-39 or Acts 8 as the norm.

Confirmationists and Pentecostals alike see Acts 8 as the norm, whereby Confirmationists focus on the apostolic laying on of hands through which the Holy Spirit is received;[140] Pentecostals focus on the second receiving of the Holy Spirit (the first being at conversion), in which it is truly a *second* blessing.[141] Turner opts for the other interpretation and takes Acts 2:38-39 as the norm, which brings us directly to the importance of the role of the reader in interpretation.

---

139 Turner, *Power from on High*, 352-360. This is a rather short section which builds on Turner's preparatory work in the previous chapters of his monograph.
140 See especially N. Adler, *Taufe und Handauflegung: Eine exegetisch-theologische Untersuchung von Apg 87:14-17* (Münster: Aschendorf, 1951).
141 See Menzies, *Development*, and the next chapter of this dissertation.

3.9.2 The substantial properties of the text
In his treatment of Acts 8 Turner now deviates from his normal procedure and "jumps" to Eco's box nine, in which value judgments are made. That is: ideological coloring comes to the surface. It is exactly here where is determined whether the text is interpreted, or whether the text is used for one's own purposes.[142] Turner lists six different types of explanation for Acts 8:[143]

1. **Source critical explanation.** The reason for the "departure from the norm of Acts 2:38" is a rather clumsy redaction of two independent sources. Turner dismisses this explanation with the words of Geoffrey Lampe, who calls it a "desperate thesis".[144] There is scholarly consensus about Luke's freedom as an editor, so he could have easily made Acts 8 compatible to the norm in Acts 2;
2. **Inadequate Samaritan faith.** This explanation originates with James Dunn.[145] Dunn argues that the Samaritans had faith in Philip, rather than in Christ. This faith was based on miracle working (just as was the case with Simon Magus) and as such was not genuine faith. Turner opposes this view and argues that Luke describes the Samaritan episode as a "typical missionary success".[146] According to Turner there is no indication that Luke understood Philip's preaching as deficient. In fact, Turner concludes that the "defective faith tumbles on linguistic and contextual evidence, and then shatters on the observation that it is the laying on of apostolic hands with prayer (…) which imparts the Spirit. The very implication of the apostle's prayer is that they accept the Samaritan faith as authentic."[147]
3. **A second gift of the Spirit.** If the Samaritan faith was adequate as Turner argues, than a logical consequence would be that the reception of the Spirit in 8:17 was a *second* reception (the first being at their baptism in 8:12). The primary sparring partner for Turner here is G.R. Beasley-Murray, who in his *Baptism in the New Testament* argues along these lines.[148] Beasley-Murray carefully distinguishes between the Spirit of Acts 2:38 (conversion) and 8:17 (charismata). Again on the basis of linguistic and

---

142 Eco, *Lector in fabula*, 233-236.
143 Turner, *Power from on High*, 361-373.
144 Turner, *Power from on High*, 361.
145 Dunn, *Baptism in the Spirit*, 63-68.
146 Turner, *Power from on High*, 363.
147 Turner, *Power from on High*, 367.
148 G.R. Beasley-Murray, *Baptism in the New Testament* (Grand Rapids, MI: Eerdmans, 1962), 118-119.

contextual evidence this is refuted by Turner. Turner argues Luke only knows of *one* reception of the Spirit. Acts 8:16 explains that this reception did not yet occurred, so Acts 8:17 equals (the norm) in Acts 2:38.

4. **A Hellenistic-Pauline conversion-initiation pattern.** This explanation originates from Michel Quesnel and comprises the preservation of two historically distinct initiation paradigms: baptism ἐπί (upon) or ἐν (in) the name of Jesus (modeled on John the Baptist), and baptism εἰς (into) the name of Jesus (as witnessed in the epistles).[149] Reason for this distinction is an assumed Hellenistic-Pauline cautiousness for the Spirit of prophecy (the charismatic Spirit). Turner dismisses this explanation of Acts 8 on linguistic grounds: Luke varies in his style of writing, so upon/in/into the name of Jesus are interchangeably. And, Turner argues, according to Luke there was no split between Philip and the apostles. Philip, Peter and John all came from the same mother church where only the Spirit of prophecy was known.

5. **A narrative-critical solution.** F.S. Spencer tried to solve the Acts 8 episode with the narrative term "forerunner-culminator", in which the relationship of Philip-Peter is modeled after the John-Jesus relationship in Luke's Gospel and paralleled by the Apollos-Paul relationship in Acts.[150] Turner understands this as a literary description of the narrative structure, rather than as an explanation of the Acts 8 episode in which the Spirit is bestowed upon the Samaritans by Peter and John.

6. **The gift of the Spirit as a donum superadditum of empowering for mission.** Here we approach a specific Pentecostal model especially advocated by Roger Stronstad, James Shelton and Robert Menzies.[151] According to this model Luke saw the promise/gift of the Spirit as essentially a charismatic empowering for mission. This empowering is distinct of and subsequent to conversion.[152] Turner notes three important problems: a)

---

149 Michel Quesnel, *Baptisés dans l'Esprit* (Paris: Cerf, 1985); Turner, *Power from on High*, 369-371.
150 F.S. Spencer, *The Portrait of Philip in Acts* (Sheffield: JSOT, 1992), 211-241; Turner, *Power from on High*, 371.
151 For other Pentecostal views and a clear explanation between "two-stage" and "one-stage" Pentecostals, see: Turner, "Interpreting the Samaritans of Acts 8: The Waterloo of Pentecostal Soteriology and Pneumatology?", *Pneuma* 23 (2001), 265-268.
152 Turner, *Power from on High*, 371-372. See also the monographs and articles by Stronstad, Shelton and Menzies as mentioned in the bibliography at the end of this dissertation and Turners response to Shelton: "'Empowerment for Mission?'The Pneumatology of Luke-Acts: An Appreciation of James B. Shelton's *Mighty in Word and Deed*", *VE* (1994), 103-122. See also Turner, "Waterloo", 265-286.

the context of the passage in Acts 8 is significant silent about mission; b) Luke has a much broader understanding of the working of the Spirit than empowering for mission alone and c) this Pentecostal model explains the time lapse between baptism and reception of the Spirit, but does not explain why there is no gap between baptism and the reception of the Spirit in Acts 2:38 (which is the norm, according to Turner).
The cornerstone for this Pentecostal explanation is their view of the laying on of hands. This is interpreted as a commission or ordination for the missionary task. Turner argues that the transfer of authority (as one of the interpretations of laying on of hands) is not in view here in Acts 8. The accounts in 6:6, 13:3, 14:23 are all about transfer of authority (respectively the apostles to the seven; Antioch church to Paul and Barnabas; Paul to the elders). The accounts in Acts 8:16-19 and in 19:6 are exceptions and do not deal with a transfer of authority, but rather with a transfer of "power" or in these two specific instances with a transfer of the Holy Spirit.

In his preliminary conclusion, Turner states that for Luke this delaying of reception of the Spirit is perhaps "anomalous", but is not seen as "problematic" (contra Dunn and Beasley-Murray). Turner opts for the interpretation that somehow God sovereignly withheld his Spirit, so that the leadership of the Jerusalem church could approve this extension of salvation beyond Jerusalem. As an example Turner mentions the apostles themselves: they were believers during Jesus' ministry and after His resurrection and ascension, but only received the Holy Spirit at Pentecost.[153]

3.9.3 Preliminary deductions and possible implications
We can deduce some practical and interpretive facts from Turner's treatment of the Samaritan episode in Acts 8. It is clear that for Turner Acts 2:38-39 provides the norm. Believers only once receive the Spirit. This is the "Spirit of prophecy" which is the soteriological Spirit as well as the charismatic Spirit. On the basis of Acts 8 it is highly improbable that Luke thought of a "two-stage" pneumatology, in which believers first receive the soteriological Spirit and second receive the charismatic Spirit. It is also improbable that Luke thought of one Spirit baptism, exclusively for an empowerment for mission. Beneath this second interpretation (of which Robert Menzies is a proponent, see chapter 4 of this dissertation), lies an "inadequate soteriology" (Turners words).[154]

---

153 Turner, *Power from on High*, 374.
154 Turner, "Waterloo", 268-270.

We can conclude that beneath the surface of interpretation of the Samaritan episode, two aspects are crucial for the reader's interpretation. The first aspect is the "richness" of the readers soteriology, that is what does it all include or not? Turner embraces a very rich soteriology, based on Luke 1-2 and Jesus' inaugural address in Luke 4.[155] Here we clearly see that the "soteriological material" from Luke 1-2 and 4 has to a certain degree been "narcotized" (to use Eco's terminology) and now comes to the surface in Turner's interpretation of Acts 8. The second aspect is the reader's interpretation of the laying on of hands. Does this ritual have the same meaning despite the difference in context? Turner's answer to this is negative and he meticulously searches for the right meaning in the given context.

3.10 The Damascus event (Acts 9)
3.10.1 The actualized text
There are a couple of textual issues in this episode of Acts 9:1-19. First there is the word κύριος in verse 5. Is this a normal way of greeting one another? Or is this the sign of Paul's conversion, because he addresses Jesus as Lord?

Another textual issue is whether the καὶ πλησθῇς πνεύματος ἁγίου ("that you might be filled with the Holy Spirit") from verse 17 is Lukan or not. Turner does admit that the sense (aorist subjunctive instead of an aorist indicative) is unusual, but states that the vocabulary is Lukan.[156]

3.10.2 The substantial properties of the text
There are various interpretations, all based on the textual issues mentioned above. Howard Ervin defends the traditional Pentecostal interpretation in which the κύριος in verse 5 shows that Paul is converted and that he is baptized in the Spirit (second blessing) when Ananias prays for him in verse 17.[157] Turner dismisses this interpretation as "an over-simplification" because "Lord" was a normal way of addressing one another and if Paul was genuinely converted, why would he be asking "Who are you?"[158]

---

155 Turner, "Waterloo", 269-270, 275-276.
156 Turner, *Power from on High*, 377n.83.
157 Howard M. Ervin, *Conversion-Initiation and the Baptism in the Holy Spirit. A Critique of James D.G. Dunn's 'Baptism in the Holy Spirit'* (Peabody, MA: Hendrickson, 1984), 41-50.
158 Turner, *Power from on High*, 375.

While following the topic and therewith the narrative structure of the text, Turner does admit that there is a possibility Paul came to faith while reflecting on his Divine encounter and before Ananias came to him. But his "conversional commitment" or the "completion of his conversion-initiation" occurs only after Ananias guidance and with Paul's baptism.[159]

Another, also traditional Pentecostal, interpretation is made by Robert Menzies, who argues that Paul is commissioned for his ministry and that his reception of the Spirit is an empowerment for mission.[160] According to Turner this is a stronger case than Ervin's, despite Turner's own disagreement with this interpretation. Based on 9:12 and 9:17 Turner argues for the following order: "first Ananias lays hands on Paul for healing (9:12, 18); subsequently Paul is baptized and takes food (9:18)".[161] He interprets the laying on of hands is for healing alone and assumes that somewhere at or beyond the water baptism Paul receives the Spirit. This would be according to the norm in Acts 2:38.

In this interpretation Turner very closely follows the text and its narrative structure. However tempting this sequence of events is, the text does not clarify all these specific details. Admitting this, Turner seems open for the *both-and* solution of James Shelton: Paul's reception of the Spirit is both soteriological and as well an empowerment for mission.[162]

3.10.3 Preliminary deductions and possible implications
This *both-and* solution is an example of what Eco calls "bracketed extension": the meaning is not as clear as one would expect, so the exact interpretation has to become clear in the continuing narrative. In the meantime the reader's preliminary interpretation is put between brackets. This is then exactly what Turner does when he closes the section on the Damascus event with the words "his reception of the gift within the context of conversion-initiation suggests a broader understanding which we shall explore later."[163]

---

159 Turner, *Power from on High*, 375.
160 Menzies, *Development*, 260-263.
161 Turner, *Power from on High*, 376-377.
162 James B. Shelton, *Mighty in Word and Deed: The Role of the Holy Spirit in Luke-Acts* (Peabody, MA: Hendrickson, 1991), 131.
163 Turner, *Power from on High*, 378.

3.11 The Cornelius' household (Acts 10)
3.11.1 The actualized text
In an excursus Turner briefly discusses tradition and redaction in the Cornelius episode, treating two main traditions which François Bovon distinguishes. Turner however is quick to dismiss these options and argues that Peter's vision is puzzling and parabolic, instead of having a plain and simple literal meaning.[164] In addition Turner points to the almost general agreement among scholars that Luke describes the Cornelius event in close parallel with Acts 2 and so depicts a "Gentile Pentecost".[165]

3.11.2 The substantial properties of the text
Following the storyline of the Cornelius episode, it is exactly this point of general consensus among scholars which shows the plot of the story: in the 10th chapter of Acts a "Gentile Pentecost" occurs. The narrative structure of the text shows that in Luke's view it is God himself who initiates this next decisive step of inclusion of the Gentiles. It is the Spirit who confirms this at each stage (10:19-20, :44-48, 11:12, :15-18 and 15:8-9).[166]

In determining the meaning of the event Turner's primary sparring partners are Robert Menzies and James Dunn. Here we come across what Eco calls the "actantial structure" (box 8) of the text. In trying to come to a Lukan Pneumatology the meaning of the working of the Spirit is deduced from the story of Conelius. Menzies argues that the gift of the Spirit is an empowerment for mission, while Dunn argues the Spirit enables these Gentiles to experience forgiveness and enter salvation.[167] Dunn argues on the basis of three points:

1. In 10:43-44 Cornelius receives the Spirit right after hearing Peter speak of God's forgiveness. The Spirit thus constituted God's forgiveness to Cornelius;
2. The verses 11:17 and 11:18 are treated as a parallelism, explaining each other;[168]

---

164 Turner, *Power from on High*, 379.
165 Turner, *Power from on High*, 380 Turner lists three uniting factors which clearly show the similarities between Acts 2 and Acts 10. That the apostles interpreted the event in Acts 10 as a "Gentile Pentecost" is confirmed by Acts 11:15-17 and 15:8 as well.
166 Turner, *Power from on High*, 380.
167 Menzies, *Development*, 267; Dunn, *Baptism*, 70-82; Turner, *Power from on High*, 381.
168 11:17 So if God gave them the same gift as us (…) / 11:18 (…) God has granted even the Gentiles repentance to life.

3. Approximately the same can be said of 15:8-9 in which verse 9 is equivalent to verse 8 and actually explains and clarifies verse 8.[169]

Turner, however, disagrees with Dunn on these three points. Concerning the first point, Turner does not equate the receiving of the Spirit with God's forgiveness. In his later article Dunn formulates it more cautiously when he states that the Spirit is an "embodiment" or "transmitter" of God's forgiveness.[170] Turner argues on the basis of 11:14 and 15:7 that Peter's words resulted in faith and 15:8 then means that God gave them the "Spirit of prophecy".

With regard to the second point Turner does admit there is a *mild* parallelism (emphasis is mine), however he finds the equation between the gift of the Spirit and the gift of repentance forced. Verse 18b is interpreted by Turner as a conclusion to the whole episode of 11:3-17.

The same can be said about Dunn's third point, concerning the verses 8-9 in Acts 15. The question here is whether the phrases "giving the Holy Spirit to them" (:8) and "He purified their hearts by faith" (:9) describe the same divine action. Turner argues that verse 9b does not intent to clarify verse 8b, but "to provide the grounds for the conclusion in 15:10-11."[171] The argument is that God cleansed or purified their hearts by faith, rather than through their Torah commitment. God's gift of the Spirit to these Gentiles proves that (from God's perspective) they were clean at heart and as such could receive the Spirit of prophecy.

In response to Menzies, Turner has two arguments that indicate that the Spirit "has more to do with salvation, than Menzies is prepared to admit."[172] Despite the different order of events (conversion, reception of the Spirit, water baptism), Turner notes that in the Cornelius episode Luke turns to the "norm" of Acts 2:38-39. The gift of the Spirit is immediately associated with repentance, conversion and water baptism. The interpretation (on basis of 10:2, 4, 22, 31, 33) that Cornelius was already converted is refuted by Turner. This interpretation does not do justice to the narrative development and makes Peter the apostle who confirmed Cornelius' faith and not the one who preached to Cornelius. The retelling

---

169 15:8 God, who knows the heart, showed that He accepted them by giving the Holy Spirit to them, just as he did to us. / 15:9 He made no distinction between us and them, for He purified their hearts by faith.
170 Dunn, "Baptism in the Spirit: A Response to Pentecostal Scholarship", *JPT* 3 (1993), 13.
171 Turner, *Power from on High*, 383.
172 Turner, *Power from on High*, 384. He elaborates on these two arguments on pages 384-387.

of the Cornelius episode in chapters 11 and 15 of Acts confirms that Cornelius was converted while listening to Peter. The positive picture of Cornelius is probably best understood when acknowledging that he was a Gentile God-fearer or semi proselyte, but not yet a Christian convert.

Turner's second argument in response to Menzies concerns "Peter's remembering" of the words by John the Baptist "you will be baptized with the Holy Spirit", which Luke wrote down in Acts 11:16. On basis of this "remembrance" Turner argues that the terminology "baptism in the Spirit" was not widely used in the early church, whether it be an initiation (so Dunn) or an empowering (so Menzies). So Luke deliberately lets Peter remember the words of John the Baptist to parallel the Cornelius event with the promise of John the Baptist and as such with Pentecost in Acts 2. Because of the context of 11:1-18, it is precisely here that Luke writes about Peter's "remembrance". According to Turner Luke understands the pouring out of the Spirit as the instrument (executive power) for the Messiah to cleanse and restore Israel. Turner already interpreted it in this way in Luke 3:16-17 and Acts 1:5 (see above in §3.3 and §3.7). It is exactly because this interpretation of cleansing and restoring, why Peter understands that the Gentile household of Cornelius also fits into God's plan of salvation. Peter's mysterious vision was about cleansing and restoring. The pouring out of the Spirit on Cornelius' household confirms this. Acts 15:8-9 accentuate this line of interpretation when Peter says: "God (…) accepted them by giving the Holy Spirit to them, just as He did to us. He made no distinction between us and them (…)."

This case of the Cornelius episode clearly shows that Turner takes "the middle-of-the-road" position in the debate whether the Spirit in Luke-Acts is the soteriological Spirit (so Dunn) or the empowerment-for-mission Spirit (so Menzies). Instead of the *either-or* position, Turner takes the *both-and* position.

3.11.3 Preliminary deductions and possible implications
The example mentioned above whether Cornelius was already converted to Christian faith before Peter came is an excellent example of a premature interpretation. The questions the reader could have had about Cornelius positive picture painted by Luke in 10:2, 4, 22, 31 and 33 should have been put between brackets, as Eco mentions in box 5 of his model. Only after further reading of the narrative it is possible to give a more solid interpretation of these verses.

However, as Eco describes in box 10, during the reading process the reader creates possible worlds in his mind. If there is a certain discrepancy between this possible world and the actual world, then it is up to the reader to cooperate with the text and to believe the world of the text. If in the actual world the outpouring of the Spirit is a second experience subsequent to conversion, than the reader will try to solve this issue. Just as is the case in classical Pentecostalism. However, the other way around is true as well. If the reader is convinced that in the actual world the outpouring of the Spirit occurs at conversion, then the issue in the world of the text has also to be solved.

According to Eco's model the reader has to choose to cooperate with the narrative and the possible world of the narrative. Any discrepancies with the actual (real) world have to be narcotized until the developing narrative provides answers. In my opinion Turner does read Luke's narrative the way Eco proposes, as a cooperative reader. Before jumping to conclusions with regard to Cornelius' positive picture, Turner narcotizes this and continues reading only to come to an interpretation after reading Acts 11 and 15, in which the story of Cornelius is retold, with some interesting additions (see above, Acts 11:16 'Peter's remembering' and Acts 15:8-9 'just as He did to us'). So in following the narrative Turner comes to the interpretation that the outpouring of the Spirit on Cornelius household is closely tied to the conversion of this household.

3.12 The Ephesian disciples (Acts 19)
3.12.1 The actualized text
There is not much to be said about the expression of the text. The only issue which Turner lightly addresses is the words τινας μαθητάς (certain disciples) in 19:1. This choice of words strongly suggests Luke had Christian disciples in mind, because of Luke's use elsewhere of this rather technical term for believers. It further could be that the Ephesian disciples were Apollos's disciples because of the mentioning of John's baptism. Turner however rejects this view, foremost based on the plot of the text.

3.12.2 The substantial properties of the text
In a close reading of the text Turner concludes that Luke does not connect the Ephesian disciples with Apollos, but rather contrasts them with each other: Apollos is zealous in the Spirit, whereas the Ephesian disciples have not even heard of the Spirit; the Ephesian disciples are 'rebaptised', Apollos is not.[173] On this basis, Turner's conclusion is then straightforward: according to Luke, these Ephesian disciples were not

---
173 Turner, *Power from on High*, 389.

Christians at all.¹⁷⁴ Turner's assumption regarding the plot of the story is that these Ephesian disciples were disciples of John, were baptized in John's baptism of repentance and were still awaiting the Coming One about whom John had preached. In verse 4 Paul then explains the Gospel to them and in response to their affirmative answer to the Gospel they are (re)baptized and receive the Holy Spirit with the laying on of hands by Paul. Other attempts to understand this text and the developing plot are:

1. The Ephesian disciples are genuine Christians, who did not yet receive the Holy Spirit as their empowerment (for mission);¹⁷⁵
2. The Ephesian disciples are Apollos's disciples but needed to be slightly corrected in their faith;¹⁷⁶
3. e Ephesian disciples are "semi-Christians".¹⁷⁷

As stated above, according to Turner the most natural reading of the narrative and understanding of the plot is to conclude that the Ephesian disciples were not yet Christians.¹⁷⁸ Here we see that Turner in his understanding and interpretation of the text, discovers what Eco calls the discursive and narrative structures of the text (boxes 4 and 6 in Eco's model). In continuing his interpretation of the text, Turner now presses a little further and makes some abstract observations. Here we see that Turner moves to box 8 from Eco's model and comes to the box of actantial structures. It seems that for Luke it is apparently possible to have some sort of "believing" without having received the Holy Spirit. Turner distinguishes this "Ephesian" event from the Samaritan episode, because the Samaritans had already heard the Gospel, while here Paul preaches to them (19:4), after which they are being baptized and receive the Holy Spirit. Brought to an abstract level one can conclude that the whole package of conversion-initiation consists of (a) hearing and accepting the kerygma of Jesus; (b) water baptism and (c) the reception of the Holy Spirit. All this is consistent with the norm of Luke 2:38-39. Here we see that Turner moves to a normative aspect of the Luke-Acts narrative where it concerns conversion-initiation.

---

174 Turner, *Power from on High*, 390.
175 This is the classical Pentecostal stance to proof a second necessary Spirit experience.
176 So for instance Menzies, Kim and Shepherd. See Turner, *Power from on High*, 388n.118.
177 So E. Käsemann, "The Disciples of John the Baptist in Ephesus", in: *Essays on New Testament themes* (London: SCM, 1964), 136-148.
178 So also Dunn, *Baptism in the Holy Spirit*, 83-85.

Contra Menzies, Turner does not interpret the laying on of hands of Paul as some sort of commissioning in the missionary task and the as such the reception of the Spirit as the empowerment for this missionary task.[179]

3.12.3 Preliminary deductions and possible implications

Up until now Turner has been very cautious to posit premature claims regarding the normative working of the Holy Spirit, whether it is a second blessing, an empowering for mission or "just" as soteriological evidence. All the Spirit passages (as mentioned and treated throughout this entire chapter) have been subjected to thorough research, whereby some poignant questions have been put between brackets. In his treatment of this last literary knot or cluster of πνεῦμα texts, Turner takes position and "removes the brackets". The vital question is whether Luke saw speaking in tongues as a normative event and a necessary evidence of being filled with the Holy Spirit. Turner argues that the expectancy in Judaism concerning the reception of the Spirit was dramatic and experiential: reception of the Spirit should be accompanied with certain charismata.[180] He understands Pentecost as a unique salvation-historical event where this dramatic reception of the Spirit took place. In the Samaritan episode a new stage in the Acts 1:8 program has been reached and confirmed by the visible, dramatic and experiential outpouring of the Spirit upon the Samaritan believers. The same is true in the Cornelius episode, where it shows that even Gentile believers can receive the Holy Spirit in all its fullness as God had promised. Turner designates these events as "important turning points" and states that these were important turning points because of the *legitimation* of these new believers (emphasis is mine).[181] However, according to Turner, this does not mean that Luke regarded speaking in tongues as normative and evidential for the reception of the Spirit. The rather "normal" group of the Ephesian disciples receiving the Spirit are explained by Turner as a closure of one of Luke's sub-plots concerning the promise of baptism in the Spirit.[182] Furthermore he argues that Luke in 19:6 does not explicitly state that each believer spoke in

---

179 Menzies, *Development*, 271-277; Turner, *Power from on High*, 393.
180 Turner, *Power from on High*, 393.
181 Turner, *Power from on High*, 394.
182 Turner here follows W.H. Shepherd, *The Narrative Function of the Holy Spirit as Character in Luke-Acts* (SBL 147; Atlanta, GA: Scholars, 1994), 229. Turner, *Power from on High*, 396.

tongues (Luke would have used ἕκαστος), but only shows that the reception of the Spirit was accompanied by visibility. Some spoke in tongues, others prophesied, all of these gifts would have been interpreted as initial evidence of their reception of the Spirit. To conclude we can summarize that for Luke such dramatic and experiential signs were normal but not normative.

3.13 Conclusion
3.13.1 The Role of the Reader: Max M.B. Turner
Turner is meticulous in his research and keenly aware of the pitfalls of a too easily application of texts or a reading into the text of present day experiences. Assessing Turner's work through the model of Umberto Eco, as we have done in this chapter, we can come to the following conclusions:

1. Turner is meticulous in cooperating with the text. With a keen eye for detail, background, context and intertextuality, he reads and rereads the text in front of him and turns out to be a "model reader", namely a cooperative reader;
2. Turner does spend responsible attention to the text in front of him: textual issues are addressed and tried to be solved without jumping to conclusions. However, already in this first step of reading, exegetical choices are made which do determine the continuing reading process and cooperation with the narrative;
3. Turner's main focus is in the intensions of the text, that is boxes 4, 6, 8 and 9 from Eco's model. Especially boxes 4 and 6 receive considerable attention: little by little the textual meaning is determined and narrative structures are made visible. Due to Turner's excellent work in these boxes 4 and 6, it is possible to distinguish a Lukan Pneumatology which is firmly rooted in the history of the people of Israel. This contributes to one of Luke's overall theological themes of *promise and fulfillment*;
4. When it comes to the application of the text and adding possible value judgments to the text, Turner remains reluctant and careful not to do this prematurely. His careful reading through the narrative is characterized by first assessing the data and diverse possible interpretations. Only after this is done, he "jumps" to boxes 9 and 10 of Eco's model. On basis of the gathered data and close reading and rereading of the text, Turner then does not hesitate to draw conclusions and propose applications for the individual Christian believer and the Church today.

3.13.2 Lukan Pneumatology according to Max M.B. Turner
After the thorough reading, rereading and interpreting of the Lukan narrative, Turner comes to his conclusions in regard to Lukan Pneumatology. As an overall interpretive framework (or as Eco would call it *the narrative structure*) Turner uses the theme of the New Exodus: the people of God are led into a New Exodus by a Spirit-endowed Person to become a cleansed and restored eschatological community. This Spirit-endowed Person is a prophet-like-Moses and Davidic Messiah through whom the Spirit of God is working to "preach Good News to the poor, proclaim liberty to the captives and the recovery of sight to the blind, to set at liberty the oppressed and to proclaim the acceptable year of the Lord" (the theological themes of Jubilee). This Spirit-endowed Person proves to be Jesus of Nazareth who promises and fulfills in due time the outpouring of the Spirit of God on his followers. Within this interpretive framework of the New Exodus, Jesus inaugural address (Luke 4) and Peter's Pentecost speech (Acts 2) both serve as programmatic texts.

The Holy Spirit is typified as the Old Testament "Spirit of Prophecy" and shows the presence of God in (miraculous) power, revelation and wisdom. Turner has a very rich concept of salvation: it is not only redemption from sin and guilt, but also an ongoing participation in worship, life and witness. It is the Holy Spirit who works all this through the believing individual, as well as it is the Holy Spirit who cleanses and restores. This is both for the spiritual benefit of the believing individual as well as for the community. Turner's conclusions concerning Lukan Pneumatology are as follows:

1. Based on his reading of Luke-Acts, Turner comes to the conclusion of a "one stage model" of Spirit reception: the Holy Spirit is received at conversion;
2. urner interprets Acts 2:38-39 as the Lukan norm for Spirit reception. This means that conversion, water baptism and the reception of the Holy Spirit are all part of one package;
3. he Spirit received with conversion-initiation is the *potential* of a broad range of charismata. The realization of this potential comes only through obedient discipleship and expectant prayer. Those are the people who Luke describes as being "full of the Holy Spirit";
4. The different sequence in the Samaritan and Cornelius episodes (Acts 8 and 10) are interpreted and explained as clearly marked new phases in salvation-history which required a convincing and visible outpouring of the Holy Spirit – just as was the case with the disciples in Acts 2;

5. The laying on of hands should be interpreted anew in every distinct context. It cannot be treated as a rule that it always means *commissioning* or *confirmation* or *a transfer of power*;
6. The evidence of Spirit reception can be a diversity of charismata. Speaking in tongues and prophesying *can* be part of this and are, by Luke, regarded as normal, but not as normative;
7. The Holy Spirit in Luke-Acts serves to cleanse and restore the individual believer and the community to become God's empowering presence in this world.

CHAPTER 4
THE MODEL APPLIED (2):
ROBERT P. MENZIES

4.1 Introduction
Robert P. Menzies completed his Ph.D. in New Testament studies in 1989 at the University of Aberdeen, Scotland, under supervision of I. Howard Marshall. His dissertation was published in 1991 as *The Development of Early Christian Pneumatology with Special Reference to Luke-Acts*. Later, in 1994, this volume was significantly revised and made accessible for a wider audience and published as *Empowered for Witness: The Spirit in Luke-Acts*.
Both of these volumes and the relevant articles by Robert Menzies on Lukan Pneumatology form the basis of this present chapter.

Robert Menzies lectured at Asia Pacific Theological Seminary in the Philippines and the Assemblies of God Theological Seminary in the United States. He is currently director of Synergy, a rural outreach organization in South West China. Together with his father William W. Menzies, he served as a missionary in the Philippines and they also wrote the book *Spirit and Power, Foundations of Pentecostal Experience* together. The most recent publications by Robert Menzies are: *The Spirit and Spirituality: Essays in Honor of Russell P. Spittler* (2004), *The Language of the Spirit: Interpreting and Translating Charismatic Terms* (2010) and *Pentecost: This Story is Our Story* (2013).

Menzies' dissertation consists of three parts. Firstly he thoroughly discusses the Spirit in early Judaism, then he focuses on Luke-Acts in which he discusses the different πνεῦμα clusters and subsequently he discusses some relevant Pauline texts in part III. with a discussion of some.

In the revised volume, *Empowered for Witness*, these last chapters on Paul are replaced by two chapters on the significance of Lukan Pneumatology for the church today. This significance is discussed from a Pentecostal perspective, focusing on the "issue of subsequence" and speaking in tongues (glossolalia) as the initial evidence for the baptism in the Spirit.

Before discussing all the relevant Lukan passages, Menzies makes clear that his method is redaction-critical, that he assumes Luke knew the Gospel of Mark and the written source Q and that the Book of Acts is produced in the same way as the Gospel: using a variety of written and/or oral sources.

These various aspects determine how Menzies reads and interprets Luke-Acts and will show his specific role as reader and interpreter.

4.2 The infancy narratives (Luke 1-2)
4.2.1 *The actualized text*
While reading the text of the infancy narratives, Menzies shows the need for a rather broad *encyclopedic competence*.

To rightly interpret the infancy narratives, the reader needs some knowledge of Early Judaism as well as the overall theology of Luke-Acts. This poses the old hermeneutical question where to start: with a part of the story or with the whole story?

Menzies starts with a synchronic analysis of the Lukan text and tries to distinguish between sources and Lukan redaction. He admits the difficulty of determining sources behind the text of Luke 1-2, but he does focus on the clusters of πνεῦμα texts and then indicates that Luke used traditional material, which he shaped for his own narrative: "Luke has selected, organized, and modified the traditional material at his disposal."

According to Menzies, in regard to the πνεῦμα texts, it is therefore possible to "distinguish between tradition and Lukan redaction." Subsequently the Lukan redaction then "provides important insight into Luke's unique perspective on the Spirit."

In relation to the birth of John, Menzies argues that both of the Spirit phrases (1:15, 17) can be omitted without a significant altering of the narrative.

In some way, the same is the case with the mentioning of the Spirit in the life of Simeon (2:25-27), Menzies takes these as Lukan redactions, although he admits it is a "hypothesis".

The same is true about Anna, the prophetess. The Spirit is not mentioned in the text, however because of the word prophetess, Menzies interprets this as evidence that the Spirit was working in her.

So concerning the text proper, Menzies does make distinctions between traditional sources and Lukan redaction. Based on these (hypothetical) Lukan redactions, Menzies builds his interpretation of the textual meaning and determines the topic of the infancy narratives. This is a rather problematic method to apply to the infancy narratives, because they are Lukan Sondergut. A synoptic comparison with Mark and/or Matthew is not possible. Perhaps starting with the whole story of Luke-

Acts to find some interpretive keys for the infancy narratives would be a more solid approach here.

4.2.2 The substantial properties of the text

The textual meaning of the infancy narratives, according to Menzies, is "to emphasize the pneumatic and prophetic character of John's ministry and to strengthen the links between John and Jesus."
Because of the repetition of ἐπλήσθη πνεύματος ἁγίου (1:41, 67), describing Elisabeth's and Zechariah's filling with the Spirit, Menzies concludes that a person's filling with the Spirit leads to prophetic or inspired speaking. So the topic of the text is to show the relationship between the filling of the Spirit and prophetic speaking.
In addition, with the instances of the mentioning of the Spirit in relation to Simeon, Menzies interprets the Spirit of prophecy as "granting special revelation, guidance, and inspiring speech."
So the meaning and therewith the topic of the narrative in Menzies' interpretation is still about the prophetic Spirit, however the working here is broader than only prophecy. Menzies also interprets the mentioning of Anna being a prophetess as another confirmation that the text of the infancy narratives has the prophetic Spirit as topic. He then concludes that "the Spirit is inextricably related to prophetic phenomena."

The only exception is in Luke 1:35, where the Spirit seems to have a creative function instead of or in addition to the already mentioned prophetic function. Based on Matthew 1:18-20, Menzies argues that there was a tradition about the role of the Spirit in the birth of Jesus. Luke probably included this tradition to strengthen the parallel between John and Jesus. Following Schneider, Menzies agrees that Luke minimizes the contrast between the Spirit's creative and prophetic working.

However, in his interpretation Menzies does not take Luke 1:35 as a redundant piece of synonymous parallelism (his choice of words), but argues that the use of δύναμις is theologically motivated.

This interpretive move made by Menzies has direct consequences for the reading of the remainder of the narrative of Luke-Acts. Menzies does not equate δύναμις with the Holy Spirit, but argues that according to Luke the Spirit points to prophetic activity (such as inspired speech), and the δύναμις points to healings and exorcisms.

To justify this reading Menzies uses quite a lot of other Lukan passages which, in his opinion, underline this interpretation. If we apply Eco's model to this reading, then it becomes obvious that Menzies "jumps" to the narrative and even actantial structures of the text (boxes 6 and 8 in Eco's model), before determining the story of the text (box 4). In a cooperative reading, as Eco proposes, the normal way would be to "narcotize" this possible parallelism between δύναμις and πνεῦμα. In the further reading of the narrative this then could be verified or falsified.

Menzies explains the difference between δύναμις and πνεῦμα as a nuanced difference and sees the Spirit as being the source of power. He concludes: "Each produces a specific nexus of activities and when Luke refers to both a broader range of activities is envisioned", and shows this with the following figure:

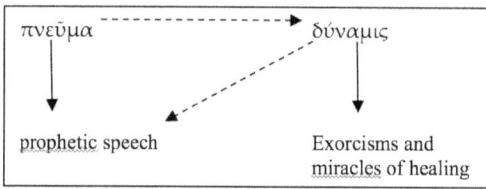

In his interaction with the other Lukan πνεῦμα and δύναμις texts (Luke 1:17, 4:14, 24:49, Acts 1:8, 10:38), Menzies focuses on the narrative structure behind the text.[1] According to Menzies, Luke's purpose with the parallel statement in 1:35 is to join the traditional creative role of the Spirit with his own understanding of the prophetic role of the Spirit. As such the emphasis moves from the miraculous birth to Mary's prophetic proclamation in 1:46-55. In short, according to Menzies in his story Luke does sustain the Spirit's creative role, but he uses δύναμις for this, so he can accentuate the prophetic role of πνεῦμα. What we observe here is a circular reasoning in which 1:35 is interpreted with the help of other Lukan πνεῦμα and δύναμις texts without taking into account their specific contexts. Subsequentlly these interpretations of other Lukan πνεῦμα and δύναμις texts are used to validate Menzies' interpretation of 1:35. A further significant detail is that Menzies does not mention possible Isaianic allusions (for instance 32:15) to 1:35, whereas most commentators do so.[2]

---

1 One can raise the objection that Menzies does not treat every instance of δύναμις in Luke-Acts, and as such perhaps lacks a full Lukan understanding of the use of δύναμις. In total Luke uses δύναμις some 25 times in both of his volumes: Moulton, *Concordance to the Greek Testament*, 232.
2 Brown, *Birth of the Messiah*, 311-312 (he does not refer to Isaiah 32:15, but 11:1-2 and 4:2-3); Marshall, *Gospel of Luke*, 70; Nolland, *Luke 1-9:20*, 54; Bock, *Luke 1:1-9:50*, 121n.37 and Green, *Gospel of Luke*, 90.

4.2.3 Preliminary deductions and possible implications
In summarizing his findings, Menzies concludes that there must have been a distinction between the pneumatology of the primitive church and Luke's pneumatology: the first being more charismatic, the latter being prophetic. He comes to this conclusion by separating δύναμις and πνεῦμα. Subsequently Menzies argues that Luke keeps the two understandings of the working of the Spirit separate: an Old Testament understanding of πνεῦμα as the prophetic Spirit. And a Hellenistic understanding of δύναμις as miracle working power.³ He concludes:

> "In short, the primitive church, following in the footsteps of Jesus, broadened the perceived functions of the Spirit of God so that it was viewed not only in traditional Jewish terms as the source of prophetic power, but also as miracle-working power. Luke, on the other hand, retained the traditional Jewish understanding of the Spirit as the Spirit of prophecy and, with the term δύναμις, incorporated a Hellenistic mode of expression to speak of miracle-working power."⁴

Based on the story of the infancy narratives, the first deduction Menzies makes is that there were two different views of the Holy Spirit. Luke prefers the traditional Jewish one of those two different views. In addition to this, Menzies describes the implication of this finding for the overall theological homogeneity of Luke-Acts.⁵ He rejects the scheme of three different epochs in Luke-Acts, which originated from Hans Conzelmann. In contrast to Conzelmann, Menzies argues that the infancy narratives are of "vital importance for understanding Luke's pneumatology as a whole."⁶ He acknowledges that both *form* and *content* of the infancy narratives point to God's fulfillment of promises (emphasis is Menzies'). However, this fulfillment is not a decisive mark of a different epoch; it is the inauguration of the eschaton, which finds its further development in the continuing narrative of Luke-Acts. So the second deduction Menzies

---

3 Menzies, *Development*, 128-129.
4 Menzies, *Development*, 129. Menzies seems to be in a rather isolated position with this explanation. The most natural reading of 1:35 remains to be a parallelism. Gabriel provides *one* answer to Mary's question and explains that the child to be born will be holy. The immediate context is about God's creative power (Spirit), providing holiness. A direct link to inspired speech seems awkward, because it is only later in the narrative (verse 47) that Mary starts speaking.
5 Menzies, *Development*, 130-134 (section five).
6 Menzies, *Development*, 134.

makes is that the infancy narratives cannot be seen in isolation from the rest of Luke-Acts. To put it in other words: in the infancy narratives Luke introduces the Spirit of prophecy, which provides the basis for the further development of a Lukan pneumatology.

4.3 The ministry of John the Baptist (Luke 3:1-20)

4.3.1 The actualized text

In his treatment of the ministry and person of John the Baptist, Menzies limits himself to the promise in Luke 3:16b-17 (αὐτὸς ὑμᾶς βαπτίσει ἐν πνεύματι ἁγίῳ καὶ πυρί: οὗ τὸ πτύον ἐν τῇ χειρὶ αὐτοῦ διακαθᾶραι τὴν ἅλωνα αὐτοῦ καὶ συναγαγεῖν τὸν σῖτον εἰς τὴν ἀποθήκην αὐτοῦ, τὸ δὲ ἄχυρον κατακαύσει πυρὶ ἀσβέστῳ). Concerning the text Menzies argues that the Q tradition presents these words correctly.[7] The omission of καὶ πυρί by Mark is, according to Menzies, because of the positive picture Mark presents of the Gospel. Mark does not mention any judgment or wrath, but rather pictures the ministry of John the Baptist as essentially Christological: pointing to the unique status of Jesus as the Spirit baptizer.[8]

4.3.2 The substantial properties of the text

In Menzies' understanding of the text, he takes James Dunn as his primary sparring partner.[9] He follows Dunn in the acceptance of the baptism in Spirit and fire as being *one* baptism: one baptism with a positive and a negative side. In comparison with Mark and Matthew, Menzies then states that Mark and Luke highlight the positive side of this baptism, whereas Matthew portrays the more negative side.[10] However, on other aspects Menzies does not agree with Dunn. He disagrees with Dunn's portrayal of *individuals* who repent, receive the Spirit (as a cleansing agent) and enter the Kingdom of God.[11] Dunn's use of the Qumran scrolls and Isaiah 4:4 are not appropriate to use in the eyes of Menzies. Menzies distinguishes between the use of spirit in 1QS and 1QH. He follows P.

---

7 Menzies, *Development*, 135-136; *Empowered for Witness*, 123.
8 Menzies, *Development*, 141.
9 James D.G. Dunn, *Baptism in the Holy Spirit. A Re-examination of the New Testament Teaching on the Gift of the Spirit in Relation to Pentecostalism Today* (London: SCM, 1970) and 'Spirit-and-Fire-Baptism', *NovT* (1972), 81-92.
10 Menzies, *Development*, 137.
11 "The cleansing envisioned is not the purification or moral transformation of the individual, as Dunn suggests; rather, it involves a cleansing of Israel by means of separation: the righteous (grain) shall be separated from the unrighteous (chaff)." Menzies, *Development*, 139.

Wernberg-Møller and M. Treves, and argues that the two spirits in 1QS 3:13-4:26 are human dispositions: good and evil as opposing forces.[12] Later Menzies states that "several factors speak against the appropriateness of reading John's prophecy against the background provided by the scrolls of Qumran."[13] The scrolls do contain references to the cleansing work of the Spirit of God, but do not mention any judgment as is the case in the promise of John the Baptist. It is obvious that this is Menzies' reading of the texts and his application to the promise of John the Baptist. Not all will agree with such a reading and application.[14] This is an example of the role of the reader who chooses that certain reading and/or interpretation which, in his opinion, fits best. In addition Menzies suggests that the promise of John the Baptist refers to the collective people of Israel and not to the individual as James Dunn does.[15]

So to summarize, according to Menzies the topic in this episode is about John the Baptist promising one baptism (of which Spirit and fire are two aspects) which is for the collective people of Israel and consists of cleansing instead of judgment. Menzies then continues and substantiates this interpretation by comparing Luke with the Gospels of Mathew and Mark. Here we see that he uses source and redaction criticism to show the narrative structure which is beneath the surface of the topic of this episode. The omission of καὶ πυρί in Mark, leads Menzies to the conclusion that Mark interpreted the message of John the Baptist in a largely positive manner. Mark's purpose was Christological: Jesus is unique in his status as the Spirit-baptizer. Matthew, on the contrary, follows Q more closely then Luke does and accentuates the judgmental aspect of the promise of John. Matthew's purpose is to warn not to reject Jesus, because future judgment and destruction will happen. Menzies does not yet make any

---

12 Menzies, *Development*, 78-79; *Empowered for Witness*, 72-73.
13 Menzies, *Development*, 137; *Empowered for Witness*, 125.
14 See for instance William P. Atkinson, *Baptism in the Spirit: Luke-Acts and the Dunn Debate* (Eugene, OR: Wipf and Stock, 2011), 48-50.
15 Menzies, *Development*, 137-138; *Empowered for Witness*, 126. It is rather strange that Menzies will not elaborate on this collective aspect of the promise when treating the different texts in the Book of Acts. If the promise of John the Baptist finds its fulfillment or initial fulfillment in Acts, why is it then that Luke does not pay attention to the judgment part of the promise? And why is it that Luke narrates on individuals being filled with the Spirit? And if, in Menzies' interpretation, the Spirit inspires for speech or empowers for mission, that these aspects are omitted in the promise of John the Baptist? It seems that Menzies treatment of Luke 3:16b-17 raises more questions than answering them.

value judgments, but by comparing the synoptic Gospels he focuses on their different perspectives of the message of John the Baptist.

4.3.3 Preliminary deductions and possible implications
From this comparison between the synoptics, Menzies elaborates on the specific purpose of the Lukan version of John's promise. He does ask himself the question why Luke then used καὶ πυρί as well, if only he wanted to focus on the positive side of Spirit baptism?[16] His answer is that for Luke the metaphor of the winnowing fork is of utmost importance: because this metaphor focuses on the *sifting* of grain and chaff. It is here that Menzies looks ahead to the Book of Acts and as a forecast illustrates that Acts 1:5, 8 and 11:16 are exactly about this sifting. To put it in Menzies' own words:

> (...) Luke understood the Pentecostal bestowal of the Spirit to be the means by which the righteous remnant would be separated from the chaff. (...) Luke clearly interprets the sifting activity of the Spirit of which John prophesied to be accomplished in the Spirit-directed mission of the church and its Spirit-inspired proclamation of the Gospel (Acts 1.5, 8; 11.16). Thus the mission of the church anticipates the final act of messianic judgment."[17]

To press things one step further, Menzies argues that the driving force behind this mission of the church is the Spirit. The Spirit who inspires people to proclaim the Gospel. To put it in other words: the Spirit of prophecy inspires speech and does not "purify or morally transform the individual".[18]

Although Menzies does not elaborate any further on the mission of the church, one can deduce from this initial interpretation that Menzies continues to see this as the mission of the church today. He does not limit himself to the early church alone. So cautiously, we see a first glance of the world structures which Eco's mentions in the 10th box of his model.

---

16 Menzies, *Development*, 142.
17 Menzies, *Development*, 144.
18 Menzies, *Development*, 140; *Empowered for Witness*, 126.

4.4 The baptism and subsequent testing of Jesus (Luke 3:21-22, 4:1-14)

4.4.1 The actualized text
With regard to the text of Jesus' baptism (3:21-22) Menzies argues that Luke depended on Mark alone. Menzies subscribes the minor variations to Lukan redaction and designates these redactions as literary and stylistic rather than theological. This is not the case with the temptation account. In Luke 4:1 and 4:14, Luke's redactions are clearly theological in nature. Especially in regard to Luke's distinctive view of the Holy Spirit. Menzies argues that Luke had access to Mark and Q, but added significant changes: in 4:1 Jesus is described as being full of the Holy Spirit (Ἰησοῦς δὲ πλήρης πνεύματος ἁγίου) and led by the Holy Spirit into the wilderness (καὶ ἤγετο ἐν τῷ πνεύματι ἐν τῇ ἐρήμῳ). In Luke 4:14 we find a Lukan redaction which closes the temptation episode on the one hand and introduces the following narrative on the other hand. The use of δύναμις corresponds with the exorcism performed by Jesus in 4:31-37 (note the recurrence of δύναμις in 4:36).

4.4.2 The substantial properties of the text
In interpreting the story of Jesus' baptism, Menzies does not attach much value to the Lukan changes of Jesus receiving the Spirit *after* baptism and in accompaniment with prayer.[19] He interprets them as a shift in emphasis, rather than a shift in the content of the story. However, the descending of the dove and the sound of the heavenly voice are treated more extensively. On the mysterious appearance of the dove, Menzies discusses some possible interpretations, but he does not elaborate on the possible significance for the story of Jesus' baptism.[20] The heavenly declaration is interpreted by Menzies as confirmation of Jesus being the Messiah-King and Servant of Israel, based on the references to Psalm 2:7 and Isaiah 42:1. In relation to the anointing with the Spirit, Menzies does not interpret this in adoptionistic terms: Jesus becoming the Messiah or Son of God. Instead he argues that through the reception of the Spirit Jesus "is equipped for his messianic task (…) the voice identifies an already existing status."[21] So according to Menzies, the story of the text is about Jesus

---

19 Menzies, *Development*, 149.
20 Menzies, *Development*, 149-150. In my own opinion it could be that the dove should be seen and interpreted as a sacrificial animal, pointing forward to Jesus' sacrificial death. This would also link the heavenly voice with the command in Gen. 22:2, especially when one takes into account the keywords ἀγαπητός and υἱός.
21 Menzies, *Development*, 152-153; *Empowered for Witness*, 137-138.

being equipped for his ministry on earth. This equipping takes place through the anointing with the Holy Spirit. To put it in his own words:

> "(...) I conclude that the Jordan event represents the inauguration of Jesus' messianic task, not the beginning of his sonship or messiahship. Similarly, the heavenly declaration, as a confirmation of Jesus' existing status, constitutes Jesus' call to begin his messianic mission. The important corollary for this study is that Jesus' pneumatic anointing, rather than being the source of his unique filial relationship to God or his initiation into the new age, is the means by which Jesus is equipped for his messianic task."[22]

This leads to the conclusion that in Luke's eyes (and Menzies' interpretation) the Holy Spirit in Luke-Acts is to equip for ministry. Or in Menzies' words: to empower for mission.[23] According to Menzies, the subsequent temptation narrative actually confirms this. The mentioning of the Spirit in 4:1 links this narrative to the previous account of Jesus' baptism. However, Luke mentions (in contrast with Mark and Matthew) the Holy Spirit for a second time in this verse and accentuates that Jesus is full of the Holy Spirit. Menzies interprets this addition as Luke's confirmation that he saw the Jordan event as the moment that Jesus was filled with the Spirit. Menzies writes:

> "I suggest that with the insertion of this phrase Luke has consciously edited his source in order to emphasize the fact that Jesus' experience at Jordan was the moment at which he 'was filled with the Spirit'. In this way Luke was able to bring out the continuity between Jesus' experience of the Spirit and that of the early church."[24]

The second mentioning of the Spirit (4:14) causes Menzies to conclude that there is a "unique pneumatic significance" which Luke attaches to the

---

22 Menzies, *Development*, 153-154; *Empowered for Witness*, 138.
23 Unfortunately Menzies does not spend any time to discuss the relationship between Christology and Pneumatology in this text. He does not elaborate on the (first) role of the Spirit at Jesus' birth and the subsequent (second) role of the Spirit at Jesus' baptism. The compelling question, which Menzies leaves aside, is: how do these two events relate to each other?
24 Menzies, *Development*, 157; *Empowered for Witness*, 141. Menzies does not elaborate on the question whether Jesus needed to be filled again. That is: Jesus' birth is caused by the Spirit, but somehow he needed a subsequent filling before embarking on his mission. As such this is prototypical for the disciples in Acts 2.

temptation account.²⁵ Menzies then elaborates on this unique significance and argues that Jesus did not overcome the temptations by the Spirit, but by Jesus' own obedience to scripture (note the triple use of γέγραπται). From this he draws that it is not the Spirit who is the source of obedience, but that it is Jesus' obedience to his messianic task that makes Him worthy to be a man of the Spirit. This interpretation is corroborated by Menzies' own discussion of the relevant rabbinic texts.²⁶ Regrettably Menzies does not elaborate on this sequence. If I understand him correctly, he does argue that obedience precedes reception of the Spirit. Based on his interpretation of the rabbinic texts this means that obedience to the law makes one worthy of the Spirit. In anticipation on his further work, it seems like a person *first* has to be worthy *before* he can receive the Spirit. To put it differently: one *first* has to be a servant of God or belong to the people of God, *before* the reception of the Spirit.

4.4.3 Preliminary deductions and possible implications
In this episode of Jesus' baptism and subsequent temptation in the desert, we see that Menzies jumps to boxes 7, 9 and 10 in Eco's model. Menzies interprets the sequence of events happening to Jesus (water baptism, filling with the Spirit, leading in the desert) as a clear Lukan theological sequence which carries prescriptive claims for the church today: "just as Jesus was empowered by the Spirit at the Jordan, so it was also for the early church at Pentecost and beyond; and so it must be for the church to which Luke writes."²⁷ This is actually what Eco calls "inferential walks":²⁸ Menzies already knows about the Pentecost story in Acts 2 and with this information he returns to the text of Luke 4. Although a value judgment is not explicitly stated, one can derive from the phrase "so it must be for the church to which Luke writes" the conclusion that Menzies does not interpret the empowerment of the Spirit as optional.²⁹

---

25 Menzies, *Development*, 160.
26 Menzies, *Development*, 161. For Menzies' treatment of the rabbinic passages see 92-96 and 104-108.
27 Menzies, *Development*, 157; *Empowered for Witness*, 142.
28 Eco, *Lector in fabula*, 154-157; *The Role of the Reader*, 32, and see above in §2.5.
29 In addition see Menzies, *Development*, 157n.1 in which he writes "Of course the parallels are not exhausted with Pentecost." This note is omitted in *Empowered for Witness*.

4.5 Jesus' inauguration address (Luke 4:14-30)

4.5.1 The actualized text

Like most New Testament scholars, especially those writing on Luke-Acts and/or the Spirit, Menzies sees the episode of Jesus' inaugural address as the cornerstone of Luke's theology. In comparison to the Gospel of Mark, Luke not only moves this episode forward in his gospel so that Jesus' ministry starts with it, but he also combines his major theological themes in it. Menzies does not think that Luke used Mark 6:1-6 as a source (he agrees with Max Turner on this), but that there probably circulated a traditional account of Jesus teaching in the Nazareth synagogue.[30] He further leaves this discussion aside and then proceeds to focus on Luke 4:18-19, because these are the verses of his primary concern. In his analysis of Luke 4:18-19 in comparison to the LXX text of Isaiah 61:1-2, he comes to some "striking divergences:"[31]

a. The omission of the phrase ἰάσασθαι τοὺς συντετριμμένους τῇ καρδίᾳ;
b. The insertion of ἀποστεῖλαι τεθραυσμένους ἐν ἀφέσει from Isaiah 58:6;
c. The καλέσαι of the LXX has been altered to κηρύξαι;
d. The omission of the final phrase in the LXX, καὶ ἡμέραν ἀνταποδόσεως.

I will discuss these divergences in the next section. Based on previous work by David Hill, Menzies does not doubt the historicity of this episode and argues that it was quite possible for Jesus to enter the synagogue and read from the scroll of Isaiah.[32] He however does not find it likely that Jesus himself altered the text, so Menzies describes its alterations to Luke's redactional creativity and his theological and especially pneumatological purposes.[33]

4.5.2 The substantial properties of the text

To unravel the plot and story of this episode, Menzies continues to focus on these four alterations of the text. He argues that it was not on structural grounds that the phrase "to heal the broken hearted" from Isaiah 61:1 was omitted, but he follows Martin Rese in his conclusion that Luke,

---

30 Menzies, *Development*, 163; *Empowered for Witness*, 146. For an overview of different opinions regarding the use of Mark and/or a traditional source see: Nolland, *Luke 1-9:20*, 191-195 and Marshall, *The Gospel of Luke*, 179-180.
31 Menzies, *Development*, 163-174.
32 Menzies, *Development*, 164; *Empowered for Witness*, 146; David Hill, "The Rejection of Jesus at Nazareth (Luke 4.16-30)", NovT 13 (1971), 161-180.
33 Menzies, *Development*, 175.

because of the omission, accentuates the Spirit as being the prophetic Spirit instead of the power to perform miracles.[34] It is here, with the omission of "to heal the broken hearted", that we come across the important role of the reader in interpreting the story. Menzies interprets that it was Luke who deleted this phrase and so accentuated the prophetic role of the Spirit. Turner, on the other hand, argues that Luke had access to a traditional source where the phrase was already missing.[35] The key question here concerns the background of the Spirit in Judaism: what acts were generally acknowledged as being suitable to subscribe to the Spirit? Menzies follows Schweizer and Rese and sticks to the more narrow interpretation that the Spirit inspires to speak. He undergirds this with an appeal to the infancy narratives, where Luke obviously ties the Spirit to speech.[36] Turner, on the other hand, holds to a broader concept of the Spirit of prophecy and includes miracles and works of power. In addition he argues that the omission of the Isaianic phrase stems from Luke's source.[37] In this instance the "inferential walks" determine the reader's (opposite) interpretations: both take their own understanding of the Jewish concept of the Spirit of prophecy to the text under scrutiny, and let this understanding determine their (distinct) interpretations.

With regard to the insertion of "to proclaim freedom to the prisoners" the same distinction between Menzies and Turner appears: Menzies subscribes it to Lukan redaction, Turner understands it as being part of a traditional source, used by Luke. Menzies argues that this insertion by Luke is an emphasis on the liberating power of Jesus' preaching and as such ties it to inspired speech.[38]

This same line of reasoning is used by Menzies to explain the change from καλέσαι to κηρύξαι, and his explanation of the abrupt ending of the last sentence is, according to Menzies, not that relevant because of the indifference as to whether it belonged to a traditional source or if it was Luke's. In discovering the story of this episode Menzies builds upon his previous work on the Spirit in Judaism and argues that Luke altered the text of 4:18-19 for the benefit of his own theological purpose. The alterations point to the working of the Spirit in such a way that to be Spirit

---

34 Menzies, *Development*, 166-167; Martin Rese, *Alttestamentliche Motive in de Christologie des Lukas* (SNT 1; Güttersloh: Gütersloher Verlagshaus, 1969), 214.
35 Turner, *Power from on High*, 224-225.
36 Menzies, *Development*, 170.
37 Turner, *Power from on High*, 224-225.
38 Menzies, *Development*, 173.

filled means one is empowered to speak. In this concrete instance it is Jesus at the start of his earthly ministry who claims to be empowered by the Spirit and as a result his preaching is inspired.[39]

4.5.3 Preliminary deductions and possible implications
Menzies does cooperate with the story of the text in a high degree and because he uses source criticism as a methodology it is only natural that he focuses on the assumed Lukan redactions. In this episode his interpretation is very closely tied to his methodology and to his pre-understanding of the Spirit in Judaism. Menzies' interpretation actually verifies his understanding of the Spirit in Judaism. His conclusion that the Spirit of prophecy inspires to speak is in accordance with the infancy narratives and as such seems to be a clearly Lukan theological distinctive. However, contrary to Turner, Menzies does not elaborate on the core elements of this Isaianic citation.[40] The Christological and missiological focus are left aside and the relation to the miracles performed by Jesus is only discussed superficially. So despite the fact that Menzies primarily focuses on Lukan Pneumatology, it seems rather odd that he leaves aside the relationship with Lukan Christology. Another lack in his treatment of Jesus' inaugural address is the "year-of-jubilee" terminology. Is there a relation between this terminology and the way Luke wants his readers to understand the role of the Spirit?

So although Menzies does cooperate with the story of the text, there still remain some questions and discrepancies. Only the continuation of the Lukan narrative will make clear whether this is the only possible interpretation of Luke's understanding of the Spirit.

4.6 Jesus' general sayings about the Spirit (Luke 10:21, 11:13 [11:20], 12:10-12)
4.6.1 The actualized text
Besides the πνεῦμα clusters in the first chapters of the Gospel of Luke, πνεῦμα occurs in four other instances in the Gospel: 10:21, 11:13 and 12:10, 12. For matters of convenience I have designated these occurrences as 'general sayings about the Spirit' and I will briefly discuss these in this section.

10:21. There are several variant readings of this verse in the manuscripts and based on external evidence and the LXX use of ἀγαλλιᾶσθαι

---

39 Menzies, *Development*, 174-177.
40 For Turner's view see above in §3.5.3.

with a preposition, Menzies prefers the reading of ἠγαλλιάσατο ἐν τῷ πνεύματι τῷ ἁγίῳ καὶ εἶπεν.[41] In comparing this verse with Matthew 11:25b, Menzies concludes that Matthew has the original Q version and Luke altered this by replacing ἀποκριθεὶς for ἠγαλλιάσατο.

11:13. In the episode of 11:1-13, according to Menzies it is Luke who altered the original ἀγαθά (Mt.7:11b = Q) into πνεῦμα ἅγιον, thereby breaking the parallelism from verse 13a with verse 13b.[42]

11:20. In his treatment of Jesus' general sayings about the Spirit Menzies as well includes the saying in 11:20, despite the fact that Luke does not use πνεῦμα here. In contrast to the Matthean "Spirit of God" (12:28), Luke has "finger of God". Because of Luke's frequent use of the Spirit, this seems a rather odd alteration. However, Menzies explains (and thus interprets) this as a Lukan emphasis that the prophetic Spirit is not to be associated with exorcisms.[43]

12:10-12. After a thorough comparison between Mark, Matthew and Luke, Menzies concludes that Matthew used the Q saying to put it in the Markan context, where Luke somehow conflates both traditions. He then argues (convincingly) that because of the best fit in the context, Matthew has taken the original Q context, while Luke has taken it to put it in another context.[44]

4.6.2 The substantial properties of the text

10:21. According to Menzies, the Lukan redaction in this verse shows that Luke attaches the joyful praise of Jesus to the working of the Spirit. This is consistent with the Psalms in the Old Testament and the infancy narratives in Luke 1-2. Luke's alteration reflects "his distinctive prophetic pneumatology."[45]

11:13. In his interpretation of this Lukan redaction, Menzies argues that the story here is about Luke anticipating the post-resurrection experience of the church. It is only at Pentecost that God will give his Holy Spirit. The relevance of this text then is for the post-Pentecostal church. It is here that Menzies cautiously moves from his interpretation to the application for the church today (this is also the post-Pentecostal church):

---

41 Menzies, *Development*, 178n.2.
42 Menzies, *Development*, 181-182. Contra Turner, who chooses another variant reading: πνεῦμα ἀγαθόν (Turner, *Power from on High*, 340n.61).
43 Menzies, *Development*, 189.
44 Menzies, *Development*, 190-191.
45 Menzies, *Development*, 180.

the promise from 11:13 cannot be an initiatory or soteriological promise, but it is an exhortation for praying to receive the Spirit. This reception of the Spirit is an ongoing practice: it has to be experienced on an ongoing basis.[46]

11:20. The pertinent question in this instance is whether ἐν δακτύλῳ θεοῦ is original or not. The opinions vary and Menzies argues that this phrase is not original from Luke, but because of Luke's "reluctance to associate the Spirit directly with activities which do not correspond to strictly prophetic categories (e.g. exorcisms and miracles of healing)" he altered the original πνεῦμα to ἐν δακτύλῳ θεοῦ.[47] Instead of trying to investigate why Luke does so, Menzies assumes it is because Luke does not want to associate the Spirit with miracles and/or exorcisms. Here we see that Menzies' presupposition colors his exegesis of Luke 11:20 so that the role of the reader is determinative in the interpretation of this text. For a more thorough treatment of this text see Edward J. Woods, *The 'Finger of God' and Pneumatology in Luke-Acts*.[48]

12:10-12. In considering the story of the text, Menzies states that the meaning of this saying in Mark and Matthew is clear: "to 'blaspheme against the Holy Spirit' is to attribute to the agency of Satan the exorcisms which Jesus performs by the Holy Spirit."[49] However, the Lukan context differs and two possible interpretations are briefly discussed. The first is that 'blasphemy against the Spirit' should be seen as an offense to the Christian mission. The phrase then is an encouragement for the disciples. The second interpretation is that the saying is aimed at Christians who do not listen to the voice of the Spirit and refuse to witness in the midst of persecution.[50] Menzies opts for the second interpretation and argues that the context shows this story is about acknowledging Christ in the midst of persecution.

4.6.3 Preliminary deductions and possible implications
The foremost deductions Menzies makes from these general sayings about the Spirit are in connection with 11:20 and 12:10-12. In comparing the Lukan text with Mark and Matthew, he interprets the alterations in

---

46 Menzies, *Development*, 184-185.
47 Menzies, *Development*, 191; *Empowered for Witness*, 163.
48 Edward J. Woods, *The 'Finger of God' and Pneumatology in Luke-Acts* (JSNTSup 205; Sheffield, Sheffield Academic, 2001).
49 Menzies, *Development*, 192.
50 Menzies, *Development*, 193.

the Lukan text as a Lukan redaction. A Lukan redaction to emphasize the working of the Spirit in relation to speech contrary to exorcism. It seems like Menzies places greater emphasis on his conviction that for Luke the meaning of the working of the Spirit could not be attached to exorcisms. Due to his use of source criticism other possible interpretations are set aside. This leads Menzies to the conclusion that for Luke the Spirit only inspires speech.

4.7 The promise of the Spirit (Luke 24 – Acts 1)
4.7.1 The actualized text
The specific texts concerning the promise of the Spirit are Luke 24:47-49 and Acts 1:4-8. It is widely recognized that these passages close the ministry of Jesus (the Gospel) and introduce the ministry of the church (Acts).[51] The parallel statements combine the Gospel and the Book of Acts, with the textual linkage being ὁ ἐπαγγελία τοῦ πατρός (the promise of the Father). Menzies assumes there is some core of traditional material, based on the parallels in Matthew and John. However, the content of this traditional source is "exceedingly difficult, if not impossible, to ascertain."[52] So he takes the text as it is in front of him to show the literary and theological significance for Luke.

4.7.2 The substantial properties of the text
According to Menzies the topic of these parallel statements in Luke 24 and Acts 1 is Jesus commissioning his disciples. The narrative structure behind the text probably stems from Isaiah 49:6, in which the Servant of the Lord is addressed to be a light for the nations and to bring salvation to the ends of the earth. After explaining that Jesus' passion and resurrection are rooted in scripture, it is now shown that the coming mission is rooted in scripture as well. The disciples' question about the restoration of the kingdom of Israel in Acts 1:6 is interpreted by Menzies as a literary

---

51 William S. Kurz, *Acts of the Apostles* (Catholic Commentary on Sacred Scripture; Grand Rapids, MI: Baker Academic, 2013), 25-29; Ben Witherington III, *The Acts of the Apostles. A Socio-Rhetorical Commentary* (Grand Rapids, MI: Eerdmans 1998), 105; Green, *The Gospel of Luke*, 856; Bock, *Luke 9:51-24:53*, 1942-1943 and *Acts*, 36-58; Nolland, *Luke 18:35-24:53*, 1120 and R.C. Tannehill, *The Narrative Unity of Luke-Acts: A Literary Interpretation* (Philadelphia, PA: Fortress, 1986, 1990), 298-301. See also the table in Arie W. Zwiep, *The Ascension of the Messiah in Lukan Christology* (NovTSup 87: Leiden, New York, Köln: Brill, 1997), 118.

52 Menzies, *Development*, 199.

device to accentuate the wide scope of the mission: to the ends of the earth.[53]

The disciples can only participate in this mission after they receive 'the promise of the Father', which will result in them being clothed with power. Menzies then interprets the Holy Spirit and the promise of the Father as being interchangeable and sees this as being the source of the power (δύναμις). The question Menzies asks himself is why Luke uses "the promise of the Father" to designate the Holy Spirit. Acts 1:4 implies that Jesus spoke earlier to his disciples about this promise, and according to Menzies the only Lukan texts that can be considered for this are Luke 11:13 or 12:12. Menzies does not elaborate on these possibilities, but instead focuses on an adequate Old Testament background. He finds this background in Joel 3:1-5a (LXX) and sees this passage as Luke's motivation to use the terminology 'the promise of the Father'. The promise was received at Pentecost and this event is interpreted by Luke (in Peter's speech) by referring to the Joel text. Next to this Menzies points to Luke's insertion of λέγει ὁ θεός in Acts 2:17, and interprets this as Luke's desire to emphasize that the promise comes from the Father.[54] It is here that we see the role of the reader in this argument. Menzies does not elaborate on this Lukan insertion; neither does he treat the textual differences from other manuscripts.[55] If Luke would have made an abundantly clear relation with the promise of the Father, why did he not insert "says the Father" in 2:17 instead of "says God"?

Menzies' third argument stems from the closure of Peter's Pentecost speech where the word ἐπαγγελία occurs in Acts 2:39. He argues that the word promise echoes the words from the Joel prophecy (Joel 3:5a) and as such is connected to Acts 2:17-21, where Peter cites (slightly altered) this prophecy. However, Menzies does make an important interpretative distinction here. He states that the ἐπαγγελία from Acts 2:39 concerns the Spirit of prophecy *as well as salvation* (italics are mine).[56] Whereas the ἐπαγγελία in Luke 24:49, Acts 1:4 and Acts 2:33 point to the first part of the Joel prophecy (Joel 3:1) and only concerns the Spirit of prophecy, the

---

53 Menzies, *Development*, 199-200.
54 Menzies, *Development*, 203, 217.
55 See for instance, Salter, *Power of Pentecost*, 4.
56 Menzies, *Development*, 203; *Empowered for Witness*, 171. It is interesting that Menzies contradicts himself here, because elsewhere he states: "(…) that Luke never attributes soteriological functions to the Spirit (…)"in: William W. Menzies and Robert P. Menzies, *Spirit and Power. Foundations of Pentecostal Experience* (Grand Rapids, MI: Zondervan, 2000), 70.

ἐπαγγελία in Acts 2:39 points as well to the second part of the Joel prophecy (Joel 3:5) and concerns also salvation. So to prove that the Spirit and the promise are interchangeable Menzies uses the repetition of the word ἐπαγγελία and ties this to the Joel text. However, when it comes to the exact *interpretation* of the ἐπαγγελία, Menzies makes a distinction: in one and the same context (Acts 2), he first interprets the Spirit as being the Spirit of prophecy; and in the latter instance he interprets the Spirit as being the Spirit of salvation. He does justify this distinction in interpretation by focusing on the audience. The first audience was the disciples of Jesus (Luke 24:49, Acts 1:4, Acts 2:33); the second audience was unconverted bystanders (Acts 2:38-39). This distinction is important for Menzies because it sustains his specific view on Lukan Pneumatology.

To summarize, according to Menzies the story here is about Jesus commissioning his disciples, whereby the promise of the Father is the same as the Holy Spirit. The outpouring of this Spirit was prophesied by Joel and is an enabler to fulfill the mission as was already stated by Isaiah (in 49:6). The exact interpretation of the Spirit (prophecy or salvation) then depends on the audience addressed: if the audience is unconverted, the Spirit of salvation is meant. If the audience already is converted, the Spirit of prophecy is meant. One can question whether this line of reasoning is solid exegesis. Can one make such a sharp distinction in the working of the Spirit from the Joel prophecy? Does such a sharp distinction do justice to the text under scrutiny (first the Joel text and secondly Acts 2)? Or must we conclude that this is a somewhat arbitrary distinction to corroborate Menzies' more limited view of the Spirit in Luke-Acts?

4.7.3 Preliminary deductions and possible implications
Apparently it is possible for Menzies to interpret the same promise/Spirit in a different manner, dependent on the addressed audience. It is here that we do see some interpretive moves: in box 7 of his model Eco describes the so called "forecasts" and "inferential walks". In interpreting the promise/Spirit, Menzies forecasts that it concerns the Spirit of prophecy. That is: the Spirit that empowers for mission. This is confirmed by the story which is about Jesus commissioning his disciples. However, at the end of Peter's Pentecost speech in Acts 2 this interpretation is falsified, so it urges Menzies to interpret differently. Because of Luke's use of the Joel text, Menzies "makes a trip outside the Lukan text" only to return to the Lukan text with the Joel information. This is what Eco calls "inferential

walks". Other scholars such as Dunn, Bruce and Carson "wander" out of the Lukan narrative as well, only to use other Old Testament texts.[57]

The model of Eco shows that the more well-read a reader is, the greater the chance to bring extra weight to the text under scrutiny. As the encyclopedic competence of the reader increases, the more he has to be alert to the limits of interpretation which are in the text itself.

4.8 Pentecost: the outpouring of the Spirit (Acts 2)

4.8.1 The actualized text

Obviously the text of Acts 2 is of profound importance for a Lukan Pneumatology. Menzies treats the description of the Pentecost account (2:1-13) in just a few pages, only to give more attention to the Joel text in Acts 2:17-21. Within this episode he discusses the alterations between the Lukan text in Acts 2:17-21 and the LXX text of Joel 3:1-5a. Respectively the following alterations are discussed by Menzies:[58]

1. In verse 17 the alteration of μετὰ ταῦτα to ἐν ταῖς ἐσχάταις ἡμέραις;
2. In verse 17 the insertion of λέγει ὁ θεός;
3. A stylistic modification in verse 17 is the inversion of the two καὶ οἱ sentences: in Acts the young men (νεανίσκοι) are placed before the old men (πρεσβύτεροι);
4. In verse 18 γε and μου (2x) are inserted;
5. In verse 18 καὶ προφητεύσουσιν is inserted;
6. In verse 19 the words ἄνω, σημεῖα and κάτω are inserted. The use of σημεῖα with τέρατα is typical for Luke.[59]

4.8.2 The substantial properties of the text

In interpreting these alterations and thereby determining the story of the text, Menzies first elaborates on the theological significance of the alterations, and subsequently discusses the question whether the Pentecost event has to be interpreted as a new Sinai.

Theological significance. The prominent theological conclusions Menzies draws are with respect to the alterations mentioned above. He first dismisses the view that according to Luke the disciples enter 'the last days' with Pentecost. Menzies interprets the infancy narratives as the beginning of the eschaton. He states that the pouring out of the Spirit is

---

57 Menzies, *Development*, 204n.2.
58 Menzies, *Development*, 213-223; *Empowered for Witness*, 178-189.
59 Menzies, *Development*, 221n.5.

an event of the end times instead of the ushering in of a new age.⁶⁰ Menzies subscribes this first alteration in verse 17 to the hand of Luke and interprets it as a stylistic variant to the ἐν ταῖς ἡμέραις ἐκείναις in verse 18.⁶¹ The λέγει ὁ θεός is as well attributed to Lukan redaction and Menzies links this with the ἐπαγγελία τοῦ πατρός in Luke 24:49 and Acts 1:4. However, one can ask himself the question why Luke uses θεός instead of πατρός?⁶² The use of the latter would have strengthened the parallel. Anyway, the theological and interpretive significance here is that Luke accentuates that the Spirit comes from God.

The insertions in verse 18 are interesting and here the interpretive responsibility of the reader comes to the surface. Menzies follows the consensus regarding the double μου in the Lukan text. In the Joel text literal slaves are in view, as being another segment of Jewish society who will receive the Spirit. In the Lukan text of Acts "the terms become religious metaphors which include and give further definition to the groups previously mentioned."⁶³ In his elaboration on this, Menzies then makes a significant interpretive remark. He states that the alteration from slaves to servants means that the gift of the Spirit is only for those who already "*are members of the eschatological community of salvation*."⁶⁴ This means that membership of the eschatological community is a presupposition for receiving the Spirit and not dependent on receiving the Spirit (contra James Dunn, who defends the latter view).⁶⁵ The next significant interpretive move has to do with an issue of translation in verse 18:

καί γε ἐπὶ τοὺς δούλους μου καὶ ἐπὶ τὰς δούλας μου ἐν ταῖς ἡμέραις ἐκείναις ἐκχεῶ ἀπὸ τοῦ πνεύματός μου, καὶ προφητεύσουσιν.

The γε at the beginning of verse 18 is translated by Menzies as "indeed" thereby confirming that *servants* parallel the previously mentioned *people*. However, the γε can also be translated as "even", thereby signaling the exceptional status of servants.⁶⁶

---

60 Menzies, *Development*, 216. So also Turner, *Power from on High*, 352 and Salter, *Power of Pentecost*, 4.
61 Menzies, *Development*, 217; *Empowered for Witness*, 181.
62 MSS A, ℵ, B have ὁ θεός, D and E have κύριος. See Salter, *Power of Pentecost*, 4n.11.
63 Menzies, *Development*, 218.
64 Menzies, *Development*, 219 (emphasis is mine).
65 Menzies, *Development*, 219; Dunn, *Baptism in the Holy Spirit*, 22.
66 Menzies, *Development*, 219-220; *Empowered for Witness*, 183. Menzies argues here

The last two insertions are briefly treated by Menzies where προφητεύσουσιν is designated as a parallel with verse 17 and as such emphasizes that the Spirit produces prophetic inspiration. The inserted words in verse 19 refer to a series of divine acts which are universal in nature (above…below).[67]

According to Menzies the narrative structure of this text (box 6 in Eco's model) shows Luke's hermeneutical key to understanding the Pentecost event. The Joel text serves to show that Luke understands the Spirit as the Spirit of prophecy, which produces inspired speech and also grants insight through visions and dreams.[68] This Spirit is universally available to people *who already belong to the community of God*, and thus Luke sees the church as a community of prophets. The Pentecost event is not the beginning of the end of times; however it certainly is one of the signs of the last days.

A new Sinai. A popular interpretation of the outpouring of the Spirit at Pentecost is to read and interpret it against the background of the giving of the law at Mount Sinai. Before rejecting this interpretation, Menzies first lists the following three important arguments in favor of this interpretation:[69]

1. When Luke wrote Acts, the feast of Pentecost was a feast of the remembrance of the giving of the law on Sinai;
2. There are literary allusions in the Pentecost account which refer to the Sinai tradition (most prominent the sound of wind and the image of fire);
3. The interpretation that Acts 2:33-34a is based on Psalm 67:19 (LXX) and as such parallels Moses ascending Sinai and giving the law, with Jesus ascending into heaven and giving the Spirit.

As mentioned above, Menzies disagrees with this interpretation and explains that Pentecost was a festival of harvest and only in later times, long after the destruction of the temple, Rabbis in the second and third century associated Pentecost with the giving of the law at Sinai.[70] He does admit that

---

with T. Holtz, *Untersuchungen über die alttestamentlichen Zitate bei Lukas* (TU 104; Berlin, Akademie, 1968),10-11, who opts for the translation "even". That "even" is the primary choice of interpretation is confirmed by BDAG, 190. See also Bock, *Acts*, 114 and Salter, *Power of Pentecost*, 10.

67 Menzies, *Development*, 221-223.
68 Menzies, *Development*, 224.
69 Menzies, *Development*, 229-231; *Empowered for Witness*, 189-190.
70 Menzies, *Development*, 231-235; *Empowered for Witness*, 190-191.

in some sectarian circles Pentecost was regarded as a covenant renewal, but argues that generally speaking Pentecost was celebrated as a harvest festival.[71] With regard to the words and images used by Luke (wind, fire, heaven, language, word, voice) Menzies explains that these are not solely dependent on the Sinai account. These terms are common terms to describe a theophany and are not limited to the giving of the law.[72] In his consideration of the relevance of Psalm 67:19 (LXX) Menzies shows that all the evidence points to a rather shallow connection between Psalm 67:19 and Acts 2:33. The repetition of catchwords is not limited to Psalm 67:19, but these are all frequently used in Luke-Acts. Besides this the explicit key term used in Psalm 67:19, δόματα, is missing in the text of Acts.

After examination of these arguments Menzies concludes that Luke did not present Pentecost as a "new Sinai". Luke viewed the gift of the Spirit as the source of prophetic inspiration, not as some sort of inner law which would lead to a renewal of the recipient's ethical life.[73]

4.8.3 Preliminary deductions and possible implications
This third part of Eco's model of the cooperative reader (boxes 5, 7 and 10) lead us into the possible implications and deductions which the reader makes. In Robert Menzies' discussion of Acts 2, the chapter on Pentecost, he does not make straightforward value judgments or implications for the reader today. He however does provide some interpretations which will prove to be fundamental to his overall conclusions regarding Lukan Pneumatology. Whereas the Joel prophecy states that the outpouring of the Spirit is universal in scope, Menzies limits this to people who already are a member of the community of God. He does not elaborate on a certain sequence of conversion, reception of the Spirit or so, but he paves the way for the doctrine of a second subsequent filling with the Spirit. This is confirmed by the debatable translation of γε in verse 18. He further firmly denies that this Spirit of prophecy has anything to do with cleansing or Ez. 36 as a background.[74] However, in his treatment of the promise of John the Baptist in Luke 3:16-17, he proposes an interpretation which holds a collective cleansing of the people of God. Unfortunately he

---

71 Contra Turner who gives more weight to the book of Jubilees then Menzies does. Turner does not argue that it was a "hard fact" that Pentecost was associated with the giving of the law, but he states that "it was very much in the air in the period covered by Acts", Turner, *Power from on High*, 280-282.
72 Menzies, *Development*, 236-239.
73 Menzies, *Development*, 244.
74 Menzies, *Development*, 225-226.

does not take this into account while discussing the Acts 2 episode. In addition Menzies is determined to show that Pentecost does not signify a new Sinai. There might be some allusions to Sinai, but not in the sense that the outpouring of the Spirit is some sort of new internal law which will transform a person's ethical life.

Excursus: Acts 2:38[75]
So far Menzies has reached his prominent conclusion about the Spirit in Luke-Acts. In Menzies' view Luke shows that the Spirit is the source of prophetic power and enables God's servants for mission. In Chapter 11 of *The Development of Early Christian Pneumatology*, Menzies respectively treats other Spirit texts from the Book of Acts, which I will discuss below. However, of great importance is his discussion of Acts 2:38 which is used by other scholars to show that Luke sees the Spirit as well as the Spirit of salvation (see above in the *Forschungsbericht*). With regard to Acts 2:38 Menzies argues that the promised gift of the Spirit refers to the promise from the Joel prophecy and as such is the Spirit of prophetic enabling. Luke 24:49, Acts 1:4 and 2:33 are used to accentuate this interpretation. According to Menzies the close connection with water baptism in 2:38 does not prove that soteriological or initiation functions are as well part of the gift of the Spirit. It might be that for Luke water baptism and reception of the Spirit are normally closely knit together, but Luke does not develop this elsewhere. Menzies then interprets 2:38 as that the promise of the Spirit is only for those who are already converted and baptized. As such "repentance and water baptism are the normal prerequisites for reception of the Spirit".[76] This interpretation of Acts 2:38 confirm Menzies in his earlier conclusion that the Spirit in Luke-Acts is only for those who already are converted. Max Turner, on the other hand, also argues that the Spirit in Acts is the prophetic Spirit from the Joel prophecy. However, he asks himself the question whether this interpretation means that the Book of Acts implies that other functions of the Spirit (such as for example soteriological functions) are not in view.[77]

So in my focus on the role of the reader we here have a typical example of the reader's presuppositions or foreknowledge. Or to put it in Eco's

---

75 Menzies, *Development*, 246-248. Menzies' primary opponents are James Dunn and Jacob Kremer.
76 Menzies, *Development*, 247. However, that this opposes Luke's narrative in Acts 9:17-18 and 10:47 is not mentioned by Menzies.
77 Turner, *Power from on High*, 348.

words: the encyclopedic competence of the reader. In regard to the Pauline corpus scholars agree on the soteriological functions of the Spirit. The pertinent question, however, is whether this was also in Luke's mind (so Turner) or whether it was totally absent (so Menzies).

4.9 The Samaritans (Acts 8)
4.9.1 The actualized text
In approximately twelve pages (248-260) in his *Development of Early Christian Pneumatology*, Menzies discusses the episode of Acts 8. In this episode we read about the Samaritans coming to faith and their baptism afterwards (verse 12). Hearing this news, the Jerusalem church sends Peter and John as delegates and they pray for the Samaritans to receive the Holy Spirit. The reception of the Spirit is accompanied with the laying on of hands. Menzies does not discuss the text of this episode. He treats the text as it is in front of him and then takes James Dunn as his primary sparring partner to evaluate and interpret the story of the Samaritan conversion and subsequently their reception of the Holy Spirit. Dunn argues that the Samaritans were not yet Christian: their faith was somehow defective, that is why the apostles had to come.[78] Menzies, on the other hand, reads the story with different eyes and comes up with a different interpretation.

4.9.2 The substantial properties of the text
According to Menzies the story of the Samaritans in Acts 8 is an excellent example to show that for Luke the reception of the Spirit is not necessarily tied to conversion-initiation. Due to Luke's redactional capacity it is untenable that this story is a conflation of different sources. Menzies continues that if Luke did not edit this text, than it must have implications for his pneumatology. The various scholarly attempts to "ease the problem" are all firmly put aside by Menzies. The unique exception of Acts 8 in salvation-history is dismissed because it is unlikely in Menzies' eyes and the text does not support it.[79] The argument that the Samaritans were not without the Spirit but without spiritual gifts (so Beasley-Murray) is rejected by Menzies, based on vs.16.[80] James Dunn's argumentation that the Samaritans were not really Christians before the reception of the

---

78 Dunn, *Baptism in the Holy Spirit*, 63-68.
79 Menzies, *Development*, 250-251.
80 Menzies, *Development*, 252. For the full argument of Beasley-Murray, see: G.R. Beasley-Murray, *Baptism in the New Testament* (Grand Rapids, MI: Eerdmans, 1962), 118-120.

Spirit is rejected by Menzies as well.[81] In answer to the different proposed solutions Menzies is crystal clear: "Acts 8:4-25 poses an insoluble problem for those who maintain that Luke establishes a necessary link between baptism/Christian initiation and the gift of the Spirit."[82]

On the other hand, Menzies argues, this sequence in Acts 8 perfectly fits the story of the reception of the Spirit in Luke-Acts. As already was the case in Acts 2, Luke does believe that the gift of the Spirit is a supplementary gift given to those who already are Christians. That is: those people who already are incorporated in the community of believers. In his description of Acts 8 it is clear that Luke compares (or even parallels) this gift of the Spirit with the reception in Acts 2 and as such designates that this supplementary gift of the Spirit is an empowerment for mission. That is essentially what the story in Acts 8 is about.

4.9.3 Preliminary deductions and possible implications

Once the story of the text (narrative structure, Eco's box 6) is determined, Menzies elaborates and assumes that also in Acts 8 the gift of the Spirit was accompanied with prophecy and speaking in tongues.[83] Here we have an excellent example of what Eco calls "inferential walks". Based on his foreknowledge (Eco's terminology is: encyclopedic competence) of Acts 2, Menzies assumes prophecy and tongues in Acts 8, although the text does not explicitly state this. Eco explains this as for instance in the narrative "x-does-so-and-so" and the result of this is "y", and then the reader will conclude "if-x-takes-action-then-the-result-is-y."[84] Translated to the situation in Acts 8 Menzies assumes that *if people receive the Spirit then they prophesy and speak in tongues as a consequence.*[85] The contrast then is striking when it comes to the laying on of hands. Here Menzies does not make the assumption that the laying on of hands was part of the reception of the Spirit. He interprets this instance in Acts 8 as a confirmation that the reception of the Spirit is an empowerment for mission and substantiates this conclusion with reference to Acts 6:6, 9:17 and 13:3. He however explicitly states that the gift of the Spirit is often granted apart from the rite. My own cautious conclusion in this instance is that the role of the reader is a bit

---

81 Menzies, *Development*, 252-256.
82 Menzies, *Development*, 257.
83 Menzies, *Development*, 258. He refers to some eight other scholars who make this assumption as well.
84 Eco, *Lector in fabula*, 155.
85 Emphasis is mine to accentuate the specific role of the reader in this instance.

elusive when it is not constrained by the limits of the text. The text does not mention tongues and/or prophecy, so there is a limit to our interpretation: we simply do not know. However, because of Menzies' encyclopedic competence, he *assumes* that the Samaritans spoke in tongues and prophesied. This is convenient because it fits the classical Pentecostal view on the reception of the Spirit. On the other hand however, when it comes to the laying on of hands Menzies separates it from the reception of the Spirit so that it fits his view on ordination and empowerment for mission. Because of this interpretive move by Menzies, it is all the more striking that he does not elaborate on this commissioning or ordaining. In Acts 8 we read about apostles (Peter and John) who do so, only one chapter later in Acts 9 it is a disciple, Ananias. What about apostolic succession? Or certain conditions before someone can be ordained and by whom? Unfortunately these (present day) questions are left aside by Menzies. His line of reasoning is dependent on the separation between the reception of the Spirit and the laying on of hands. The text however does not detach the laying on of hands and the reception of the Spirit, and as such the text provides limits to what seems to be a classical confirmationist point of view. This example shows the importance of limits provided by the text itself and the varying degrees in which the reader takes these limits into account.

4.10 The Damascus event (Acts 9)
4.10.1 The actualized text
Following the narrative of Acts and arriving at the next πνεῦμα cluster, Menzies only spends three and a half pages (260-263) of his *Development of Early Christian Pneumatology* to discuss the Damascus event from Acts 9. The leading question Menzies asks himself is whether the Damascus event is about Paul receiving the Spirit at his conversion or receiving the Spirit as a commissioning. Menzies points to the importance of this event for Luke, because the description of the event in Acts 9 recurs in Acts 22 and 26. He dismisses the probability of three different underlying sources for these three stories. The variations in these three accounts are due to Luke's literary style and redactional activity. So the three accounts all "supplement and complement one another."[86]

4.10.2 The substantial properties of the text
Having reached the conclusion mentioned above, Menzies continues to focus on Paul's reception of the Spirit. In his discussion of this episode,

---
86 Menzies, *Development*, 261.

Menzies connects it to Acts 22:12-16 and Acts 26:12-18 and observes that Paul's reception of the Spirit is closely linked to Ananias. Here we see that intertextuality plays an important role in determining the plot of the story. Because of the interconnectedness of those three passages in Acts, Menzies does not hesitate to call the story of Acts 9 the "Ananias episode."[87] So in his interpretation of the Damascus event, while comparing with the other two repetitions of the story, Menzies concludes that Acts 9 is principally an account of the commissioning of Paul as a missionary. The "abundant evidence" for this interpretation comes from the way the story is modeled: after commissioning stories from the Old Testament and other Ancient Near Eastern Texts.[88] In 9:17 Paul receives the Spirit and already in 9:20 he is preaching the Gospel, which is used by Menzies to sustain his interpretation. According to Menzies, Luke shows that the reception of the Spirit is a prerequisite for preaching, this, in his opinion, is in correspondence with Acts 2 and Acts 8. That is why he can conclude that for Luke the Spirit is an empowerment for mission.

4.10.3 Preliminary deductions and possible implications
In his progression through the Book of Acts, it seems that Menzies is swifter in drawing conclusions. Contrary to the model of the cooperative reader in which Eco suggests that a reader and interpreter puts discrepancies between brackets (box 5), Menzies tries to find solutions based upon his previous conclusions. His treatment of the episode of the Damascus event shows this. One of the foremost questions should be what this story is about. As Eco shows in his model in boxes 4 and 6, the reader determines the possible meaning(s) of the text, only to verify or falsify this meaning in a closer scrutiny of the text. Determining the narrative structure and the topic of the text are of vital importance before interpreting the text. According to Menzies the text is about Ananias, specifically the role of Ananias in commissioning Paul for his mission. However, one can argue that the Damascus event is about Saul. Taking into account the whole structure of the Book of Acts it becomes clear that the person of Saul is introduced in Acts 7:58, only to make a greater and more significant entry in Acts 9. And subsequently dominates the second half of the Book of Acts. The pertinent question of when the conversion of Saul took place is conveniently left aside by Menzies. So in this episode

---

87 Menzies, *Development*, 262.
88 Menzies, *Development*, 262. However, in the corresponding footnote Menzies contradicts himself by referring to a thesis which has been severely criticized (Menzies' words).

it seems that the text leaves much more space for other interpretations than Menzies addresses.

4.11 The Cornelius' household (Acts 10)
4.11.1 The actualized text
In his treatment of the conversion of the Cornelius household (pages 264-267 of *Development of Early Christian Pneumatology*) Menzies does not elaborate on the text proper. Just as above in his treatment of the Damascus event, he takes the summaries of Acts 10 into account and consequently discusses Acts 10 together with the summaries in 11:15-17 and 15:8-10.

As a point of general consensus among scholars Menzies mentions the significance of this episode as a validation for the Gentile mission. This is the only point of consensus. In regard to a Lukan view of the Spirit there is a variety of conflicting interpretations. Proponents of a soteriological view of the Spirit use this episode as a proof text. Menzies however, claims that "this interpretation is wide of the mark" and that the reception of the Holy Spirit is a "sign of salvation, but not the means".[89] In determining the story of the text Menzies focuses foremost on the summaries of this episode and discusses the verses in Acts 11:15-17 and 15:8-10. This is a rather odd way of treating the Cornelius episode. Instead of a close reading of the narrative in Acts 10, Menzies chooses to take some sort of "short cut" by focusing on the summaries of this episode.

4.11.2 The substantial properties of the text
Menzies admits that in this episode of the Cornelius' household conversion is accompanied with the reception of the Spirit, in contrast to the Samaritan episode in Acts 8. He however holds strictly to his previously established view of Lukan pneumatology and states that the Spirit-baptism of the Cornelius household is a sign of God's acceptance of these Gentiles. God accepted them as his servants and as such He granted them the Spirit which resulted in inspired speech. It seems that a previously established grid now is used to interpret Acts 10. This appears to be a rather forced interpretive move, especially when Menzies questions the exegesis of those who hold to a more soteriological view of the Spirit in Luke-Acts. He does so by focusing on the alleged parallelisms in Acts 11:17a-18b and 15:8-9:

---

[89] Menzies, *Development*, 264; *Empowered for Witness*, 215. Menzies quotes Jacob Kremer as his opponent in this interpretation, who argues that the reception of the Holy Spirit is sign (Zeichen) *and* means (Mittel) of salvation.

Acts 11:17-18
:17 So if God gave them the same gift he gave us who believed in the Lord Jesus Christ, who was I to think that I could stand in God's way?";
:18 When they heard this, they had no further objections and praised God, saying, "So then, even to Gentiles God has granted repentance that leads to life (μετάνοια εἰς ζωὴν)."[90]

Especially James Dunn argues that the μετάνοια εἰς ζωὴν has to be equated with the reception of the Spirit.[91] Menzies, on the contrary, argues that μετάνοια is a prerequisite for the reception of the Spirit, which he substantiates by pointing to Acts 2:38 and 5:31-32.[92] To simplify this: it is Jesus who saves, forgives sins and brings people to conversion, which makes them *servants* of God. Being a servant of God, one is eligible for receiving the Holy Spirit.

Acts 15:8-9
:8 God, who knows the heart, showed that he accepted them by giving the Holy Spirit to them, just as he did to us;
:9 He did not discriminate between us and them, for he purified their hearts by faith.[93]

In addition to Acts 11 mentioned above, Dunn argues that both verses from Acts 15 are synonymous: "Peter is obviously saying the same thing in two ways."[94] So the giving of the Holy Spirit is equated with the cleansing or purifying of the hearts. Menzies however argues the opposite way: because of the purification of hearts (premise) God granted them the Holy Spirit (deduction). And exactly this way of reasoning fits perfectly in Menzies' earlier established Lukan pneumatology. Here we see that because of the encyclopedic competence of the reader the interpretations vary, or are even opposite of each other.

Although Menzies admits that in this story of Cornelius conversion and the reception of the Spirit are closely connected, he fails to elaborate on this connection. Several questions come to mind: could there be a connection with Acts 2:38? And if so, in what way should we interpret

---

90 Both quotations are from the New International Version.
91 Dunn, *Baptism in the Holy Spirit*, 81.
92 Menzies, *Development*, 266.
93 Both quotations are from the New International Version.
94 Dunn, *Baptism in the Holy Spirit*, 81.

this close connection between conversion and reception of the Spirit? If Luke wanted to stress that the reception of the Spirit is an empowerment for mission, why then is there not the slightest sign of Cornelius engaging in missions? The usage of Menzies' previously established pneumatological grid on this passage leaves us with more questions than answers. This shows the defining role of the reader in determining the story and its interpretive consequences for an overall view of a Lukan pneumatology.

4.11.3 Preliminary deductions and possible implications
Based notably on the parallel with the outpouring of the Spirit at Pentecost in Acts 2 (see Luke's references in 10:47, 11:15-17, 15:8), Menzies deduces that the Gentiles received the same gift: the Spirit of prophecy. This Spirit is a sign of God's acceptance and means that the Gentiles will participate in the mission of the church. Menzies assumes that the Cornelius household, as well as the Samaritans from Acts 8 and the church in Antioch (Acts 13), from now on participate in the mission as well. This underlines his interpretation of the Spirit in Luke as being an empowerment for mission. Although not explicitly stated in his *Development of Early Christian Pneumatology*, elsewhere Menzies argues that this baptism in the Spirit is normative for Christians today, evidenced by speaking in tongues.[95] This shows that, in Menzies' interpretation, the world of the text resembles the world today and as such experiencing the outpouring of the Spirit as Luke describes it, can be (or should be?) experienced in the church today. In short: Menzies sees Jesus as *exemplar*, followed by the apostles and subsequently followed by first century as well as 21st century Christian believers.

4.12 The Ephesian disciples (Acts 19)
4.12.1 The actualized text
According to Menzies the final verses of chapter 18 (Acts 18:24-28) belong to the story of the Ephesian disciples. It is in these verses that Luke describes the origin of the Ephesian church and starts telling his audience about Apollos. Because of the unusual description of Apollos as an evangelist, it matches the description of the Ephesian disciples in 19:1-7.[96] Before embarking on his own interpretation of the story of the text, Menzies

---

95 William W. Menzies, Robert P. Menzies, *Spirit and Power. Foundations of Pentecostal Experience* (Grand Rapids, MI: Zondervan, 2000).
96 Menzies, *Development*, 268; *Empowered for Witness*, 218.

briefly discusses the contributions of Ernst Käsemann[97] and Eduard Schweizer.[98] He opposes the thesis of Käsemann that Luke modified his sources to picture an ideal and unified church. The transformation of Apollos and the Ephesian disciples to immature Christians then serve "to smooth the rivalry between the Baptist community and the church."[99] The thesis of Schweizer that Luke misinterpreted the traditional source and his objective to emphasize the temporal continuity from Judaism to Christianity is as well opposed by Menzies.[100]

4.12.2 The substantial properties of the text
According to Menzies Luke shaped the original accounts of this story, however this does not necessarily mean that Luke has been unfaithful to the history and tradition of the accounts. Menzies assumes that there were groups of former disciples of John the Baptist, who converted to Christianity. Apollos was probably one of them and Menzies views the Ephesian disciples in Acts 19 to be converts of Apollos.[101] Somehow along the way there had been a misunderstanding because they were not baptized in the name of Jesus. It then is Paul who explains this to the Ephesian disciples, baptizes them and after the laying on of hands they receive the Holy Spirit. From this reconstruction of the story Menzies deduces that:

1.) The Ephesian disciples (as well as Apollos) were already Christians, that is: disciples of Jesus;
2.) Paul commissions them by his laying on of hands, so that they become his fellow-workers in the mission of the church.[102]

---

97 Ernst Käsemann, "The Disciples of John the Baptist in Ephesus" in: E. Käsemann, *Essays on New Testament Themes* (SBT 41; London: SCM, 1964), 136-148.
98 Eduard Schweizer, "Die Bekehrung des Apollos, Apg 18,24-26" in: E. Schweizer, *Beiträge zur Theologie des Neuen Testaments: Neutestamentliche Aufsätze (1955-1970)* (Zürich: Zwingli Verlag, 1970), 71-79.
99 Menzies, *Development*, 268; *Empowered for Witness*, 219.
100 Menzies, *Development*, 269.
101 Menzies, *Development*, 272
102 Menzies, *Development*, 271; *Empowered for Witness*, 220-221.

Despite attempts of Klaus Haacker,[103] James Dunn[104] and J.K. Parrat,[105] Menzies' interlocutors, Menzies holds to the conclusions mentioned above. It seems that the most important fact for his thesis is whether the Ephesian disciples already were Christians or not. Based on the use of the words μαθητάς in verse 1 and πιστεύσαντες in verse 2 Menzies reads the story as the Ephesians being disciples of Jesus, who were not taught about the Holy Spirit. This reading substantiates his previous established view of Lukan pneumatology: the gift of the Spirit is not a necessary element in conversion.[106]

4.12.3 Preliminary deductions and possible implications
Once again Menzies does not yet make the step to apply his research to the actual world and/or the church today. His way of treating the data from Acts 19 substantiates his already established Lukan view of the Spirit and corresponds with the previous mentioned πνεῦμα clusters in Acts 2, 8, 9 and 10.

As mentioned above, the key for his argumentation is found in 19:1-2. However, it seems that the other three readers (Haacker, Dunn and Parrat) have a strong case as well. Haacker argues that from Luke's point of view it could not be possible to be a disciple without having received the Spirit;[107] Dunn reads the question by Paul in verse 2 as a "question of suspicion": how can it be that you are disciples but have not heard of the Spirit?;[108] and Parrat reads Acts 19:4 as Paul's instruction to the Ephesians to believe in Jesus.[109] So this poses us a real problem. If there are altogether limits of interpretation *within* the text itself, then these are treated substantially different by all four readers. I hope to elaborate on this issue in the concluding chapter of this dissertation.

For now, we can establish what Menzies' role is. Approaching the end of the πνεῦμα clusters in the Book of Acts, Menzies does not gather more information or puts possible solutions "between brackets" as Eco calls it. He assesses the text and proposes a possible solution for this episode on the Ephesian disciples. A solution that fits within his already established

---

103 K. Haacker, "Einiger Fälle von 'erlebter Rede' im Neuen Testament, *NovT* 12 (1970), pp.70-77.
104 Dunn, *Baptism in the Holy Spirit*, 83-89.
105 J.K. Parratt, "The Rebaptism of the Ephesian Disciples", *ExpTim* 79 (1968), pp.182-183.
106 Menzies, *Development*, 275; *Empowered for Witness*, 224.
107 Menzies, *Development*, 273; *Empowered for Witness*, 222.
108 Menzies, *Development*, 273-274; *Empowered for Witness*, 222-223.
109 Menzies, *Development*, 274-275; *Empowered for Witness*, 223-224.

Lukan Pneumatological framework. In Menzies' interpretation Luke separates the reception of the Spirit from conversion. Luke describes the Ephesians as disciples and believers, they were granted forgiveness. Later they were endowed with the prophetic Spirit and enabled (laying on of hands) to partake in the mission of Paul. Menzies elaborates and states that these Ephesian disciples stayed close with Paul (Acts 19:9, 30, 20:1) and assumes they were probably part of the eldership in the Ephesian church (Acts 20:17, 28).[110] The phrase from Acts 20:28 "(…) the flock of which the Holy Spirit has made you overseers" is tied to Acts 19:6, the moment they received the Holy Spirit. Menzies concludes this episode by stating: "In each instance the Spirit comes upon the individual or group as a prophetic endowment enabling the recipient(s) to participate effectively in the mission of which has been entrusted to the prophetic people of God."[111]

4.13 Conclusion
4.13.1 The Role of the Reader: Robert P. Menzies
Robert Menzies is a keen scholar with a Pentecostal heart. In several of his writings one will discover an above average interest in the Gospel of Luke and the Book of Acts, wholly consistent with the various Pentecostal communities. His interest in the practice of the church and missions, probably stem from his own experience as a missionary.[112] In his dissertation he is precise in his methodology and therewith his scholarly work. Central to this study is the question whether "Luke follows Paul in attributing soteriological significance to the gift of the Spirit?"[113] Menzies uses redaction and source criticism as methodology, which influences his way of reading the narrative of Luke-Acts. For the Gospel of Luke this is rather easily done because of the comparison with the Gospels of Mark and Matthew. The so called "Lukan Sondergut" provides a good picture of Luke's view on the Spirit. However, when it concerns the Book of Acts, this methodology is more difficult to apply. Menzies' tendency in his exegesis of the relevant episodes in Acts is to rely heavy on his previously established position based on the Gospel of Luke. If, in a certain episode in Luke-

---

110 Menzies, *Development*, 276-277; *Empowered for Witness*, 225.
111 Menzies, *Development*, 277; *Empowered for Witness*, 225.
112 See for instance Robert P. Menzies, "The Persecuted Prophets: A Mirror Image of Luke's Spirit-Inspired Church", in: I.H. Marshall, Volker Rabens and Cornelis Bennema (eds.), *The Spirit and Christ in the New Testament & Christian Theology* (Grand Rapids, MI: Eerdmans, 2012), 52-70.
113 Menzies, *Development*, 18; *Empowered for Witness*, 17.

Acts, the opinions vary whether a source was traditional or distinctively Lukan, Menzies opts for the latter.[114] Assessing Menzies' work through the model of Umberto Eco, we can conclude the following:

1. When it comes to the text proper, as Eco describes in boxes 1-3, Menzies does give responsible attention to the text itself and possible textual variations;
2. Because of his preparatory work on the Spirit in Early Judaism, the encyclopedic competence of Menzies is enormous. Codes and subcodes in the narrative of Luke-Acts are read and interpreted through "Early Judaism glasses";
3. When it comes to determine the framework of the text (Eco: narrative structures) Menzies gives notably more time to the Gospel than to the Book of Acts;
4. Generally speaking it seems that Menzies' treatment of the Book of Acts is "one large inferential walk": he takes the interpretation of the Gospel (his encyclopedic competence) with him while interpreting the Book of Acts. This can be and should be profitable, however it can as well be a burden. Menzies does not reckon with this last aspect of his encyclopedic competence in his interpretation of the relevant passages in the Book of Acts;
5. Once and a while Menzies seems to jump to boxes 5, 7 and 8 to predict a certain outcome of his study or to show relevance for the actual world. Most of the applications and value judgments however are kept for the third part of his dissertation.

Based on Eco's model we can conclude that Menzies is a cooperative reader. It seems however that this cooperation is more on Menzies' terms, than on the terms provided by the narrative of Luke-Acts. For instance the Book of Acts is a narrative, so it seems a missed opportunity not to determine the narrative structures of the different episodes in Acts. Menzies, on the contrary, reads and interprets Acts with the Gospel in mind, instead of treating the narrative of Acts on its own merits. It appears to be that Menzies' encyclopedic competence troubles his cooperation with the text of Acts. That is: his previously established view of the Spirit in Early Judaism and his conclusions with regard to the Spirit from the Gospel (these form Menzies' encyclopedic competence) all color his interpretation of the πνεῦμα clusters in the Book of Acts. This leads me to the conclusion that Menzies sometimes cooperates with the text on his own predetermined terms.

---

114 See above in §§4.2.1, 4.5.2 and 4.6.2.

4.13.2 Lukan Pneumatology according to Robert P. Menzies
Summarizing the work of Menzies we can conclude that as an overall theme Menzies sees the Spirit in Luke-Acts as the Spirit of Prophecy. According to Menzies this means that from Luke's point of view the Spirit is the source for prophetic inspiration through which the people of God are empowered for effective service (mission). After determining an Early Jewish view of the Spirit, Menzies takes this "foreknowledge" to the text of Luke-Acts. The narrative of Luke-Acts is read through the mold of "the prophetic Spirit" and subsequently applied to Christian believers and the church today. Unfortunately only the last two chapters of *Empowered for Witness* are designated to current day questions. In these last two chapters Menzies argues that a first step is to listen to the New Testament writers (biblical theology), in this case Luke. A subsequent step is to ask our contemporary questions (systematic theology), such as the question if baptism in the Spirit is evidenced by speaking in tongues.[115] Due to this distinction between biblical theology and systematic theology Menzies shows that tongues should accompany the reception of the Spirit. His conclusion is: "The normative character of evidential tongues thus emerges, not from Luke's primary intent, but rather as an implication from Luke's prophetic pneumatology and Paul's complementary perspective."[116]

Unfortunately Menzies fails to describe what the exact relation is between receiving the Spirit as an empowerment for missions and the speaking in tongues. How does speaking in tongues empower the Christian believer for mission? So despite the fact that Menzies thoroughly treats the πνεῦμα clusters in Luke-Acts, there still remain some questions. Summarizing Menzies' view concerning Lukan Pneumatology we can conclude as follows:[117]

1. The gift of the Spirit is distinct from conversion;
2. Luke never attributes soteriological functions to the Spirit;[118]

---

115 Menzies, *Empowered for Witness*, 244-248.
116 Menzies, *Empowered for Witness*, 252.
117 These conclusions are primarily based on the explicit elaboration on the issues of subsequence and evidential tongues by Menzies in chapters 13 and 14 of *Empowered for Witness*. It is striking that in these chapters Menzies frequently uses Gordon Fee as his primary sparring partner, while Fee is only mentioned once in parts I and II of his dissertation.
118 These are Menzies' exact choice of words in *Empowered for Witness*, 237; In his dissertation he concludes: "The soteriological dimension is entirely absent from the pneumatology of Luke", *Development*, 316.

3. Therefore, Luke does not follow Paul in attributing soteriological significance to the gift of the Spirit;
4. The Spirit in Luke-Acts is the source of power for effective witness, not cleansing and/or justification;
5. The initial physical evidence of the reception of the Spirit (or in Pentecostal terminology "Baptism in the Spirit) is speaking in tongues.[119]

These conclusions regarding Lukan Pneumatology can be designated as "classical Pentecostal". However some questions remain unanswered. Questions concerning the topics Menzies does not address. For instance, treating Jesus as *exemplar* leaves aside the question of Jesus' uniqueness. In what way was Jesus unique compared to the apostles and later Christian believers? And more relevant to the current subject: in what way describes Luke Jesus as *exemplar* or as unique in his ministry? And as I already mentioned above: what is the exact relation between speaking in tongues and the empowerment for mission? Contemporary church related issues such as ordination and the laying on of hands are left aside. Menzies' role as a reader and interpreter of the Lukan narrative is distinctive and commendable, but in the end it is obvious that he reads and interprets as a *Pentecostal* scholar. So it is not surprising that his conclusions perfectly fit the classical Pentecostal stance on (Lukan) pneumatology.

---

119 This conclusion is drawn from the 14th chapter of Menzies' *Empowered for Witness*. He however prefers to speak of "accompanying sign": Menzies, *Empowered for Witness*, 253n2.

CHAPTER 5
THE MODEL APPLIED (3): William S. Kurz

5.1 Introduction

William S. Kurz is a Roman Catholic scholar who earned his Ph.D. in 1976 from Yale University. He is a professor of New Testament at Marquette University where he has taught for more than 35 years. He specializes in the exegesis and interpretation of the New Testament, with a special focus on Luke-Acts and the Johannine writings. His focus in interpretation of scripture is narrative criticism and canonical criticism, and this makes it interesting and worthwhile to compare him with Max Turner and Robert Menzies. Besides this Kurz is a devout Catholic and in his writings he shares about his personal experiences in faith. This certainly will color his way of reading and interpreting and will shed some light on his role as a reader of Luke-Acts. Martin Mittelstad calls Kurz a "Charismatic Catholic" and he regrets that the work of Kurz receives so little attention within the Pentecostal community.[1] Publications of Kurz on Luke-Acts are *The Acts of the Apostles* (1983, revised in 1989), *Following Jesus: A Disciples Guide to Luke and Acts* (1984, revised in 2003), "Narrative Models for Imitation in Luke-Acts" (1990), *Reading Luke-Acts: Dynamics of Biblical Narrative* (1993), "From the Servant in Isaiah to Jesus and the Apostles in Luke-Acts to Christians Today: Spirit-Filled Witness to the Ends of the Earth" (2008) and most recently a Catholic Commentary on the Book of Acts: *Acts of the Apostles* (2013).[2] Besides

---

1 Martin W. Mittelstadt, *Reading Luke-Acts in the Pentecostal Tradition* (Cleveland, TN: CPT, 2010), 89.
2 William S. Kurz, *The Acts of the Apostles* (CBC 5; Collegeville, MN: Liturgical, 1983); *Following Jesus: A Disciples Guide to Luke and Acts* (Ann Arbor, MI: Servant, 1984), "Narrative Models for Imitation in Luke-Acts" in: D.L. Balch, W.A. Meeks and E. Ferguson (eds.), *Greeks, Romans, and Christians: Essays in Honor of Abraham J. Malherbe* (Minneapolis, MN: Fortress, 1990), 175-194; *Reading Luke-Acts: Dynamics of Biblical Narrative* (Louisville, KY: Westminster/Fort Knox, 1993); "From the Servant in Isaiah to Jesus and the Apostles in Luke-Acts to Christians Today: Spirit-Filled Witness to the Ends of the Earth" in: M.F. Foskett and O.W. Allen Jr. (eds.), *Between Experience and Interpretation: Engaging the Writers of the New Testament* (Nashville, TN: Abingdon, 2008) and *Acts of the Apostles* (Catholic Commentary on Sacred Scripture; Grand Rapids, MI: Baker Academic, 2013).

these publications several of his books and commentaries are translated in Hungarian, Italian, Spanish and Polish. So with William Kurz we have an international oriented scholar who is a prolific author on Luke-Acts.

For this chapter I will again follow the different πνεῦμα clusters in Luke and Acts and use the model of Umberto Eco to deduce what is the role of the reader, in this instance the Catholic scholar William S. Kurz. However, in addition to this fixed outline of the chapter I will start with an extra section on Kurz' methodology because his approach of the Lukan narrative is slightly different to that of Turner's and Menzies'.

5.2 Methodology: Kurz' dynamic reading of Luke-Acts
5.2.1 Introduction
Where Max Turner and Robert Menzies selected a historical critical methodology, William Kurz approaches the text of Luke-Acts from a literary point of view. Designating the historical critical method with words as "dissatisfaction", "crisis" and a "paradigm shift" Kurz legitimizes his literary approach.[3] One of Kurz' main objections is that the different historical critical methods (source, form, redaction, composition and canonical criticism) all treat the biblical texts from a historical perspective: "They still did not focus on how these texts are read in the twentieth century."[4] According to Kurz literary criticism is able to bridge the gap between dogmatics and exegesis on the one hand and on the other examine the narrative as a narrative regardless of vigorous debates about different types of genre. That is why he chose to apply literary criticism to the narrative of Luke-Acts and it is evident this choice has consequences for his reading of the text.

5.2.2 The expression of the text
As far as the text proper is concerned, Kurz treats Luke-Acts as a canonical two volume biblical narrative and as such its purpose reaches beyond the first century readers.[5] The author, called "Luke", designed both volumes as a continuation of the biblical narratives from the Greek Old Testament, and because of this both volumes were intended to become a part of the Christian Bible. According to Kurz this means the narrative should

---

3 Kurz, *Reading Luke-Acts*, 3.
4 Kurz, *Reading Luke-Acts*, 4.
5 With the term 'canonical' Kurz emphasizes the unity of the Bible, Old and New Testament, and subsequently the unity of the Gospel of Luke and the Book of Acts. Kurz, *Reading Luke-Acts*, ix-2.

be read "from a faith stance within the church, not solely from a historical or academic perspective."[6] In another context Kurz does not hesitate to firmly state that the Bible is God's inspired word, that it contains living words and that the message of Luke-Acts remains important for this present day.[7] Biblical narratives can serve for present day Christian imitation. He however warns for (what he calls) abuses such as "proof-texting" (for instance the use of Acts 8:14-17 to proof a necessary second reception of the Spirit or to proof the sacrament of confirmation) and the gathering of texts relating to a particular contemporary question (for instance different texts relating to homosexuality).[8] Kurz appreciates the academic approach to the Bible and finds the historical-critical approach necessary in order to prevent anachronisms, but argues that beyond the academic approach the biblical texts need to be applied directly to life. And in this application he holds firmly to a Catholic tradition of interpreting the biblical texts.[9] Kurz for instance states "Catholics interpret Acts within the context of the whole of Sacred Scripture as it has been elucidated in the Church's creeds, dogma, worship, sacraments and tradition; we take into account the perspective of saints, scholars, and Church teaching, both ancient and modern."[10] So besides the narrative critical method, Kurz as well uses a Catholic angle from which he approaches the text. This is what Eco calls *ideological overcoding* in box 1 of his model. Kurz consciously approaches the text from a Roman Catholic angle.

5.2.3 Codes and subcodes in the text
When it comes to the codes and subcodes in the text Kurz focuses on Christian addressees. As Eco calls it, it is the encyclopedic competence (the ability to recognize the codes and subcodes in the text) of the reader which contributes to a proper understanding of the text. A model reader will recognize, understand and interpret the author's codes and subcodes sufficiently. In Kurz's opinion the model reader of Luke-Acts is a Christian reader:

> "The gaps in Luke and Acts that are meant to be filled are gaps that would occur to Christian readers, and they are meant to be filled from a Christian

---

6   Kurz, *Reading Luke-Acts*, 6.
7   Kurz, *Following Jesus*, 7; *The Acts of the Apostles* (1983), 5; *Acts of the Apostles* (2013), 19.
8   Both examples are Kurz's: Kurz, *Following Jesus*, 9-10.
9   Kurz, *Following Jesus*, 12-13; *Acts of the Apostles* (2013), 19-20.
10 Kurz, *Acts of the Apostles* (2013), 19.

perspective. The points of view of the text, both in its original setting and in its later context as part of the Christian Bible, are grounded in and express Christian faith. The most empathetic reading of the text would therefore ordinarily proceed from Christian faith and experience."[11]

Especially when the narrative concerns faith, miracles and the identity of Jesus, Kurz argues that the model reader is that reader who approaches the text from a Christian faith perspective. He continues that because of Christian catechesis and experience these readers will much easier fill the different gaps in the Lukan narrative. For instance Luke does not explicitly state that Jesus was baptized by John, on the contrary before Jesus' baptism (Luke 3:21) Luke had already told his audience that John had been taken captive by Herod (Luke 3:19-20). However, the well informed reader or model reader (Kurz would argue the catechized Christian reader) already knows that it is John who baptized Jesus. They recognize Luke's flash forward in verses 19-20, before Jesus' baptism is mentioned. In addition to this Kurz argues that a good knowledge of the Greek Old Testament is presupposed by the author of Luke-Acts.[12] This is because of the many allusions, examples and similarities with Old Testament stories and persons which are referred to in the Lukan narrative. Kurz consistently mentions the Greek Old Testament, which in my opinion is not exactly common ground for the average catechized Christian reader. I could imagine Kurz means the Old Testament (in that translation which is suitable for the present day reader), but not the Greek Old Testament. If Kurz does mean here *the original readers* of the Lukan narrative, then he seems to contradict himself because of his own criticism on historical criticism. He does not hesitate to use words as "historical-critical elitism" and "academic scribes [who] lock the scriptures into the distant past" in his conclusion.[13] Somehow it seems that for determining the right model reader we both need historical as well as literary criticism.

5.2.4 Circumstances of utterance
Kurz argues that because Luke-Acts belongs to the Christian canon a much wider audience is expected than only the original implied readers (see above). This relativizes the importance of the original circumstances in which Luke and Acts were created: because Luke and Acts are canoni-

---

11 Kurz, *Reading Luke-Acts*, 15.
12 Kurz, *Reading Luke-Acts*, 16.
13 Kurz, *Reading Luke-Acts*, 16.

cal a much wider audience is expected instead of only the original implied readers.¹⁴ Instead of focusing on the actual author, Kurz uses the concept of the implied author. He discovers four different implied authors in the text of Luke-Acts: a *histor* (a careful historical investigator), a Christian apologist, a master of both Hellenistic and biblical styles of Greek and a travel companion on Paul's later journeys (because of the "we" sections in Acts).¹⁵ With regard to the readers Kurz argues as well that it is impossible to determine the original readers of Luke-Acts. He states: "once a writing is made public, the writer can no longer control or even predict who will read it."¹⁶ This is why Kurz does not spend much time to discuss possible readers or a particular community to which Luke wrote. In a quick overview he mentions as addressees a Gentile Christian community, a Jewish Christian community, an apologetic to non-Christian Romans or a Pauline defense against Jewish or Jewish Christian charges of apostasy.¹⁷ He however does not elaborate on this, simply because there is no consensus. The same is true of a possible geographical location of the Lukan community. Kurz names a couple of cities, but only because they are mentioned in the Lukan narrative. He somehow concludes with the option that Luke-Acts might have been intended for more than one community, as some sort of "ecumenical narrative".¹⁸ In conclusion we can say that when it comes to the circumstances of utterance there is no consensus on place, date or occasion of writing. Kurz does not spend a great deal of time on these issues, but rather focuses on the text of the narrative itself, with its implied readers and implied author. All with the purpose of what the text of Luke-Acts has to say to the present day (Roman Catholic) Christian community.

5.2.5 Conclusion
Already at the beginning of this chapter we can conclude that the reading of Luke-Acts by William Kurz is heavily colored by a certain number of presuppositions. He is very open in how he approaches the narrative of Luke-Acts and in what he sees as the right parameters in the meaning and application of the narrative. Firmly rooted in the Catholic tradition, the proper interpretation should be in accordance with the creeds, dogma

---

14 Kurz, *Reading Luke-Acts*, 10.
15 Kurz, *Reading Luke-Acts*, 10-12.
16 Kurz, *Reading Luke-Acts*, 12.
17 Kurz, *Reading Luke-Acts*, 12-13.
18 Kurz, *Reading Luke-Acts*, 13.

and sacraments. Christian faith and academics do not exclude each other, however when it concerns the application of the biblical text, faith has to be preferred. After reviewing these presuppositions it will be all the more interesting to treat the different πνεῦμα clusters in Luke-Acts to discover what the typical role of the reader William Kurz looks like.

5.3 The infancy narratives (Luke 1-2)
5.3.1 The actualized text
The text of the infancy narratives in Luke 1-2 is seen by Kurz as a larger prologue to the Gospel and its sequel, the Book of Acts.[19] The prologue proper, Luke 1:1-4, is treated separately by Kurz.[20] Kurz argues that one of the main functions of the infancy narratives is to foreshadow later events in the narrative. For instance Simeon's prophecy in Luke 2:29-35 foreshadows the Jewish division over Jesus being the Messiah and the subsequent spread of the Gospel to the Gentiles. At the end of the Book of Acts Paul refers as well to Isaiah in which he accentuates the foretold division between those who would and those who would not believe in Christ. This leads Kurz to conclude that it is a recalling of Simeon's prophecy and as such provides some sort of a closure to the two-volume narrative.[21] However, there is some incompletion of the narrative as well which leaves the pious from Israel with only a partial fulfillment of their expectations.[22] So the infancy narratives provide some clues and foreshadowing of events to happen later on in the narrative, some of those clues provide a closure to the story, others however leave the reader with an open ending or partial fulfillment.

5.3.2 The substantial properties of the text
In his understanding of the text of the infancy narratives, Kurz focuses on the narrator of the story and his relation to the intended reader(s). In contrast with the prologue of 1:1-4, in which the narrator is a *histor*, the narrator of the infancy narratives is some sort of omniscient third person who tells the story from a bird's eye perspective. His writing is "unpolished biblical Greek: heavily Semitic in sentence structure and full of Septuagintal expressions."[23] All this is analogous with the biblical tradition.

---

19 Kurz, *Reading Luke-Acts*, 19.
20 Kurz, *Reading Luke-Acts*, 18-19, 39-44.
21 Kurz, *Reading Luke-Acts*, 29.
22 Kurz, *Reading Luke-Acts*, 30.
23 Kurz, *Reading Luke-Acts*, 46.

The purpose, according to Kurz, is to provide the readers with background information and an orientation how to interpret the narrative to come. In accordance with Hellenistic biographies and biblical historiography, the narrator writes about the parentage and circumstances of birth of the main character of the narrative. He chooses to do so about John the Baptist and Jesus. The story is about pious Jews (Zechariah, Elizabeth, Simeon, Anna) who eagerly await God's promises to save his people. Kurz rightly points to the fact that Zechariah and Elizabeth are depicted as righteous Israelites, despite the fact of Elizabeth's barrenness which was commonly interpreted as a curse from God.[24] The miraculous births of both the main characters show the importance of these characters. In addition John is referred to as a great prophet (in resemblance of Elijah, Luke 1:17) and Jesus as Son of the Most High, whose (Davidic) reign will never end (Luke 1:32-33). The Holy Spirit plays an important part in the lifes of both characters: John was filled with the Spirit from his mother's womb and Jesus was conceived through the Holy Spirit overshadowing Mary. Besides these important aspects of the main characters, the omniscient narrator also informs the readers about the results of Jesus' ministry. Even before his baptism and inaugural address in Luke 3-4, the narrator gives away that there will be rejection as well as acceptance of Jesus and that Jesus will be a light to the Gentiles. So according to Kurz, the structure of the text (mainly shown by the omniscient narrator) shows that the story of the infancy narratives is about the introduction of the main character of Luke-Acts. This main character is born under special circumstances and out of a pious ancestry. His ministry will invoke opposite reactions among the people. And perhaps among the readers of the narrative?

5.3.3 Preliminary deductions and possible implications
It is beyond doubt that Kurz treats the world of the text as the actual world. In his gathering of information from the infancy narrative, he does not once put any discrepancies between brackets. John being filled with the Spirit already in his mother's womb and Mary becoming pregnant through the overshadowing of the Holy Spirit are both understood just as it is described by Luke. The forecasts and inferential walks as Eco calls them in box 7 of his model are limited to what Kurz calls the foreshadowing of events. Considering the fact that Kurz treats the infancy narratives as the extended prologue to the whole narrative of Luke-Acts, it is safe to argue that Kurz interprets the infancy narratives preliminary from box 7.

---

24 Kurz, *Reading Luke-Acts*, 46.

That is: all of Luke 1-2 is meant to stir the reader to predict a certain outcome or continuation of the story. What will happen with both of the main characters? Why is Jesus described as superior to John? How will it come to pass that some will accept Jesus, but others will reject Him? Only if one continues reading these questions will be answered and forecasts will be verified or falsified. With the knowledge of all of the narrative in mind Kurz already answers some of these questions and is a such able to designate the infancy narratives as the larger prologue or one great foreshadowing of events to come.

Besides this, it is crystal clear that Kurz 'wanders out of the text' and relates to present day stories. This is exactly what Eco describes in box 10 of his model: the reader Kurz chooses to cooperate with the text of the narrative and does not hesitate to apply the text to the contemporary world. For instance in his *Following Jesus*, Kurz deduces from the infancy narratives one of the basic themes of Luke-Acts, called "God's Initiating Love". In it he makes some direct applications to present day readers: [25]

1. God begins our Christian way. Even before our birth, He prepares the circumstances;
2. God intervenes in our everyday lives;
3. Similar to the story of Luke-Acts, we as well can look back in retrospect and see that God prepared the way for our mission;
4. Just as was the case with Mary, God's plan for us depends on our "yes": we have to cooperate with God's plan;
5. The calling of John is our calling as well: preparing the way for Jesus and pointing to Him;
6. Simeon's prophecy of doom gives us hope, but also prepares us for hardships.

Kurz constantly varies between the story of the infancy narratives, present day applications and the example of his own life and ministry. He does admit that "these beliefs directly contradict some of the most pervasive worldviews today."[26] However, he chooses to cooperate with the text and the world of the text and as such performs the role of a model reader. The infancy narratives show God's initiating love: in history with John and Jesus, and in the present day with contemporary readers.

---

25 Kurz, *Following Jesus*, 17-22.
26 Kurz, *Following Jesus*, 18.

5.4 The ministry of John the Baptist (Luke 3:1-20)

5.4.1 The actualized text
Based on commentaries by John Nolland, Joseph Fitzmyer and François Bovon, Kurz argues that the text of the episode about John the Baptist is placed within world history, as was common practice among historians (Luke 3:1-2, Acts 26:26b).[27] The allusion in the text to the call of Jeremiah (Luke 3:2, Jer. 1:1) and the citation from Isaiah 40 (Luke 3:4-6) are interpreted by Kurz as a biblical backdrop for the story that follows. Apparently the author of Luke-Acts wanted to place his narrative deliberately in the context of world history on the one hand and in sequence with biblical history on the other. This perfectly fits Kurz's canonical approach of the narrative of Luke-Acts.

5.4.2 The substantial properties of the text
The story of the ministry of John the Baptist is primarily about John being the one who prepares for the ministry of Jesus. It is in this way that Kurz interprets the story and explains the non-chronological reference to John's later imprisonment by Herod (Luke 3:19-20). With this flash forward the author "completes one plot line (John's) before turning to another (Jesus')."[28] Although Kurz does not discuss the promise of John the Baptist about "the coming one who will baptize with the Holy Spirit and fire" (Luke 3:16), this promise fits well in the story of John being Jesus' precursor. Unfortunately this is all there is to say about John's promise. Kurz does not treat this verse as for example Turner and Menzies do. He leaves it aside and as far as he is concerned the ministry of John is purely preparatory for the ministry of Jesus. This is according the Lukan style of foreshadowing what is to come in the remaining of the narrative. The first main character (John) has to make place for the second and more important main character: Jesus.

5.4.3 Preliminary deductions and possible implications
The promise of John the Baptist is not treated separately by Kurz. In contrast with Max Turner and Robert Menzies, he does not elaborate on the

---

27 Kurz, *Reading Luke-Acts*, 47, endnotes 10 and 11, 195. The used commentaries are: John Nolland, *Luke 1-9:20* (WBC 35a; Dalles, TX: Word, 1989), Jospeph A. Fitzmyer, *The Gospel According to Luke (I-IX). Introduction, Translation and Notes* (AncB 28a; Garden City, NY: Doubleday, 1985) and François Bovon, *Das Evangelium nach Lukas: 1. Teilband, Lk. 1,1-9,50* (EKK 3,1; Zürich, Neukirchen-Vluyn: Benziger Verlag, Neukirchener Verlag, 1980).
28 Kurz, *Reading Luke-Acts*, 47.

possible meanings of the promised baptism with Spirit and fire. Kurz only relates to this promise in his recent commentary on the Book of Acts in which he explains Acts 1:5 and shows the relation between this verse and Luke 24:49 and Luke 3:16.[29] According to Kurz the promise of John the Baptist is a significant contrast between his own baptism in water and the coming baptism in Spirit. Based on the meaning of baptism in Greek (dip, drench, immerse), Kurz argues that it recalls Old Testament promises in which God would pour out his Spirit like water on thirsty ground.[30] This is interpreted by Kurz as a vivid image of what would occur at Pentecost (Acts 2): "The disciples […] would be immersed in God's own life!" He explains that the promise (John's promise in Luke 3:16 and its repetition in Acts 1:5) "will be realized at Pentecost and then in Christian baptism, which involves both water and the Spirit's indwelling and empowerment."[31] In an aside in his commentary, Kurz wanders out of the text and refers to a comment of Pope Benedict XVI in which he states that Pentecost is the "crowning moment of Jesus' whole mission" and that we should rediscover this baptism in the Holy Spirit. In this quotation baptism, confirmation and prayer to the Virgin Mary are all closely related.[32] So here we clearly do see that Kurz' role of reading the text of Luke and Acts is closely interwoven with his own denominational points of view. There where the text of neither Luke 3:16 or Acts 1:5 mention the close combination of Spirit baptism with water baptism, Kurz does. As a matter of fact he adds the practices of the Roman Catholic church of confirmation and praying to the Virgin Mary and as such shows his presuppositions about the promise of John the Baptist. This shows that in his reading of the text, Kurz adds Catholic doctrines to his interpretation of the text which subsequently show the role of this particular reader.

5.5 The baptism and subsequent testing of Jesus (Luke 3:21-22, 4:1-14)
5.5.1 *The actualized text*
The text of Jesus' baptism is construed to have its sole focus on Jesus. The apocalyptic language and the mentioning of Jesus praying give an extra dimension to this event. Because of the voice from heaven declaring "you are my beloved Son, with you I am well pleased" the emphasis is on Jesus'

---

29 Kurz, *Acts of the Apostles* (2013), 29.
30 Kurz, *Acts of the Apostles* (2013), 29. Kurz refers to Isa 32:15, 44:2-3; Ezek. 39:29; Joel 3:1 and Zech. 12:10.
31 Kurz, *Acts of the Apostles* (2013), 29.
32 Kurz, *Acts of the Apostles* (2013), 30.

divine sonship. The subsequent genealogy then focuses on Jesus' earthly lineage. The text of the temptation episode is traditional material and is told from an omniscient point of view. The climax of the temptations takes place in Jerusalem which corresponds with Luke's overall story in which the climax of Jesus' ministry is in Jerusalem as well. By explicitly mentioning the Jordan river, Luke links the temptation episode to Jesus' baptism and the whole of the episode is framed by a double reference to "the Spirit" (full of the Holy Spirit in 4:1 and in the power of the Spirit in 4:14).

5.5.2 The substantial properties of the text
According to Kurz, the story of Jesus' baptism and subsequent genealogy contextualize Jesus' divine sonship. On the one hand Jesus is clearly presented as Son of God, as already revealed to Mary through the words of the angel in Luke 2:26-38 where words are used as "Son of the Most High", "Holy One" and "Son of God". This is confirmed at Jesus' baptism through the voice from heaven. On the other hand the genealogy presents Jesus' earthly descent and according to Kurz "demythologizes" the title Son of God. Kurz means that Jesus was human also and that He is described from above, as well as from below.[33] The narrative then is structured to show two aspects of the main character: the divine aspect as well as the human aspect. Kurz argues that these different points of view, one from above and the other from below, are meant to complement and not contradict each other.

The framing of the temptation episode by the double Spirit reference shows, according to Kurz, the role of the Spirit in the start of Jesus mission.[34] The purpose of Jesus being led into the desert was "to fast and sort out in prayer just what his mission was and how he was to exercise it."[35] Kurz knows the story and ties some of the events here to later events in the narrative. Eco calls this forecasts and inferential walks in box 7 of his model. Because Kurz knows the remainder of the narrative he interprets the "leaving of the devil for an opportune time" in 4:13 as a cliffhanger or foreshadowing of the passion narrative. It is there, in the passion event, that the devil will return to Jesus. What Eco argues that the reader can conclude "if-x-takes-action-then-the-result-is-y" we clearly see in the temptation narrative: if the devil tempts, then Jesus answers from scripture

---

33 Kurz, *Reading Luke-Acts*, 48.
34 Kurz, *Following Jesus*, 25.
35 Kurz, *Following Jesus*, 26.

(note the triple γέγραπται in 4:4, 8 and 10).³⁶ Box 8 of Eco's model is about determining actantial structures and reducing characters to propositions. This is what Kurz is doing when he extensively shows the parallels between Jesus' life and ours and between Jesus' temptations and ours. Experiencing the Holy Spirit is often accompanied with encountering the devil or evil spirits.³⁷ Jesus shows the contemporary reader how to overcome the devil's temptations. "He [Jesus] shows us the danger of trying to keep control over God's power and gifts, of trying to use worldly power as a shortcut to spiritual success, and of rushing ahead of God's will for us by reading biblical texts out of context."³⁸ In summary, according to Kurz the story is about balancing Jesus' divine and human side and showing how to counter temptations of the devil.

5.5.3 Preliminary deductions and possible implications
Again, as we have seen before, Kurz directly draws some lines of interpretation between the story in Luke's narrative and the present day world.³⁹ He does not hesitate to illustrate this with examples from his own life and to apply some of the principles to the 21ˢᵗ century reader. Just as we do not tell every detail of our own life, so does Luke filter and only shares some of the important things of Jesus' life. Luke made some changes in the order of events because he did not write as a secular historian, but had pastoral purposes with his narrative.⁴⁰ In this episode, these important things are Jesus' baptism, his genealogy and the temptations in the desert. Jesus' baptism and experience with the Holy Spirit is interpreted by Kurz as a "datable turning point" and explained by his own experience with the Holy Spirit. Kurz writes:

> "I longed to experience personally the power of the Holy Spirit to enable me to touch souls as a priest. When I was able to surrender my own ideas about how to do things, God overwhelmed me with his love. That love was so overpowering that I was confident that he wanted me to be a priest.[…] A similar datable turning point changed Jesus' life and began his active mission of preaching."⁴¹

---

36 Eco, *Lector in fabula*, 155 and see §2.5 above.
37 Kurz, *Following Jesus*, 25-27.
38 Kurz, *Following Jesus*, 27.
39 Kurz, *Following Jesus*, 23-28.
40 Kurz, *Following Jesus*, 23.
41 Kurz, *Following Jesus*, 24-25.

Here we see Kurz reading back his own experience into the narrative of Luke. The world of the text coincides with the actual world and vice versa. Kurz continues to focus on the role of the Holy Spirit and argues that it was the role of the Spirit which got Jesus started in his mission, led him in the desert and taught Jesus to distinguish between temptations and his real call. This is the same role the Holy Spirit plays in the life of contemporary readers. Kurz jumps to boxes 9 and 10 in the model of Eco and constantly adds value judgments to his reading of the text. In this way he uncovers the elementary ideological structures of the text and finds direct applications for his own life and the lives of his readers. This reading of the text prominently shows the role of the reader, because the uncovered elementary ideological structures are *Kurz's reading* of the text. The question remains whether the original author intended the same elementary ideological structures.

5.6 Jesus' inauguration address (Luke 4:14-30)
5.6.1 The actualized text
Contrary to Max Turner and Robert Menzies, Kurz does not elaborate on the use of Luke's conflated quotation from Isaiah 58 and 61. His only mentioning of Isaiah 61 is to explain that Luke uses this text "to provide intertextual depth to his portrait of Jesus as Spirit-anointed and prophet".[42] And the rather superficial remark that it was Jesus who in this referral to Isaiah presented the character of his mission.[43] Unfortunately Kurz fails to describe and elaborate on this intertextual depth. Especially his narrative critical approach calls for a more thorough analysis of the conflated quotation in Luke 4:18-19. Why did Luke choose to use these verses from the Old Testament? What was his purpose in using this image for Jesus and how does it recur in the remaining of the Lukan narrative? Kurz leaves these questions unanswered and fails to elaborate on the conflated Isaianic quotation. So concerning the text proper Kurz does not spend much time or effort in analyzing Jesus' inaugural address, despite the fact that he does call it "programmatic".[44]

5.6.2 The substantial properties of the text
According to Kurz, the main emphasis in this episode is on the foreshadowing of the ministry of Paul in the Book of Acts. Through accentuating

---
42 Kurz, *Reading Luke-Acts*, 49.
43 Kurz, *Following Jesus*, 29.
44 Kurz, *Reading Luke-Acts*, 49.

the reputation and reception of Jesus and his teaching in synagogues, the parallel here is made with Paul, especially with his custom to go into synagogues (Acts 17:2). Kurz sustains this parallel in both of his commentaries on Acts and points to the almost identical Greek phrases in Luke 4:16 and Acts 17:2 (κατὰ τὸ εἰωθός).[45] So Jesus' inaugural address is one of the events which will be echoed in the Book of Acts. In his pointing to this parallel Kurz relies on the article written by Susan Marie Praeder, 'Jesus-Paul, Peter-Paul and Jesus-Peter Parallelisms in Luke-Acts: A History of Reader Response'.[46] However, at the end of her paper Praeder closes with a firm warning:

> "The practice of parallel reporting in the twelve studies suggests that they were formed through a process of parallel reading that involved selective reading, remembering and forgetting, looking backward and forward in the text and to other texts, and long and painstaking reading. All of this can be carried too far. Selective reading of Luke-Acts can be so selective that it becomes reading of a short form of the text that is supposed to substitute for the long form of the text. Remembering and forgetting and looking backward and forward are part of any reading process. In parallel reading similarities are remembered or sought out for remembering. This process can result in remembering too much that should have been forgotten and forgetting too much that should have been remembered. The search for textual similarities and the constructing, studying, and testing of parallel reports make for long and painstaking reading. A serious question is whether this long process brings readers of Luke-Acts closer to the text and all its complications or to a simplified form of the text that lends itself to solutions."

It seems to me that Kurz opts for the short reading which Praeder mentions, because in both of his books he only spends one page to Jesus' inaugural address. Kurz recognizes that it is programmatic, but fails to work this out. The conflated quotation is a very difficult issue and it remains vague why Luke chose to use Isaiah 58 and 61 in the way he did. Through Kurz' short reading he exactly does what Praeder warns for: a selective reading which results in a simplified form of the text. Here we clearly come across the role of the reader Kurz. The reader Kurz selects and simplifies the text. In the model of Umberto Eco it is shown that in boxes 4

---

45 Kurz, *The Acts of the Apostles* (1983), 75; *Acts of the Apostles* (2013), 262.
46 S.M. Praeder, 'Jesus-Paul, Peter-Paul and Jesus-Peter Parallelisms in Luke-Acts: A History of Reader Response', *SBL Seminar Papers*, vol.23 (1984), 23-39.

and 6 plot and story of the text are determined. Subsequently in boxes 8 and 9 the focus is on the narrative structure and possible deductions from this structure which can lead to an ideological structure. Kurz wastes an opportunity to dig a little deeper and shed some light on the narrative structure and topic of this episode. This results in a simplified reading of this programmatic text.

5.6.3 Preliminary deductions and possible implications
Concerning the implications of this episode Kurz focuses on the mission of Jesus. Jesus is the Spirit anointed person who comes with the good news of salvation. This salvation contains sight to the blind, other physical healings and forgiveness from sin and guilt. The setting free of the captives is interpreted by Kurz as exorcism.[47] In quoting 2 Corinthians 6:2 (In an acceptable time I have heard you, and in the day of salvation I have helped you [Isaiah 49:8]), Kurz seems to imply that this Isaianic text from the second Servant Song links the suffering Servant from Isaiah with Jesus and with Paul. Again, he does not elaborate on this linkage despite the fact that various other scholars did.[48] Especially the question whether Luke had the year of Jubilee in mind or not is an interesting issue to elaborate on. Perhaps the intertextual depth extends itself beyond the conflated Isaianic quotation to Isaiah 49 and Leviticus 25 as well.[49] According to the model of Eco the reader could make an "inferential walk" (box 7) and show his or her knowledge of a promised year of jubilee and see whether this would be verified or falsified in the remaining of the Lukan narrative. Kurz however constrains himself on the one hand to the foreshadowing motif of Paul going into synagogues in the Book of Acts, and on the other hand he sees in 4:29 a foreshadowing of the passion of Jesus. In his application of the text he directly applies the quotation from Isaiah to the present day readers. That is: Jesus has come with the good news of salvation for us today. His healing, forgiving and setting free is for

---

47 Kurz, *Following Jesus*, 29.
48 Kurz, Following Jesus, 29. In his *Reading Luke-Acts* Kurz does not mention 2 Cor. 6:2. Other scholars who elaborated on this linkage are for instance: Hans Conzelmann, *Die Mitte der Zeit. Studien zur Theologie des Lukas* (Tübingen: Mohr Siebeck, 1953), 29-31; Ralph P. Martin, *2 Corinthians* (WBC 40; Waco, TX: Word, 1986), 167-169; I.Howard Marshall, *The Gospel of Luke* (NIGTC; Grand Rapids, MI: Eerdmans/Paternoster, 1978), 184; Darrell L. Bock, *Luke 1:1-9:50* (BECNT; Grand Rapids, MI: Baker, 1994), 410-411; Murray J. Harris, *The Second Epistle to the Corinthians* (NIGTC; Grand Rapids, MI: Eerdmans/Paternoster, 2005), 459-462.
49 Marshall, *The Gospel of Luke*, 184; Bock, *Luke 1:1-9:50*, 410-411.

contemporary people. "All we have to do is to accept him and let him save us" shows Kurz' direct application.[50] He herewith limits the application of the text to salvation, spiritually and physically. Any mentioning about the Spirit, receiving the Spirit or anointment with the Spirit is omitted in contemporary application. The working of the Spirit in this episode is limited to the uniqueness of Jesus as Messiah and Christ.

5.7 Jesus' general sayings about the Spirit (Luke 10:21, 11:13, 12:10-12)
With regard to Kurz' reading of Jesus' general sayings about the Spirit I can be very short: these sayings are completely left aside. It is fair to acknowledge that it is not Kurz' intention to treat every πνεῦμα text with the purpose to determine a Lukan pneumatology. However, in his overall treatment of Luke-Acts and his distinctive literary approach, it would have proven worthwhile to look at these general sayings as well. Kurz' primary interest is in the journey motif, which we find in the Gospel of Luke. From Luke 9:51 the motif of Jesus' journey to Jerusalem provides the background for his teaching (and the general sayings about the Spirit) while he is on the way to Jerusalem. In a few pages Kurz elaborates on this motif of journeying to Jerusalem and concludes that this journey forms the framework for Luke and that it culminates in a rather emotional ending when Jesus weeps over the city and subsequently enters it (Luke 19:41-45).[51] Unfortunately Kurz does not elaborate on this journey motif or ties it to Paul's journey in Acts 19:21-21:17. Charles Talbert and Susan Marie Praeder do elaborate on both these journeys: where Talbert interprets them as an intentional correspondence by the author, Praeder is more cautious and only sees a relation in content between both journeys.[52] In his more popular work, *Following Jesus*, Kurz spends a few pages on Luke 12 and focuses on two parables with the common theme of trusting in God.[53] Just before these two parables we read about Jesus' warning of blasphemy against the Spirit (12:10) and the encouragement that the Spirit will teach (διδάσκω) when the apostles are brought before synagogues, rulers and authorities (12:12). This encouragement is taken up by Kurz in his commentaries on the Book of Acts. In his treatment of

---

50 Kurz, *Following Jesus*, 29.
51 Kurz, *Reading Luke-Acts*, 51-54.
52 Charles H. Talbert, *Literary Patterns, Theological Themes and the Genre of Luke-Acts* (SBL Monograph Series 20; Missoula, MT: Scholars, 1974), 16-20 and Praeder, 'Jesus-Paul, Peter-Paul and Jesus-Peter Parallelisms in Luke-Acts', 36-37.
53 Kurz, *Following Jesus*, 65-68.

Acts 4:8, he points to this general Spirit saying in Luke 12:12 and concludes this was a prophetic saying of Jesus only to be fulfilled when Peter and John were taken captive by the local authorities: "Here, in fulfillment of Jesus' prophetic instructions, Peter is filled with the Holy Spirit as he answered them. His response manifests Spirit-inspired wisdom and boldness."[54] Kurz does not deduce any principle from this instance for Christians or the church today. He does not elaborate on the working of the Spirit or fulfillment with the Spirit as well. With regard to the warning of blasphemy against the Spirit, Kurz spends a few pages to elaborate on this with the primary point that the Book of Acts shows us that sinning against the Spirit is worse than sinning against Jesus.[55] His focus is on the urgency of accepting God's love and believing in Jesus.

It seems to me that in the case of Jesus' general sayings about the Spirit Kurz could have been more cooperative with the text of the narrative. In a rather superficial way the echo of Luke 12:12 is mentioned in Acts 4:8, and Luke 12:10 is explained in a rather devotional way. The remaining sayings (Luke 10:21, 11:13) however are neglected. In this instance the model of Eco shows a reader who does not cooperate with this part of the text. Whether this has consequences for the continuing reading and interpreting of the narrative of Luke-Acts remains to be seen.

5.8 The promise of the Spirit (Luke 24 – Acts 1)
5.8.1 The actualized text
The explicit verses which deal with the promise of the Spirit are in Luke 24:47-49 and Acts 1:4-8. Kurz focuses on the ending of the Gospel which overlaps and leads into the prologue of Acts. The narrative in both volumes deals with Jesus' last words before the ascension. According to Kurz, the incompatibilities of the Gospel's ending and the beginning of Acts need to be subscribed to the different purposes Luke had in mind. The Gospel ends with the disciples worshipping in the temple, which provides a neat *inclusio* with the beginning of the Gospel, where Luke as well starts with worship in the temple. In the beginning people expect a savior, at the end people rejoice in the coming of the savior. Assuming that Acts was written later, it needed a fitting preface which recounted the Gospel's ending and led into Luke's second volume about the continuation of the story. The connection between both the Gospel's ending and the preface

---

54 Kurz, *Acts of the Apostles* (2013), 79 and *Acts of the Apostles* (1983), 30. The quotation above is from the most recent commentary.
55 Kurz, *Following Jesus*, 96-98.

of Acts is the promise of the Spirit. In his conclusion on the narrators in the Gospel, Kurz writes:

> "Thus it is written that the Messiah would suffer and rise from the dead on the third day and that repentance, for the forgiveness of sins, would be preached in his name to all the nations, beginning from Jerusalem (24:45-49, RNAB). This refers not only back to his passion and resurrection (thus summarizing the Gospel), but also forward to the events of Acts and the spread of the Gospel. This statement by Jesus functions as hinge between the two Lukan volumes, the Gospel and Acts, ground both in scripture. The narrator shows Jesus continue by calling them his witnesses and promising the Holy Spirit, which he terms the promise of his Father, for whose power they are to wait in Jerusalem (24:48-49). With this proleptic word by Jesus, the stage is set for the events of Acts."[56]

5.8.2 The substantial properties of the text
For the topic of the text Kurz focuses primarily on the text of Acts 1. The narrator in Acts 1 calls to mind different biblical clues for the intended audience. First there is the allusion to Elisha who witnesses Elijah's departure (2 Kings 2:9-14) and subsequently as his successor receives Elijah's spirit. The same event is anticipated in Acts 1: the disciples witness Jesus' ascension and will afterwards receive the Holy Spirit at Pentecost.[57] In addition Kurz points to the appearance of the two men in white clothes and finds in it an echo of the angelic figures at the empty tomb (Luke 24:4). In Luke the women stared into an empty tomb, in Acts the men stare into an empty sky. Both the women in the Gospel and the men in Acts are encouraged not to look for Jesus, but to return to Jerusalem and prayerfully wait for the next phase in God's plan of salvation.

However, the most extensive treatment of Acts 1:8 is in Kurz' article written in a Festschrift honoring Luke Timothy Johnson. In his 'From the Servant in Isaiah to Jesus and the Apostles in Luke-Acts to Christians Today: Spirit-Filled Witness to the Ends of the Earth' Kurz relates to the servant motif in Isaiah.[58] The servant of the Lord in Isaiah can refer to

---

56 Kurz, *Reading Luke-Acts*, 71-72.
57 Kurz, *Reading Luke-Acts*, 74-75.
58 William S. Kurz, 'From the Servant in Isaiah to Jesus and the Apostles in Luke-Acts to Christians Today: Spirit-Filled Witness to the Ends of the Earth' in: Mary F. Foskett and O. Wesley Allen jr. (ed.), *Between Experience and Interpretation: Engaging the Writings of the New Testament* (Nashvill, TN: Abingdon, 2008), 175-194.

both individuals and to the people of Israel as a collective, so this makes it perfectly suitable for Luke to apply this servant motif to Jesus in the Gospel and the collective of God's people in the Book of Acts. The task of the servant, as well in Isaiah as in Acts, is to witness to God.[59] Acts 1:8 is part of Jesus' answer to his disciples and serves the so called 'misunderstanding motif' in Luke-Acts. Because of the misunderstanding about the coming of the Kingdom, the narrator can teach the audience and readers about the promise of the Spirit and the purpose of the Spirit's coming.[60] Besides the geographical meaning of 'to the ends of the earth' (Spain, Ethiopia, Rome), Kurz stresses the meaning of witnessing to all nations including Gentiles. He sees in this an echo of Isaiah 49:6 (LXX has ἕως ἐσχάτου τῆς γῆς, these are the exact same words Luke uses in Acts 1:8 and Acts 13:47) and writes: "Like the servant of Second Isaiah, the disciples, *when empowered by the Holy Spirit*, will be witnesses to the Lord to the ends of the earth."[61] Although Kurz does not engage in the debate whether the Spirit in Acts is soteriological or an empowerment for mission, the latter option strongly comes in view here.

In his summary of the servant role as witness, Kurz lists four observations which demonstrate how he reads the story:[62]

1. It is God who calls someone as a servant and witness;
2. Servants and witnesses do not act from their own power, but are empowered by God who fills them with the Holy Spirit;
3. Servants are sent by God to all nations;
4. Servants will encounter suffering while witnessing to all nations.

Noteworthy is the fact that Kurz adds to his third observation that "The servant commission is essentially a missionary one (...)".[63] Closely tied to his Theocentric observations (God calls, God empowers through his Spirit, God sends) this strongly suggests that Kurz primarily interprets the role of the Spirit as an empowerment for witness. This is corroborated by Kurz' comments found in both of his commentaries on the Book of Acts.[64] In his recent commentary on Acts Kurz accentuates this

---

59 Kurz, 'Servant in Isaiah', 177.
60 Kurz, 'Servant in Isaiah', 177-178 and Kurz, *Reading Luke-Acts*, 151.
61 Kurz, 'Servant in Isaiah', 178-179, emphasis is mine.
62 Kurz, 'Servant in Isaiah', 186-188.
63 Kurz, 'Servant in Isaiah', 187.
64 Kurz, *Acts of the Apostles* (2013), 30-34 and *Acts of the Apostles* (1983), 17.

conclusion of empowerment by quoting Pope Benedict XVI and Pope Paul VI.[65]

5.8.3 Preliminary deductions and possible implications

In box 5 of his model of the cooperative reader, Eco describes the reader's use of "putting certain things between brackets" and the reader's belief or disbelief of the text.[66] It is evident that Kurz believes the text of Luke 24:47-49 and Acts 1:4-8 and applies it as such to Christians today. Already the title of the article about the Isaianic Servant motif makes this abundantly clear. The primary role for Christians today is being a witness. This can only be accomplished by *waiting* for God's empowerment with the Holy Spirit. This aspect of waiting returns in Luke 24:49 and Acts 1:4-8, and is explained by Kurz as essential: "Aware of the great needs of the world and a multitude of ministry opportunities, we can be tempted to rush out and try to accomplish things on our own rather than waiting for the Holy Spirit's empowerment and guidance."[67] Paralleling Jesus' promise of the empowerment with the Spirit (Acts 1:8) with Jesus' own baptism in the Jordan and the Spirit descending on him (Luke 3:21-22), Kurz concludes that as well as the latter event inaugurated Jesus' public ministry, so will the first inaugurate the apostle's public ministry.

5.9 Pentecost: the outpouring of the Spirit (Acts 2)

5.9.1 The actualized text

With Acts 2 a major new plot section begins, introduced with the words ἐν τῷ συμπληροῦσθαι, which is linked by Kurz with the exact same phraseology at the start of the travel narrative in the Gospel (Luke 9:51).[68] He argues that these words echo the prophecy from Jeremiah 25:11-12 (LXX), which would be interpreted as the beginning of a new stage in God's preordained plan and in using these specific words Luke would catch the attention of his intended audience.[69] The modified text of the Joel quotation in Acts 2:17-21 is not treated that extensively by Kurz as is done by Max Turner and Robert Menzies. Kurz does mention the modifications,

---

65 Kurz, *Acts of the Apostles* (2013), 30, 34. Pope Benedict XVI uses the words of 'baptism with the Holy Spirit' and speaks about regeneration, purification and the extinguishing of evil. As such this could imply he interprets the baptism with the Holy Spirit as soteriological as well as an empowerment for mission.
66 Eco, *Lector in fabula*, 99-101 and see above in §2.5.2.
67 Kurz, *Acts of the Apostles* (2013), 33.
68 Kurz, *Reading Luke-Acts*, 77; *Acts of the Apostles* (2013), 44.
69 Kurz, *Reading Luke-Acts*, 77-78.

but suffices by referring to other redactional studies.⁷⁰ So in regard to the text proper, Kurz limits himself and makes some general narrative remarks about possible parallelisms, echoes and the omniscient narrator of the story.

5.9.2 The substantial properties of the text
The topic of the Pentecost episode in Acts 2 can be summarized by some sort of "promise and fulfillment" framework.⁷¹ In his various publications, Kurz walks through the text of the second chapter of Acts and focuses on the theme of promise and fulfillment. Echoes, allusions, parallels and the use of Old Testament scripture all point to the promise in the past and its fulfillment in the Pentecost story. The filling with the Holy Spirit as described in Acts 2:3-4, refers to the promise in Acts 1:8, Luke 24:49 and especially Luke 3:16, because of the repetition of the word "fire" (πῦρ).⁷² Both Jesus in Luke 3 and the disciples in Acts 1-2 are in prayer, while the outpouring of the Holy Spirit occurs. After this Jesus delivers his inaugural address in Luke 4, and Peter does so in the remaining part of Acts 2. Both speeches are programmatic for the subsequent ministries of Jesus in the Gospel and for the apostles in Acts.⁷³ The phenomena of wind and fire in Acts 2:3-4 are interpreted by Kurz in a similar vein to the theophanies on Mount Sinai with Moses and Elijah. The presence of the different nationalities among the audience signify that most of the world was present and witnessed a reversal of the Babel curse (language confusion) when hearing the apostles speak in their own languages.⁷⁴ In listing all these allusions Kurz shows that the story of Acts 2:1-13 is pregnant with Old Testament imagery and that God's promises are about to be fulfilled.

---

70 Kurz, *Reading Luke-Acts*, 79; *Acts of the Apostles* (2013), 50-53.
71 See for instance William S. Kurz, "Promise and Fulfillment in Hellenistic Jewish Narratives and in Luke and Acts" in: David P. Moessner (ed.), *Jesus and the Heritage of Israel: Luke's Narrative Claim upon Israel's Legacy* (Luke the Interpreter of Israel, vol.1; Harrisburg, PA: Trinity, 1999), 147-170. Other monographs in which the topic of promise-fulfillment is discussed are for instance: Mark L. Strauss, *The Davidic Messiah in Luke-Acts. The Promise and its Fulfillment in Lukan Christology* (LNTS 110; Sheffield: Sheffield Academic, 1995) and Kenneth Duncan Litwak, *Echoes of Scripture in Luke-Acts. Telling the History of God's People Intertextually* (JSNT Sup.282; London, New York: T&T Clark, 2005).
72 Kurz, *Acts of the Apostles* (2013), 44-45; *Acts of the Apostles* (1983), 21.
73 Kurz, *Following Jesus*, 123.
74 Kurz, *Acts of the Apostles* (2013), 44-45; *Acts of the Apostles* (1983), 21.

Peter's speech explains the event of Pentecost and elaborates on the fulfillment theme, using Old Testament scripture to substantiate this explanation. The adapted Joel prophecy and parts from Psalms 16 and 110 are quoted by Peter to show that it is the risen Jesus who is the promised Messiah, who is Lord and who is now seated at the right hand of God pouring out his Spirit on his disciples.[75] The alterations from the Joel prophecy are explained by Kurz as an indication that the last days have arrived, the eschatological fulfillment of Old Testament prophecies. The added phrase "and they shall prophesy" in 2:18 is interpreted by Kurz as Peter's explanation of their tongue speech and as such it is the Holy Spirit who inspires their speech.[76] The addition of "above" and "below" in 2:19 is an emphasis on the continuation of the miracle working power of God's servants: Moses in the Old Testament, Jesus in the Gospels and now the disciples in Acts.[77] According to Umberto Eco the primary concern of the cooperative reader should be the actantial structures in the text and his deduction of some abstract value judgments from these structures.[78] It seems like Kurz reads and interprets the text of Acts 2 in a fluent continuation with the Old Testament history of God and the people of Israel. This history culminates into the life and ministry of Jesus, which is not the end but only sets the stage for the final phase in God's plan of salvation. In this final phase it is through the empowerment of the Holy Spirit that the disciples then and Christians now, are able to engage in the missionary enterprise.

When it concerns value judgments Kurz is cautious to give some normative principles. He however does focus on the church and uses the text of Acts to pass on some of his thoughts:

1. The gift of speaking in tongues is positively valued by Kurz. Based on Acts 2 he interprets it as a missionary phenomenon and equates it with prophecy. The tongue speech in Acts 10:46 and 19:6 is interpreted differently, more in line with 1Cor. 12-14, being a gift of prayer and praise. This latter meaning of tongue speech is explained as being important for personal spiritual growth and Kurz cautiously refers to Romans 8:26-27 to substantiate this.[79]

---

75 Kurz, *Acts of the Apostles* (2013), 50-58; *Acts of the Apostles* (1983), 22-25.
76 Kurz, *Following Jesus, 124; Acts of the Apostles* (2013), 50.
77 Kurz, *Acts of the Apostles* (2013), 52.
78 Eco, *Lector in fabula*, 231 and above in §2.5.2.
79 Kurz, *Following Jesus, 124; Acts of the Apostles* (2013), 46.

2. With regard to soteriology Kurz does subscribe moral, ethical and soteriological attributes to the working of the Spirit. He writes that the Holy Spirit is indispensable for our faith and salvation, that Acts 2 provides a model for contemporary Christians and that Christians today receive the Holy Spirit in baptism and confirmation. In connection with this, Christian virtues and the fruit of the Spirit are mentioned, all to resemble the character of Jesus.[80]
3. Contrary to Max Turner and Robert Menzies, Kurz spends some of his writing on the person of Mary. The mentioning of Mary in Acts 1:14 is reason for Kurz to focus on this very important person within Roman Catholicism. According to Kurz Luke mentions Mary "to demonstrate that just as Mary had received the Holy Spirit so that Jesus could be born, so Mary received the Spirit when the church was born."[81] Kurz continues to state that it is a tragic mistake to downplay the role of Mary in the life of contemporary Christians and actually calls for a renewed devotion to Mary as mother of the church.[82]

To summarize, Kurz seems to cautiously propose a middle of the road position in the debate whether the Spirit in Acts is primarily soteriological or meant as an empowerment for mission. He superficially touches these subjects, but shifts his attention foremost to the individual Christian believer or the church as a whole and encourages his readers to live a life full of the Holy Spirit. Exceptional, but not surprising, is Kurz' attention to the Catholic tradition and the person of Mary. He repeatedly refers to the Catechism, speeches of the Pope and Vatican II.[83] And in a personal touch Kurz stresses the importance of Mary in his own spiritual life.[84]

In summary, according to Kurz the topic of Acts 2 is the outpouring of the Holy Spirit, legitimized by Peter in his speech on the basis of promises from the Old Testament. The narrative structure concerns the theme of promise and fulfillment, then and now. The implicit normative claim seems to be that contemporary Christians should be filled with the Spirit, participate in a "new evangelization" and resemble the character of Christ through the fruit of the Spirit. In this, the role of Mary and the Catholic Church (especially in administering the sacrament of confirmation) are indispensable.

---

80 Kurz, *Acts of the Apostles* (2013), 46-49; *Following Jesus*, 120.
81 Kurz, *Following Jesus*, 121.
82 Kurz, *Following Jesus*, 121-122.
83 Kurz, *Following Jesus*, 122-23; *Acts of the Apostles* (2013), 44, 47, 49, 51.
84 Kurz, *Following Jesus*, 122.

5.9.3 Preliminary deductions and possible implications
It is clear that Kurz cooperates with the world of the text. His reading of Acts 2 does not show any signs of postponing a certain interpretation. So, to speak in Eco's terminology, Kurz does not put certain things between brackets or wanders out of the text.[85] Kurz "jumps" back and forth from the text to the actual world, applying events from the text to the world of the (Roman Catholic) church and Christians today. In this process of application Kurz directs his attention to the need of the Holy Spirit in his own spiritual growth and that of others. Charismatic gifts such as speaking in tongues have proven their importance in praying, ministering to people in need and in administering the sacraments.[86] According to Kurz the church today needs charismatic gifts to let God be in charge of the church. The following quotation illustrates best how Kurz cooperates with the world of the text and puts it in correlation to the church today:

> "To be truly open to the Holy Spirit, Catholics must accept God's revelation as he has given it in Scripture, fostered it in tradition, and protected it, by the teaching authority of the church, from misinterpretation. We must acknowledge God's revelation as he continues to apply it to our own contemporary circumstances. The reception of the Holy Spirit at Pentecost marked the beginning of the church. Reception of the same Spirit continues to be necessary to revivify the church today. As the Holy Spirit gave to the first Christians the gifts the church needed, so today the Spirit is giving us gifts that the church needs."[87]

So to summarize, Kurz sees a clear continuation of the "promise-fulfillment" theme from the Old Testament to Luke-Acts to the church today. As a matter of fact, one could say that according to Kurz the church today is, or should be, a part of the story of Pentecost in Acts 2.

5.10 The Samaritans (Acts 8)
5.10.1 The actualized text
The text of Acts 8:4-25 is introduced by the transitional text of 8:1-3.[88] In this paragraph Luke describes the scattering of the people from Jerusalem to Judea and Samaria, due to persecution which broke out in Jerusalem.

---

85 Eco, *Lector in fabula*, 99, 154-157 and above in §2.5.3.
86 Kurz, *Following Jesus*, 125-126.
87 Kurz, *Following Jesus*, 127.
88 Kurz, *Acts of the Apostles* (1983), 43; *Reading Luke-Acts*, 84.

This scattering of the people is used for the expansion of the Gospel (Acts 8:1, 4, 11:19), starting with Philip in Samaria. This scattering due to persecution is explained by Kurz as irony in the story: the intention to suppress the Gospel leads to the spread of the Gospel.[89] Kurz accentuates the irony and relates it to the initial promise by Jesus in Acts 1:8, however it is not the apostles who will spread the Gospel, but actually all those others except the apostles, who stayed in Jerusalem (Acts 8:1).[90] According to Kurz, the scattering as a result from persecution provides a framework for the text in which the stories of Philip (Acts 8), Paul (Acts 9) and Peter (Acts 10) are told. Acts 8:4 and 11:19 form the parameters for this framework as they refer to the tragic death of Stephen. The bottom line according to Kurz is: "Nothing can stop the spread of God's word, not even persecution."[91] So concerning the expression of the text, Kurz focuses on the narrator's point of view and the literary devices the author used in telling the story.

5.10.2 The substantial properties of the text
In determining the story and narrative structures of Acts 8:4-25, Kurz seems to tie these to the three main characters in this episode: Philip, the apostles (Peter and John) and Simon the magician. All three play an important part in this episode and all three fulfill their respective roles in the overall narrative of Acts.

Philip is first mentioned in Acts 6:5 and is now introduced as the first missionary outside Jerusalem, thus serving as a hinge between the first part of Acts about the Jerusalem church and the second part of Acts about the gradual fulfillment of Acts 1:8. The story of Philip shows that persecution cannot stop the expansion of the Gospel and that it even crosses the boundaries of ethnicity. In continuation with the Gospel Philip's preaching is accompanied with miracles and exorcisms and results in belief and baptism.[92] Even Simon the magician seems to come to faith, but serves as an antagonist later in the story.

Not surprisingly Peter and John receive the most attention by Kurz. Acts 8:14-17 is the classical text for the Roman Catholic sacrament of confirmation.[93] It is through the laying on of hands by the apostles that

---

89 Kurz, *Reading Luke-Acts*, 144.
90 Kurz, *Reading Luke-Acts*, 144; *Acts of the Apostles* (2013), 137.
91 Kurz, *Reading Luke-Acts*, 89.
92 Kurz, *Acts of the Apostles* (2013), 137-139; *Acts of the Apostles* (1983), 43.
93 See http://www.vatican.va/archive/ccc_css/archive/catechism/p2s2c1a2.htm for the text of the Catechism.

the newly converted Samaritans receive the Holy Spirit. Kurz interprets this as the apostolic approval of the converts from Samaria and as a completion of their initiation into the church:

> "Luke underlines apostolic authority in the early church by stressing the continuity between the first conversions in Jerusalem at the hand of the apostles and the laying on of hands by Peter and John, which completed the incorporation of the Samaritans into the Church."[94]

When it concerns the sacrament of confirmation, we have a perfect example of Kurz putting this dogma between brackets. He does not mention it in the ongoing text of his commentary, but instead saves it for an "aside" to briefly elaborate on this sacrament of the Catholic church.[95]

Following the text of the episode Kurz continues to write about Simon the magician. According to Kurz it is typically Lukan to contrast Christian miracles with non-Christian magic.[96] The Samaritans were in awe and wonder about Simon's miracles, but now that Philip arrived and preached the Gospel he won over the Samaritans. They believed and were baptized, even Simon himself. Later in the story it appears that Simon was only interested in the power and miracles provided by the Holy Spirit, and he offered money to Peter and John. The story has some sort of open ending, because the text does not make clear whether Simon repents or not. He only asks Peter to pray for him (Acts 8:24). The value judgment Kurz bases on this episode is that there is an "essential distinction between magic and God's gifts. Magic is something the practitioner can control through methods or techniques, and can even buy."[97]

So the story of Philip in Acts 8 fits the overall outline of the Book of Acts, which we find in Acts 1:8. Irony is found in the fact that the apostles stay in Jerusalem, however they are needed to provide the essential gift of the Spirit, which leads to the Roman Catholic sacrament of confirmation. This gift of the Spirit is completely the opposite of non-Christian magic and not for sale.

---

94 Kurz, *Acts of the Apostles* (2013), 141-142.
95 The goal of the series in which Kurz' commentary is published is to "offer scholarship illumined by faith (…) within the living tradition of the church" (preface, pages 8-9). To accomplish this there are several "asides" titled "Biblical Background" and "Living Tradition" as well as a section called "Reflection and Application" at the end of each discussed episode.
96 Kurz, *Acts of the Apostles* (2013), 139n.8.
97 Kurz, *Acts of the Apostles* (2013), 142.

5.10.3 Preliminary deductions and possible implications
The Samaritan episode from Acts 8 provides us a perfect example of the role of the reader in interpreting the text. As mentioned above, Kurz puts the Roman Catholic sacrament of confirmation between brackets, only to elaborate on it a little later in his commentary. According to Kurz we find the origin of the sacrament of confirmation in this Samaritan episode. It "completes baptism and in a certain way perpetuates the grace of Pentecost in the church."[98] He refers to the Catechism and is positive about preparing young people to receive their confirmation. However, in another "aside" just one page earlier in his commentary, Kurz elaborates on God's freedom in giving the Spirit in relation with water baptism. Kurz correctly states that the text of Acts shows variety in the relationship between water baptism and the reception of the Spirit. His conclusion from this textual evidence is that it "illustrates God's freedom in pouring out his Spirit whenever he chooses." However, referring to Catholic tradition Kurz interprets that "a person receives the Holy Spirit initially in baptism and then in a fuller way through the laying on of hands at confirmation."[99]

Here we see what Eco calls "inferential walks": the reader walks out of the text, only to return with information from other texts or sources or experiences to interpret the text.[100] The text itself does not mention any prescriptive act to receive the Holy Spirit. Actually, Kurz himself admits that Acts shows a wide variety in the relationship between baptism and the reception of the Holy Spirit. Kurz' interpretation of this episode is clearly colored by his Roman Catholic tradition. The intriguing question remains whether the text of Acts as a whole and specifically Acts 8, leaves room for such a prescriptive interpretation resulting in the sacrament of confirmation or not.

In the closing paragraph on this section (titled: reflection and application), Kurz evaluates the sacrament of confirmation and asks himself why it is that so many baptized and confirmed Catholics do not show the effects of the reception of the Spirit. He does not doubt the sacrament, but argues that the beneficiary should exhibit a personal appropriation of the sacrament. He writes: "Nevertheless, the fruits of the sacraments also depend on the disposition of the one who receives them. The dispositions needed for the sacraments to bear fruit include faith in Jesus, turning

---
98   Kurz, *Acts of the Apostles* (2013), 143.
99   Kurz, *Acts of the Apostles* (2013), 142.
100 Eco, *Lector in fabula*, 154-157; *The Role of the Reader*, 32. See also above in §2.5.3.

from sin, and the desire to do God's will."[101] Kurz then concludes that the Book of Acts can awaken a new desire to experience the effects of the sacraments and he refers to Luke 11:9-13 where Jesus' disciples are encouraged to pray the Father for the Holy Spirit.

5.11 The Damascus event (Acts 9)
5.11.1 The actualized text
Kurz's focus on the text is from the narrator's point of view, where he compares the story of Acts 9 with the retelling of this story in Acts 22 and 26. He distinguishes between an "extradiegetic omniscient narrator" in Acts 9 and an "intradiegetic character narrator" in the episodes in Acts 22 en 26.[102] The extradiegetic narrator has the advance of some sort of objectivity. He describes the feelings and events of both the main characters in the story, Saul and Ananias. He clearly narrates from a Christian point of view (Jesus is "the Lord", Paul is a "chosen instrument") and makes sure the story is rooted in biblical tradition (the allusion to Tobit 11:12).[103] In Acts 22 and 26 Paul himself serves as the intradiegetic narrator and retells the event from Acts 9 from his own perception. Differences between the three versions of the story are because of the different audiences and purposes of each story. Redaction critics had already concluded this, but Kurz adds that literary criticism shows that the story in Acts 9 should be treated as the authoritative version of the story. Authoritative because of the omniscient point of view of the narrator.[104]

5.11.2 The substantial properties of the text
In defining the topic of this Acts 9 episode, Kurz's primary focus is on Saul, specifically the conversion of Saul. The fact that this event is retold twice in Acts shows the importance of this event.[105] The story is closely linked to the ending of the episode about Stephen, proceeding with the theme of the persecution of the church. The δὲ...ἔτι in 9:1 links this episode to the

---

101 Kurz, *Acts of the Apostles* (2013), 144.
102 Kurz, *Reading Luke-Acts*, 86-87, 126-131. The term "extradiegetic" means that the story is told from the outside, someone not partaking in the story. The term "intradiegetic" means the opposite: the story is told by someone who is part of the story.
103 Kurz, *Reading Luke-Acts*, 127-128; *Acts of the Apostles* (1983), 48; *Acts of the Apostles* (2013), 156.
104 Kurz, *Reading Luke-Acts*, 131.
105 Kurz, *Acts of the Apostles* (1983), 46-47; *Acts of the Apostles* (2013), 151. Contra Robert Menzies, who sees the person of Ananias as the primary person of interest in this episode.

previous mentioning of Saul persecuting the church in 8:1-3.[106] The story then develops and has as its focal point Saul's encounter with the risen Jesus, which is not without consequences. The encounter in 9:3-6 is reminiscent of Old Testament theophanies such as described in Ezekiel 1 and Daniel 10. This provides a certain depth to the story and places it within the biblical tradition. The word κύριος in verse 5 is at first translated by Kurz as the normal "sir", but because of the context (a voice from heaven) he later corrects himself and uses "Lord".[107] The explanation for this shift is due to the context: because the voice is from heaven the proper translation should be "Lord" according to Kurz. Unfortunately Kurz fails to elaborate on this translation and does not seem to be aware of the Pentecostal doctrine of the "second blessing" which among other things is based on this interpretation of the κύριος in verse 5.[108] It further becomes clear that the person of Ananias is just an instrument in God's hands and that the red thread of the story is Paul's new mission: bringing the Gospel to the Gentiles. So instead of persecuting Christians in Damascus, Paul's mission changes into bringing the Gospel to the Gentiles. The reason for this dramatic change of course is the theophany on the road to Damascus. Kurz however is remarkably silent about Paul's conversion, the subsequent laying on of hands by Ananias' and Paul's reception of the Holy Spirit. He describes these events without thoroughly interpreting them. It seems that Kurz reads the laying on of hands by Ananias as an instrument for Paul's healing: "Ananias comes in and lays hands on him for him to regain his sight. [...] First Saul is healed from his blindness, a sign of his inner spiritual enlightenment."[109] Kurz does not write about a possible commissioning of Paul by Ananias, or the reception of the Spirit through the laying on of hands. The Catholic sacrament of confirmation seems to fit in this episode as well (conversion, baptism, laying on of hands, reception of the Holy Spirit), however Kurz does not mention this at all in his commentary. In comparison with Max Turner and Robert Menzies' treatment of this episode (see above in §3.10 and §4.10) this seems a bit odd and a missed opportunity for Kurz to add some depth to his interpretation of this passage.

---

106 Kurz, *Reading Luke-Acts*, 127; *Acts of the Apostles* (2013), 151.
107 Kurz, *Acts of the Apostles* (2013), 152.
108 See the discussion above in §3.10.2. "Second blessing" is the popular terminology within Pentecostal circles to describe a necessary and normative second filling with the Holy Spirit which is evidenced by speaking in tongues.
109 Kurz, *Acts of the Apostles*, 154-155.

5.11.3 Preliminary deductions and possible implications
As already mentioned above, according to Kurz the story of Acts 9 is about the new mission of Paul: bringing the Gospel to the Gentiles. Kurz underlines this interpretation of the story by referring back to the Gospel of Luke (Luke 2:32 and 21:12) and looking forward to Acts 13 and 26.[110] That the Gospel would be preached to the Gentiles was already prophesied by Simeon in Luke 2:29-32 and the remainder of Acts will show that the Gospel will as well be preached before kings and governors. Due to these interpretive flashbacks and flash forwards, Kurz discovers an intertextual depth in this story, which subsequently colors his reading of the text of this episode. Box 7 in Eco's model of the cooperative reader shows the possible forecasts and inferential walks of the reader.[111] To arrive at the hypothesis that the story of Acts 9 is about the new mission of Paul, Kurz wanders out of the text of Acts 9 by referring back to the Gospel of Luke and looking forward to the remainder of Acts.[112] This foreknowledge of the whole of the narrative of Luke-Acts provides Kurz with the necessary information to determine the topic of Acts 9. A positive aspect of this approach is that Kurz keeps a keen eye on the whole of the story of Luke-Acts. A less positive aspect is that the interpretation of Acts 9 tends to be a bit superficial. There is much more to say about this episode than just Paul receiving a new mission.

5.12 The Cornelius' household (Acts 10)
5.12.1 The actualized text
The text of this episode actually starts in 9:32 where, according to Kurz, the narrative of Acts switches between the main characters of the story: Paul and Peter.[113] Acts 9:31 is a typically Lukan summary, which closes the previous section about S/Paul and simultaneously paves the way for the other main character: Peter.[114] Acts 9:31-43 informs the reader about Peter's ministry in Lydda and Joppa and its closing verse (43) places Peter in Joppa, which sets the stage for the next episode about the Cornelius' household. The Cornelius' episode is in Kurz's words "a major turning

---
110 Kurz, *Acts of the Apostles* (2013), 154-155.
111 See above in §2.5.3 and Eco, *Lector in fabula*, 154-157.
112 Kurz treats Acts 9:9 more or less in the same manner: based on Philippians 3:7-9 he concludes that "Saul's heart was captured by the Lord", Kurz, *Acts of the Apostles* (2013), 153.
113 The Greek ἐγένετο δέ is frequently used by Luke to introduce a new episode (see for instance: Acts 4:5, 8:1, 9:19, 14:1, 16:16, 19:1,23, 28:17), Kurz, *Reading Luke-Acts*, 87.
114 Kurz, *Reading Luke-Acts*, 87.

point in Acts".[115] Kurz sees some sort of parallel between the introduction of Cornelius as a devout centurion in Acts 10:1-2 and the story about the devout centurion in Luke 7:1-10. Subsequently the angel's assurance in 10:4 (Cornelius' prayers have been heard by God) is paralleled with Luke 1:13, in which the angel reassures Zechariah (whose prayers as well have been heard by God).[116] In addition to these parallels Kurz highlights the repetition of Cornelius' vision (first in 10:3-6 and later the retelling in 10:30-32), which shows the importance of this vision. Kurz compares this with Paul retelling the event of his calling (Acts 9) in Acts 22 and 26. It seems typical for the narrative of Acts that certain events are described and later retold to accentuate the importance of these events. In this manner different points of view are shown to the reader which can contribute to the understanding and interpretation of the text.[117] The same technique is used when it concerns the outpouring of the Holy Spirit upon Cornelius and his household. At first this is told by the omniscient narrator in Acts 10:44-48 and later retold by Peter in Acts 11:15-17 and more or less referred to in 15:8-9. Through Peter's remembrance of the promise of John the Baptist (Acts 11:16) it seems that a major Lukan theological theme comes to the surface in his two volume narrative: Jesus is savior for Jew *and* Gentile, confirmed by the outpouring of the Holy Spirit on *all* flesh.[118] Kurz deliberately ties this episode of Cornelius and Peter's retelling in Acts 11 to the prologue of Luke's Gospel in Luke 1:3-4, stating that "God has reached out beyond the chosen people to save all flesh."[119] Because of the mentioning of the outbreak of persecution after Stephen's stoning in Acts 11:19 Kurz argues convincingly that this is where the story about Peter ends.[120] So the text proper is about the other main character in Acts, Peter, and starts in Acts 9:32 until Acts 11:18.

---

115 Kurz, *Reading Luke-Acts*, 87; *Acts of the Apostles* (1983), 51; *Following Jesus*, 142.
116 Kurz, *Reading Luke-Acts*, 87-88; *Acts of the Apostles* (1983), 51; *Acts of the Apostles* (2013), 168.
117 Kurz, *Reading Luke-Acts*, 88.
118 It seems to me that Peter's remembrance of the promise of John the Baptist is a very deliberate move of the author of Luke-Acts, which serves as a key to understand the previous passages about the outpouring of the Spirit. In this way Peter's remembrance is a climax which unfolds a very important aspect of Luke's Pneumatology and as such shows one of the various theological themes of Luke-Acts.
119 Kurz, *Reading Luke-Acts*, 89.
120 Kurz, *Reading Luke-Acts*, 89.

5.12.2 The substantial properties of the text
According to Kurz the topic of the Cornelius' episode is that "God shows no partiality" (Acts 10:34). This theme comes regularly to the surface in Kurz's various writings.[121] The occasion for this topic is Peter's vision in 10:10-16. Peter hears the heavenly voice three times, only to be left in bewilderment. He does not understand what the vision is about until later in the story when the three servants of Cornelius arrive and they travel together to the house of Cornelius, where Cornelius tells about his vision. Peter then understands the meaning of his own vision (verse 28, 34) and starts explaining the Gospel to Cornelius and all present. The topic that God shows no partiality is grounded in the Old Testament (in Acts 10:34 Peter refers to Deuteronomy 10:17) and in this story it is then applied to the relationship between Jew and Gentile. Kurz elaborates on this topic by the "aside" in his commentary and provides some depth to the Greek word προσωπολήμπτης and the text in Deuteronomy.[122] Eco shows in his model that after establishing the topic of the text the cooperative reader moves beyond the text by using abstract terminology and even adding value judgments (boxes 8 and 9 in his model).[123] Kurz' reading of the Cornelius' episode clearly shows that he does so. After his short treatment of the Deuteronomy text he refers to various other Old and New Testament texts (Rom. 2:11-12, 2Chron. 19:7, Sir. 35:11-14). The statement "like God himself, his people are also to show no partiality" is underlined by a quotation from Leviticus 19:15 and via the example of Jesus (who did not show partiality) Kurz arrives at James 2:1-4 where the Christian community is summoned to impartiality.[124] This reading and application of the topic of the Cornelius' episode becomes even clearer in Kurz' more popular book *Following Jesus*. There he explicitly writes about the struggle to accept changes. As an example he mentions the Roman Catholic Mass which was supposed to be in Latin, but is now in English. In addition Kurz writes about the previous warning not to touch the sacred host, but that it is now given in the hand.[125] Kurz continues to write that some changes might perplex us but we must recognize that some "are God's will for a new situation."[126] When facing difficult changes in the

---

121 Kurz, *Reading Luke-Acts*, 88; *Following Jesus*, 151; *Acts of the Apostles* (1983), 53-54; *Acts of the Apostles* (2013), 175-176.
122 Kurz, *Acts of the Apostles* (2013), 176.
123 Eco, *Lector in fabula*, 229-244 and above in §2.5.2.
124 Kurz, *Acts of the Apostles* (2013), 176.
125 Kurz, *Following Jesus*, 148-149; *Acts of the Apostles* (1983), 53.
126 Kurz, *Following Jesus*, 150.

church today, the Cornelius' episode can be of comfort to the present day church. In his application of the biblical text Kurz does not start with the episode in Acts, but uses the story for present day examples. He adds that "God's word in Scripture" and "the official teaching of the church" function as a check in determining whether changes are God's will or not. Kurz does not hesitate to draw a direct line between Peter then and the Roman Catholic Pope now: "He, like Peter, has learned to affirm some changes, and to condemn others."[127] In his short discussion of Acts 10:34-35 Kurz translates the "no partiality" from the text to the current day obligation of being hospitable: "The same God who calls us to family-type community also calls us to treat with genuine hospitality strangers or others not in the community."[128] The relation of this topic of showing no partiality to the outpouring of the Spirit in 10:44 is, according to Kurz, obvious. The fact that these Gentiles receive the Spirit in the same way as the apostles at Pentecost, is the pre-eminent example of God showing no partiality.

5.12.3 Preliminary deductions and possible implications
In his reading of the Cornelius episode Kurz does not so much put certain things between brackets (box 5 in Eco's model). He however does wander out of the text and uses his own encyclopedic knowledge (box 7) to come to some observations and interpretations which are coherent with the actual world (box 10). In his discussion of Peter's speech to the Cornelius' household (10:34-43), Kurz focuses on Jesus' anointing with the Holy Spirit: the Spirit was with Jesus from his conception, but at his baptism the Spirit empowered Jesus for his ministry.[129] The parallel is drawn with the church in the Book of Acts and the readers of Luke-Acts, such as the church today:

> "[…] Jesus worked miracles not only as God […] but also as a Spirit-empowered man, who is therefore a model for all his disciples. This enables Luke and Acts to underline the continuity between wonder-working prophets like Moses and Elijah, the miraculous prophetic ministry of Jesus, and the miracles of his Spirit-empowered followers like Peter, Stephen, and Paul in Acts. Peter and others imitated Jesus' healings as part of their prophetic witness to

---
127 Kurz, *Following Jesus*, 150.
128 Kurz, *Following Jesus*, 151.
129 Kurz, *Acts of the Apostles* (2013), 178.

God's saving message; so such works are likewise possible for Spirit-empowered Christian readers of Luke-Acts."[130]

This rather lengthy quote shows Kurz' interpretive way of reading the text. He takes the characters from the text as models which need to be imitated by Christians today. On the one hand this shows a far-reaching cooperation with the text which firmly applies the text to the world today. On the other hand the question remains whether this exact modeling and imitation was actually meant by the original author or whether this modeling and imitation can be found in the narrative and actantial structures of the text under scrutiny. To put it in other words and use the imagery of the game of chess: is this modeling and imitation a legitimate move to make and does the text allow such a move?

Although Kurz does not explicitly write about his theological view on the working of the Spirit, the interpretation above strongly suggests Kurz views the Spirit as a necessary empowerment for believers to engage in mission and miracles. On the other hand however, Kurz as well writes about the Spirit as the soteriological Spirit. The Gentiles (Cornelius' household) are cleansed by the Spirit of God, "God reaches out to forgive and cleanse sinners."[131] Kurz argues that circumcision is not necessary anymore, because the Spirit of God purifies those who were seen as unclean.[132] So besides the empowerment for mission, there is as well a cleansing aspect in the outpouring of the Spirit. Once again, Kurz does not explicitly take position in the debate whether the Spirit in Luke-Acts is an empowerment for mission or soteriological, but from his interpretation and application of the Cornelius episode we can deduce that Kurz leaves room for both positions. Or perhaps even combines these positions when it concerns the household of Cornelius and the church today.

5.13 The Ephesian disciples (Acts 19)
Just as was the case with Jesus' general sayings about the Spirit in Luke 10-12 (see above in §5.7), I can as well be very short about the Ephesian disciples. In some brief passages in his different writings, Kurz treats this episode with some cursory consideration.[133] He seems to take for granted

---

130 Kurz, *Acts of the Apostles* (2013), 178.
131 Kurz, *Following Jesus*, 143, 154.
132 Kurz, *Acts of the Apostles* (1983), 51.
133 Kurz, *Reading Luke-Acts*, 97-98; *Acts of the Apostles* (1983), 81-82 and *Acts of the Apostles* (2013), 291-292.

that the twelve were deficient Christians or not at all Christians: "This rules out the possibility that they could be full-fledged Christians, since Christian initiation entails receiving the Spirit as Jesus' disciples did at Pentecost."[134] This is more or less the same interpretation as Turner's (see above in §3.12) and a different interpretation than Menzies' (see above in §4.12). Kurz loosely ties this episode about the Ephesian disciple to the previous Appolos' account (Acts 18:24-28) reading it as a "split-screen approach" by the omniscient narrator.[135] In his 1983 commentary Kurz argues that "the main point is clear" being that Paul's followers corrected Apollos' teaching. Kurz finds it possible that the Ephesian disciples were the reason that Apollos needed further instruction.[136] In his more recent commentary Kurz does not mention any possible connection at all between the episode about Apollos and the Ephesian disciples. His reading and interpretation of this episode is rather straightforward: Paul comes across these disciples from Ephesus, they probably believed in John the Baptist's message and were baptized in John's baptism. Paul elaborates and explains that they have to believe in the One coming after John, Jesus. They believe and are being baptized in the name of Jesus, and after Paul lays his hands on them they receive the Holy Spirit and as a result prophesy and speak in tongues. In addition to the Turner's and Menzies' interpretation of this episode, Kurz adds (in all three of his books) the observation that in verse 7 is spoken of about (ὡσεί) twelve men.[137] He interprets this as a correspondence to the twelve apostles among the 120 in Acts 1 and 2 and sees it as a hint to the twelve tribes of Israel: "In Scripture the number twelve often symbolizes the people of God."[138] To conclude: this is very much what Kurz has to say about the Ephesian disciples. Due to Kurz' last remark about the approximate number of twelve men hinting back to Acts 1 and 2, I am inclined to see some sort of *inclusio* here. Acts 19 is the last occurrence of people being filled with the Spirit in Luke-Acts. Somehow the *inclusio* hints back to Acts 2 where the disciples were filled, but as well forms a neat closure of one of Luke's subthemes, which started in the beginning of the Gospel with the promise of John the Baptist (Luke 3:16). Max Turner seems to argue this

---

134 Kurz, *Acts of the Apostles* (2013), 291.
135 Kurz, *Reading Luke-Acts*, 97.
136 Kurz, *Acts of the Apostles* (1983), 81.
137 Kurz, *Reading Luke-Acts*, 98; *Acts of the Apostles* (1983), 82; *Acts of the Apostles* (2013), 292.
138 Kurz, *Acts of the Apostles*, 292.

way as well.¹³⁹ Especially because Kurz uses literary criticism as his methodology, it seems a missed opportunity that he does not spent some more words to open up this episode. It would have provided his interpretation with some intertextual depth and a satisfying ending of 'Luke's theology of the Spirit'.

5.14 Conclusion
5.14.1 The Role of the Reader: William S. Kurz
The reader Kurz is foremost a Catholic reader. His reading of Luke-Acts prominently shows this Catholic angle: he regularly refers to the tradition of the Catholic church, the catechism, sacraments and statements made by the Pope. In short you can say that William Kurz is a devout and proud Catholic and he does not hesitate to show this in his reading and interpretation of the text. In addition Kurz is somewhat critical towards the academic reading of the text, especially when it concerns those scholars who use historical criticism as their primary methodology.¹⁴⁰ These scholars seem to "lock the Scriptures" for the ordinary Christian reader and forget to address contemporary concerns. Kurz tries to 'solve' this by using a literary critical approach himself. This is a commendable effort and shows where his passion is: interpreting the word of God for contemporary (Catholic) Christian believers. However a slight inconsistency needs to be mentioned and is that Kurz on the one hand is critical towards the various historical oriented methods, but on the other hand admits that his own work (*Reading Luke-Acts as Biblical Narrative*) "does not ignore but builds on the insights from historical criticism".¹⁴¹ So despite his criticism Kurz himself does use the insights from this research in his own work. Because Kurz' literary critical approach and Luke being a storyteller with Luke-Acts as the narrative result (see above in §1.2.1), Eco's model provides an excellent opportunity to assess Kurz' distinctive reading of Luke-Acts. As a result we can conclude the following:

1. Kurz is a cooperative reader in the sense that he reads and interprets the text of the narrative in order to apply the text of the narrative to present day issues. He does not hesitate to use events from his own life as an example;

---

139 Turner, *Power from on High*, 396-397.
140 Kurz, *Reading Luke-Acts*, 16.
141 Kurz, *Reading Luke-Acts*, 5.

2. Because of Kurz' emphasis on literary-criticism little attention is spent on the text itself, as Eco refers to in boxes 1-3 in his model;
3. In determining the story of the text, Kurz is eager to interpret and apply for the present day reader. The historical and theological side of the text is often left aside in favor of application. This results in an excellent cooperation with the text. However, it simultaneously raises the question whether Kurz spends responsible attention to the distinctive historical and theological aspects of the text;
4. The weight of Kurz' work is in application. His reading is pregnant with ideological insights and value judgments. In many cases normative statements are made for the benefit of contemporary readers.

To summarize, Kurz seems to be preoccupied with the "discipling" effect of the text. His primary focus is how contemporary readers of Luke-Acts can understand and interpret the narrative in order to be better disciples of Jesus Christ. This discipling desire is prominent in his *Following Jesus*, and this is also the desire in his more academic works such as *Reading Luke-Acts* and in both of his commentaries on Acts. With the purpose of discipleship in mind, Kurz acts as a cooperative reader whose presupposition is that the narrative of Luke-Acts is relevant, actual and applicable for the Christian reader today. Unfortunately this particular cooperation with the text results in a rather superficial treatment of some thorny theological issues such as second blessing, ordination and evidential tongues.

5.14.2 Lukan Pneumatology according to William S. Kurz
As already mentioned, it is not Kurz' purpose to write a Lukan pneumatology. However, in his treatments of the various πνεῦμα passages, we can deduce his view of the working and the role of the Holy Spirit in Luke-Acts and the importance for the contemporary reader. We can summarize Kurz' conclusions concerning Lukan Pneumatology as follows:

1. Kurz sees the promise of John the Baptist reiterated in Acts 1:5 and 1:8, and fulfilled at Pentecost in Acts 2. The continuous fulfilling of this promise occurs at the water baptism and confirmation of the Christian. This involves the Spirit's indwelling in and empowerment of the Christian;
2. The Holy Spirit is meant as an empowerment for mission and ministry, just as was the case with Jesus' baptism and subsequent reception of the Holy Spirit and the outpouring of the Holy Spirit at Pentecost on the disciples. Both of these events are taken as *exemplars* for Christians today and Kurz encourages Christians to wait for such an empowerment of the Spirit;

3. In Kurz' interpretation of Luke-Acts the Holy Spirit is also the soteriological Spirit. He argues that due to apostolic authority Christians receive the Holy Spirit at water baptism and confirmation. His leading argument here is more dependent on the Catholic tradition and doctrine, than on the narrative of Luke-Acts;
4. In addition Kurz does not hesitate to call the Spirit the charismatic Spirit. This charismatic Spirit is needed for prayer, spiritual growth and in ministry. The speaking in tongues in Acts 2 are interpreted as a missiological phenomenon, whereas speaking in tongues in Acts 8 and 19 are interpreted along the line of 1Cor.14, for the edifying of the individual believer.

In short we can conclude that Kurz' reading and interpretation of the πνεῦμα clusters in Luke-Acts result in a pneumatology which takes neither side of the soteriological or empowerment debate, but includes both. Kurz' main purpose is the spiritual growth of the present day Christian believer and to encourage this spiritual growth water baptism and confirmation are needed, as well as charismatic gifts for personal growth and an empowerment of the Spirit to be an effective witness.

CHAPTER 6

THE ROLE OF THE READER: LIMITS AND POSSIBILITIES OF INTERPRETATION

6.1 Introduction

In the *Forschungsbericht* of this dissertation we have seen that in the past forty-five years some consensus on Lukan pneumatology has been reached. Scholars agree that the author can be described as historian, theologian and storyteller at the same time: Luke-Acts tells us a theological story embedded in history. That First-Century Judaism serves as the primary background for this story is agreed on, as well as the close relation between the Holy Spirit and mission in Luke-Acts. However in certain issues this consensus proved to be thin or superficial and the areas of disagreements outnumbered the areas of consensus. It seemed that a lot had to do with hermeneutics and especially the role of the reader. Based on the same text (the narrative of Luke-Acts) different readers could come up with different, sometimes opposite, conclusions. This stresses the importance of hermeneutics. In chapter two I gave an overview of hermeneutical developments: from behind the text issues (*Einleitungs-* and *Einführungsfragen*) the shift was made to the text itself (New Criticism, Structuralism) and eventually to the reader of the text (reader-response strategies).[1] At one end of the spectrum there is the issue of *authorial intent*: what exactly did the author intended to say in his text? This original meaning should coincide with the present day interpretation. At the other end of the spectrum we find the reader or interpretive community who *produces* meaning: without a reader there is no interpretation. All this shows that the shift in the past century has been enormous. In §2.2 I discussed the development of various theories which describe the role of the reader during the process of interpretation. Terminology such as implied reader (*implizite Leser*), discovery of meaning (*Sinnkonstitution*), filling in the gaps or blanks, actualization of the text were all used to describe the role of the reader or the role of the interpretive community.[2] However it was Umberto Eco who actually developed a

---

1 See above in §2.1.
2 The German terminology is from Wolfgang Iser, *Der implizite Leser*.

model to gain insight in the process of reading and interpreting a text. Eco's model shows how the interpretive choices are made by the reader. This way transparency in the role and therewith influence of the reader in interpreting a text is acquired. Eco's model of the cooperative reader is especially suitable for narrative texts. And that is what scholars agree on: Luke-Acts is a narrative, the writer (Luke) can be designated as *storyteller*. Eco's position is that a narrative text needs the cooperation of the reader and that such a text is written to invoke a certain response from its readers. The comparison is made with the game of chess.[3] The rules of chess are fixed. Just as the board and the pieces which are used to play with. However, each different player can play in his own manner. Within the given set of rules there are multiple options and possibilities to move the pieces. The analogy with reading a narrative is that the text is fixed, however each different reader focuses on different aspects and responds differently to the narrative. So far so good, but the opposite is true as well: there are things the game of chess is not meant for. It can be used to be proudly displayed, but never played with. It can be used by little children as toys, but that is not the purpose of the game. With regard to Luke-Acts, Eco gives the following example:

> "To interpret a text means to explain why these words can do various things (and not others) through the way they are interpreted. But if Jack the Ripper told us that he did what he did on the grounds of his interpretation of the Gospel according to Saint Luke, I suspect that many reader-oriented critics would be inclined to think that he read Saint Luke in a pretty preposterous way. Non-reader-oriented critics would say that Jack the Ripper was deadly mad – and I confess that, even though feeling very sympathetic with the reader-oriented paradigm [...] I would agree that Jack the Ripper needed medical care."[4]

This illustration shows the significance of a model which makes the process of reading and interpreting transparent. In other words: to fully understand and comprehend a certain interpretation we have to gain insight in the reading process. Eco's model of the cooperative reader provides this insight. In chapters three, four and five we have treated three different scholars. Three well informed readers, all three from different denominational backgrounds and all three with different reading

---

3 Eco, *Lector in fabula*, 152-154, 217-218.
4 Eco, *Interpretation and Overinterpretation*, 24.

strategies and subsequent interpretations of the Lukan πνεῦμα clusters. But what exactly are the limits and possibilities of interpretation? Are all three scholars equally right in their interpretation? Do all three operate within the boundaries of the text? Or are they *over-interpreting* the text and in doing so exceeding the limits of interpretation? To determine a satisfactory answer to these questions we do need some criteria to evaluate their respective interpretations. Unfortunately Eco's model of the cooperative reader does not provide us with some solid criteria of what the limits of interpretation are and whether a reader exceeds these limits or not. However, this does not mean that any interpretation is possible. It does not mean that there is an unlimited amount of different interpretations. Eco calls this *unlimited semiosis* and phrases it as follows:

> "(…) unlimited semiosis does not lead to the conclusion that interpretation has no criteria. To say that interpretation (as the basic feature of semiosis) is potentially unlimited does not mean that interpretation has no object and that it 'riverruns' merely for its own sake. To say that a text has potentially no end does not mean that every act of interpretation can have a happy end."[5]

So despite the fact that different interpretations are possible or that different interpretive choices are made, this does not mean that the possibilities are endless or that every interpretation is a responsible interpretation. Eco's model of the cooperative reader provides insight in the reading process and as such determines the role of the reader in his interpretation of the text. In regard to criteria to determine the limits of interpretation Eco does not leave us totally empty-handed. It is possible to deduce some criteria for the reading process from Eco's various writings. Instead of criteria it is perhaps better to use the word observations. From Eco's writings we can deduce some observations about the limits of interpretation. Because every text is different and every reader is different it is slightly impossible to produce a 'once and for all' set of solid criteria to which every reader must submit. However, in closely observing the reader and the text it is possible to determine whether a reader exceeds the limits of responsible interpretation or not. Eco's own example of Jack the Ripper (see above) illustrates this. The basics of Eco's model can be summarized as follows:

---

5 Eco, *Interpretation and Overinterpretation*, 23-24.

1. For a proper understanding and interpretation of the text the reader needs to immerse oneself in the world of the author. This is necessary to determine the author's reading strategy and discover the codes the author has put in the text;[6]
2. The next step for the reader is to immerse himself in the world of the text. It is here that the reader can discover the model reader which the original author had in mind;[7]
3. The encyclopedic competence of the reader then determines whether or not the limits of interpretation are exceeded. The reader's encyclopedic competence should be compatible with the author's purpose of the text and the model reader for which he created the text.[8]

If we translate these three basics of Eco's model to a workable set of criteria we can conclude that a cooperative reader should:

1. Take the text itself as his starting point. This is after all the material to work with, the material to read and to interpret;
2. Take the piece of text under scrutiny (a certain episode or passage), determine the right story of this text and let this story be in accordance with the narrative in its entirety;
3. Determine whether he has to do with an open or a closed text. A closed text is limited in its possible interpretations, an open text provides more possible interpretations.

The first two criteria are about the text. The original author wrote the text in specific circumstances (social, cultural, political), with a specific purpose in mind. He used a reading strategy in which a model reader is incorporated so that the actual reader understands and interprets correctly as long as he cooperates alongside the model reader the author had in mind. The limits of interpretation then are set by the text and the (presumed) encyclopedic competence of the reader. If the reader has a rather large encyclopedic competence he will be aware of different interpretive possibilities and a rather wide range of limits. Compare this to the more

---

6 Eco, *Lector in fabula*, 70-75; Eco, *The Role of the Reader*, 7-8; Zwiep, *Tussen tekst en lezer II*, 348-350.
7 Eco, *Lector in fabula*, 70-75, 80-82; Eco, *The Role of the Reader*, 7-11; Eco, *Interpretation and Overinterpretation*, 64-65.
8 Eco, *Lector in fabula*, 99-105; Eco, *The Role of the Reader*, 7-11; Zwiep, *Tussen tekst en lezer II*, 348-357.

practiced chess player. He will have more strategies at his disposal than the less practiced chess player. The same is true for the experienced reader: due to his larger encyclopedic competence he has a wider range of interpretations at his disposal. However, the negative side of a large encyclopedic competence is the danger of *overinterpretation* or *ideological overcoding*.[9] The experienced reader cannot approach the text with an open mind anymore. Because of his wide knowledge he is biased in his approach and interpretation of the text and as such can exceed the limits of interpretation. Determining the right topic and story of the text should prevent such an overinterpretation.

The last criterion is about the nature of the text. An open text leaves the reader with more interpretive possibilities, whereas in a closed text the author guides the reader by limiting the possible interpretations.[10] In an open text the limits of interpretation are more problematic. There are open ends within the text and plot lines are not fully developed, whether on purpose or not. A certain degree of (creative) cooperation from the reader is required. In a closed text the author determines in his text how the story will unfold and what the exact (one and only) interpretation should be. This is part of the plot of the narrative and such a plot has a clear set of interpretive limits. The biblical narrative of Luke-Acts is a mixture of both sorts of texts. An example of a closed text is for instance the regulations for heathen Christians in Acts 15:1-20. This is a closed set of prescriptions. An example of an open text is the episode right after Jesus' inaugural address, Luke 4:28-30, where Jesus can walk unharmed through an angry crowd. How was this possible?[11] This mixture of open and closed texts in Luke-Acts make it difficult to establish firm limits of interpretations. An open text naturally leaves room for various possible interpretations. This leads to the conclusion that there is a certain bandwidth in possible interpretations. As present day readers we are not always happy with such a bandwidth, because we are inclined to search for the one-and-only correct interpretation of a biblical text. However, the narrative of Luke-Acts leaves room for a rather large bandwidth of interpretations. An example of a guideline Luke uses as a reading strategy

---

9 Eco, *Lector in fabula*, 111-112; Eco, *The Role of the Reader*, 22.
10 Eco, *The Open Work*, *The Role of the Reader* and *Lector in fabula*, 75-78. See also Zwiep, *Tussen tekst en lezer II*, 342. And see above in §2.4 for examples of a closed and an open text.
11 For an extensive treatment of this episode see: Bruce W. Longenecker, *Hearing the Silence: Jesus on the Edge and God in the Gap – Luke 4 in Narrative Perspective* (Eugene, OR: Cascade, 2012).

is his use of frequent references and allusions to the Old Testament. These provide a certain depth to the narrative and directs the reader in his interpretation of the text. To summarize this set of criteria in a thesis, I argue that for a sound and responsible interpretation of the biblical narrative it is necessary to determine whether a text is open or closed, to rightly establish the story of the episode and to let it be in accordance with the narrative in its entirety.

In the previous three chapters I discussed all three scholars along the lines of the ten established πνεῦμα clusters in Luke-Acts. These ten clusters are what Eco calls "literary knots" (above in §2.4). The knots in an open text leave room for multiple possible interpretations. Six out of these ten πνεῦμα clusters are of great significance in construing a Lukan pneumatology. The respective interpretations of these six clusters determine the building blocks for the construing of a Lukan pneumatology. In all of these six πνεῦμα clusters Turner, Menzies and Kurz show their own distinctive reading and interpretation of the text. In their reciprocal interaction the role of each scholar will become vividly clear and therewith the insight whether the scholar in question exceeds the limits of interpretation or not. From the Gospel of Luke the three clusters are Luke 1-2, 3 and 4. Luke 1-2 form some sort of introduction to Lukan pneumatology, the key in Luke 3 is the promise of John the Baptist and Luke 4 is programmatic for Jesus' ministry in the remainder of the Gospel. From the Book of Acts chapters 2, 8 and 10 will be discussed. Acts 2 is programmatic for the working of the Spirit after Jesus' ascension and Acts 8 and 10 show the development of the working of the Spirit when ethnic boundaries are crossed. By focusing on these six episodes we can gain insight in the role of the reader and determine whether he exceeds the limits of interpretation or not while construing a Lukan pneumatology.

6.2 Luke 1-2: The Infancy Narratives
All three scholars do agree on the importance of the infancy narratives. Despite their different approaches of the text, all three are convinced that these two chapters of *Lukan Sondergut* provide a prolonged prologue to the whole of the Lukan narrative. Various theological themes are cautiously introduced only to be worked out in the remainder of the story. Somehow in the infancy narratives the stage is set for much more to happen. It is as well clear that in these infancy narratives the Holy Spirit has a leading role in comparison to the rest of the Gospel. However, the question is how distinctively Lukan this role of the Spirit is in comparison to the Old Testament background of the Gospel. From a literary point of

view, Kurz focuses on the omniscient narrator of the infancy narratives and states that the manner in which these narratives are written stem from a biblical tradition. Various pious Jews are described, a barren woman who miraculously becomes pregnant and several Isaianic quotations firmly put the story in the biblical tradition of the Old Testament. When it concerns the Holy Spirit, the Old Testament background is not in question. However, especially Turner and Menzies have different and opposite opinions about what exact characteristics can be categorized under the heading 'Spirit of prophecy'. Both scholars base their opinions on their own research of the Old Testament and Intertestamental use of the Spirit of prophecy. Turner opts for a more broader understanding of the Spirit of prophecy, including various elements such as charismatic wisdom, revelation, guidance, praise and prophetic speech (see above in §3.2.1), whereas Menzies on the contrary limits the meaning of the Spirit of prophecy to inspired speech (see above in §4.2). These (opposite) findings are taken to the text of Luke-Acts. In his model of the cooperative reader, Eco calls this foreknowledge the encyclopedic competence of the reader. But this competence can as well be a burden to rightly understand the text. The reader's presuppositions color their reading and interpretation of the text and as well their cooperation with the text. Luke 1:35 illustrates this the best:

> The angel answered, "The Holy Spirit will come upon you, and the power of the Most High will overshadow you. So the holy one to be born will be called the Son of God."[12]

The crucial question here is whether these words of the angel Gabriel should be taken as a parallelism or not. If yes, than Holy Spirit and power of the Most High are equated (so Turner), if not than Holy Spirit and Power of the Most High are two different things (so Menzies). If we take the original Greek words it looks like this:

Πνεῦμα ἅγιον ἐπελεύσεται ἐπὶ σέ,
καὶ δύναμις ὑψίστου ἐπισκιάσει σοι

Parallelism as a figure of speech means there is "similarity in structure of a pair of words, phrases, clauses, or syntactical arrangements."[13] In addition

---

12 The quotation is taken from the New International Version.
13 James L. Resseguie, *Narrative Criticism of the New Testament. An Introduction* (Grand Rapids, MI: Baker Academic, 2005), 56.

Bailey and Vander Broek point to the specific form of this story in Luke 1:26-38 and describe it as a commissioning story:

> "Indispensable to this type of story are the elements (a word, phrase, or a block of material) of confrontation, commission, and reassurance. The confrontational component depicts a divine representative or person who issues an authoritative commission to someone in the story; the commission is issued to make the recipient an agent of a higher authority; the reassurance is apparently designed to eliminate any remaining resistance from the person being commissioned."[14]

Comparing the episode from Acts 9 and this episode from Luke 1, they conclude a rather flexible pattern "including two descriptions of reassurance (30 and 35-37), one after Mary's initial reaction and one after her protest."[15] They further argue that the form of such a story is descriptive and the interpreter should focus on the purpose, namely "to commission someone to carry out a divinely-instigated task."[16] Applying this to Luke 1:35 in a natural reading it seems that Luke wanted to state the same thing, but used different concepts. So from a narrative perspective the most logical explanation is that we do have here a parallelism which equates Holy Spirit with power.[17] The question remains if Luke meant this figurative, as a way of speaking, and as such used the literary device of a parallelism. Or did Luke had a specific purpose in mind to equate or divide power and Holy Spirit? Menzies (see above in §4.2.2) interprets this passage as a Lukan redaction to theologically divide power and Holy Spirit. The latter inspires prophetic speech and the former instigates exorcism and miracles of healing. Menzies mainly uses other Lukan texts to substantiate this interpretation. Due to the fact that most commentators interpret 1:35 as a parallelism and that from a narrative point of view this

---

14 James L. Bailey and Lyle D. Vander Broek, *Literary Forms in the New Testament. A Handbook* (Louisville, KY: Westminster/John Knox, 1992), 144.
15 Bailey and Vander Broek, *Literary Forms*, 146.
16 Bailey and Vander Broek, *Literary Forms*, 146.
17 In my own opinion this logical explanation is reinforced when 1:35 is interpreted with the whole of the infancy narratives in mind. One of Luke's purposes in paralleling John's and Jesus' births is to accentuate that Jesus is more important, He is the long awaited savior. John was filled with the Spirit in his mother's womb and would act in the power of Elijah; Jesus, on the contrary, is conceived by the Holy Spirit and power of the Most High. Through this parallel the reader is naturally inclined to interpret the birth of this last person as more important.

is the most natural reading of the story, I am inclined to think that Menzies here exceeds the limits of interpretation. The model of Eco shows that Menzies does not narcotize the possible meaning of power to come to a full understanding later in the narrative, but he interprets directly and mostly based on his own foreknowledge. Unfortunately this colors the remaining of Menzies' interpretation of the Lukan narrative and will result in a particular Lukan pneumatology in which Holy Spirit and power are separated. This shows that despite the fact that Menzies properly examined the world of the author and the world of the text, his encyclopedic competence results in a rather unnatural interpretation of the promise in Luke 1:35.

6.3 Luke 3: The Promise of John the Baptist
The promise of John the Baptist in Luke 3:16-17 has caused a lot of debate among various scholars.[18] There is agreement about the obvious contrast between the ministry of John and the ministry of Jesus. This is in continuation with the previous established parallel in the infancy narratives: John and Jesus are paralleled only with the purpose to show that Jesus is the greater one. John seems to be aware of this and refers to the coming one who is stronger, greater (ἰσχυρότερός). All three scholars, Turner, Menzies and Kurz, agree on this contrast. Kurz especially aims on the narrative importance of this episode and argues that Luke firmly puts the story in world history as well as in biblical history. The promise in 3:16-17 as such is not discussed by Kurz, although it neatly fits the picture of John being the lesser one, being Jesus' precursor. In their reading of the narrative Turner and Menzies engage in the scholarly debate about the content and meaning of John's promise. Both agree that this baptism in Spirit and fire concerns one baptism and functions as a contrast to John's ministry of water baptism (see above in §3.3 and §4.3).[19] Various questions are

---

18 James D.G. Dunn, *Baptism in the Holy Spirit. A Re-examination of the New Testament Teaching on the Gift of the Spirit in Relation to Pentecostalism Today* (London: SCM, 1970); idem, 'Spirit-and-Fire-Baptism', *NovT* (1972); I.H. Marshal, The Gospel of Luke (NIGTC; Grand Rapids, MI: Paternoster/Eerdmans, 1978), 144-148; John Nolland, *Luke 1-9:20* (WBC 35a; Dallas, TX: Word, 1989), 151-154; Robert L. Webb, "The Activity of John the Baptist's Expected Figure at the Threshing Floor (Mathew 3:12=Luke 3:17)", *JSNT* 43 (1991); idem, *John the Baptizer and Prophet* (Sheffield: JSOT, 1991); Darrell L. Bock, *Luke 1:1-9:50* (BECNT; Grand Rapids, MI: Baker Books, 1994), 320-325 and Joel B. Green, *The Gospel of Luke* (NICNT; Grand Rapids, MI: Eerdmans, 1997), 180-182.
19 Turner explicitly uses the term "hendiadys" to strengthen that Spirit and fire are combined in one baptism, Turner, *Power from on High*, 173-175.

imposed on the text: does the promise concern individuals or a collective group of people? Or perhaps both? Should the promise be understood eschatologically or not? Should we read and interpret the promise literally or not? In answering these questions and therewith interpreting the text Turner, Menzies and Kurz interpret differently. Although Kurz does not elaborate on the promise as such, his relative silence is an interpretation as well. It is in his discussion of Acts 1:5 that he refers back to John's promise.[20] In this flashback Kurz interprets the promise of John the Baptist as being fulfilled at Pentecost and subsequently fulfilled in Christian water baptism: "This promise will be realized at Pentecost, and then in Christian baptism, which involves both water and the Spirit's indwelling and empowerment."[21] So in his interpretation of John's promise Kurz actually contradicts himself: John's promise in Luke 3:16-17 serves as a contrast between his ministry (water baptism) and the ministry of Jesus (Spirit baptism). A literary critical approach only confirms this contrast. Already in the infancy narratives of Luke 1-2 John and Jesus are paralleled, only to enlarge the contrast between both: Jesus will be the main character of the subsequent narrative. However, in his interpretation of the promise, Kurz ties water baptism and Spirit baptism together and substantiates this by quoting Pope Benedict XVI who refers to the Roman Catholic sacraments of (water) baptism and Confirmation. In addition to this readers are encouraged "to ask the Virgin Mary to obtain a renewed Pentecost for the church again today".[22] This interpretation is a very clear example of moving far beyond the textual evidence and reading back Church traditions (water baptism, Confirmation) and present day issues (a lukewarm church?) in the text. In this instance Kurz exceeds the limits of interpretation and lets the world today and church tradition govern the interpretation of the text. The world of the author and the world of the text seem to have disappeared in Kurz's interpretation.

Turner and Menzies approach the promise of John the Baptist from a slightly different angle and focus on the meaning of Spirit and fire. Especially the judgment part (fire) of the promise has their attention. Menzies interprets the promise as being addressed to the collective of the people of Israel instead of individuals (contra James Dunn, see above in §4.3.2). The baptism in Spirit and fire will bring about a cleansing on the people of Israel. This cleansing is not a judgment, but rather a sifting of the people

---

20 Kurz, *Acts of the Apostles* (2013), 26-30.
21 Kurz, *Acts of the Apostles* (2013), 29.
22 Kurz, *Acts of the Apostles* (2013), 30.

of Israel, a sifting between the righteous and the wicked.[23] In his comparison with Mark and Matthew, Menzies seems to imply that every Gospel writer accentuates another aspect of John's promise: Mark is positively oriented and Christological in his focus; Matthew accentuates the judgment aspect of the promise, while Luke sees it as a promise of cleansing. This cleansing then is interpreted by Menzies as a sifting: the righteous people of Israel (grain) will be sifted from the unrighteous people of Israel (chaff).[24] Menzies presses this interpretation one step further by stating that the way in which this cleansing will happen is through "Spirit-inspired oracles uttered by the Messiah, blasts of the Spirit which would separate the wheat from the chaff".[25] It is here that Menzies stretches his interpretation of the promise, because it is simply not stated *how* the Messiah will execute this promise.

Of the three scholars, Turner is the most comprehensive in his discussion of the promise of John the Baptist (*Power from on High*, 170-187). He finds the interpretation of the meaning of this promise in its purpose. The means of baptism is different and as such forms a contrast: John baptized in water, the Stronger One will baptize with Spirit and fire. However, both have the same purpose: cleansing of sin, repentance.[26] This interpretation is based upon the Old Testament background (especially Isaiah 4:2-6, 9:2-6, 11:1-4 and Malachi 3:2b-3) and Turner's shift from the general meaning of the words βαπτίζω and πτύον.[27] This interpretation leads Turner to conclude that in John's mind the Stronger One would not pour out the Spirit on Israel, but would come to cleanse Israel. This would be possible because the Stronger One himself was endowed with the Spirit.[28] This leads to the conclusion that "the Spirit is clearly in some sense soteriological necessary".[29] In the unfolding of the narrative of Luke-Acts it will become clear that the fulfilment of this promise will come "in an unanticipated way, mainly beyond Pentecost (Acts 1:5; 11:15-18)".[30] It seems to me that of the three scholars discussed, Turner is the one who remains within the limits of interpretation provided by the text. His interpretive

---

23 Menzies, *Development*, 140; *Empowered for Witness*, 126 and see above in §4.3.2 and §4.3.3.
24 Menzies, *Empowered for Witness*, 125-128.
25 Menzies, *Development*, 140; *Empowered for Witness*, 128.
26 Turner, *Power from on High*, 183.
27 See above in §3.3.2.
28 Turner, *Power from on High*, 184-185.
29 Turner, *Power from on High*, 186.
30 Turner, *Power from on High*, 187.

move to deviate from the general meaning of πτύον (fork like shovel) to spade, seems to be justified by the immediate context of cleaning out the threshing floor. The only discrepancy remains within the narrative of Luke-Acts itself: if the meaning of John the Baptist's promise was about a Spirit endowed Messianic figure who would come to cleanse and restore, why then does Luke refer to Joel's prophecy in Acts 2:17 and uses the words "pouring out" in regard to Pentecost? Or could it be that on the one hand the focus of the promise of John the Baptist is on the *person* who will come, the Stronger One? While on the other hand in the Pentecost episode the focus is on *the way* this person baptizes with Spirit and Power?

I conclude this section on the promise of John the Baptist with a last personal remark. In reading and interpreting Luke 3:16-17 none of the three discussed scholars point back to the prophecy spoken by Simeon in Luke 2:34-35. Simeon refers to Isaiah 8:14 and clearly states that the destiny of Jesus will be to divide, to sift: note the words falling and rising in Luke 2:34. In my opinion this already hints to the promise of John the Baptist and corroborates the interpretation of a Stronger One who will come to cleanse Israel. This textual link favors the interpretation of John's promise based on the purpose of this promise instead of an interpretation based on the manner in which this purpose will be accomplished.

6.4 Luke 4: Jesus' inaugural address

In general most scholars consider Luke 4:14-30 to be a programmatic text in the Gospel. This also applies to Turner, Menzies and Kurz. All three consider Jesus' inaugural address to be programmatic or a "corner stone" text.[31] In the concerning sections above (§3.5, §4.5 and §5.6) it was already made clear that the reading and interpretation of this particular episode in Luke 4 shows the importance of the role of the reader. One might argue that the role of the reader here is decisive for one's view of Lukan pneumatology. Specifically in the reading of this episode the reader is forced to make some interpretive decisions which will affect their further reading of the Lukan narrative and therewith their view of Lukan pneumatology.

Kurz is remarkably silent about this episode. He briefly discusses the intertextual depth that the Isaianic quotation brings to the text and suffices with the remark that this shows the character of Jesus' mission.

---

31 Menzies, *Empowered for Witness*, 145.

In addition he points to the (alleged) parallelism with Paul in the Book of Acts (see above in §5.6) and concludes that the words from Isaiah characterize Jesus' mission first and later the mission of the disciples. Because of his relative silence it is difficult to exactly know how Kurz understands this passage. However silence does speak as well. Kurz interprets the narrative of Luke-Acts primarily from a birds eye view. In such a reading it is slightly impossible to discuss every detail. His purpose is to draw some narrative critical lines, highlight certain parallelisms and once in a while elaborate on certain details. Unfortunately this Isaianic quotation is interpreted rather superficially. Perhaps a more cooperative way of reading the text is to narcotize the various possible approaches of the Isaianic quotation and just read on in the Lukan narrative. Such a reading is certainly suitable for a first or second reading of the narrative, however for an in-depth study of Luke's theology and especially his pneumatology such narcotizing will not suffice and will not prove to be satisfactory. This shows the difference between Kurz on the one hand and Turner and Menzies on the other. Kurz's approach is excellent for a first or second time reading in which it covers the broad line of Luke's story.

Both Turner and Menzies take another approach. They choose to discuss and interpret the Isaianic quotation in depth and use their respective interpretations to establish their view on Lukan pneumatology. It is in this sense that the interpretation of this passage (together with some passages from Acts) is decisive for one's view on Lukan pneumatology. In the separate treatments of Turner and Menzies above (§3.5 and §4.5) it became clear that the key issue in interpreting this passage is the question whether Luke used a traditional source or sources (so Turner) or whether Luke redacted the Isaianic quotation for his own theological purposes (so Menzies). Both of these interpretive choices have their respective consequences. Turner argues that Luke used traditional sources which show that as well as in the Old Testament and in early Judaism there was a rather broad view on the working of the Spirit. According to Turner themes such as Jubilee, a New Exodus and restoration of the people of Israel seem to dominate the image of this Isaianic quotation in Jesus' inaugural address. Such an understanding makes it possible for the working of the Spirit to include healing miracles and exorcisms.[32]

In contrast Menzies argues that Luke did use some traditional material, however Menzies assigns the alterations in the Isaianic quotation to

---

32 Turner, *Power from on High*, 265-266.

the hand of Luke.³³ These alterations point towards a distinctive Lukan view of the Spirit, a prophetic view of the Spirit: the Spirit who inspires for speech. So Menzies' interpretation of this passage results in a rather narrow view of the working of the Spirit.

The compelling question then is: who is right? Two well-informed readers read and interpret the same text, but come with different, opposing, interpretations of this text.

Umberto Eco distinguishes between an 'open' text and a 'closed' text and as already discussed above (§2.4) in reality a text is often of combination of both.³⁴ Reading the narrative of Luke-Acts and particularly this episode of Jesus' inaugural address in Luke 4 there are both open parts as well as closed parts in this text. The closed parts are about geography and Jesus' location: the synagogue in Nazareth, Galilee (4:14-16) and that he is reading from Isaiah (verse 17). The open part has to do with the content of Jesus' reading and the meaning of this content. So in their interpretations of the text, Turner and Menzies discuss an open text. Characteristic for an open text is that multiple answers or interpretations are possible. An open text demands the creative interaction of the reader with this text. Eco's model is called the model of the *cooperative* reader. It is assumed that author and reader will cooperate with each other to come to the most satisfying interpretation. An open text demands a certain response from the reader. In this particular episode we read that the audience present responds in a certain way to Jesus' reading and interpretation (verse 21) of this Isaianic quotation. It seems that this invokes the readers of the Lukan narrative to respond as well. Turner and Menzies do. Both in their respective ways, with their respective and opposing interpretations. However, within the given context both of these interpretations make sense. Both of these interpretations are possible. The analogy with the game of chess is obvious: different moves are possible within a given setting of the pieces. This is not a postmodern or relativistic approach that 'every reader makes his own truth out of the text', but it is inherent to the open character of this specific passage. The limits of interpretation are exceeded if one for instance interprets that murder belonged to the ministry of Jesus (see Eco's example of Jack the Ripper above in the introduction). To put it in other words: when the text (or the narrative as a whole) does not give an

---

33 Menzies, *Empowered for Witness*, 145-148, 155-156.
34 Eco, *The Open Work*, *The Role of the Reader*. See also Zwiep, *Tussen tekst en lezer II*, 342.

occasion for a certain interpretation (such as murder belonging to Jesus' ministry), but this interpretation is nevertheless made, the interpreter exceeds the limits of interpretation.

Menzies concludes that the working of the Spirit is rather narrow, limited to inspiring speech. Whereas Turner's conclusion is that the working of the Spirit is broader and that various themes come to the surface in this passage.

These conclusions should be sufficient for an in-depth reading of this Lukan passage. Both scholars cooperate with the text and both come with an interpretation of this text. But although these conclusions are sufficient, I do not find them particularly satisfactory. Luke as the (implied) author of Luke-Acts must had some sort of model reader in mind. A reader who would cooperate with the text in that sense that Luke intended the reader to cooperate. What exactly did Luke have in mind when writing this passage? Unfortunately it is impossible to answer that question. Turner and Menzies both built upon their knowledge and research of the Old Testament and early Judaism. They extracted a view of the Spirit and with this information approached the Lukan text. Their encyclopedic competence is comprehensive and as such forms the key for their respective interpretations of this passage. A recommendation for further research could perhaps be to study this background of the Spirit of prophecy.

To conclude this section it is only fair to say that Kurz opts for a rather superficial reading, foremost from a birds eye perspective. Turner and Menzies do not hesitate to firmly study the passage and its background and in my opinion both stay within the limits of interpretation, because both respect the boundaries given by the text and the narrative in its entirety. Although the result is that both scholars interpret differently.

6.5 Acts 2: Pentecost
From the programmatic text in the Gospel of Luke, we continue to focus on the programmatic text in the Book of Acts: Acts 2, the outpouring of the Holy Spirit or the Pentecost episode. Turner treats the whole of chapter 2 in a very extensive way, whereas Menzies confines himself to the altered Joel quotation in Acts 2:17-21 and Kurz' treatment is limited to some general remarks on Pentecost and the outpouring of the Spirit. He however is comprehensive in regard to the application of the Pentecost event to the present day church. He stays within the limits of interpretation because he limits himself to the boundaries of the text, he uses however the whole of the biblical canon and frequently uses the angle of the

(Catholic) church tradition to interpret. An example of the latter is that Kurz is the only one who includes Mary in his treatment of Acts 2. Understandable as this is from the (Catholic) church point of view, I do think he gives her more attention than the text allows.

Applying Eco's model to all three scholars, it is obvious that in their respective reading of the Pentecost episode, Turner is the most cooperative reader of the text. In chapter 10 of his *Power from on High*, he consecutively determines the textual meaning (box 6), the narrative structure (box 8) and the ideological structure (box 9) of the Pentecost episode. The textual meaning is about the outpouring of the Spirit, whereas the narrative structure is found in the purpose of Peter's speech. This purpose is more Christological than Pneumatological in nature and leads Turner to the ideological structure of the narrative: in the Pentecost episode the image of Jesus as the Davidic Messiah and prophet-like-Moses is shown. This is an excellent illustration of a well-informed reader who cooperates with the narrative under scrutiny. Whether the text allows such an extensive cooperation has to be determined. Especially Menzies argues against any Sinai allusions, thereby diminishing the prophet-like-Moses image of Jesus in this episode. The three arguments in favor of a Sinai allusion are all three mentioned and subsequently discussed by Menzies (see above in §4.8).[35] Before treating the three Sinai arguments, Menzies is bold in his introduction when he states that proponents of the Sinai allusions view the gift of the Spirit in essence as a new, interior, law – written on the heart. He continues: "This line of interpretation is admittedly incompatible with *my* assessment of Luke's understanding of the Pentecost gift" (emphasis is mine).[36] So what exactly is at stake here? Are Sinai allusions incompatible with the text of Acts 2 and as such exceed the limits of interpretation? Or are Sinai allusions incompatible with Menzies' interpretation of the text and his view of Lukan pneumatology?

The first argument is whether the Pentecost festival, during the time of Luke, was associated with the giving of the law at Sinai. Hard evidence for this association comes from Rabbis Jose ben Halafta (c. AD 150) and Elezar (c. AD 270).[37] Menzies rightly observes that this evidence is late. So it is not convincing that during Luke's time Pentecost was already associated with the giving of the law. Turner on the other hand argues

---

35 Menzies, *Empowered for Witness*, 189-201.
36 Menzies, *Empowered for Witness*, 190.
37 Turner, *Power from on High*, 280-282; Menzies, *Empowered for Witness*, 190-191. Dates are taken from Turner and Menzies.

that such an association was not suddenly and unexpectedly established: there had to be some traditional association before it could be officially determined. In addition Turner points to 2 Chron. 15:10-12 and to Jubilees 6:19 as evidence to a celebration of covenant renewal, which Menzies, in his turn, dismisses as minor connections.[38] Another link between Pentecost and Sinai seems to be confirmed by the Qumran community that annually renewed the covenant (1QS 1:8-2:18, 4Q266), however Philo and Josephus are silent about any associations between Pentecost and the giving of the law.[39] Reviewing this evidence it seems to me that it is rather thin to conclude only on the τὴν ἡμέραν τῆς πεντηκοστῆς from Acts 2:1 that Pentecost was associated with the giving of the law at Sinai. This correlates with Menzies' conclusion, so based on this text from Acts 2:1 the limits of interpretation seem to be overstretched. However, there are more arguments to be reviewed.

The second argument concerns alleged parallels between Sinai and Acts 2:1-13. Menzies starts with three cautious statements Samuel Sandmel made in his article "Parallelomania":[40]

1. Similiarities in texts do not necessarily mean literary dependence;
2. Distinctions are often more important than similarities;
3. Be aware of anachronistically reading late Rabinnic similarities in New Testament texts.

Subsequently Menzies discusses the alleged miracles and imagery parallels. He argues that the differences between Sinai traditions weigh heavier than the similarities (terms like wind, fire, heaven, language, voice, word). He does admit that these terms could come from a similar milieu, only to dismiss this possibility a little later because these similar terms are not unique to the Sinai tradition.[41] Turner agrees with Menzies that there is no literary parallel between Sinai traditions and the Pentecost episode and as such that "there is no direct literary dependence of Luke on any of these accounts."[42] Turner then proceeds and states that the question is not so much about literary dependence or not, but whether a reader of Acts 2

---

38 Turner, *Power from on High*, 281; Menzies, *Development*, 233 and *Empowered for Witness*, 191.
39 Turner, *Power from on High*, 281; Menzies, *Empowered for Witness*, 191-192.
40 S. Sandmel, "Parallelomania", *JBL* 81 (1962), 1-13; Menzies, *Empowered for Witness*, 193-194.
41 Menzies, *Empowered for Witness*, 195.
42 Turner, *Power from on High*, 283.

would recognize some Sinai content in the Pentecost episode? To put it in other words: does the Pentecost episode *sounds* like Sinai? According to Turner it does. He lists six points of similarity why the Pentecost episode would remind the reader of the Sinai event.[43] So according to Turner's interpretation it is part of Luke's reading strategy that the model reader would think of the giving of the law at Sinai.

The third argument which is discussed by Menzies and Turner is whether there is a Moses typology in the text of the Pentecost episode or not.[44] Not surprisingly both scholars disagree whether there is or there is not a Moses typology to be found in the Pentecost event. Menzies argues that this is not the case, foremostly following Darell Bock's discussion of Barnabas Lindars.[45] The key issue at stake is whether Acts 2:33 is a Lukan redaction (so Menzies and Bock), or if Luke modified an already existing tradition (so Turner).[46] In addition Menzies notices the absence of any reference to Moses or the law in Acts 2. As a result Menzies concludes that the outpouring of the Spirit in Acts 2 does not resemble the story of Moses ascending Mount Sinai and later descending with the law. As such it cannot be sustained that the Holy Spirit acts as a new law written within the hearts of the people. Menzies stays with his earlier conclusion that the Spirit in Luke-Acts "is the source of prophetic inspiration, and as such, the Spirit of mission."[47]

Unlike Menzies, Turner argues that Luke's redaction can be a modification instead of an addition. In that case there is an allusion to Moses ascending Mount Sinai to receive the law and descending giving the law to the people of God. Turner holds to a loose correspondence between the two events of Sinai and Pentecost. He does not stretch his arguments to the degree that the law and the Spirit are equivalent. The importance for Lukan pneumatology is that the parallel between Sinai and Pentecost suggests that Pentecost "is viewed as part of the fulfillment and *renewal* of Israel's covenant, and so ensure that the gift of the Spirit will have a vital role in Israel's restoration" (emphasis is Turner's).[48]

---

43 Turner, *Power from on High*, 284-285.
44 Menzies, *Empowered for Witness*, 198-201; Turner, *Power from on High*, 285-289.
45 Menzies, *Empowered for Witness*, 200; Darrell L. Bock, *Proclamation from Prophecy and Pattern: Lucan Old Testament Christology* (Sheffield: Sheffield Academic, 1987), 181-186.
46 What is meant here is whether Psalm 67:19 (LXX; 68:19 MT) has been of influence on Luke writing Acts 2:33 or not.
47 Menzies, *Empowered for Witness*, 201.
48 Turner, *Power from on High*, 289.

The result of both these opposite interpretations for Lukan pneumatology is that in Menzies' case he can hold to the more narrow view of the Spirit as being the missiological Spirit. Turner on the other hand maintains the broader view of the Spirit which includes restoration and renewal and as such has soteriological features in his view of the Spirit in Luke-Acts.

In his treatment of Acts 2, Kurz plainly states that Pentecost originally was a harvest festival but later became a remembrance of God giving the law at Mount Sinai. Without further elaboration he poses this as a fact and exactly adds what Menzies denies: "The celebration of the gift of the law now embraces the giving of the new law in the Spirit (Rom. 8:2), the writing of the law on the heart (Jer. 31:31-34; 2Cor. 3:2-6)."[49] In addition Kurz is the only one who mentions the popular idea that the event of speaking in different tongues is a reversal of the Babel curse (Gen. 11:1-9). He also mentions Mary and calls for a renewed attention to Mary as being the "mother of the church".[50] Kurz does not elaborate on an alleged Moses typology, he however does stress resemblances with Sinai, Moses and Elijah.[51]

The poignant question is: are all three scholars equally right in their respective interpretations of the Pentecost episode?

Fact is that all three scholars read and interpret the same story differently. The above mentioned basics of Eco's model of the cooperative reader are the reader's cooperation with the world of the author, the world of the text and the reader's encyclopedic competence. Turner is the most and Kurz the less comprehensive in regard to these three criteria. Menzies is in the middle. In his interpretation Kurz encourages individuals and the church as a whole to revalue the filling with the Holy Spirit, water baptism and the apostolic mission of the church. In all this the role of Mary is important and should not be underestimated. My own assessment is that Kurz moves too quickly to the actual world. Although his statements may be true and his encouragements praiseworthy, in his interpretation he lacks a solid foundation in the Pentecost episode. Kurz would gain in his interpretation and application if it were more rooted in the world of the author and the world of the text. Now it seems that Kurz' interpretive possibilities are limitless, which is not the case.

Menzies does an outstanding job in his interpretation of Acts 2. He reinforces his previous findings on the Spirit, namely that the Lukan

---

49 Kurz, *Acts of the Apostles* (2013), 44.
50 Kurz, *Following Jesus*, 121-122 and see above in § 5.9.
51 Kurz, *Acts of the Apostles* (2013), 45, 50, 52, 54.

Spirit is the Spirit who inspires speech: the missiological Spirit. However, it seems to me that Menzies constructs his interpretation in such way that it corroborates his earlier findings on Lukan pneumatology, resulting in a rather narrow view of the working of the Spirit in Luke-Acts. In his argumentation with regard to a possible Moses typology he states that the context of Acts 2 nowhere mentions the law, Sinai or Moses. In this Menzies is correct. However, with regard to a possible soteriological working of the Spirit, the context does mention this in Acts 2:21 and 2:37-40. So if Menzies finds that the context is important for the proper interpretation, than it seems he is falling in his own sword when it comes to his own restriction of the Spirit in Luke-Acts as being *only* the missiological Spirit. To conclude: Menzies limits himself to a narrower Lukan pneumatology, where the text of Acts 2 provides more possibilities for interpretation.

Turner discusses the text of the Pentecost episode meticulously on all three levels of Eco's model. The danger however is that Turner's encyclopedic competence becomes an enemy. Because of his wide knowledge of the world of author and text a more natural reading of the Pentecost episode seems somehow impossible. I must admit, Turner is very cautious to push the Moses typology too far (contra Kurz, who does this without hesitation), but he is very anxious as well to proof that Jesus is the prophet-like-Moses. Interestingly is that on the level of proposing value judgments (which according to Eco is the most important aspect of the cooperative reader[52]), Turner's judgment is that Jesus is depicted as the prophet-like-Moses, the Messiah who leads his people into a new Exodus which results in a renewed and restored community. The open text of Acts 2 leaves room for various possible interpretations. All three scholars use this room in their own respective way. It seems that the role of the reader is decisive in the interpretation of the text.

6.6 Acts 8: The Samaritans

The Acts 8 episode where the Samaritans come to faith, are baptized and receive the Spirit (verses 12, 15-16) is very interesting from the readers perspective and in regard to Lukan pneumatology as well. It is with solid reasons that Max Turner used "Waterloo" in the title of his extensive article about this episode. It all depends whether you identify with Napoleon or with Wellington...[53]

---

52 Eco, *Lector in fabula*, 231 and see above in § 5.5.2.
53 Max Turner, "Interpreting the Samaritans of Acts 8: The Waterloo of Pentecostal Soteriology and Pneumatology?", *Pneuma 23* (2001), 265-286.

The Acts 8 episode raises a serious problem in Lukan pneumatology as well as in Lukan soteriology. The issue at hand is the time gap between the Samaritans' conversion and baptism (verse 12) and their Spirit reception (verses 15-16). This time gap raises the next issue: whether or not apostolic authority is necessary for the reception of the Spirit, which subsequently raises the issue of the meaning of the laying on of hands. All three scholars take a stand on these issues. All three scholars read, interpret and conclude what solution fits these problems best. And all three scholars come with a different solution.

William Kurz starts his reading and interpreting of this passage with the big picture: the story is about the spread of the Gospel. Even persecution cannot stop this. There is actually irony in the story because the result of persecution is the spread of the Gospel.[54] This overview keeps Kurz from losing himself in several details of interpretation, however the flipside of this is a rather shallow foundation for his theological and doctrinal remarks. He correctly states that in Acts there is variety in the way the Spirit is received (at, after or before water baptism), and concludes that God has freedom in the way He chooses to pour out the Spirit.[55] With regard to the interpretation of Acts 8, he refers to Catholic tradition: "Catholic tradition has interpreted these texts to mean that a person receives the Holy Spirit initially in baptism and then in a fuller way through the laying on of hands at confirmation."[56] Kurz then elaborates on this Catholic tradition and states that the laying on of hands by Peter and John here in Acts 8 is the origin of the Catholic sacrament of confirmation. So, to conclude: Kurz solves the problem(s) of Acts 8 based on the text of Acts 8 and Catholic Tradition. I have to admit that based *only* on the text of Acts 8 such an interpretation is possible. The story tells us about conversion, baptism and a later reception of the Holy Spirit through the hands of apostolic leadership. The story tells about new people who are initiated into the church. However, how can Kurz conclude that the Spirit is initially received at baptism? Where the text of Acts 8 clearly states that the Samaritan believers had not yet received the Spirit. So here we have a serious discrepancy in soteriology which Kurz unfortunately does not address. In addition this is the only occurrence in Luke-Acts

---

54 Kurz could have referred here to Acts 5:38-39 to strengthen his case in determining the story of the text, he however does not do so.
55 Kurz, *Acts of the Apostles* (2013), 142.
56 Kurz, *Acts of the Apostles* (2013), 142.

where apostles lay on hands to impart the Holy Spirit.[57] This seems a little meager for a doctrine of confirmation. Properly speaking Kurz reads and interprets the text of Acts 8 within its limits, that is the limits of the text. He however does not engage with the whole of the narrative of Luke-Acts. Based on Acts 8 alone the doctrine of confirmation is possible. But if one takes into account the whole story of Luke-Acts, it seems to me that the doctrine of confirmation is based on a rather small part of Luke-Acts. Because it is not compatible with the whole story of Luke-Acts I do think Kurz exceeds the limits of interpretation. Kurz actually admits this, when he states that there is "some variety in the relationship between baptism and the receiving of the Holy Spirit."[58] If there is variety how then is it possible to come to a (normative) doctrinal application of this text? In this instance Kurz is not consistent in his interpretation. He shows that his interpretation is not limited to the text itself, but stretches beyond the text to Church doctrine. And within the boundaries of Roman Catholic doctrine, the doctrine of confirmation is a proper interpretation of the Acts 8 passage. However, based on the entire narrative of Luke-Acts the doctrine of confirmation seems far-fetched. Robert Menzies reads and interprets the Acts 8 passage in a different way. In his interpretation he primarily interacts with George Beasley-Murray and James Dunn reacting to their proposed solutions of the Acts 8 problem of the time gap between conversion and the reception of the Holy Spirit.[59] Crucial in Menzies' interpretation and relation to Lukan pneumatology is the problem of the time gap between the Samaritan's conversion and baptism, and their reception of the Spirit. This problem is not a problem for Menzies, but perfectly fits his view on Lukan pneumatology: the Spirit in Luke-Acts is the Spirit of prophetic empowering and mission and is only received *after* people are already part of the community of God through conversion and baptism. Interpreting the passage in this way (in correlation with Lukan pneumatology) Menzies argues that the Spirit is supplementary and parallels the Samaritan episode with the Pentecost event.[60] The Samaritans received the Spirit in the same way as the apostles did at Pentecost. Menzies' line of reasoning is from Jesus' Jordan experience to

---

57 The other instances of laying on of hands in Acts are in Acts 9:17 and 19:6, where respectively Ananias and Paul lay on hands. Both do not belong to the original twelve apostles, so it seems a little farfetched to speak of *apostolic* tradition.
58 Kurz, *Acts of the Apostles* (2013), 142.
59 See above in §4.9.
60 Menzies, *Empowered for Witness*, 211-212.

the disciples' Pentecost experience to the Samaritan episode. All were already saved, so their subsequent reception of the Spirit had nothing to do with soteriology, but is all about a prophetic empowerment for mission.[61] At first sight this seems a very attractive and coherent solution for the problem which rises from the Samarian episode. It is appealing, it takes the whole of Luke-Acts in account and it is applicable for the church today. However, as reader and interpreter, does Menzies engage enough with the worlds of author and text? And does his encyclopedic competence serve as an improvement or as a burden in his interpretation of this Acts 8 passage?

Just as Max Turner takes Acts 2:38 as the norm in Lukan soteriology and pneumatology, so does Menzies take Acts 8 as the normative passage. Instead of reading, rereading and narcotizing some unsolved issues (as Eco proposes in his model of the cooperative reader, see above in §2.5.2), Menzies' *focus* is on the unsolved issue.[62] It seems that the problem in Acts 8 dominates the interpretation of Acts 8. My impression is that Menzies is eager to hold to his own construed Lukan pneumatology, which, to be honest, fits the text and his interpretation of the text of Luke-Acts well. So based on the text of Luke-Acts the proposed Lukan pneumatology of Menzies is possible. The question however remains whether it was Luke's original intention to write a pneumatology or to prescribe a fixed *ordo salutis*. The text of Acts 8 gives room for such an interpretation, but was this Luke's reading strategy as well? I do not think so. The entire narrative of Acts shows a variety in conversion, reception of the Spirit and water baptism. This hints to the fact that it was not Luke's intention to provide his readers with a fixed *ordo salutis*. Luke (I think deliberately) does not try to solve the Samaritan problem. He could easily have done so because of his redactional skills. But he does not. Why then is it that Luke in his narrative allows such a (for our reading) problematic time gap between conversion and baptism and the reception of the Holy Spirit through the praying and the laying on of hands by the apostles Peter and John?

In my opinion Menzies does not sufficiently determine the story of Acts 8. His interpretation is ruled by the problem of the time gap between

---

61 To make things even more complicate, within Pentecostalism there are differences between those who advocate a "two-stage" pneumatology and those who advocate a "one-stage" pneumatology. For an elaboration on these differences see Turner, "Waterloo", 266-268.

62 With the term "narcotizing" Eco means that possible meanings are kept in mind until a certain meaning can be actualized, see Eco, *Lector in fabula*, 114; *The Role of the Reader*, 27.

conversion and reception of the Holy Spirit. The question is whether this 'problem of the time gap' is central to the story of Acts 8 or not. I think it is not. The story in Acts 8 is about the spread of the Gospel (as Kurz convincingly stated). It is about the Gospel crossing ethnic, social and cultural borders: from Jew to Samaritan. Because of Menzies' eagerness to solve the 'problem of the time gap' he misses the red thread of the story in Acts 8. A story which will be continued in the subsequent chapters.

In addition to this it seems that Menzies has a rather strong case building his argument on the examples of Jesus at the Jordan river, the apostles at Pentecost and the Samaritans in Acts 8. All were already saved and receive the Spirit after some time. The question however is if this is the right paradigm and beyond that, if it should function as a normative paradigm. I strongly disagree with this. I think Menzies treats unique events in salvation history as blueprints for normative events in the Christian life today. If this is a proper way of interpreting these events I would like to ask Menzies: 'What about the virgin birth? What about Christ's crucifixion?' Are these unique events in salvation history normative for the Christian today? In his treatment of Acts 8 Menzies exceeds the limits of interpretation because his focus is on the problem this episode raises in our modern mindset. Instead his focus should be on the story of Acts 8: the spread of the Gospel accompanied by the reception of the Holy Spirit. The manner in which this happens seems of secondary importance to Luke.[63]

Max Turner treats the Acts 8 passage extensively in the above mentioned article with the ambiguous "Waterloo" in the title. His purpose in this article is to challenge Pentecostal soteriology and pneumatology. Turner's opinion is that Pentecostals assume a rather shallow picture of salvation in Luke-Acts. According to Turner salvation is far more than "initial justification and entry into the people of God, destined for resurrection and eschatological bliss."[64] Based on this shallow concept of salvation it is true that the Samaritans were saved (8:12) and later received the Spirit (8:15-16) as their empowerment for mission. In such an interpretation there is no room for any soteriological working of the Spirit in Luke-Acts.[65] According to Turner this poor picture of salvation in Luke-Acts

---

63 This is proven by the variety in Spirit reception in the text of Acts. See Kurz, *Acts of the Apostles* (2013), 142.
64 Turner, "Waterloo", 269.
65 Soteriological in that sense that the Spirit brings about "justification, "forgiveness of sins" and incorporation in the people of God", Turner, "Waterloo", 268. The question is

leads to an incorrect interpretation of the Samaritan episode in Acts 8. Turner has a broader view of salvation which is especially based on Luke 1-2 and Luke 4. He argues that salvation encompasses God's presence which transforms, liberates and cleanses the nation of Israel with the purpose to be a light to the nations.[66] This broad interpretation of salvation is recently sustained by Justo González, who elaborates on Luke's use of the words Savior and salvation.[67] Turner looks back to the beginning of the Gospel and with this knowledge (in Eco's terms: encyclopedic competence) he approaches the Samaritan episode. His broad interpretation of salvation in Luke-Acts is leading in this approach and this broad interpretation of salvation requires the Spirit's presence. It is through the received Spirit that transformation, liberation and cleansing are worked out and experienced. So, to summarize, Turner takes the faith and baptism of the Samaritans as genuine; he however assumes that the Samaritans did not yet experience "anything of God's transformative presence and power as a result of their belief and baptism", that is why the apostles prayed for the "unexpectedly delayed gift of the Spirit."[68] To conclude: Turner takes into account the whole story of Luke-Acts, especially the broad interpretation of salvation, and with this encyclopedic competence he approaches the Samaritan episode in Acts 8. This approach is coherent with the whole story of Luke-Acts and therefore neatly fits within the limits of interpretation.

Reviewing these three scholars and their respective interpretation of the Samaritan episode from Acts 8, I must conclude that it is and remains a difficult passage to interpret. Because Luke-Acts is a two-volume story and a continuing narrative I do think it is important to determine the story of Acts 8. This is what Eco's model shows in boxes 4 and 6. In a natural reading the reader / interpreter searches for structures in the text which reveal the plot of the text. This helps understanding the text and determining the story of the text. The crucial question is: what is this text about? What is the story of this text? In the case of Acts 8 answering these questions is only possible in dialogue with the whole of the narrative of Luke-Acts. When you take Acts 1:8 as an outline for Acts as a whole, then

---

if the Spirit in Luke-Acts has anything to do with salvation or not? It is in this sense that *soteriological Spirit* is used, see also §1.4.2 in the *Forschungsbericht* of this dissertation.
66 Turner, "Waterloo", 269, 271.
67 Justo L. González, *The Story Luke Tells. Luke's Unique Witness to the Gospel* (Grand Rapids, MI: Eerdmans, 2015), 61-64.
68 Turner, "Waterloo", 271.

Acts 8 tells the reader about the further expansion of the Gospel. Kurz convincingly states that despite persecution the Gospel spreads. Or perhaps we have to put it more firmly: God is using the persecution initiated by the death of Stephen to spread the Gospel. I think this is the red thread which runs through chapters 8 to 10. This is what Luke wants his readers to adapt from the story. The Samaritans and later the Ethiopian in Acts 8, Saul the persecutor becomes Paul the missionary in Acts 9 and then Cornelius' household in Acts 10 all show that the Gospel is spreading from Jerusalem to Samaria to the ends of the world. It is with this narrative structure in mind that we have to read and interpret the Samaritan episode. Philip went to Samaria and the Samaritans believe the Gospel and are baptized. That their faith is genuine can be deduced from the fact that neither Peter nor John tries to correct or improve their faith.[69] Max Turner correctly engages with the whole narrative of Luke-Acts and 'takes' the already discovered broad interpretation of salvation into the Samaritan episode. William Kurz interprets with (Roman Catholic) church tradition in mind and properly interprets within the limits of Acts 8, he however loses touch with the whole Lukan narrative. Robert Menzies' interpretation at first hand seems appealing, he however uses a very narrow concept of salvation and I doubt whether this was also Luke's concept of salvation.

6.7 Acts 10: Cornelius' Household

The episode in Acts 10 about the household of Cornelius is another intriguing marker in the Lukan narrative when it concerns the working of the Holy Spirit. And again it is an episode where interpretive opinions vary and contradict each other. Consensus about this episode is that it can be labeled as the "Gentile Pentecost". This is where scholars agree on: Acts 10 shows that the outpouring of the Spirit is not only a promise for Israel, but for Gentiles as well.

Just as was the case in Acts 8 the key issue for interpretation is to rightly determine what the story of the text is about. The model of Eco shows that the cooperative reader puts a great deal of effort into searching for the right topic and therewith the story of the text. Once the story is determined, the reader / interpreter can move beyond the story to discover actantial structures and add value judgments to come to an appropriate application of the text.

---

69 Contra Dunn, *Baptism in the Holy Spirit*, 55-68 ; Turner, "Waterloo", 271 and *Power from on High*, 362-367; Menzies, *Empowered for Witness*, 207-210.

William Kurz convincingly shows that this episode is part of the story of that other main character in Acts: Peter. As leader of the twelve apostles Peter is most fit as an eyewitness for this new turn in salvation history. Peter's vision (10:9-17) serves as a key passage to understand the topic of the story which, according to Kurz, is that God shows no partiality. Based on this topic Kurz proceeds to value this quality of God and argues that this same quality should apply to the people of Israel (Lev. 19:15) and for the church today.[70] He even stretches this application of impartiality to the acceptance of certain changes within the church. Kurz proves to be a cooperative reader in his interpretation of this episode and neatly reads and interprets along the lines of Eco's model. So far we see that Kurz follows the narrative and the story of this episode and as such cooperates with the story. However, there is another criterion for Kurz. And that is the tradition and history of the (Roman Catholic) church. So besides the text under scrutiny and the whole narrative of Luke-Acts, Kurz as well uses his knowledge of the Catholic Church tradition. His encyclopedic competence is not limited to the text, circumstances and background of the writing of the text, but includes Catholic Church tradition as well. For the interpretation within his own church tradition this is suitable and applicable to use. However, when focusing on the reading strategy the author put in the text, it is most certain that Luke did not have the Catholic church in mind. So to conclude, Kurz neatly stays within the limits of interpretation when it concerns the story of the text and its primary application (God shows no partiality). He however exceeds the limits when bringing his church tradition into the text, how understandable this may be considering Kurz' own calling as a priest within the Roman Catholic Church.

In his discussion of the Cornelius' episode in Acts 10, Robert Menzies is very concise and actually jumps to the short summaries in Acts 11:15-17 and 15:7-10. Despite the fact that these summaries touch the heart of the matter concerning the Holy Spirit in the Cornelius' episode, it provides too little information to actually determine what the story in Acts 10 is about. The point Kurz makes, that God shows no partiality, is totally missed by Menzies. Instead he focuses on both summaries and tries especially to solve the problem raised by James Dunn, who sees the Spirit not only as an empowerment, but as the soteriological Spirit as well. Menzies contradicts himself in his limited discussion of Acts 10, he admits the close relation between Spirit baptism and conversion in the Cornelius

---

70 Kurz, *Acts of the Apostles* (2013), 176 and see above in §5.12.2.

episode, but does not bother to elaborate on this close relation.[71] Instead he jumps to conclusions and tries to refute the soteriological dimension by a different interpretation of both summaries in Acts 11 and 15. It is clear that Menzies' focus is on the Holy Spirit in Luke-Acts, the working of the Spirit and how this is applicable to Christians today. His angle for reading and interpreting Luke-Acts is pneumatology. That is the reason why he limits himself to the few verses from the Cornelius passage (10:44-48) and both the summaries. So he can subsequently address those interpretations which do not fit his previous established view of Lukan pneumatology. To me this seems like reading and interpreting the other way around. Just as Kurz includes Catholic tradition in his interpretation of the text, Menzies includes Pentecostal tradition in his interpretation. The Pentecostal doctrine of the working of the Spirit is leading in his reading of the Lukan narrative. Menzies own zeal for missions colors his interpretation. It is beyond any doubt that the power of the Holy Spirit is indispensable for Christian mission. However, the question is whether this is the point Luke wanted to make in his narrative. And whether Luke's sole purpose within these episodes of the Samaritans (Acts 8) and the Cornelius household (Acts 10) was to encourage Christians to be filled with the Holy Spirit because of an empowerment for mission.

Just as Menzies does, Max Turner also focuses on the summaries of the Cornelius episode in Acts 11 and 15. Turner, however, starts with the narrative proper and sees the parallel between Peter's vision in which he is permitted to eat unclean food and the development of the story in which unclean people are permitted to become part of the people of God. At the end of the story there is a redefinition of 'the people of God'. God himself takes this decisive step and it is the Spirit who legitimates it.[72] This interpretation is wholly congruent with the story of Acts 10 and underlines the interpretation of William Kurz who designates it as God not showing partiality. To elaborate on the nature of the gift of the Spirit, Turner needs 11:15-17 and 15:7-10 for his interpretation. He points to the strong comparison with Pentecost in Acts 2, depicting this Cornelius episode as "Gentile Pentecost" and subsequently argues that it was the Spirit of prophecy that was received by the Cornelius household. Peter preached the Gospel of salvation (10:34-43, 11:14, 15:7) which resulted in faith (15:9) and the outpouring of the Holy Spirit (10:44, 11:15, 15:8). Turner does not equate the gift of the Spirit with repentance, but interprets 11:15-18

---

71 Menzies, *Empowered for Witness*, 215.
72 Turner, *Power from on High*, 378-380.

as the conclusion of Peter's explanation to the other apostles, which clearly shows that God gave "repentance unto life" not only to believing Jews, but to Gentiles as well. The outpouring of the Spirit is the proof of this. Turner continues that it is God who had cleansed the hearts of these Gentiles and that is the reason why they are eligible for Spirit reception. The revolution here is that it is not by Torah obedience, but by God cleansing their hearts through faith (15:8). God accepted them. According to Turner this is wholly in line with the norm as stated in Acts 2:38.[73]

In his interpretation Turner closely follows the story and the development within the narrative. Together with his interpretation of both the summaries he comes to his conclusion that the Holy Spirit is the "executive power" through which the Messiah cleanses and restores his people, including Gentiles. Just as William Kurz did Turner closely follows the narrative, determines what the story is about and only then comes with his interpretation. He operates within the limits of the textual possibilities and is sensitive for Peter's remembrance of the promise of John the Baptist (11:16), through which this episode is tied to Acts 1:5 and Luke 3:16-17. There where William Kurz focuses more on Church tradition and application of the 'God shows no partiality' topic, Turner chooses a more theological angle and determines that the people of God consists of believing Jews and believing Gentiles. It is God who accepts both, based on 'repentance unto life'. The Holy Spirit is the executive power for this (new) life. The Spirit of prophecy functions apparently as the new identity marker.

6.8 Conclusion

Based upon Eco's model of the cooperative reader I argued above in the introduction that "for a sound and responsible interpretation of the biblical narrative it is necessary to determine whether a text is open or closed, to rightly establish the story of the episode and to let it be in accordance with the narrative in its entirety". If, at the end of this closing chapter, we assess all three scholars according to this thesis it brings us to the next conclusions.

Max Turner
Turner's degree of cooperating with the text is high: he is meticulous in his research and his strengths in cooperating with the text are found on the level of boxes 4, 6 and 8 from Eco's model. He spends considerable

---

73 Turner, *Power from on High*, 384.

attention to determine the story and structure of the text, he is sensible to the narrative as a whole and only then comes with his (theological) conclusions. He is creative in his cooperation with the text in the sense that he uses images as 'prophet-like-Moses' and the 'Davidic-Messiah' to describe the main character in the Gospel of Luke: Jesus, the Spirit endowed person. In the Book of Acts this working of the Spirit is extended to Christ followers, whereas Acts 2:38 serves as the normative text. The Spirit is received at conversion, has a broad range of charismata and its purpose is to cleanse and restore so that the people of God become and act as God's empowering presence in this world.

In addition, Turner's encyclopedic competence is immense, primarily in regard to Luke-Acts. But also in regard to the Old Testament background of Luke-Acts, especially concerning the Spirit of prophecy. Turner is very much aware of different theological insights and does not hesitate to eventually interpret from a theological angle. So, compared to the criteria above in §6.1 Turner cooperates well with the passage at hand and the narrative as a whole. He uses his encyclopedic competence to gain depth in his interpretations and is aware of limits and possibilities in interpretation, without crossing the line.

Solely based on Turner's more academic work *Power from on High*, one can (correctly) argue that there should be more attention for the practical implications of his research. Boxes 8, 9 and 10 from Eco's model deal with this aspect of interpreting the text and urge the reader to make value judgments. These value judgments are meager in *Power from on High*. On the contrary in his more accessible *The Holy Spirit and Spiritual Gifts*, Turner spends almost half of this monograph to discuss spiritual gifts today. As he concludes in this monograph he is a proponent of "a *via media* in spirituality between Pentecostalism and more traditional forms of Christianity."[74] In his reading and interpreting of the Lukan narrative he lays the foundation for such a *via media*. He does so convincingly and with theological sensitivity. Of course one can object and argue that this *via media* was Turner's approach from the beginning and he reads and interprets with this purpose in mind. If this is the case he still does so convincingly and with great sensitivity for the whole story of Luke-Acts.

Robert Menzies
Menzies also is meticulous in his research. Especially in his *Development of Early Christian Pneumatology* he spends a great deal in establishing the

---

74 Turner, *Holy Spirit and Spiritual Gifts*, 346.

(possible) background of Lukan pneumatology, particularly the meaning of Spirit of prophecy. However, at certain points in his research it seems like Menzies takes a shortcut. For example, the exact meaning or range of meanings of the Spirit of prophecy is not univocal. Menzies chooses for a rather narrow meaning because this fits his view of Lukan pneumatology. The interpretation of the parallelism in Luke 1:35 is dismissed as not being a parallelism, so to prevent the equation between the Holy Spirit and power. And the obvious connection between conversion and the reception of the Spirit in the Cornelius episode (Acts 10) is circumvented by Menzies' focus on the summaries of this episode in Acts 11 and 15. This leads me to the conclusion that Menzies' encyclopedic competence sometimes serves as a burden. It seems like he already has some sort of predetermined manner of the working of the Spirit in mind and in his reading and interpretation of the crucial Lukan passages then works towards confirming this. I suspect that this is because of Menzies' Pentecostal background and his zeal for mission. Personally I find this zeal for mission commendable and I am encouraged by it. However, for a theological sound interpretation of the narrative under scrutiny, I think the text of the narrative should be the starting point and not one's personal experience. As Eco's model shows, the cooperative reader starts with the world of the author and the text of the narrative. It is then a matter of reading and interpreting, *of cooperating with the text*, instead of using the text to substantiate one's own experiences. Menzies does cooperate with the text, however to a lesser extent then Turner does. At crucial moments Menzies lacks to let the specific episode be in accordance with the whole of the narrative. To use Eco's terminology from box 7 of his model: Menzies does not use the narrative in its entirety to sufficiently verify or falsify his forecasts and therewith theological statements.[75]

William Kurz
Kurz takes a different angle to read and interpret the Lukan narrative. His approach is literary critical and as such he is keenly aware of the importance of the whole narrative of Luke-Acts. This approach is combined with a canonical point of view and a high value of the Catholic church tradition. He does not hesitate to use his own experiences in his life as a Christian believer and in his calling as a Catholic priest to illustrate his interpretation of certain passages. This makes his work readable and applicable, but the question remains whether he uses the text in a proper

---

75 Eco, *Lector in fabula*, 149.

way. He cooperates with the text, but the center of gravity in his interpretation is in boxes 9 and 10 of Eco's model. Kurz is fast to apply and illustrate. His interpretation is filled with ideological structures and his purpose in reading and interpreting seems to be to encourage Christians and to revive the Catholic church. This purpose actually governs Kurz' reading and interpretation of the Lukan narrative. It seems that Kurz distances himself a bit from academic interpretation of the Bible and tries to read, interpret and apply from a (Catholic) church perspective. In this he differs from Turner and Menzies, however the question is if he is wrong in this. Or if he is a less cooperative reader. I think not. It seems that Kurz aims to let the Church community read, interpret and apply the biblical narrative. In this way the biblical story engages with the personal story of the reader. The result is a creative cooperation with the text. A disadvantage of this way of interpreting the text is that theological issues seem to disappear to the background or to disappear at all. In ambiguous matters Kurz lets the Catholic church tradition decide. This sometimes results in contradictory statements or a 'jumping to conclusions' and overall makes his theological efforts a little shallow. Concerning the working of the Spirit Kurz can conclude that the reception of the Spirit is necessary for personal spiritual growth and as an empowerment for the church to be a witness of the Gospel.

So to summarize at the end of this chapter, we can conclude that the use of Eco's model provides us insight in the specific role the reader plays in interpreting a text. Dependent of the sort text, open or closed, a certain degree of cooperation of the reader is demanded. This cooperation is recognized by a thorough reading of the specific passage and determining the topic or story of this passage. This story then should be congruent with the entire narrative to avoid any contradictions. The degree of cooperation is affected by the encyclopedic competence of the reader. This competence can strengthen the interpretation, but can be a burden as well which results in jumping to conclusions or let one's own preference be decisive. The foremostly open character of the Lukan narrative demands a creative cooperation from the reader / interpreter. The Lukan story calls for a response. And that is exactly what all three scholars do. Kurz and Menzies seem to focus more on the possibilities in interpretation and are demonstrable influenced by their respective denominational backgrounds. This sometimes results in contradictions, a preference to let church history decide or a debatable theological conclusion. Turner seems to focus more on the limits of interpretation and is very cautious to jump to (applicable) conclusions. This leads to a sound and balanced Lukan pneumatology, but could have gained weight in interaction with the church community.

In the next and concluding chapter I will visualize the cooperation of the reader and the bandwidth in interpretation. All three scholars have their own place within this bandwidth. All with their respective advantages and disadvantages. I will conclude that only within this bandwidth an interpretation of Biblical literature can be labeled as *responsible*.

CONCLUSION

Introduction
The aim of this study has been to determine the role of the reader in construing a Lukan Pneumatology. Through the various sub-questions (see above in the introduction) we explored the current status of Lukan Pneumatology in scholarly research (chapter 1, *Forschungsbericht*). We also described Eco's model of the cooperative reader as a useful method to gain insight into the role of the reader during the process of reading and interpreting a text (chapter 2, the role of the reader). Subsequently three different scholars were followed in their respective reading and interpreting of the Lukan πνεῦμα texts. These πνεῦμα texts were clustered in ten "literary knots" from the Gospel of Luke and the Book of Acts. These ten passages were subsequently discussed through the reading of the respective scholars. This is how we applied Eco's model and gained insight into the interpretive choices these three scholars made (chapters 3, 4 and 5). This helped us understand the reading and interpretation of the three scholars. Understanding the interpretation of these scholars does not necessarily mean that we *share* their respective interpretations.

That brings us to the topic of criteria. What criteria are used to determine whether a text is correctly interpreted or not? As discussed in the previous chapter (chapter 6), are there limits to the interpretation of a text or are there limitless possibilities to interpret the text? We determined that there is a certain bandwidth in interpretation. The sort of text determines the extent of this bandwidth. Eco makes a distinction between an open text and a closed text. An open text has a rather large bandwidth or range of possible interpretations. On the contrary a closed text has a small bandwidth and is limited in the range of possible interpretations. After determining whether a text is open or closed, the reader / interpreter needs to focus on the passage under scrutiny and rightly determine the narrative structure (story) of this passage. This story should be in accordance with the whole of the narrative. Subsequently the encyclopedic competence plays a role in interpreting the text. It makes quite a difference if a text is read for the first time or if one is already familiar with the text. These various steps in the process of reading and interpreting determine the degree of cooperation of the reader with the text. Schematically this looks as follows:

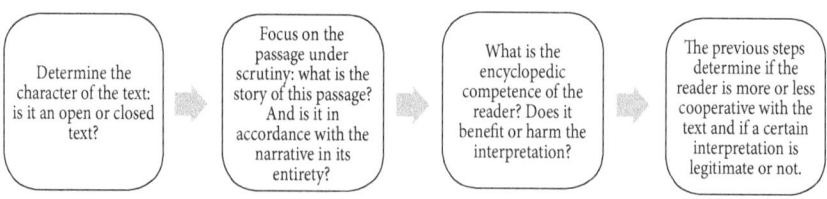

However the question remains what is a right, or better formulated, a *responsible* interpretation?

How to responsibly interpret Biblical literature

Van den Brink and Van der Kooi discuss the Bible in chapter 13 of their *Christelijke Dogmatiek*.[1] In their discussion of the historical-critical method and modernism, they use the image of a "gap" or "gorge". There is a gap between the history of the Biblical stories and our own history. A gap between the objective biblical scholar and the believing biblical scholar. And as a result of this there is a gap between the academic world and the church community.[2] Postmodernism and the development of reader-response theories pointed towards the reader of the Biblical text. The plurality of readers led to a plurality of interpretations. The image which is used here is that of a swamp. A swamp of relativity because there are no universal criteria to determine if a certain interpretation is right or wrong.[3] Is it possible to get out of this swamp and to come to a responsible interpretation? I think it is. It is on purpose that I use the term *responsible* instead of right or wrong. Epithets such as right or wrong tend to create polarization, whereas we can agree about a responsible interpretation, but disagree with the interpretation as such. In using the model of Umberto Eco we can *understand* the role of the reader. This should lead to an *understanding* of the reader and the interpretive choices this reader makes. At the same time the model of Eco showed that the range of possible interpretations is not unlimited. Within the text there are limits of interpretation. Based upon the encyclopedic competence of the reader there are limits as well. Little encyclopedic competence will lead to a limited number of interpretations or inversely, several possibilities of interpretation if the reader has a depth of encyclopedic competence. In addition the danger exists that too much encyclopedic competence serves

---

1 Gijsbert van den Brink and Kees van der Kooi, *Christelijke Dogmatiek* (Zoetermeer: Boekencentrum, 2012), 483-516. English translation is forthcoming in 2016.
2 Van den Brink, Van der Kooi, *Christelijke Dogmatiek*, 488-493.
3 Van den Brink, Van der Kooi, *Christelijke Dogmatiek*, 494-495.

as a burden in the interpretation of the text. In the sense that too much is read into the story of the text instead of the story just being the story. So for a responsible interpretation it is important to interpret within the range of possible interpretations. This next picture visualizes the bandwidth:

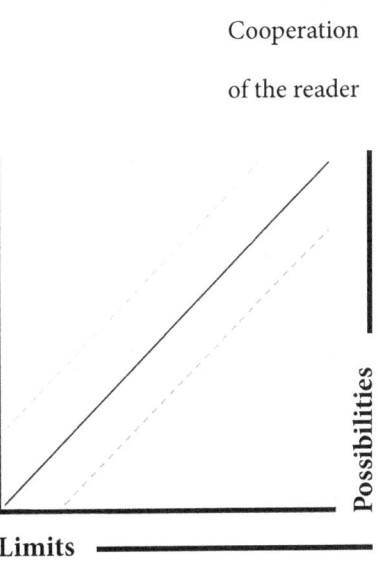

The horizontal axis represents the limits of interpretation whereas the vertical axis represents the possibilities of interpretation. Right in the middle the diagonal line shows the most balanced interpretation. Surrounding this diagonal line is the range or bandwidth of interpretation. Should a reader be inclined to move too much towards the possibilities he exceeds the bandwidth of a responsible interpretation and allows himself too much freedom. The danger of relativism looms: the reader who creates his own meaning out of the tex Another danger is the use of a biblical story for proof-texting or validating one's own experiences. This could even lead to the extremes of power abuse or a domination of people. The other extreme is an inclination towards the limits of interpretation. This leads to a rigid view of the biblical narrative which can lead to biblicism, legalism and fundamentalism. People will be judged upon the right or wrong beliefs they have on certain matters. The Biblical narrative then becomes more of a measuring stick than a narrative which begs for a response.

For a responsible interpretation of Biblical literature it is necessary that the reader closely follows the steps outlined in the diagram above in the introduction. This diagram shows the criteria as discussed in chapter 6. Criteria which establish the range or bandwidth of interpretation. A responsible interpretation of Biblical literature is that interpretation which remains within the range between the limits and the possibilities of interpretation. This range also prevents the interpreter from "drowning in the swamp", it provides a guideline for interpretation. It so to say serves as a lifeguard and guide to find a way through the swamp.

Up till now I have only focused on the text itself. The model of Eco shows the way the reader deals with the text. The outlined steps in the diagram above all deal with the text. The bandwidth between limits and possibilities in interpretation are about the text. However, praxis shows there is more than the text alone which plays a role in interpretation. In the experience of reading and interpreting the text it shows that readers use more guidelines for their interpretation then the text shows. Sometimes church history is used or a certain cultural setting. A particular community of Christians can establish their own habits and use these in their interpretation of the text. We have already seen, that the history, creeds, and catechism of the Roman Catholic Church are important in William Kurz' treatment of the text. In addition the missionary zeal and Pentecostal background of Robert Menzies color his interpretations. Max Turner is academically oriented and careful in discussing particular applications of the text. In the next section I will give a brief assessment of all three scholars and situate them within the bandwidth of interpretation.

A brief assessment of Max Turner, Robert Menzies and William Kurz
Max M.B. Turner
Because Max Turner is highly cooperative as a reader I would place him rather high along the diagonal line in the visualization above. In terms of limits and possiblities Turner has a tendency to focus on the limits of interpretation; this places him on the right side of the diagonal line, but still within the bandwidth. We have already seen in chapter 3 that Turner is very keen on the text itself. He is consciously aware of various limits and possibilities in interpretation. For instance in his treatment of the Pentecost episode in Acts 2 he carefully investigates if there could be some Sinai allusion, he disucsses Menzies' arguments and comes with a cautious conclusion that Pentecost is not an allegory of the Sinai episode, but that there is some correspondence which suggests that Pentecost can be viewed as "the fulfilment and renewal of Israel's covenant".[4] Turner notices the possibilities within the text, he however safely chooses to stay within the limits the text provides. He is not only cooperative with the text but his large encyclopedic competence enables him to thoroughly discuss several arguments from other scholars and engage with (possible) background of the episode under scrutiny. His treatment of the promise of John the Baptist in Luke 3:16-17 shows this. After carefully discussing the text of this promise he comes with his interpretation of a metaphori-

---

4 Turner, *Power from on High*, 289.

cal meaning of baptism with Spirit and fire and suggests that it points to an eschatological cleansing of the people of Israel. His translation of πτύον being a spade instead of a fork-like shovel corroborates this intepretation. Unfortunately this is not followed by some sort of exposition of the practical implications for this promise for Christians or the church today. Are there any such practical implications? The church in general could have benefitted from additional exposition. Because Turner does not elaborate on this I place him on the limits side of the diagonal line instead of the possibilities side.

Robert P. Menzies
In comparison to Max Turner, Robert Menzies is a little less cooperative as a reader and therefore I would place him a little lower along the diagonal line. And unlike Turner, Menzies has a tendency to focus on the possibilities of interpretation. That puts him on the left side of the diagonal line, however still within the bandwidth. Menzies' discussion of the episodes in Acts 8, 9 and Acts 19 especially show his cooperation with the text in this direction of the possibilities. In Menzies' opinion the Spirit in Luke-Acts is an empowerment for mission. In those instances that the text speaks about the laying on of hands (Acts 8:17, 9:17 and 19:6), Menzies assumes that this is an act of commissioning for service, for mission. Because in these contexts the laying on of hands is not for healing (with 9:17 as an exception), it must be, according to Menzies, for a commissioning for mission.[5] This could be so, however the text does not explicitly state this and the context does not (except in the case of Saul/Paul) elaborate on a Samaritan (Acts 8) or Ephesian (Acts 19) participation in mission. Menzies' interpretation of Acts 19 that the group of disciples stayed with Paul and eventually were part of the group of elders in the Ephesian church is an interesting train of thought and could be a possibility, but in my opinion no more than that because there is simply no hard evidence for such an assumption.[6]

Menzies' interpretation of the relevant Lukan passages raise a serious problem when Jesus and his ministry are treated as an *exemplar* to be (normatively) followed by Christians today (see above in §4.11.3 and §4.13.2). I understand the reasoning that Jesus sets an example for Christians today, a worthy example which needs to be followed. But to identify Christians today with Jesus and his unique ministry stretches the interpretation of the

---

5 Menzies, *Empowered for Witness*, 212.
6 Menzies, *Empowered for Witness*, 225.

text too far. Christians should be full of the Spirit, they should participate in mission, they will suffer, but this does not mean that this all will be *in the exact way* as it happened to Jesus. In my opinion Menzies does not do justice to the unique persons and aspects in salvation history. As far as I am concerned Menzies here even exceeds the possible interpretations with the danger of a division between Christians who follow Jesus, but in different manners.

William S. Kurz
William Kurz inclines to the possibilities side within the bandwidth of interpretation. He is less cooperative with the text as such and focuses on the application of the text. In the visualization of the bandwidth I would therefore place Kurz just as Menzies on the left side of the diagonal line and a bit lower because of his less cooperative reading. But again, just as Menzies and Turner, Kurz stays within the bandwidth so his interpretation is responsible. The center of gravity in Kurz' interpretation of the Lukan narrative is on application. The disadvantage of this is that he spends less attention to the text itself and as a consequence misses some difficult issues the text raises. He for instance only touches the surface in his treatment of Luke 3 and 4, respectively the promise of John the Baptist and Jesus' inaugural address. He does not elaborate on the relation between water baptism and spirit baptism (see above in §5.4), but only states that they are related. The possible relation between Jesus' words in Luke 4:14-19 and the year of Jubilee and/or the suffering Servant in Isaiah is briefly mentioned but not worked out. These examples are characteristic for Kurz' work: he briefly discusses the text and then illustrates this with possible applications. These applications are almost all related to the Catholic Church. This shows that besides the text, Kurz takes the Catholic Church also as a "guide through the swamp". In his context as a priest within the Catholic Church this is adequate and permissable to do. It shows an extra boundary for the interpretive bandwidth. However in some cases the Church boundary does not coincide with the textual boundary. This for instance is the case in Acts 8, the Samaritan episode. Based only on this episode the Catholic sacrament of confirmation makes sense. This interpretation is possible because in this instance Kurz does not interact with the whole story of Luke-Acts or even with the canon. It is possible for Kurz to stress God's freedom in giving the Spirit as He desires, and on the next page defend the Catholic sacrament of confirmation.[7] We must acknowledge, however, that in Kurz' reading of

---

7 Kurz, *Acts of the Apostles* (2013), 142-143.

Luke-Acts the Roman Catholic *Traditionsbegriff* plays an import role.[8] Within Roman Catholicism the correct interpretation of the Bible originates with the apostles and is in tradition passed on and administered through the *magisterium*. So, as I already hinted at above, besides the text of Luke-Acts, there is the living tradition which serves as an interpretive guide to correctly understand and apply the biblical text. When we take this *Traditionsbegriff* into account we can only fully understand and appreciate the work of Kurz. Appealing in Kurz' approach is his interaction with the whole story of the Bible. He does not hesitate to interact with other books or authors. These interactions then demonstrate Kurz' point of view on the unity of the Bible and the value of the whole of the canon. The purpose of Kurz' writings is to edify Christians and encourage them to read the Bible and grow in discipleship (especially obvious in *Following Jesus* and the Living Tradition sidebars in his recent commentary on Acts). The benefit of this is accessible work for the Christian believer, however the disadvantage is a superficial treatment of the various texts from a scholarly point of view.

Concluding remarks
At the end of this research we can conclude that the role of the reader in construing a Lukan pneumatology is crucial. Not in the sense that the reader creates meaning out of the text, but in the sense that the reader interprets the meaning of the text. There are rules of interpretation, there are limits within the text, and there are possibilities within the text. The part of the reader in his cooperation with the text and the use of his encyclopedic competence all play a huge role during the process of reading, rereading, interpreting and eventually determining the meaning of a text. This crucial role of the reader comes with an enormous responsibility. The reader's responsibility is to stay within the bandwidth allowed, the bandwidth that is found within the possible interpretations that the text offers. This responsibility begs the reader / interpreter to consequently determine the character of the text under scrutiny, to carefully focus on

---

8 For *Tradtionsbegriff*, see: Van den Brink, Van der Kooi, *Christelijke Dogmatiek*, 76-77, 360-361, 499-500; Heinrich Denzinger, *Enchiridion Symbolorum: A Compendium of Creeds, Definitions, and Declarations of the Catholic Church* (San Francisco CA: Ignatius, 11854, 432012); Francis Schüssler Fiorenza, 'Systematic Theology: Tasks and Methods' in: F. Schüssler Fiorenza and John P. Galvin (eds.), *Systematic Theology. Roman Catholic Perspectives* (Minneapolis, MN: Fortress, 1991, 22011), 54-58; Richard Boeckler, *Der moderne römisch-katholische Traditionsbegriff* (Göttingen: VandenHoek & Ruprecht, 1967); Ludwig Ott, *Grundriss der* Katholischen Dogmatik (Freiburg: Herder, 1952).

the passage at hand while not losing sight of the entire narrative and to constantly be aware of his own encyclopedic competence to prevent harmful interpretations and applications. This bandwidth of interpretation shows the extent of a responsible interpretation. Outside this bandwidth an interpretation is simply wrong. The reader / interpreter cannot simply make anything out of the text or create his own meaning. There are limits to the possible interpretations. This conclusion does not solve the disagreements in Lukan pneumatology. It perhaps does not even contribute to a wider consensus in Lukan pneumatology. However, it does show the responsibility of the interpreter and the possible range of interpretation. It does help to understand the various interpretations of the Lukan πνεῦμα clusters and based on the criteria mentioned above it is possible to determine whether an interpretation is responsible or not. In my opinion all three of the discussed scholars succeeded to responsibly interpret the biblical narrative of Luke-Acts. Although I pointed out that in some cases a certain scholar crossed the boundaries, the overall picture is that all three scholars cooperate with the text albeit in their own respective manner. Through the use of Eco's model of the cooperative reader we gained understanding in their respective interpretive choices. This understanding does not mean that we share all of these interpretive choices. That is the consequence of a certain range in possible interpretations.

There is one more thing what needs to be said here and could possibly instigate further research. All three of the discussed scholars are not only readers and interpreters. All three are authors as well. I deduced their reading of the Lukan narrative from their writings. All three have written with a specific purpose and audience in mind. They have written for a special reference group. One question remains and is beyond the scope of this present research to be properly answered: in what way did the specific reference group of these three scholars influence their reading and interpretation of the Lukan narrative? This question could prove to be worthwhile for further research to investigate if a specific reference group or purpose attributes (positively or negatively) to the encyclopedic competence of the reader / interpreter of the Lukan narrative.

In respect towards future research I hope that the discipline of biblical studies will benefit from Eco's model and that it will instigate further theological debate about the importance of the role of the reader in interpretation. It is my wish that both the academy and the church will benefit from responsible interpretations of the biblical narrative.

APPENDIX 1
PNEUMA AND ITS DERIVATES IN THE GOSPEL OF LUKE

1:15 ἔσται γὰρ μέγας ἐνώπιον [τοῦ] κυρίου, καὶ οἶνον καὶ σίκερα οὐ μὴ πίῃ, καὶ πνεύματος ἁγίου πλησθήσεται ἔτι ἐκ κοιλίας μητρὸς αὐτοῦ,

1:17 καὶ αὐτὸς προελεύσεται ἐνώπιον αὐτοῦ ἐν πνεύματι καὶ δυνάμει Ἠλίου, ἐπιστρέψαι καρδίας πατέρων ἐπὶ τέκνα καὶ ἀπειθεῖς ἐν φρονήσει δικαίων, ἑτοιμάσαι κυρίῳ λαὸν κατεσκευασμένον.

1:35 καὶ ἀποκριθεὶς ὁ ἄγγελος εἶπεν αὐτῇ, Πνεῦμα ἅγιον ἐπελεύσεται ἐπὶ σέ, καὶ δύναμις ὑψίστου ἐπισκιάσει σοι· διὸ καὶ τὸ γεννώμενον ἅγιον κληθήσεται, υἱὸς θεοῦ.

1:41 καὶ ἐγένετο ὡς ἤκουσεν τὸν ἀσπασμὸν τῆς Μαρίας ἡ Ἐλισάβετ, ἐσκίρτησεν τὸ βρέφος ἐν τῇ κοιλίᾳ αὐτῆς, καὶ ἐπλήσθη πνεύματος ἁγίου ἡ Ἐλισάβετ

1:47 καὶ ἠγαλλίασεν τὸ πνεῦμά μου ἐπὶ τῷ θεῷ τῷ σωτῆρί μου,

1:67 Καὶ Ζαχαρίας ὁ πατὴρ αὐτοῦ ἐπλήσθη πνεύματος ἁγίου καὶ ἐπροφήτευσεν λέγων

1:80 Τὸ δὲ παιδίον ηὔξανεν καὶ ἐκραταιοῦτο πνεύματι, καὶ ἦν ἐν ταῖς ἐρήμοις ἕως ἡμέρας ἀναδείξεως αὐτοῦ πρὸς τὸν Ἰσραήλ

2:25,26,27 Καὶ ἰδοὺ ἄνθρωπος ἦν ἐν Ἰερουσαλὴμ ᾧ ὄνομα Συμεών, καὶ ὁ ἄνθρωπος οὗτος δίκαιος καὶ εὐλαβής, προσδεχόμενος παράκλησιν τοῦ Ἰσραήλ, καὶ πνεῦμα ἦν ἅγιον ἐπ' αὐτόν· καὶ ἦν αὐτῷ κεχρηματισμένον ὑπὸ τοῦ πνεύματος τοῦ ἁγίου μὴ ἰδεῖν θάνατον πρὶν [ἢ] ἂν ἴδῃ τὸν Χριστὸν κυρίου. καὶ ἦλθεν ἐν τῷ πνεύματι εἰς τὸ ἱερόν· καὶ ἐν τῷ εἰσαγαγεῖν τοὺς γονεῖς τὸ παιδίον Ἰησοῦν τοῦ ποιῆσαι αὐτοὺς κατὰ τὸ εἰθισμένον τοῦ νόμου περὶ αὐτοῦ

3:16 ἀπεκρίνατο λέγων πᾶσιν ὁ Ἰωάννης, Ἐγὼ μὲν ὕδατι βαπτίζω ὑμᾶς· ἔρχεται δὲ ὁ ἰσχυρότερός μου, οὗ οὐκ εἰμὶ ἱκανὸς λῦσαι τὸν ἱμάντα τῶν ὑποδημάτων αὐτοῦ· αὐτὸς ὑμᾶς βαπτίσει ἐν πνεύματι ἁγίῳ καὶ πυρί·

3:22 καὶ καταβῆναι τὸ πνεῦμα τὸ ἅγιον σωματικῷ εἴδει ὡς περιστερὰν ἐπ' αὐτόν, καὶ φωνὴν ἐξ οὐρανοῦ γενέσθαι, Σὺ εἶ ὁ υἱός μου ὁ ἀγαπητός, ἐν σοὶ εὐδόκησα

4:1 Ἰησοῦς δὲ πλήρης πνεύματος ἁγίου ὑπέστρεψεν ἀπὸ τοῦ Ἰορδάνου, καὶ ἤγετο ἐν τῷ πνεύματι ἐν τῇ ἐρήμῳ

4:14 Καὶ ὑπέστρεψεν ὁ Ἰησοῦς ἐν τῇ δυνάμει τοῦ πνεύματος εἰς τὴν Γαλιλαίαν. καὶ φήμη ἐξῆλθεν καθ' ὅλης τῆς περιχώρου περὶ αὐτοῦ

4:18 Πνεῦμα κυρίου ἐπ' ἐμέ, οὗ εἵνεκεν ἔχρισέν με εὐαγγελίσασθαι πτωχοῖς, ἀπέσταλκέν με κηρύξαι αἰχμαλώτοις ἄφεσιν καὶ τυφλοῖς ἀνάβλεψιν, ἀποστεῖλαι τεθραυσμένους ἐν ἀφέσει

4:33 καὶ ἐν τῇ συναγωγῇ ἦν ἄνθρωπος ἔχων πνεῦμα δαιμονίου ἀκαθάρτου, καὶ ἀνέκραξεν φωνῇ μεγάλῃ

4:36 καὶ ἐγένετο θάμβος ἐπὶ πάντας, καὶ συνελάλουν πρὸς ἀλλήλους λέγοντες, Τίς ὁ λόγος οὗτος, ὅτι ἐν ἐξουσίᾳ καὶ δυνάμει ἐπιτάσσει τοῖς ἀκαθάρτοις πνεύμασιν, καὶ ἐξέρχονται

6:18 οἳ ἦλθον ἀκοῦσαι αὐτοῦ καὶ ἰαθῆναι ἀπὸ τῶν νόσων αὐτῶν· καὶ οἱ ἐνοχλούμενοι ἀπὸ πνευμάτων ἀκαθάρτων ἐθεραπεύοντο

7:21 ἐν ἐκείνῃ τῇ ὥρᾳ ἐθεράπευσεν πολλοὺς ἀπὸ νόσων καὶ μαστίγων καὶ πνευμάτων πονηρῶν, καὶ τυφλοῖς πολλοῖς ἐχαρίσατο βλέπειν

8:2 καὶ γυναῖκές τινες αἳ ἦσαν τεθεραπευμέναι ἀπὸ πνευμάτων πονηρῶν καὶ ἀσθενειῶν, Μαρία ἡ καλουμένη Μαγδαληνή, ἀφ' ἧς δαιμόνια ἑπτὰ ἐξεληλύθει

8:29 παρήγγειλεν γὰρ τῷ πνεύματι τῷ ἀκαθάρτῳ ἐξελθεῖν ἀπὸ τοῦ ἀνθρώπου. πολλοῖς γὰρ χρόνοις συνηρπάκει αὐτόν, καὶ ἐδεσμεύετο ἁλύσεσιν καὶ πέδαις φυλασσόμενος, καὶ διαρρήσσων τὰ δεσμὰ ἠλαύνετο ὑπὸ τοῦ δαιμονίου εἰς τὰς ἐρήμους

8:55 καὶ ἐπέστρεψεν τὸ πνεῦμα αὐτῆς, καὶ ἀνέστη παραχρῆμα, καὶ διέταξεν αὐτῇ δοθῆναι φαγεῖν

9:39 καὶ ἰδοὺ πνεῦμα λαμβάνει αὐτόν, καὶ ἐξαίφνης κράζει, καὶ σπαράσσει αὐτὸν μετὰ ἀφροῦ καὶ μόγις ἀποχωρεῖ ἀπ' αὐτοῦ συντρῖβον αὐτόν:

9:42 ἔτι δὲ προσερχομένου αὐτοῦ ἔρρηξεν αὐτὸν τὸ δαιμόνιον καὶ συνεσπάραξεν: ἐπετίμησεν δὲ ὁ Ἰησοῦς τῷ πνεύματι τῷ ἀκαθάρτῳ, καὶ ἰάσατο τὸν παῖδα καὶ ἀπέδωκεν αὐτὸν τῷ πατρὶ αὐτοῦ

9:55 στραφεὶς δὲ ἐπετίμησεν αὐτοῖς // variant reading (!)

10:20-21 πλὴν ἐν τούτῳ μὴ χαίρετε ὅτι τὰ πνεύματα ὑμῖν ὑποτάσσεται, χαίρετε δὲ ὅτι τὰ ὀνόματα ὑμῶν ἐγγέγραπται ἐν τοῖς οὐρανοῖς Ἐν αὐτῇ τῇ ὥρᾳ ἠγαλλιάσατο [ἐν] τῷ πνεύματι τῷ ἁγίῳ καὶ εἶπεν, Ἐξομολογοῦμαί σοι, πάτερ, κύριε τοῦ οὐρανοῦ καὶ τῆς γῆς, ὅτι ἀπέκρυψας ταῦτα ἀπὸ σοφῶν καὶ συνετῶν, καὶ ἀπεκάλυψας αὐτὰ νηπίοις: ναί, ὁ πατήρ, ὅτι οὕτως εὐδοκία ἐγένετο ἔμπροσθέν σου

11:13 εἰ οὖν ὑμεῖς πονηροὶ ὑπάρχοντες οἴδατε δόματα ἀγαθὰ διδόναι τοῖς τέκνοις ὑμῶν, πόσῳ μᾶλλον ὁ πατὴρ [ὁ] ἐξ οὐρανοῦ δώσει πνεῦμα ἅγιον τοῖς αἰτοῦσιν αὐτόν

11:24 Ὅταν τὸ ἀκάθαρτον πνεῦμα ἐξέλθῃ ἀπὸ τοῦ ἀνθρώπου, διέρχεται δι' ἀνύδρων τόπων ζητοῦν ἀνάπαυσιν, καὶ μὴ εὑρίσκον, [τότε] λέγει, Ὑποστρέψω εἰς τὸν οἶκόν μου ὅθεν ἐξῆλθον
11:26 τότε πορεύεται καὶ παραλαμβάνει ἕτερα πνεύματα πονηρότερα ἑαυτοῦ ἑπτά, καὶ εἰσελθόντα κατοικεῖ ἐκεῖ, καὶ γίνεται τὰ ἔσχατα τοῦ ἀνθρώπου ἐκείνου χείρονα τῶν πρώτων

12:10-12 καὶ πᾶς ὃς ἐρεῖ λόγον εἰς τὸν υἱὸν τοῦ ἀνθρώπου, ἀφεθήσεται αὐτῷ: τῷ δὲ εἰς τὸ ἅγιον πνεῦμα βλασφημήσαντι οὐκ ἀφεθήσεται ὅταν δὲ εἰσφέρωσιν ὑμᾶς ἐπὶ τὰς συναγωγὰς καὶ τὰς ἀρχὰς καὶ τὰς ἐξουσίας, μὴ μεριμνήσητε πῶς ἢ τί ἀπολογήσησθε ἢ τί εἴπητε: τὸ γὰρ ἅγιον πνεῦμα διδάξει ὑμᾶς ἐν αὐτῇ τῇ ὥρᾳ ἃ δεῖ εἰπεῖν

13:11 καὶ ἰδοὺ γυνὴ πνεῦμα ἔχουσα ἀσθενείας ἔτη δεκαοκτώ, καὶ ἦν συγκύπτουσα καὶ μὴ δυναμένη ἀνακύψαι εἰς τὸ παντελές

23:46 καὶ φωνήσας φωνῇ μεγάλῃ ὁ Ἰησοῦς εἶπεν, Πάτερ, εἰς χεῖράς σου παρατίθεμαι τὸ πνεῦμά μου: τοῦτο δὲ εἰπὼν ἐξέπνευσεν

24:37-39 πτοηθέντες δὲ καὶ ἔμφοβοι γενόμενοι ἐδόκουν πνεῦμα θεωρεῖν. καὶ εἶπεν αὐτοῖς, Τί τεταραγμένοι ἐστέ, καὶ διὰ τί διαλογισμοὶ ἀναβαίνουσιν ἐν τῇ καρδίᾳ ὑμῶν; ἴδετε τὰς χεῖράς μου καὶ τοὺς πόδας μου ὅτι ἐγώ εἰμι αὐτός: ψηλαφήσατέ με καὶ ἴδετε, ὅτι πνεῦμα σάρκα καὶ ὀστέα οὐκ ἔχει καθὼς ἐμὲ θεωρεῖτε ἔχοντα.

APPENDIX 2
PNEUMA AND ITS DERIVATES IN THE BOOK OF ACTS

1:2 ἄχρι ἧς ἡμέρας ἐντειλάμενος τοῖς ἀποστόλοις διὰ πνεύματος ἁγίου οὓς ἐξελέξατο ἀνελήμφθη·

1:5 ὅτι Ἰωάννης μὲν ἐβάπτισεν ὕδατι, ὑμεῖς δὲ ἐν πνεύματι βαπτισθήσεσθε ἁγίῳ οὐ μετὰ πολλὰς ταύτας ἡμέρας

1:8 ἀλλὰ λήμψεσθε δύναμιν ἐπελθόντος τοῦ ἁγίου πνεύματος ἐφ᾽ ὑμᾶς, καὶ ἔσεσθέ μου μάρτυρες ἔν τε Ἰερουσαλὴμ καὶ [ἐν] πάσῃ τῇ Ἰουδαίᾳ καὶ Σαμαρείᾳ καὶ ἕως ἐσχάτου τῆς γῆς

1:16 Ἄνδρες ἀδελφοί, ἔδει πληρωθῆναι τὴν γραφὴν ἣν προεῖπεν τὸ πνεῦμα τὸ ἅγιον διὰ στόματος Δαυὶδ περὶ Ἰούδα τοῦ γενομένου ὁδηγοῦ τοῖς συλλαβοῦσιν Ἰησοῦν

2:4 καὶ ἐπλήσθησαν πάντες πνεύματος ἁγίου, καὶ ἤρξαντο λαλεῖν ἑτέραις γλώσσαις καθὼς τὸ πνεῦμα ἐδίδου ἀποφθέγγεσθαι αὐτοῖς

2:17-18 Καὶ ἔσται ἐν ταῖς ἐσχάταις ἡμέραις, λέγει ὁ θεός, ἐκχεῶ ἀπὸ τοῦ πνεύματός μου ἐπὶ πᾶσαν σάρκα, καὶ προφητεύσουσιν οἱ υἱοὶ ὑμῶν καὶ αἱ θυγατέρες ὑμῶν, καὶ οἱ νεανίσκοι ὑμῶν ὁράσεις ὄψονται, καὶ οἱ πρεσβύτεροι ὑμῶν ἐνυπνίοις ἐνυπνιασθήσονται· καί γε ἐπὶ τοὺς δούλους μου καὶ ἐπὶ τὰς δούλας μου ἐν ταῖς ἡμέραις ἐκείναις ἐκχεῶ ἀπὸ τοῦ πνεύματός μου, καὶ προφητεύσουσιν.

2:33 τῇ δεξιᾷ οὖν τοῦ θεοῦ ὑψωθεὶς τήν τε ἐπαγγελίαν τοῦ πνεύματος τοῦ ἁγίου λαβὼν παρὰ τοῦ πατρὸς ἐξέχεεν τοῦτο ὃ ὑμεῖς [καὶ] βλέπετε καὶ ἀκούετε.

2:38 Πέτρος δὲ πρὸς αὐτούς, Μετανοήσατε, [φησίν,] καὶ βαπτισθήτω ἕκαστος ὑμῶν ἐπὶ τῷ ὀνόματι Ἰησοῦ Χριστοῦ εἰς ἄφεσιν τῶν ἁμαρτιῶν ὑμῶν, καὶ λήμψεσθε τὴν δωρεὰν τοῦ ἁγίου πνεύματος

4:8 τότε Πέτρος πλησθεὶς πνεύματος ἁγίου εἶπεν πρὸς αὐτούς, Ἄρχοντες τοῦ λαοῦ καὶ πρεσβύτεροι

4:25 ὁ τοῦ πατρὸς ἡμῶν διὰ πνεύματος ἁγίου στόματος Δαυὶδ παιδός σου εἰπών, Ἱνατί ἐφρύαξαν ἔθνη καὶ λαοὶ ἐμελέτησαν κενά;

4:31 καὶ δεηθέντων αὐτῶν ἐσαλεύθη ὁ τόπος ἐν ᾧ ἦσαν συνηγμένοι, καὶ ἐπλήσθησαν ἅπαντες τοῦ ἁγίου πνεύματος, καὶ ἐλάλουν τὸν λόγον τοῦ θεοῦ μετὰ παρρησίας

5:3 εἶπεν δὲ ὁ Πέτρος, Ἀνανία, διὰ τί ἐπλήρωσεν ὁ Σατανᾶς τὴν καρδίαν σου ψεύσασθαί σε τὸ πνεῦμα τὸ ἅγιον καὶ νοσφίσασθαι ἀπὸ τῆς τιμῆς τοῦ χωρίου

5:9 ὁ δὲ Πέτρος πρὸς αὐτήν, Τί ὅτι συνεφωνήθη ὑμῖν πειράσαι τὸ πνεῦμα κυρίου; ἰδοὺ οἱ πόδες τῶν θαψάντων τὸν ἄνδρα σου ἐπὶ τῇ θύρᾳ καὶ ἐξοίσουσίν σε

5:16 συνήρχετο δὲ καὶ τὸ πλῆθος τῶν πέριξ πόλεων Ἰερουσαλήμ, φέροντες ἀσθενεῖς καὶ ὀχλουμένους ὑπὸ πνευμάτων ἀκαθάρτων, οἵτινες ἐθεραπεύοντο ἅπαντες

5:32 καὶ ἡμεῖς ἐσμεν μάρτυρες τῶν ῥημάτων τούτων, καὶ τὸ πνεῦμα τὸ ἅγιον ὃ ἔδωκεν ὁ θεὸς τοῖς πειθαρχοῦσιν αὐτῷ

6:3-5 ἐπισκέψασθε δέ, ἀδελφοί, ἄνδρας ἐξ ὑμῶν μαρτυρουμένους ἑπτὰ πλήρεις πνεύματος καὶ σοφίας, οὓς καταστήσομεν ἐπὶ τῆς χρείας ταύτης ἡμεῖς δὲ τῇ προσευχῇ καὶ τῇ διακονίᾳ τοῦ λόγου προσκαρτερήσομεν καὶ ἤρεσεν ὁ λόγος ἐνώπιον παντὸς τοῦ πλήθους, καὶ ἐξελέξαντο Στέφανον, ἄνδρα πλήρης πίστεως καὶ πνεύματος ἁγίου, καὶ Φίλιππον καὶ Πρόχορον καὶ Νικάνορα καὶ Τίμωνα καὶ Παρμενᾶν καὶ Νικόλαον προσήλυτον Ἀντιοχέα,

6:10 καὶ οὐκ ἴσχυον ἀντιστῆναι τῇ σοφίᾳ καὶ τῷ πνεύματι ᾧ ἐλάλει

7:51 Σκληροτράχηλοι καὶ ἀπερίτμητοι καρδίαις καὶ τοῖς ὠσίν, ὑμεῖς ἀεὶ τῷ πνεύματι τῷ ἁγίῳ ἀντιπίπτετε, ὡς οἱ πατέρες ὑμῶν καὶ ὑμεῖς

7:55 ὑπάρχων δὲ πλήρης πνεύματος ἁγίου ἀτενίσας εἰς τὸν οὐρανὸν εἶδεν δόξαν θεοῦ καὶ Ἰησοῦν ἑστῶτα ἐκ δεξιῶν τοῦ θεοῦ

7:59 καὶ ἐλιθοβόλουν τὸν Στέφανον ἐπικαλούμενον καὶ λέγοντα, Κύριε Ἰησοῦ, δέξαι τὸ πνεῦμά μου

8:7 πολλοὶ γὰρ τῶν ἐχόντων πνεύματα ἀκάθαρτα βοῶντα φωνῇ μεγάλῃ ἐξήρχοντο, πολλοὶ δὲ παραλελυμένοι καὶ χωλοὶ ἐθεραπεύθησαν:

8:15 οἵτινες καταβάντες προσηύξαντο περὶ αὐτῶν ὅπως λάβωσιν πνεῦμα ἅγιον:

8:17 τότε ἐπετίθεσαν τὰς χεῖρας ἐπ' αὐτούς, καὶ ἐλάμβανον πνεῦμα ἅγιον.

8:18 ἰδὼν δὲ ὁ Σίμων ὅτι διὰ τῆς ἐπιθέσεως τῶν χειρῶν τῶν ἀποστόλων δίδοται τὸ πνεῦμα, προσήνεγκεν αὐτοῖς χρήματα

8:19 λέγων, Δότε κἀμοὶ τὴν ἐξουσίαν ταύτην ἵνα ᾧ ἐὰν ἐπιθῶ τὰς χεῖρας λαμβάνῃ πνεῦμα ἅγιον.

8:29 εἶπεν δὲ τὸ πνεῦμα τῷ Φιλίππῳ, Πρόσελθε καὶ κολλήθητι τῷ ἅρματι τούτῳ.

8:39 ὅτε δὲ ἀνέβησαν ἐκ τοῦ ὕδατος, πνεῦμα κυρίου ἥρπασεν τὸν Φίλιππον, καὶ οὐκ εἶδεν αὐτὸν οὐκέτι ὁ εὐνοῦχος: ἐπορεύετο γὰρ τὴν ὁδὸν αὐτοῦ χαίρων.

9:17 Ἀπῆλθεν δὲ Ἀνανίας καὶ εἰσῆλθεν εἰς τὴν οἰκίαν, καὶ ἐπιθεὶς ἐπ' αὐτὸν τὰς χεῖρας εἶπεν, Σαοὺλ ἀδελφέ, ὁ κύριος ἀπέσταλκέν με, Ἰησοῦς ὁ ὀφθείς σοι ἐν τῇ ὁδῷ ᾗ ἤρχου, ὅπως ἀναβλέψῃς καὶ πλησθῇς πνεύματος ἁγίου.

9:31 Ἡ μὲν οὖν ἐκκλησία καθ' ὅλης τῆς Ἰουδαίας καὶ Γαλιλαίας καὶ Σαμαρείας εἶχεν εἰρήνην, οἰκοδομουμένη καὶ πορευομένη τῷ φόβῳ τοῦ κυρίου, καὶ τῇ παρακλήσει τοῦ ἁγίου πνεύματος ἐπληθύνετο.

10:19 τοῦ δὲ Πέτρου διενθυμουμένου περὶ τοῦ ὁράματος εἶπεν [αὐτῷ] τὸ πνεῦμα, Ἰδοὺ ἄνδρες τρεῖς ζητοῦντές σε:

10:38 Ἰησοῦν τὸν ἀπὸ Ναζαρέθ, ὡς ἔχρισεν αὐτὸν ὁ θεὸς πνεύματι ἁγίῳ καὶ δυνάμει, ὃς διῆλθεν εὐεργετῶν καὶ ἰώμενος πάντας τοὺς καταδυναστευομένους ὑπὸ τοῦ διαβόλου, ὅτι ὁ θεὸς ἦν μετ' αὐτοῦ.

10:44-47 Ἔτι λαλοῦντος τοῦ Πέτρου τὰ ῥήματα ταῦτα ἐπέπεσεν τὸ πνεῦμα τὸ ἅγιον ἐπὶ πάντας τοὺς ἀκούοντας τὸν λόγον. καὶ ἐξέστησαν οἱ ἐκ περιτομῆς πιστοὶ ὅσοι συνῆλθαν τῷ Πέτρῳ, ὅτι καὶ ἐπὶ τὰ ἔθνη ἡ δωρεὰ τοῦ ἁγίου πνεύματος ἐκκέχυται· ἤκουον γὰρ αὐτῶν λαλούντων γλώσσαις καὶ μεγαλυνόντων τὸν θεόν. τότε ἀπεκρίθη Πέτρος, Μήτι τὸ ὕδωρ δύναται κωλῦσαί τις τοῦ μὴ βαπτισθῆναι τούτους οἵτινες τὸ πνεῦμα τὸ ἅγιον ἔλαβον ὡς καὶ ἡμεῖς;

11:12 εἶπεν δὲ τὸ πνεῦμά μοι συνελθεῖν αὐτοῖς μηδὲν διακρίναντα. ἦλθον δὲ σὺν ἐμοὶ καὶ οἱ ἓξ ἀδελφοὶ οὗτοι, καὶ εἰσήλθομεν εἰς τὸν οἶκον τοῦ ἀνδρός·

11:15-16 ἐν δὲ τῷ ἄρξασθαί με λαλεῖν ἐπέπεσεν τὸ πνεῦμα τὸ ἅγιον ἐπ' αὐτοὺς ὥσπερ καὶ ἐφ' ἡμᾶς ἐν ἀρχῇ. ¹⁶ἐμνήσθην δὲ τοῦ ῥήματος τοῦ κυρίου ὡς ἔλεγεν, Ἰωάννης μὲν ἐβάπτισεν ὕδατι, ὑμεῖς δὲ βαπτισθήσεσθε ἐν πνεύματι ἁγίῳ.

11:24 ὅτι ἦν ἀνὴρ ἀγαθὸς καὶ πλήρης πνεύματος ἁγίου καὶ πίστεως. καὶ προσετέθη ὄχλος ἱκανὸς τῷ κυρίῳ.

11:28 ἀναστὰς δὲ εἷς ἐξ αὐτῶν ὀνόματι Ἀγαβος ἐσήμανεν διὰ τοῦ πνεύματος λιμὸν μεγάλην μέλλειν ἔσεσθαι ἐφ' ὅλην τὴν οἰκουμένην· ἥτις ἐγένετο ἐπὶ Κλαυδίου.

13:2-4 λειτουργούντων δὲ αὐτῶν τῷ κυρίῳ καὶ νηστευόντων εἶπεν τὸ πνεῦμα τὸ ἅγιον, Ἀφορίσατε δή μοι τὸν Βαρναβᾶν καὶ Σαῦλον εἰς τὸ ἔργον ὃ προσκέκλημαι αὐτούς. τότε νηστεύσαντες καὶ προσευξάμενοι καὶ ἐπιθέντες τὰς χεῖρας αὐτοῖς ἀπέλυσαν. Αὐτοὶ μὲν οὖν ἐκπεμφθέντες ὑπὸ τοῦ ἁγίου πνεύματος κατῆλθον εἰς Σελεύκειαν, ἐκεῖθέν τε ἀπέπλευσαν εἰς Κύπρον,

13:9 Σαῦλος δέ, ὁ καὶ Παῦλος, πλησθεὶς πνεύματος ἁγίου ἀτενίσας εἰς αὐτὸν

13:52 οἵ τε μαθηταὶ ἐπληροῦντο χαρᾶς καὶ πνεύματος ἁγίου.

15:8 καὶ ὁ καρδιογνώστης θεὸς ἐμαρτύρησεν αὐτοῖς δοὺς τὸ πνεῦμα τὸ ἅγιον καθὼς καὶ ἡμῖν,

15:28-29 ἔδοξεν γὰρ τῷ πνεύματι τῷ ἁγίῳ καὶ ἡμῖν μηδὲν πλέον ἐπιτίθεσθαι ὑμῖν βάρος πλὴν τούτων τῶν ἐπάναγκες, ἀπέχεσθαι εἰδωλοθύτων καὶ αἵματος καὶ πνικτῶν καὶ πορνείας: ἐξ ὧν διατηροῦντες ἑαυτοὺς εὖ πράξετε. Ἔρρωσθε. // variant reading (!)
16:6 Διῆλθον δὲ τὴν Φρυγίαν καὶ Γαλατικὴν χώραν, κωλυθέντες ὑπὸ τοῦ ἁγίου πνεύματος λαλῆσαι τὸν λόγον ἐν τῇ Ἀσίᾳ:

16:18 τοῦτο δὲ ἐποίει ἐπὶ πολλὰς ἡμέρας. διαπονηθεὶς δὲ Παῦλος καὶ ἐπιστρέψας τῷ πνεύματι εἶπεν, Παραγγέλλω σοι ἐν ὀνόματι Ἰησοῦ Χριστοῦ ἐξελθεῖν ἀπ' αὐτῆς: καὶ ἐξῆλθεν αὐτῇ τῇ ὥρᾳ.

17:16 Ἐν δὲ ταῖς Ἀθήναις ἐκδεχομένου αὐτοὺς τοῦ Παύλου, παρωξύνετο τὸ πνεῦμα αὐτοῦ ἐν αὐτῷ θεωροῦντος κατείδωλον οὖσαν τὴν πόλιν.

18:25 οὗτος ἦν κατηχημένος τὴν ὁδὸν τοῦ κυρίου, καὶ ζέων τῷ πνεύματι ἐλάλει καὶ ἐδίδασκεν ἀκριβῶς τὰ περὶ τοῦ Ἰησοῦ, ἐπιστάμενος μόνον τὸ βάπτισμα Ἰωάννου.

19:1-2 Ἐγένετο δὲ ἐν τῷ τὸν Ἀπολλῶ εἶναι ἐν Κορίνθῳ Παῦλον διελθόντα τὰ ἀνωτερικὰ μέρη [κατ]ελθεῖν εἰς Ἔφεσον καὶ εὑρεῖν τινας μαθητάς, // variant reading (!)
εἶπέν τε πρὸς αὐτούς, Εἰ πνεῦμα ἅγιον ἐλάβετε πιστεύσαντες; οἱ δὲ πρὸς αὐτόν, Ἀλλ' οὐδ' εἰ πνεῦμα ἅγιον ἔστιν ἠκούσαμεν.

19:6 καὶ ἐπιθέντος αὐτοῖς τοῦ Παύλου [τὰς] χεῖρας ἦλθε τὸ πνεῦμα τὸ ἅγιον ἐπ' αὐτούς, ἐλάλουν τε γλώσσαις καὶ ἐπροφήτευον.

19:12-16 ὥστε καὶ ἐπὶ τοὺς ἀσθενοῦντας ἀποφέρεσθαι ἀπὸ τοῦ χρωτὸς αὐτοῦ σουδάρια ἢ σιμικίνθια καὶ ἀπαλλάσσεσθαι ἀπ' αὐτῶν τὰς νόσους, τά τε πνεύματα τὰ πονηρὰ ἐκπορεύεσθαι. ἐπεχείρησαν δέ τινες καὶ τῶν περιερχομένων Ἰουδαίων ἐξορκιστῶν ὀνομάζειν ἐπὶ τοὺς ἔχοντας τὰ πνεύματα τὰ πονηρὰ τὸ ὄνομα τοῦ κυρίου Ἰησοῦ λέγοντες, Ὁρκίζω ὑμᾶς τὸν Ἰησοῦν ὃν Παῦλος κηρύσσει. ἦσαν δέ τινος Σκευᾶ Ἰουδαίου ἀρχιερέως ἑπτὰ υἱοὶ τοῦτο ποιοῦντες. ἀποκριθὲν δὲ τὸ πνεῦμα τὸ πονηρὸν εἶπεν αὐτοῖς, Τὸν [μὲν] Ἰησοῦν γινώσκω καὶ τὸν Παῦλον ἐπίσταμαι, ὑμεῖς δὲ τίνες ἐστέ; καὶ ἐφαλόμενος ὁ ἄνθρωπος ἐπ' αὐτοὺς ἐν ᾧ ἦν τὸ πνεῦμα τὸ πονηρὸν κατακυριεύσας ἀμφοτέρων ἴσχυσεν κατ' αὐτῶν, ὥστε γυμνοὺς καὶ τετραυματισμένους ἐκφυγεῖν ἐκ τοῦ οἴκου ἐκείνου.

19:21 Ὡς δὲ ἐπληρώθη ταῦτα, ἔθετο ὁ Παῦλος ἐν τῷ πνεύματι διελθὼν τὴν Μακεδονίαν καὶ Ἀχαΐαν πορεύεσθαι εἰς Ἱεροσόλυμα, εἰπὼν ὅτι Μετὰ τὸ γενέσθαι με ἐκεῖ δεῖ με καὶ Ῥώμην ἰδεῖν.

20:22-23 καὶ νῦν ἰδοὺ δεδεμένος ἐγὼ τῷ πνεύματι πορεύομαι εἰς Ἰερουσαλήμ, τὰ ἐν αὐτῇ συναντήσοντά μοι μὴ εἰδώς, πλὴν ὅτι τὸ πνεῦμα τὸ ἅγιον κατὰ πόλιν διαμαρτύρεταί μοι λέγον ὅτι δεσμὰ καὶ θλίψεις με μένουσιν.

20:28 προσέχετε ἑαυτοῖς καὶ παντὶ τῷ ποιμνίῳ, ἐν ᾧ ὑμᾶς τὸ πνεῦμα τὸ ἅγιον ἔθετο ἐπισκόπους, ποιμαίνειν τὴν ἐκκλησίαν τοῦ θεοῦ, ἣν περιεποιήσατο διὰ τοῦ αἵματος τοῦ ἰδίου.

21:4 ἀνευρόντες δὲ τοὺς μαθητὰς ἐπεμείναμεν αὐτοῦ ἡμέρας ἑπτά, οἵτινες τῷ Παύλῳ ἔλεγον διὰ τοῦ πνεύματος μὴ ἐπιβαίνειν εἰς Ἱεροσόλυμα.

21:11 καὶ ἐλθὼν πρὸς ἡμᾶς καὶ ἄρας τὴν ζώνην τοῦ Παύλου δήσας ἑαυτοῦ τοὺς πόδας καὶ τὰς χεῖρας εἶπεν, Τάδε λέγει τὸ πνεῦμα τὸ ἅγιον, Τὸν ἄνδρα οὗ ἐστιν ἡ ζώνη αὕτη οὕτως δήσουσιν ἐν Ἰερουσαλὴμ οἱ Ἰουδαῖοι καὶ παραδώσουσιν εἰς χεῖρας ἐθνῶν.

23:8-9 Σαδδουκαῖοι μὲν γὰρ λέγουσιν μὴ εἶναι ἀνάστασιν μήτε ἄγγελον μήτε πνεῦμα, Φαρισαῖοι δὲ ὁμολογοῦσιν τὰ ἀμφότερα. ἐγένετο δὲ κραυγὴ μεγάλη, καὶ ἀναστάντες τινὲς τῶν γραμματέων τοῦ μέρους τῶν Φαρισαίων διεμάχοντο λέγοντες, Οὐδὲν κακὸν εὑρίσκομεν ἐν τῷ ἀνθρώπῳ τούτῳ· εἰ δὲ πνεῦμα ἐλάλησεν αὐτῷ ἢ ἄγγελος

28:25 ἀσύμφωνοι δὲ ὄντες πρὸς ἀλλήλους ἀπελύοντο, εἰπόντος τοῦ Παύλου ῥῆμα ἓν ὅτι Καλῶς τὸ πνεῦμα τὸ ἅγιον ἐλάλησεν διὰ Ἠσαΐου τοῦ προφήτου πρὸς τοὺς πατέρας ὑμῶν

APPENDIX 3
THE HOLY SPIRIT IN LUKE-ACTS AND GERMAN INFLUENCES[1]

The German scholar Eduard Schweizer has had a sustaining influence on different pneumatological writings through his article in the .[2] He notices a distinction between Mark, Matthew and Luke, writing 'Lukas hat ein neues Geistverständnis.' There where Mark and Matthew see Jesus as a spiritual man, Luke describes Jesus as Lord of the Spirit.[3] Schweizer sees the Spirit in Luke-Acts foremost as the Spirit of prophecy which also makes the church a community of prophets.[4] Miracles and an inner, ethical, change are not attributed to the Spirit per se. The driving force behind miracles and healings is the δύναμις of Jesus and not the πνεῦμα of Jesus.[5] So Schweizer stands in agreement with the terminology of the Spirit of prophecy, although there are a couple of unsolved issues in relation to the soteriological function and the miraculous working of the Spirit. Max Turner discusses a couple of disagreements on Lukan pneumatology within Schweizer's work.[6]

Another influential German work in regard to Lukan pneumatology is the monograph published in 1973 by Jacob Kremer:[7] It is, as the subtitle

---

1 Due to the fact that the debate on Lukan pneumatology originated between German scholars (see above in §1.2), it is only fair to write something about several influential German works in regard to Lukan pneumatology. This excursus is a short treatment of the works by Eduard Schweizer, Jacob Kremer and Norbert Baumert. In addition the German dissertation by Helene Wuhrer is worth reading, especially those passages which deal with God speaking in Acts 8, 9 and 10. See Helene Wuhrer, (Unpublished dissertation, VU University, 2013).
2 Eduard Schweizer, 'πνεῦμα', in: G. Kittel and G. Friedrich, (Stuttgart: Kohlhammer, 1933-1978) Bd.VI, 320-453.
3 Schweizer, 'πνεῦμα',404. See also the later work of Schweizer, (Stuttgart, Berlin: Kreuz, 1978), 74-75.
4 Schweizer, 'πνεῦμα', 405-407.
5 Although Schweizer does admit that δύναμις and πνεῦμα are more or less synonyms and thus interchangeable, Schweizer, 'πνεῦμα', 405.
6 Turner, *Power from on High*, 59-61
7 Jakob Kremer, *Pfingstbericht und Pfingstgeschehen. Eine exegetische Untersuchung zu Apg 2,1-13* (SBS 63/64; Stuttgart: KBW, 1973)..

suggests, an exegetical work on Acts 2:1-13. It is a thorough work on these verses from Acts and shows the difficulties of the exact meaning of receiving the Spirit in Luke-Acts. In the debate on the Spirit in Luke-Acts, Kremer proposes a mediating position.[8] On the one hand the Spirit is universal, with the meaning that every one receives the Spirit when becoming a Christian.[9] On the other hand, Kremer acknowledges that the Spirit received at Pentecost is the Spirit who empowers for preaching.[10] Kremer tries to combine these different aspects of the Spirit, but in the end he shows how difficult it is to understand Luke's precise intentions when he writes about the working of the Spirit in his two volume work.

More recent work on the Spirit is done by Norbert Baumert in his two volume [11]and his article about 'Charism and Spirit-Baptism'.[12] In the first volume of , Baumert undertakes an extensive word study of χάρισμα.[13] The second volume deals with water baptism and spirit baptism, in which Baumert also treats Luke-Acts. He argues that the modern term 'Spirit-Baptism' is not the same as the Lukan gift of the Spirit as some endpoint of initiation.[14] 'Spirit-Baptism' is a term which refers to the individual experience of the presence and the power of the Spirit. Baumert thus places the terminology of 'Spirit-Baptism' in an experiential setting instead of a normative setting. On pages 107-118 of his second

---

8   Max Turner designates this as 'a fusion of the Spirit of prophecy and the soteriological Spirit', see Turner, , 66.
9   'Er [Luke] äußert sich in keiner Weise darüber, ob zwischen dem, was die Apostel zu Pfingsten erfuhren (eine besondere charismatische Begabung), und dem, was am Anfang des Christwerdens empfangen wird (die allgemeine Geistbegabung), ein Unterschied besteht', Kremer, , 220.
10 'Hier ist aber nicht einfach vom heiligen Geist, den sie empfangen werden (so Joh.20:22), die Rede, sondern von δύναμιν ἐπελθόντος τοῦ ἁγίου πνεύματος ἐφ᾽ ὑμᾶς (Kraft des auf euch herabkommenden Geistes)', Kremer, , 186. Later, in concluding this section, Kremer writes: 'Auf die sonst in die Urkirche mit dem Begriff "Taufe" verbundenen Wirkungen des Geistempfangs (z.B. Neuschöpfung, Heiligung, Gotteskindschaft, Unterpfand der ewigen Herrlichkeit) wird in keiner Weise hingewiesen', Kremer, , 190.
11 Norbert Baumert (2 Bände; Würzburg: Echter, 2001). See for a review of this two volume work W. Vondey, (2003), 152-154.
12 Norbert Baumert "'Charism' and 'Spirit-Baptism': Presentation of an Analysis', 12-2 (2004). This article is a summary of the results of Baumert's two volume work mentioned above.
13 The subtitle of this first volume is rightly chosen as *Entflechtung einer semantischen Verwirrung*.
14 Baumert, 'Charism' and 'Spirit-Baptism', 161 and for a thorough treatment of the Biblical data, see (vol.2), 97-140.

volume Baumert discusses 'Spirit-Baptism' (*Geisttaufe*) in Luke-Acts. He does not see the baptism of Jesus as a paradigm for the early church at Pentecost, but as an analogy instead. Later he writes:

> 'Die Urkirche weiß gut um die Besonderheit des Anfangs, und doch zugleich, daß alle den Geist empfangen können, aber nicht in der gleichen Weise. Man muß sehr genau zuschauen, was davon 'normatif' empfunden wurde. Wenn auffallende charismatische Phänomene genannt werden (Sprachengebet etc.), sind sie ein besonders deutlicher Hinweis, aber nicht ein Kriterium – auch wenn an zu nehmen ist, daß am Anfang viele diese Gabe hatten.'[15]

In other words, this is again a hermeneutical issue: What is the key to treat texts as normative or as descriptive? Was it really Luke's intention to write a normative treatment on receiving the Spirit? This brings us in the area of disagreements on the Holy Spirit in Luke-Acts and therewith on the importance of the role of the reader.

---

15 Baumert, , 110.

BIBLIOGRAPHY

Alexander, L. C. A., *The Preface to Luke's Gospel: Literary Convention and Social Context in Luke 1.1-4 and Acts 1.1* (SNTSMS 78; Cambridge: University Press, 1993) xv + 268pp.
— 'Acts and Ancient Intellectual Biography' in: Winter, B.W. and Clark, A.D. (eds.), *The Book of Acts in its Ancient Literary Setting* (BAFCS 1; Grand Rapids, MI: Eerdmans, 1994), pp.31-64.
Archer, K. J., *A Pentecostal Hermeneutic for the Twenty-First Century: Spirit, Scripture and Community* (JPTSS 28; London; New York: T&T Clark, 2004) xii + 240pp.
Atkinson, W., 'Pentecostal Responses to Dunn's Baptism in the Holy Spirit: Luke-Acts', *JPT* 6 (1995) pp.87-131.
— *Baptism in the Spirit: Luke-Acts and the Dunn Debate* (Eugene, OR: Wipf and Stock, 2011) x + 154pp.
Avemarie, F., *Die Tauferzählungen der Apostelgeschichte* (WUNT 139; Tübingen: Mohr Siebeck, 2002) xii + 559pp.
Baer von, H., *Der Heilige Geist in den Lukasschriften* (Stuttgart: Kohlhammer, 1926) 220pp.
Bailey, K. E., *Jesus Through Middle Eastern Eyes. Cultural Studies in the Gospels* (London: SPCK, 2008) 443pp.
Bailey J.L, and Vander Broek, L.D., *Literary Forms in the New Testament. A Handbook* (Louisville,
KY: Westminster/John Knox, 1992) 219pp.
Balch, D. L., Ferguson, E. and Meeks, W.A. (eds.), *Greeks, Romans and Christians: Essays in Honor of Abraham J. Malherbe* (Minneapolis, MN: Fortress, 1990) 400pp.
Barthes, R., *Le bruissement de la langue. Essais critiques IV* (Paris: Seuil, 1984) 448pp.
Bauer, W., Danker, F.W., *A Greek-English Lexicon of the New Testament and Other Early Christian Literature* (Chicago: University of Chicago Press, ³2000), lxxix + 1108pp.
Baumert, N., *Charisma – Taufe – Geisttaufe* (2 Bände; Würzburg: Echter, 2001) 320pp. + 399pp.
— "Charism' and 'Spirit-Baptism': Presentation of an Analysis', *JPT* 12-2 (2004) pp.147-181.
Beasley-Murray, G. R., *Baptism in the New Testament* (Grand Rapids, MI: Eerdmans, 1962) x + 422pp.

Beynon, G., *Experiencing the Spirit: New Testament Essentials for Every Christian* (Leicester: IVP, 2006) 160pp.
Bock, D.L., *Proclamation from Prophecy and Pattern: Lucan Old Testament Christology* (Sheffield:
Sheffield Academic, 1987) 418pp.
— *Luke* (BECNT 3A-B; Grand Rapids, MI: Baker Academic, 1994, 1996) 987 + 1162pp.
— *A Theology of Luke and Acts: God's Promised Program, Realized for All nations* (BTNTS; Grand Rapids, MI: Zondervan, 2012) 496pp.
Boeckler, R., *Der moderne römisch-katholische Traditionsbegriff* (Göttingen: Vandenhoek &
Ruprecht, 1967) 236pp.
Borgman, P., *The Way according to Luke: Hearing the Whole Story of Luke-Acts* (Grand Rapids, MI:
Eerdmans, 2006) xii + 404pp.
Bovon, F., *Das Evangelium nach Lukas: 1. Teilband, Lk. 1,1-9,50* (EKK 3,1; Zürich,
Neukirchen-Vluyn: Benziger Verlag, Neukirchener Verlag, 1980) 524pp.
— *Luke the Theologian: Fifty-Five Years of Research* (1950-2005) (Trans. Ken McKinney: Waco, TX: Baylor University Press, 2006) xiv + 681pp.
Brink van den, G. and Kooi van der, C., *Christelijke Dogmatiek* (Zoetermeer, Boekencentrum: 2012) 722pp.
Brown, R.E., *The Birth of the Messiah: A Commentary on the Infancy Narratives in the Gospels of Mathew and Luke* (New York, NY: Doubleday, 1977, 1999), 752pp.
Bruner, F. D., *A Theology of the Holy Spirit. The Pentecostal Experience and the New Testament Witness* (Grand Rapids, MI: Eerdmans, 1970) 390pp.
Cadbury, H. J., *The Making of Luke-Acts* (New York: MacMillan, 1927) 390pp.
Chilton, B. "Announcement in Nazara: An Analysis of Luke 4.16-21", in: R.T. France and D. Wenham
(eds.), *Studies of History and Tradition in the Four Gospels, II* (Sheffield: JSOT, 1986), 147-172.
Cho, Y., 'Spirit and Kingdom in Luke-Acts: Proclamation as the Primary Role of the Spirit in Relation to the Kingdom of God in Luke-Acts', *AJPS* 6-2 (2003) pp.173-197.
—

— *Spirit and Kingdom in the Writings of Luke and Paul: An Attempt to Reconcile these Concepts* (Waynesboro, GA: Paternoster, 2005) xviii + 227pp.

Collini S. (ed.), *Interpretation and Overinterpretation* (Cambridge: Cambridge University Press, 1992) ix + 155pp.

Conzelmann, H., *Die Mitte der Zeit. Studien zur Theologie des Lukas* (Tübingen: Mohr Siebeck, 1953, ⁷1993) viii + 241pp.

— *The Acts of the Apostles* (Hermeneia; orig. German; trans. J. Limburg, A.T. Kraabel and D.H. Juel; Philadelphia: Fortress, 1987) 335pp.

Cornils, A., *Vom Geist Gottes erzählen: Analysen zur Apostelgeschichte* (TANZ 44; Tübingen:

Francke, 2006) viii + 283pp.

Cullmann, O., *Heil als Geschichte. Heilsgeschichtliche Existenz im Neuen Testament* (Tübingen:

Mohr Siebeck, 1965) xii + 328pp.

Denzinger, H., *Enchiridion Symbolorum: A Compendium of Creeds, Definitions, and Declarations of the Catholic Church* (San Francisco CA: Ignatius, ¹1854, ⁴³2012) 1437pp.

Dunn, J. D. G., *Baptism in the Holy Spirit: a Re-examination of the New Testament Teaching on the Gift of the Spirit in Relation to Pentecostalism Today* (London: SCM, 1970) viii + 248pp.

— *Jesus and the Spirit: A Study of the Religious and Charismatic Experience of Jesus and the first Christians as Reflected in the New Testament* (London: SCM, 1975) xii + 515pp.

— 'Baptism in the Spirit : A Response to Pentecostal Scholarship on Luke-Acts', *JPT* 3 (1993) pp.3-27.

— *The Christ and the Spirit: Pneumatology* (vol. 2; Grand Rapids, MI: Eerdmans, 1998) xvi + 400pp.

— *Unity and Diversity in the New Testament. An Inquiry into the Character of Earliest Christianity* (London: SCM, 1977, ⁶ᵗʰ·ʳᵉᵛ·2006) xviii + 470pp.

— *The Theology of Paul the Apostle* (London, New York: T&T Clark, ¹1998, 2003) xxxvi + 808pp.

Eco, U., *A Theory of Semiotics* (AdvSem; Bloomington, IN: Indiana University Press, 1976, 1979) ix + 354pp.

— *The Role of the Reader: Explorations in the Semiotics of Texts* (AdvSem; Bloomington, London: Indiana University Press, 1979, 1984) viii + 288pp.

— *Lector in fabula. La cooperationi interpretative nei testi narrativi* (Tascabili Bompiani 27; Milan: Bompiani,1979, ¹¹2010) 250pp.

— *Il nome della rosa* (Letteraria Italiana; Milan: Bompiani, 1980) 442pp.
— "Two Problems in Textual Interpretation", *Poetics Today* (1980) pp.145-161.
— "The Theory of Signs and the Role of the Reader" *BMMLA 14.1 (1981)* pp.35-45.
— *Semiotics and the Philosophy of Language* (AdvSem; Bloomington, IN: Indiana University Press, 1984, 1986) 242pp.
— *Il pendolo di Foucault* (Letteraria Italiana; Milan: Bompiani, 1988) 661pp.
— *Lector in fabula. De rol van de lezer in narratieve teksten* (trans. Y. Boeke, P. Krone: Amsterdam: Bert Bakker, 1989) 333pp.
— *The Open Work* (trans. A. Cancogni: Cambridge, MA: Harvard University Press, 1989) xxxii + 285pp.
— *The Limits of Interpretation* (Advances in Semiotics; Bloomington, IN: Indiana University Press, 1990, 1994) 295pp.
— *L'isolo del giorno prima* (Milan: Bompiana, 1994 473pp.
— *Baudolino* (Milan: Bompiani, 2000) 637pp.
— *Sulla Letteratura* (Milan: Bompiani, 2002)359pp.
— *On Literature* (trans. M. McLaughlin: New York: Harcourt, 2002) x + 334pp.
— *Il cimitero di Praga* (Milan: Bompiani, 2010), 523pp.
Eisen, U. E., *Die Poetik der Apostelgeschichte: Eine narratologische Studie* (NTOA 58; Fribourg/Göttingen: Academic/Vandenhoeck & Ruprecht, 2006) 294pp.
Elbert, P. (ed.) *Faces of Renewal: Studies in Honour of Stanley M. Horton presented on his 70th Birthday* (Peabody, MA: Hendrickson, 1988) xxvii + 292pp.
Ervin, H. M., *Conversion-Initiation and the Baptism in the Holy Spirit. A Critique of James D.G. Dunn's 'Baptism in the Holy Spirit'* (Peabody, MA: Hendrickson, 1984) viii + 172pp.
— *Spirit-Baptism: A Biblical Investigation* (Revision of: *These are not Drunken, As Ye Suppose*, 1968; Peabody, MA: Hendrickson, 1987) 208pp.
Fee, G.D., 'Hermeneutics and Historical Precedent – A Major Problem in Pentecostal Hermeneutics', in: Spittler, R. P. (ed.) *Perspectives on the New Pentecostalism* (Grand Rapids, MI: Baker, 1976) pp.118-132.
— 'Baptism in the Holy Spirit: The Issue of Separability and Subsequence', *Pneuma* 7 (1985) pp.87-99.
— *Gospel and Spirit: Issues in New Testament Hermeneutics* (Peabody, MA: Hendrickson, 1991) 160pp.

— *Gods Empowering Presence. The Holy Spirit in the Letters of Paul* (Peabody, MA: Hendrickson, 1994) xxiv + 967pp.
Fee, G.D. and Stuart, D., *How to Read the Bible for All Its Worth. A Guide to Understanding the Bible* (Grand Rapids, MI: Zondervan, ³2003) 288pp.
Ferguson, E., *Baptism in the Early Church. History, Theology, and Liturgy in the First Five Centuries* (Grand Rapids, MI: Eerdmans, 2009) xxii + 987pp.
Fitzmyer, J. A., *The Gospel according to Luke*, 2 vols. (AncB 28-28a; New York: Doubleday, 1981-1985) xxvi + 1642pp.
— *Luke the Theologian: Aspects of His Teaching* (London: Chapman, 1989) xi + 264pp.
Foskett, M. F., Allen jr., O.W. (eds.), *Between Experience and Interpretation: Engaging the Writings of the New Testament* (Nashville: Abingdon, 2008) xvi + 262pp.
France, R. T., Wenham, D. (eds.), *Gospel Perspectives II. Studies of History and Tradition in the Four Gospels* (Sheffield: JSOT, 1986) 376pp.
González, Justo L., *The Story Luke Tells. Luke's Unique Witness to the Gospel* (Grand Rapids, MI: Eerdmans, 2015) xi + 129pp.
Grässer, E., *Das Problem der Parusieverzögerung in den synoptischen Evangelien und in der Apostelgeschichte* (Berlin: Töpelmann, 1957) viii + 234pp.
Green, J. B., *The Theology of the Gospel of Luke* (NTT 3; Cambridge: Cambridge University Press, 1995) xiv + 170pp.
— *The Gospel of Luke* (NICNT; Grand Rapids, MI: Eerdmans, 1997) xcii + 928pp.
— "Scripture and Theology: Uniting the Two So Long Divided" in: J.B. Green and M.M.B. Turner (eds.), *Between Two Horizons. Spanning New Testament Studies & Systematic Theology* (Grand Rapids, MI: Eerdmans, 2000) pp.23-43.
— and M.M.B. Turner (eds.), *Between Two Horizons. Spanning New Testament Studies & Systematic Theology* (Grand Rapids, MI: Eerdmans, 2000) x + 246pp.
— *Methods for Luke* (Cambridge: Cambridge University Press, 2010) x + 157pp.
— 'Narrative Criticism', in: Green, J. B. (ed.) *Methods for Luke* (Cambridge: Cambridge University Press, 2010) pp.74-112.
— *Hearing the New Testament. Strategies for Interpretation* (Grand Rapids, MI: Eerdmans, 1995, ²2010) xii + 432pp.

Gunkel, H., *Die Wirkungen des Heiligen Geistes nach der populären Anschauung der apostolischen Zeit und der Lehre des Apostels Paulus* (Göttingen: Vandenhoeck & Ruprecht, 1888, ³1909) viii + 109pp.

Haenchen, E., *Die Apostelgeschichte* (KEK III; Göttingen: Vandenhoeck & Ruprecht, 1956, ⁷1977) 717pp.

Hamm, D., 'The Mission Has a Church: Spirit, World and Church in Luke-Acts', in: Hinze, B. E. (ed.) *The Spirit in the Church and the World* (Maryknoll, NY: Orbis Books, 2004) pp.68-80.

Hamilton Jr., J.M., *God's Indwelling Presence: The Holy Spirit in the Old & New Testaments* (Nashville: B&H Academic, 2006), xiii + 233pp.

Harrington, W.J., *Reading Luke for the First Time* (Mahwah, NJ: Paulist, 2015) 156pp.

Harris, Murray J., *The Second Epistle to the Corinthians* (NIGTC; Grand Rapids, MI: Eerdmans/Paternoster, 2005) xxxiii+1446pp.

Haya-Prats, G., *Empowered Believers. The Holy Spirit in the Book of Acts* (Eugene, OR: Cascade, 2010) 316pp.

Hildebrandt, W., *An Old Testament Theology of the Spirit of God* (Grand Rapids, MI: Baker Academic, 1993) 256pp.

Hinze, B. E., *The Spirit in the Church and the World* (Maryknoll, NY: Orbis Books, 2004) xxi + 247pp.

Holtz, T., *Untersuchungen über die alttestamentlichen Zitate bei Lukas* (TU 104; Berlin: Akademie, 1968) 185pp.

Hunter, H. D., *Spirit-Baptism: A Pentecostal Alternative* (Eugene, OR: Wipf & Stock, 2009) 237pp.

Johnson, L. T., *The Gospel of Luke* (SPg 3; Collegeville, MN: Liturgical, 1991) xiv + 466pp.

Kaiser, W.C., 'The Indwelling Presence of the Holy Spirit in the Old Testament' *EQ 82* (2010) pp.308-315.

Kärkkäinen, V. M., 'Spirit, Mission and Eschatology. An Outline of a Pentecostal-Charismatic Theology of Mission', *Mission Studies* 16-1 (1999) pp.73-94.

— *Pneumatology: The Holy Spirit in Ecumenical, International and Contextual Perspective* (Grand Rapids, MI: Baker Academic, 2002) 195pp.

Kärkkäinen V.M. and Yong, A., *Towards a Pneumatological Theology: Pentecostal and Ecumenical Perspectives on Ecclesiology, Soteriology and Theology of Mission* (Lanham, MD: University Press of America, 2002) xxi + 294pp.

Käsemann, E., *Essays on New Testament Themes* (SBT 41; London: SCM, 1964) 202pp.
— "The Disciples of John the Baptist in Ephesus" in: E. Käsemann, *Essays on New Testament Themes* (SBT 41; London: SCM, 1964) pp.136-148.
Keck, L.E. and Martyn, J. L., *Studies in Luke-Acts* (Nashville, TN: Abingdon, 1966) 316pp.
Keener, C. S., *The Spirit in the Gospels and Acts: Divine Purity and Power* (Peabody, MA: Hendrickson, 1997) xxi + 282pp.
— *Acts: An Exegetical Commentary* (4 vols.; Grand Rapids, MI: Baker Academic, 2012-2015) 4640pp.
Kienzler, J., *The Fiery Holy Spirit: The Spirit's Relationship with Judgment in Luke-Acts* (JPTSS; Winona Lake, IN: Eisenbrauns/Deo, 2015) 254pp.
Kilgallen, J., 'Acts: Literary and Theological Turning Points', *BTB* 7 (1977) pp.177-180.
King, Paul L., *Genuine Gold: The Cautiously Charismatic Story of the Early Christian and Missionary Alliance* (Tulsa, OK: Word & Spirit, 2006) 335pp.
Kragt, P., *The Theology of Luke-Acts: Jesus as Prophet* (Ebook; Amazon digital services, 2015) 147pp.
Kremer, J., *Pfingstbericht und Pfingstgeschehen. Eine exegetische Untersuchung zu Apg 2,1-13* (Stuttgarter Bibelstudien 63/64; Stuttgart: KBW, 1973) 297pp.
Kuecker, A., *The Spirit and the 'Other'. Social Identity, Ethnicity, and Intergroup Reconciliation in Luke-Acts* (LNTS; New York/London: Bloomsbury, T&T Clark, 2011) 296pp.
Kurz, W.S., 'Narrative Approaches to Luke-Acts', *Bib* 68 (1987) pp.195-222.
— *The Acts of the Apostles* (CBC 5; Collegeville, MN: Liturgical, rev. ed. 1989) 111pp.
— 'Narrative Models for Imitation in Luke-Acts', in: Balch, D. L., E. Ferguson and W.A. Meeks (eds.) *Greeks, Romans and Christians: Essays in Honor of Abraham J. Malherbe* (Minneapolis, MN: Fortress, 1990) pp.171-189.
— *Reading Luke-Acts: Dynamics of Biblical Narrative* (Louisville, KY: Westminster/John Knox, 1993) x + 261pp.

— 'Promise and Fulfillment in Hellenistic Jewish Narratives and in Luke and Acts', in: Moessner, D. P. (ed.) *Jesus and the Heritage of Israel: Luke's Narrative Claim upon Israel's Legacy* (Luke the Interpreter of Israel, vol.1; Harrisburg, PA: Trinity International, 1999) pp.147-170.

— *Following Jesus: A Disciple's Guide to Luke and Acts* (Ann Harbor, MI: Servant, rev.ed. 2003) 140pp.

— 'From the Servant in Isaiah to Jesus and Apostles in Luke-Acts to Christians Today: Spirit-Filled Witness to the Ends of the Earth', in: Foskett, M. F. and Allen jr., O.W. (eds.), *Between Experience and Interpretation: Engaging the Writings of the New Testament* (Nashville: Abingdon, 2008) pp.175-194.

— *Acts of the Apostles* (Catholic Commentary on Sacred Scripture; Grand Rapids, MI: Baker Academic, 2013) 397pp.

Leisegang, H., *Der Heilige Geist. Das Wesen und Werden der Mystisch-Intuitiven Erkenntnis der Philosophie und Religion der Griechen* (Berlin: Teubner, 1919) 268pp.

Levison, J. R., *The Spirit in First Century Judaism* (AGAJU 29; Leiden: Brill, 1997) xiv + 302pp.

— *Filled with the Spirit* (Grand Rapids, MI: Eerdmans, 2009) xxviii + 463pp.

Lévi-Strauss, Claude, *Les Structures élémentaires de la parenté (Berlin, New York: Mouton de Gruyter, 1947, ²2002) 621pp.*

Litwak, K.D., *Echoes of Scripture in Luke-Acts. Telling the History of God's People Intertextually* (JSNT Sup. 282; London, New York: T&T Clark, 2005) xiii+256pp.

Longenecker, B.W., *Hearing the Silence. Jesus on the Edge and God in the Gap. Luke 4 in Narrative Perspective* (Eugene, OR: Cascade, 2012 xiv + 138pp.

Macchia, F. D., *Baptized in the Spirit: A Global Pentecostal Theology* (Grand Rapids, MI: Zondervan, 2006) 296pp.

Marguerat, D., *The First Christian Historian. Writing the 'Acts of the Apostles'* (SNTS 121; Cambridge: University Press, 2002) xii + 299pp.

Marshall, I. H., *Luke: Historian and Theologian* (Grand Rapids, MI: Zondervan, 1970) 238pp.

— "Acts and the 'Former Treatise'" in: Bruce Winter and Andrew Clarke (eds.), *The Book of Acts in its Ancient Literary Setting* (BAFCS volume 1; Grand Rapids, MI / Carlisle: Eerdmans /Paternoster: 1993) pp.163-182.

— *The Gospel of Luke: A Commentary on the Greek Text* (NIGTC; Grand Rapids, MI: Paternoster/Eerdmans, repr. 1995) 928pp.

Marshall I.H. and Peterson, D., *Witness to the Gospel: The Theology of Acts* (Grand Rapids, MI: Eerdmans, 1998) xvi + 610pp.

Martin, Ralph P., *2 Corinthians* (WBC 40; Waco, TX: Word, 1986) lxiii + 527pp.

Mays, J. L. (ed.) *Interpreting the Gospels* (Philadelphia: Fortress, 1981) x + 307pp.

Menzies, R. P., *The Development of Early Christian Pneumatology with Special Reference to Luke-Acts* (JSNTS 54; Sheffield: Sheffield Academic, 1991) 375pp.

— 'The Distinctive Character of Luke's Pneumatology', *Paraclete* 25 (1991) pp.17-30.

— 'Spirit and Power in Luke-Acts : A Response to Max Turner', *JSNT* 49 (1993) pp.11-20.

— 'James' Shelton's Mighty in Word and Deed: A Review Article', *JPT* 2 (1993) pp.105-115.

— *Empowered for Witness: the Spirit in Luke-Acts* (Sheffield: Sheffield Academic, 1994) 290pp.

— 'Luke and the Spirit: A reply to James Dunn', *JPT* 4 (1994) pp.115-138.

— 'The Spirit of Prophecy, Luke-Acts and Pentecostal Theology: A Response to Max Turner', *JPT* 15 (1999) pp.49-74.

— 'Luke's Understanding of Baptism in the Holy Spirit. A Pentecostal Perspective', *PentcoStudies* 6-2 (2007) pp.108-126.

— *This Story is Our Story* (Springfield, MO: Gospel Publishing, 2013) 160pp.

— *The Language of the Spirit: Interpreting and Translating Charismatic Term* (Cleveland, TN: CPT, 2010) 136pp.

Menzies, R.P. and Wonsuk Ma, *The Spirit and Spirituality: Essays in Honor of Russell P. Spittler* (JPTS 24; London: T&T Clark, 2004) 312pp.

Menzies R.P. and Menzies, W. W., *Spirit and Power: Foundations of Pentecostal Experience* (Grand Rapids, MI: Zondervan, 2000) 233pp.

Mittelstadt, M. W., *Reading Luke-Acts in the Pentecostal Tradition* (Cleveland, TN: CPT, 2010) 216pp.

Moessner, D. P. (ed.) *Jesus and the Heritage of Israel: Luke's Narrative Claim upon Israel's Legacy* (Luke the Interpreter of Israel, vol.1; Harrisburg, PA: Trinity International, 1999) x + 395pp.

Neudorfer, H.W., *Der Stephanuskreis in der Forschungsgeschichte seit F.C. Baur* (Giessen, Basel: Brunnen Verlag, 1983) 391pp.

Nietzsche, F.W., *Gesammelte Werke* (Köln, Anaconda: 2012) 976pp.
Nolland, J., *Luke 1-9:20* (WBC 35a; Dallas, TX: Word, 1989) lxvi + 454pp.
— *Luke 9:21-18:34* (WBC 35b; Dallas, TX: Word, 1993) lix + 896pp.
— *Luke 18:35-24:53* (WBC 35c; Dallas, TX: Word, 1993) lxi + 1293pp.
— 'Salvation-history and eschatology', in: Marshall, I.H., (ed.) *Witness to the Gospel. The Theology of Acts* (Grand Rapids, MI: Eerdmans, 1998) pp.63-81.
Ott, L., *Grundriss der Katholischen Dogmatik* (Freiburg: Herder, 1952) 560pp.
Parsons M.C. and Pervo, R.I., *Rethinking the Unity of Luke-Acts* (Minneapolis, MN: Fortress, 1993) x + 148pp.
Penner, T., *In Praise of Christian Origins: Stephen and the Hellenists in Lukan Apologetic Historiography* (Emory Studies in Early Christianity; New York, London: T&T Clark, 2004) xl + 400pp.
Penney, J. M., *The Missionary Emphasis of Lukan Pneumatology* (JPTSS 12; Sheffield: Sheffield Academic, 1997) 143pp.
Pervo, R. I., *Profit with Delight: The Literary Genre of the Acts of the Apostles* (Philadelphia: Fortress, 1987) xiii + 212pp.
— *Acts: A Commentary* (Hermeneia; Augsburg, MN: Fortress, 2008) 800pp.
Philips, T. E., 'The Genre of Acts: Moving Toward a Consensus?', *CBR* 4-3 (2006) pp.365-396.
Plümacher, E., *Lukas als hellenistischer Schriftsteller: Studien zur Apostelgeschichte* (SUNT 9; Göttingen: Vandenhoeck & Ruprecht, 1972) 164pp.
Powell, M. A., "Narrative Criticism" in: Joel B. Green (ed.), *Hearing the New Testament. Strategies for Interpretation* (Grand Rapids, MI: Eerdmans, 1995, ²2010) pp.240-258.
Resseguie, J. L., *Narrative Criticism of the New Testament: an Introduction* (Grand Rapids, MI: Baker Academic, 2005) 288pp.
Richard, E., *Acts 6:1-8:4 The Authors Method of Composition* (SBL Dissertations Series 41; Missoula, MT: Scholars, 1978) xiv + 379pp.
Robey, D., "Introduction: Interpretation and Uncertainty" in *Illuminating Eco. On the Boundaries of Interpretation* (ed. C. Ross, R. Sibley; Warwick Studies in the Humanities; Hampshire, Burlington, VT: Ashgate, 2004) pp.1-10.
Ross, C., Sibley, R., *Illuminating Eco. On the Boundaries of Interpretation* (Warwick Studies in the Humanities; Hampshire, Burlington, VT: Ashgate, 2004) 226pp.

Rothschild, C. K., 'Historical Criticism', in: Green, J. B. (eds.) *Methods for Luke* (Cambridge: Cambridge University Press, 2010) pp.9-41.
Salter, M.C., *The Power of Pentecost. An Examination of Acts 2:17-21* (Eugene, OR: Wipf & Stock, 2012) xxiii + 115pp.
Sandmel, S., "Parallelomania", *JBL 81* (1962) pp.1-13.
Saussure de, Ferdinand, *Cours de linguistique générale* (publ. par Charles Bally et Albert Sechehaye; Paris, Payot: 1980) 520pp.
Schnelle, U., *Einleitung in das Neue Testament* (Göttingen: Vandenhoeck & Ruprecht, 1994, [8]2013) 607pp.
Schüssler Fiorenza, F. and Galvin, J.P., (eds.), *Systematic Theology. Roman Catholic Perspectives* (Minneapolis, MN: Fortress, 1991, [2]2011) 704pp.
Schweizer, E., 'πνευμα', in: G. Kittel, G. Friedrich and O. Bauernfeind, *Theologisches Wörterbuch zum Neuen Testament* (Stuttgart: Kohlhammer, 1933-1978) Bd.VI, pp.320-453.
— *Heiliger Geist* (Stuttgart: Kreuz, 1978) 186pp.
— *Beiträge zur Theologie des Neuen Testaments: Neutestamentliche Aufsätze (1955-1970)* (Zürich: Zwingli Verlag, 1970) 288pp.
— "Die Bekehrung des Apollos, Apg 18,24-26" in: E. Schweizer, *Beiträge zur Theologie des Neuen Testaments: Neutestamentliche Aufsätze (1955-1970)* (Zürich: Zwingli Verlag, 1970) pp.71-79.
Shelton, J. B., ' "Filled with the Holy Spirit" and "full of the Holy Spirit": Lucan Redactional Phrases', in: Elbert, P. (ed.) *Faces of Renewal: Studies in Honour of Stanley M. Horton* (Peabody, MA: Hendrickson, 1988) pp.81-107.
— *Mighty in Word and Deed: The Role of the Holy Spirit in Luke-Acts* (Peabody, MA: Hendrickson, 1991) 196pp.
— 'A Reply to James D.G. Dunn's "Baptism in the Spirit, A Response to Pentecostal Scholarship on Luke-Acts"', *JPT* 4 (1994) pp.139-143.
Shepherd, W. H., *The Narrative Function of the Holy Spirit as a Character in Luke-Acts* (SBL 147; Atlanta, GA: Scholars, 1994) vii + 290pp.
Spencer, F. S., 'Acts and Modern Literary Approaches', in: Winter, B. W. (ed.) *The Book of Acts in its Ancient Literary Setting* (BAFCS 1; Grand Rapids, MI: Eerdmans, 1994) pp.381-414.
— *The Portrait of Philip in Acts. A Study of Roles and Relations* (Sheffield: JSOT, 1992) 320pp.
Spittler, R. P., *Perspectives on the New Pentecostalism* (Grand Rapids, MI: Baker, 1976) 268pp.

Strauss, M.L., *The Davidic Messiah in Luke-Acts. The Promise and its Fulfillment in Lukan Christology* (LNTS 110; Sheffield: Sheffield Academic, 1995) 413pp.

Stronstad, R., *The Charismatic Theology of St. Luke* (Peabody, MA: Hendrickson, 1984, ²2012) 144pp.

Studebaker, S. M., *Defining Issues in Pentecostalism* (Eugene, OR: Pickwick, 2008) xiv + 207pp.

Talbert, C. H., *Literary Patterns, Theological Themes and the Genre of Luke-Acts* (SBL Monograph Series 20; Missoula, MT: Scholars, 1974) 159pp.

— 'Shifting Sands. The Recent Study of the Gospel of Luke', in: Mays, J. L. (ed.) *Interpreting the Gospels* (Philadelphia: Fortress, 1981) pp.197-213.

— *Reading Luke: A Literary and Theological Commentary* (RNT; Macon, GA: Smith & Helwys, rev.ed. 2002) 304pp.

— *Reading Acts. A Literary and Theological Commentary on the Acts of the Apostles* (RNT; New York: Crossroad, 1997; Macon, GA: Smyth & Helwys, rev.ed. 2005) xxx + 288pp.

Tannehill, R. C., *The Narrative Unity of Luke-Acts: A Literary Interpretation* (2 vols.; Philadelphia, Minneapolis: Fortress, 1986-1990) xv + 352pp.; x + 393pp.

Thiselton, A.C., *New Horizons in Hermeneutics* (Grand Rapids, MI: Zondervan, 1992) xii + 703pp.

— *Thiselton on Hermeneutics: Collected Works with New Essays* (Grand Rapids, MI: Eerdmans, 2006), xv + 812pp.

— *The Holy Spirit – In Biblical Teaching, through the Centuries, and Today* (Grand Rapids, MI: Eerdmans, 2013) xiii + 565pp.

— *Systematic Theology* (Grand Rapids, MI: Eerdmans, 2015) xiv + 453pp.

Thomas, J.C., *The Spirit of the New Testament* (Leiden: Deo, 2005) 283pp.

Turner, M. M. B., 'Spirit Endowment in Luke-Acts: Some Linguistic Considerations', *Vox Evangelica* 12 (1981) pp.45-63.

— 'The Significance of Receiving the Spirit in Luke-Acts: A Survey of Modern Scholarship', *Trinity Journal* 2-2 (1981) pp.131-158.

— 'The Spirit and the Power of Jesus' Miracles in the Lucan Conception', *NovT* 33-2 (1991) pp.124-152.

— 'The Spirit of Prophecy and the Power of Authoritative Preaching in Luke-Acts: A Question of Origins', *NTS* 38-1 (1992) pp.66-88.

- '"Empowerment for Mission"? The Pneumatology of Luke-Acts: An Appreciation and Critique of James B. Shelton's Mighty in Word and Deed', *Vox Evangelica* 24 (1994) pp.103-122.
- *Power From On High: The Spirit in Israel's Restoration and Witness in Luke-Acts* (JPTSS 9; Sheffield: Sheffield Academic, 1996) 511pp.
- *The Holy Spirit and Spiritual Gifts Then and Now* (Carlisle: Paternoster, 1996) 374pp.
- 'The Spirit in Luke-Acts: A Support or a Challenge to Classical Pentecostal Paradigms?', *Vox Evangelica* 27 (1997) pp.75-101.
- 'The Spirit of Prophecy as the Power of Israel's Restoration and Witness', in: Marshall, I. H. (ed.) *Witness to the Gospel: The Theology of Acts* (Grand Rapids, MI: Eerdmans, 1998) pp.327-348.
- 'Does Luke Believe Reception of the 'Spirit of Prophecy' makes all 'Prophets'? Inviting Dialogue with Roger Stronstad', *JEPTA* 20 (2000) pp.3-24.
- 'Interpreting the Samaritans of Acts 8: The Waterloo of Pentecostal Soteriology and Pneumatology?', *Pneuma* 23-2 (2001) pp.265-286.
- 'The Work of the Holy Spirit in Luke-Acts', *Word & World* 23-2 (2003) pp.146-153.

Unnik van, W. C., 'Luke-Acts. A Storm Center in Comtemporary Scholarship', in: Keck, L. E. (ed.) *Studies in Luke-Acts* (Nashville, TN: Abingdon, 1966) pp.15-32.

Vanhoozer, K. J., *Is There a Meaning in this Text? The Bible, the Reader, and the Morality of Literary Knowledge* (Leicester, England; Grand Rapids: Apollos; Zondervan, 1998) 512pp.

Walters, Patricia, *The Assumed Authorial Unity of Luke and Acts. A Reassessment of the Evidence* (Cambridge: Cambridge University Press, 2008) xv + 256pp.

Warrington, K., *Discovering the Holy Spirit in the New Testament* (Peabody, MA: Hendrickson, 2005) x + 230pp.

Webb, R. L., *John the Baptizer and Prophet* (JSNT.SS Sheffield: JSOT, 1991) 446pp.
- "The Activity of John the Baptist's Expected Figure at the Threshing Floor (Matthew 3.12 = Luke 3.17)", *JSNT* 43 (1991) pp.103-111.

Weiss, J., *Die Predigt Jesu vom Reiche Gottes* (Göttingen: Vandenhoeck & Ruprecht, 1892, 1900, 1964) xvi + 251pp.

Williams, J. R., 'The Holy Spirit and Eschatology', *Pneuma* 3-2 (1981) pp.54-58.

Winter B.W. and Clark, A. D., *The Book of Acts in its Ancient Literary Setting* (BAFCS 1; Grand Rapids, MI: Eerdmans, 1994) 492pp.

Wright, C.J.H., *Knowing the Holy Spirit through the Old Testament* (Oxford/Downers Grove, IL: Monarch/IVP, 2006) 160pp.

Wuhrer, H., *Zum Stellenwert vom "Reden Gottes" im NT am Beispiel der Apostelgeschichte* (Unpublished dissertation, VU University, 2013) 260pp.

Yong, A., *Discerning the Spirit(s): A Pentecostal-Charismatic Contribution to Christian Theology of Religions* (JPTSS 20; Sheffield: Sheffield Academic, 2000) 392pp.

Zwiep, A. W., *The Ascension of the Messiah in Lukan Christology* (NT.S 87; Leiden, New York, Köln: Brill, 1997) xiii + 291pp.

— 'Luke's Understanding of Baptism in the Holy Spirit', in: Zwiep, A.W., *Christ, the Spirit and the Community of God: Essays on the Acts of the Apostles* (WUNT; Tübingen: Mohr Siebeck, 2010) pp.100-119.

— *Christ, the Spirit and the Community of God: Essays on the Acts of the Apostles* (WUNT; Tübingen: Mohr Siebeck, 2010) 237pp.

— *Tussen tekst en lezer. Een historische inleiding in de bijbelse hermeneutiek* (Vol. I en II; Amsterdam: VU University Press, 2009, 2013) xxiii + 453pp.; xvii + 573pp.

CPSIA information can be obtained
at www.ICGtesting.com
Printed in the USA
LVHW081749180119
604435LV00009B/30/P